MOURNING MODERNITY

SETH MOGLEN

Mourning Modernity

*Literary Modernism and the Injuries
of American Capitalism*

STANFORD UNIVERSITY PRESS

STANFORD, CALIFORNIA 2007

Stanford University Press
Stanford, California

Printed in the United States of America on acid-free, archival-quality paper

Library of Congress Cataloging-in-Publication Data
  Moglen, Seth.

  Mourning modernity : literary modernism and the injuries of American
capitalism / Seth Moglen.
      p. cm.

  Includes bibliographical references and index.
  ISBN 978-0-8047-5418-7 (alk. paper)—ISBN 978-0-8047-5419-4
(pbk. : alk. paper)
   1. American literature—20th century—History and criticism.
2. Modernism (Literature)—United States. 3. Capitalism in literature.
4. Grief in literature. 5. Dos Passos, John, 1896-1970. U.S.A.
6. United States—In literature. 7. Politics and literature—United
States—History—20th century. 8. Literature and society—United States—
History—20th century. I. Title.

PS228.M63M64 2007
810.9´358—dc22

                                                        2007000338

Typeset by Thompson Type in 10/14 Janson

Publication assistance for this book was provided by Lehigh University

"The Descent" was originally published in COLLECTED POEMS, by
William Carlos Williams, 1939–1962, VOLUME II, copyright ©1948, 1962
by William Carlos Williams. Reprinted by permission of New Directions
Publishing Corp.

"Hard Daddy"; "Letter to the Academy"; "Words Like Freedom";
"Harlem" were originally published in THE COLLECTED POEMS OF
LANGSTON HUGHES by Langston Hughes. Reprinted by permission of
Alfred A. Knopf, a division of Random House, Inc.

Part of Chapter 1 appeared as "On Mourning Social Injury" in
Psychoanalysis, Culture, and Society, 10, no. 2 (Aug. 2005). Reprinted by
permission of Palgrave Macmillan.

To my mother, Helene,
and to the memory of my father, Sig.

Contents

Acknowledgments

Many people have sustained me during the years of writing this book, and several communities have nurtured this project.

I thank my editor Norris Pope for his intellectual engagement, professionalism, and kindness. Thanks also to Emily-Jane Cohen and the rest of the staff at Stanford for shepherding the book through the production process.

For time to write and resources to pursue my research, I am grateful to Lehigh University. The English Department granted me a pretenure leave and provided much-needed funding, which was generously supplemented by Faculty Research Grants and a Frantz and Class of 1968 Fellowship. More precious than money has been the intellectual camaraderie of colleagues in the English Department and throughout the university. I am especially grateful to John Pettegrew for many hours of stimulating conversation about American radicalism, modernism, and Dos Passos—and for generously putting aside his own work to read the entire manuscript. Dawn Keetley gave valuable responses to several chapters, and I cannot thank her enough for her colleagueship and friendship. Christian Sisack, Chris Robe, and Bob Kilker provided superb research assistance at various stages of this project, and I am fortunate to have had the help of such gifted scholars at the start of their careers. I am indebted to the many Lehigh students who participated in my undergraduate and graduate seminars on American modernism: their enthusiasm and insight brought this project to life and sharpened my thinking.

I offer deep thanks to Greg Forter and Fred Moten, who provided astute readings of the whole manuscript. Each grasped the aspirations of this project and offered crucial advice about how to realize them more fully. This is a better book because of them. Many others have read portions of the manuscript, encouraged the work, or offered professional advice. Thanks, among others, to Brent Edwards, George Lipsitz, Casey Nelson Blake, Myra Jehlen, Bill Mullen, Judith Butler, Wendy Brown, Hayden White, and Jim Clifford. It has been a great pleasure to discover in the Association for the Psychoanalysis of Culture and Society a community of scholars and clinicians who believe that a socially engaged psychoanalysis can be a practice of liberation and social justice. Thanks especially to Lynne Layton, Simon Clarke, and Mark Bracher for responding to my work and to Elizabeth Young-Bruehl for her encouragement.

Portions of this book are derived from my doctoral dissertation, and I am grateful to the members of my Berkeley dissertation committee: to Carolyn Porter for her faith in the project and the inspiration of her scholarship; to the late Larry Levine for the generous gift of his joyful conversation and for teaching me much about the practice of cultural history; to Sue Schweik for her idealism and her commitment to the power of poetry; and to the late Mike Rogin, who was also raised within the Left and showed me new ways of exploring and extending the tradition. I owe thanks to many others in the Berkeley community—more than I can name here—but I am especially grateful to my sister-in-spirit, Jody Lewen and to Danny Kim for years of friendship and intense conversation about these matters. Barbara Leckie, Franny Nudelman, Ben Reiss, Susan Courtney, David Kazanjian, and many other friends and colleagues challenged me to think more clearly about literature, politics, and psychoanalysis. I thank Hilde Clark for her insight, which helped me and this project to flourish. My union brothers and sisters in the Association of Graduate Student Employees/District 65 UAW intensified my faith in the power of solidarity and in workplace democracy—and the knowledge gained with and from them has found its way into these pages.

I owe thanks to my comrades from many countries who participated in the Oxford University Socialist Discussion Group: our explorations of democratic alternatives to capitalism have strongly influenced this book. I am particularly grateful to Robin Archer, Hanjo Glock, Adam Steinhouse, Pritam Singh, Meena Dhanda, and Yuli Tamir for inspiring conversations over many years about these matters. For sustenance over an even longer period, thanks to Neal Dolan for arguing with me about modernism and everything else, to Tom Nolan for sharing my love of Dos Passos and my hope for radical community, to David Chrisman for his investment in the creative life—and to all three for their friendship and for reading the work. Ben Nathans gave me a place to live—and he has been close friend, colleague, interlocutor, reader, and adviser.

I come at last to my family, whom I thank for unstinting love, support, and inspiration. I hope that this book is true to the spirit of my grandfather, Joseph Moglen, socialist, union activist, and working-class intellectual, who first helped me to dream of justice. My father, Sig Moglen, gave me Dos Passos's *U.S.A.* to read when I was fourteen—and decades of conversation with him about political aspiration and disappointment, about personal and social vulnerability, and about the power of literature have influenced this book from first to last. For his love and companionship I give thanks; his death taught me more about grief and loss than anything I have known. To my brother Eben, I am grateful for a continuous stream of intellectual stimulation, for material generosity and professional support, and for his love. My brother Damon was my first comrade and model for all others: for his loving solidarity, his friendship, his faith in me, his engagement with my work, and for the inspiration of his crusading spirit, thanks is too small a word. Sheila Namir has been a magical recent arrival: I thank her for her astute reading of my work and for the love that animated it. My mother, Helene Moglen, made the greatest contribution of all to this project. Her love has sustained me always. Her delight in literature and her gifts as teacher and scholar have inspired me—as have her passion for justice and her talent for fostering political community. She put aside her own work to read draft upon draft of mine. She taught me what the critic's craft could be and as mentor, editor, colleague, and friend, she helped me to find my own way. I dedicate this book to her—and to the memory of my father.

Kristin Handler has been my cherished companion in all things. She read drafts of every chapter; she talked through all the arguments; she believed in the work and helped me through the rapids. I give her deepest thanks for her love, for joy, for all we have shared during these years.

Introduction

This is a book about political despair and political hope. It is an inquiry into the cultural and psychological dynamics that have caused some Americans over the last century to feel that the most destructive forces at work in their society are irresistible and that their own desires for more humane ways of living are futile or childish. It is also an inquiry into the resources that have enabled others to imagine and work toward emancipatory alternatives. Neither political hope nor political despair is the result of rational calculation; neither is transparently provoked by social circumstance. They are, rather, cultural practices that embody different modes of psychological response to social injury and injustice. This book explores the wellsprings of each in modern America.

My inquiry will focus, in particular, on the ways in which early-twentieth-century Americans understood and responded to the capitalist transformation of their society. Many perceived that the burgeoning of advanced capitalism brought benefits: dazzling new technologies, exciting forms of urban life, access to undreamt of commodities, the expanding promise of social mobility and material prosperity. But millions could also feel that the emerging economic order was inflicting terrible wounds: intensifying economic exploitation, extreme social and material inequality, the betrayal of democracy and, beneath it all, a pervasive feeling of alienation.

The formally experimental literature that we have come to call modernism—perhaps the most famous literature yet produced in the United States— is a direct response to this social transformation. It is the fundamental contention of this book that American literary modernism is, at its heart, an effort to mourn the destructive effects of modern capitalism—and to mourn, most of all, for the crisis of alienation. Modernist writers invented a set of cultural practices through which they could express and manage the loss, disappointment, and injury endured by those who lived within the emerging center of global capitalism. Their effort to grieve was deeply divided. Some writers were unable to name the social dynamics that had produced the widespread suffering they sought to record. They represented the crisis of modernity as an inexorable and mysterious trauma, and they grieved with a melancholic psychological paralysis that manifested itself as a beautiful and poignant despair. Others identified the destructive dynamics at work in their society with considerable clarity. As a result, they mourned with a fullness that enabled them to imagine how human capacities thwarted by the processes of modernization might yet be honored and cultivated in a more just society.

There are, then, two modernisms in the United States. They emerged alongside one another, in tension and in dialogue. Together, they constituted one of the most important arguments in twentieth-century American culture. This was, centrally, an argument about the suffering that had accompanied modern capitalism—a struggle between those who imagined that the alienation and injustice of modern life reflected grim and unalterable facts about human nature and those who insisted that these inhumane circumstances had been produced by a destructive social order that could be remade. This political and historical argument was conducted at the deepest emotional level and with the highest psychological stakes. For the two modernisms staged an encounter between those who felt that their deepest wishes—for love, for social solidarity, for a less alienated way of life—were inherently unrealizable illusions and those whose central aim was to explore those desires and to imagine how they might be realized. It was an encounter between two modes of response to social crisis and collective injury: an encounter between melancholia and mourning.

During the long era of the cold war, the American literary establishment canonized one half of this cultural argument and buried the other. Two generations of critics celebrated the melancholic strand of modernism, praising the literature of despair as the most sophisticated response to the crisis of modernity. They were drawn to texts that were mainly produced by writers who came from privileged segments of society and that expressed the anguish of modernity but evaded troubling political questions. These cold war critics ignored or denigrated the modernism of mourning, marginalizing works that embodied psychological and cultural strategies that facilitated hope for political change. By the middle of the twentieth century, this distorted version of the literary movement had been fully consolidated. Melancholic modernism was isolated and institutionalized as the preeminent high-cultural response to the injuries inflicted by capitalist modernization.

Over the past twenty years, a new generation of scholars has vigorously challenged the narrowness of the established modernist canon. These scholars—often referred to today as the practitioners of a "new modernism studies"—have reclaimed a wide range of previously marginalized writers and have enabled us to see the racial, gender, class, sexual, and political diversity of this influential literary movement. By retrieving this diversity, the new modernism studies has made it possible to perceive the larger and more conflicted argument at the core of American modernism. *Mourning Modernity* seeks to name that central argument and to trace its political, psychological, and aesthetic contours. My aim is to show how the dynamic conflict between two modernisms shaped the early-twentieth-century American literary field as a whole as well as the individual works within it.

In the first half of *Mourning Modernity*, it is the broader literary field that I am concerned to map. I analyze a wide range of fictions and poems in order to show how one set of works contributed principally to the modernism of mourning and another set contributed mainly to the melancholic counter-tradition. Each of these texts is to some degree internally divided, containing both mournful and melancholic aspects—but in each case, one tendency or the other is strongly dominant. In the first half of my argument, I want to reveal the dominant tendencies of these texts and to delineate the two very different structures of feeling they embodied.

Chapter One lays the historical and theoretical foundations for this enterprise. It describes the relationship between modernism and the rise of monopoly capitalism in the early twentieth century. It outlines, in broad terms, the underlying political differences between the two modernisms and indicates the effects of the cold war canonization process. In order to explain the psychological conflict on which these political differences rest, it provides a detailed theoretical model for understanding different modes of social grieving. By offering a fundamental revision of the Freudian conceptualization of mourning and melancholia, it makes these psychoanalytic terms flexible enough to account for the emotionally demanding and historically varied processes by which individuals and groups respond to vast and systematic forms of social injury.

Chapters Two and Three then offer compressed readings of a dozen major modernist works, revealing the distinct structures of feeling at odds within the tradition. In Chapter Two, I delineate the psychological, political, and aesthetic features of melancholic modernism—offering readings of four especially influential, canonical works (Eliot's *The Waste Land*, Hemingway's *The Sun Also Rises*, Fitzgerald's *The Great Gatsby*, and Faulkner's *Absalom, Absalom!*), as well as two texts with a more tenuous relation to the cold war canon (Cather's *A Lost Lady* and Toomer's *Cane*). In Chapter Three, I explore the modernism of mourning—a tradition embodied principally in the works of writers from marginalized positions within the American social order (Hurston's *Their Eyes Were Watching God*, H. D.'s *The Flowering of the Rod*, Tillie Olsen's *Yonnondio*, the poetry of Langston Hughes) but that also includes some works (such as poems by William Carlos Williams) produced by writers from more privileged backgrounds who were admitted earlier to the modernist canon.

Having offered a map of the two modernisms that reveals the political, psychological, and aesthetic argument obscured by the cold war canon, I proceed in the second half of *Mourning Modernity* to demonstrate how these two impulses contend with one another *within* an individual literary text. For the struggle between mourning and melancholia, between political hope and despair, is enacted within individual works of expressive culture—and, indeed, within individual psyches—as surely as it is within the larger society. Most literary works resolve this struggle mainly in one direction or the other, but evidence of affective and stylistic ambivalence is almost always present. At a theoretical level, I want to emphasize that the distinction between mourning and melancholia should not be understood as a binary opposition: rather, they are two psychological tendencies on a continuum of grieving. The distinction between them is substantive, since each tendency has dramatically different psychological ramifications—and, in a social setting, each has important political implications. But the two tendencies exist in tension with one another, and it is important to grasp the dynamic struggle between them in any grieving process and, therefore, within individual literary works. Toward this end, the second half of *Mourning Modernity* offers a detailed case study that explores one writer's divided effort of social mourning.

I have chosen to devote this case study to John Dos Passos's famous but neglected *U.S.A.* trilogy because it embodies the conflict between the two modernisms more fully and more visibly than any work in the American tradition. Every modernist text enacts that conflict to some degree, but in most works one impulse is sufficiently dominant that the other registers itself as an occasional, muted, often half-buried countertendency. In contrast, Dos Passos's particular representational experiment in *U.S.A.* enabled him to develop both impulses fully, systematically, and in formal separation. At a substantive level, *U.S.A.* makes exceptionally clear the political implications of these two formal and psychological strategies. Sharing the general modernist preoccupation with the alienating effects of advanced capitalism, the trilogy is explicitly concerned with the possibility of addressing those social ills through radical political action. Struggling to maintain his hope for a democratic and egalitarian political transformation in the face of mounting repression and disappointment, Dos Passos produced a work that is structured formally and psychologically by the continuous oscillation between melancholia and mourning.

Chapter Four provides a biographical account of Dos Passos's experience of the crisis of modernization—and it explores in detail the reasons for his attraction to anticapitalist political movements. It offers a revisionary, post-cold war account of the political challenges that Dos Passos faced alongside hundreds of thousands of American radicals. Placing Dos Passos's composition of *U.S.A.* within the context of that complex and evolving political history, I suggest that the trilogy was explicitly launched as an effort to mourn for the political repression of the Red Scare of the teens and 1920s. I show how that effort was overwhelmed by the author's struggle to cope with the subsequent crisis of Stalinism, which emerged within the Left itself during the period of the trilogy's composition. Chapter Five explores the biographical prose poems of *U.S.A.* as one of the most fully realized examples of the modernism of mourning. In these formally experimental biographies, Dos Passos memorialized the radicals who had been suppressed during the Red Scare. Through his own work of grieving, he extended their aspirations as a living tradition that could be embraced and developed by readers in the future. Chapter Six then analyzes the naturalist fictions of *U.S.A.*, revealing their melancholic countertendency. Like all works of melancholic modernism, these fictions employ the deterministic and misanthropic strategies of literary naturalism. Dos Passos employs these strategies in order to assert the inevitability of the Left's failure and to negate the forms of political hope that he had simultaneously cultivated in the radical biographies. In the Conclusion, I offer a brief analysis of the Camera Eye segments of the trilogy as a way of returning to the larger psychological and political conflict that has had such fateful consequences in the history of the American Left—and that structures the cultural formation of American modernism.

One of the principal tasks of any culture is to develop—and adapt—strategies of grieving. Loss comes to each of us, but how we deal with loss is a collective as well as an individual matter. We learn ways of coping with the intimate grief that follows from the death of someone we love, from romantic rejection, from personal injury and disappointment. We also learn ways of managing the bewildering forms of loss and injury that are systematically inflicted by the social orders in which we live. Any community that suffers grave harm must find or invent practices of grieving in order to understand what its members have lost, in order to affirm those aspects of the self that have been denied, in order to find an outlet for rage, in order to survive. How we grieve has everything to do with how fully we can live. Mourning is not merely a way of remembering what is past. It is also a way of honoring what continues to live inside us and of projecting thwarted possibilities into the future. In the early twentieth century, Americans invented startling new practices for grieving the suffering produced by an economic and social transformation so vast that they could hardly grasp its contours. In the expressive arts, those forms of grieving have come to be called modernism. Some of those practices—eloquent but also mystifying—have been widely disseminated and have achieved remarkable influence over the last century. Others were long buried but contain resources for sustaining hope in the future flourishing of human capacities that have been frustrated and denied. *Mourning Modernity* explores these practices of social grieving. Their dynamic interaction produced the literature of modernism. How consciously we understand the struggle between them in our own generation will have much to do with the kind of society that we ourselves can imagine and create.

MOURNING MODERNITY

PART ONE

The Two Modernisms

ONE

Modernism and Loss

The Divided Response to American Capitalism

American modernism is famously a literature of loss. This was recognized, from the beginning, by the writers we have come to call modernist and by their readers. By 1926, Gertrude Stein could tell Ernest Hemingway "you are all a lost generation"—and he could, with peculiar pride, attach it as an epigraph to his first major novel, like a mourning band or a badge of membership in a stricken fraternity. Fifteen years later, Alfred Kazin was only summarizing what had already been widely remarked about modernist writers in the United States: "Lost and forever writing the history of their loss, they became specialists in anguish."[1] While these formulations have become clichés through repetition, they are revelatory in their way. They remind us of something important: that many writers in this period experienced losses so fundamental as to have become constitutive of identity; that these men and women had lost so much that they felt themselves to *be* lost—disoriented, unmoored, cut off from the continuities of a social order that seemed itself to be shattering. These formulations point us toward something else of equal significance: that while modernists experienced their deprivations in acutely personal ways, they recognized that the traumas they were under-going were collective and social in character. They felt themselves to be grievously injured, but they knew that they were not alone in their grief and that their injuries were not purely private. It was a generation (and more) that was lost—and these writers set out to tell the parables of their collective desolation.

Many stories have been told about the origins of modernist loss. Early on, for example, critics tended to present the First World War as the primal trauma of a lost generation. But it has become apparent that, catastrophic as it was, the war was merely the tip of the iceberg and that the expatriate "men of 1914" were only a small percentage of those on board. Like some other critics, I would like to begin with a broader materialist intuition: that mod-ernism in the expressive arts, including literature, emerged in response to a staggering economic transformation. From the first half of the nineteenth century, the burgeoning of industrial capitalism tore apart the inherited structures of modern societies, undermining achieved forms of solidarity as well as entrenched social hierarchies. From their first stirrings in this period, emergent modernisms around the world sought to register the ambivalent experience of this transformation.[2]

The formally experimental, early-twentieth-century literature called mod-ernism in the United States was, more specifically, a response to a particular phase of this process of capitalist transformation. It was a response to a shift in the scale of industrial production and commodity exchange during a pe-riod when markets were becoming ever more global under the pressures of intensifying imperialism and transnational capital flows. Both contemporar-ies and subsequent commentators have conceptualized this transition as a shift from "competitive" or "market" to "monopoly capitalism."[3] The rise of monopoly capitalism produced unique cognitive difficulties, as the details of individual lived experience were less and less adequate to provide people with an accurate sense of the vast economic structures that were transform-ing their lives, palpably and often painfully. The unparalleled formal strat-egies of modernist writing were attempts to produce "cognitive maps" of socioeconomic structures that eluded both individual experience and earlier modes of literary representation.[4] As working-class modernists hastened to show, these cognitive difficulties took on a particularly desperate significance for the vulnerable majority who suffered the increasingly efficient and often violent exploitation of labor that was characteristic of monopoly capitalism. But it was not only the most exploited who struggled to get their bearings. Even the privileged found themselves and their social relations transformed by a revolution that seemed as difficult to name as it was to escape. As the logic of the market came to permeate virtually all aspects of life, as people at all levels of society strove to satisfy more and more of their desires (including the most intimate) through the consumption of commodities, subjectivity itself seemed to be remade, with something missing at its heart.

While modernism seeks, at a cognitive level, to map vast socioeconomic structures, it struggles at an affective level to record the psychic injuries that accompanied this process of economic transformation. The losses were many, and I do not wish to speak reductively about them. But I want to propose, perhaps idiosyncratically, that modernist writers in the United States converge on a rather surprising consensus about the most pervasive symptom of this painful process. They seem to suggest that modernization had produced, above all, an affective crisis—a crisis in the possibility of love. Our modernists—not just the traditionally recognized figures, but also those from socially marginalized backgrounds who have more recently been admitted to the canon—record an experience of growing alienation, a crisis in the capacity for social solidarity at the public level, and for emotional and sexual intimacy at the private. At the very moment when American writers began to place an unparalleled value on romantic and sexual connection in particular, they were insisting that the capacity to realize such intimacy was imperiled.

These writers had considerable difficulty grasping the scale of the historical transformation that had produced their painful sense of alienation. Some imagined that their own generation had endured a sudden, violent rupture from a cohesive past in which a stable social order had provided both community and intimacy. Others recognized more accurately that the dynamics of alienation had been evolving over generations and that their own experience of disaffection reflected the intensification of a long historical development. Although some imagined that modernization had simply destroyed earlier and valued forms of human connection, others were aware that they were caught in a far more paradoxical process: that the emergent social order had stimulated heightened desires for personal intimacy and for more just and satisfying social arrangements that it also harshly foreclosed.

As they struggled to understand how a transformation in the global economic order was related to their sense of intimate distress, U.S. modernists explored this crisis of alienation in many ways—and they focused on varied aspects of the social process. Most were aware that economic change had led to a revolution in the sex-gender system. While some (especially women) greeted emergent models of femininity with hopefulness, others were deeply fearful, and many (of both sexes) perceived a related crisis in masculinity that seemed to doom heterosexual connection. Other writers focused on the collapse of cultural and class hierarchies on which social cohesion, and patterns of loyalty and reciprocity, were imagined by elites to depend. Many working-class modernists were concerned with the ways in which intensifying economic exploitation entailed psychic as well as material costs for working people, including the deformation of family life and the draining of libidinal energies necessary for satisfying affective relations. To a remarkable degree, middle-class modernists represented highly commodified forms of bourgeois class ambition as socially destructive and corrosive of personal intimacy. Even African American modernists, engaged in the ongoing work of mapping the pathologies of the American racial order, recorded the emergence of a new affective crisis. In particular, they devoted increasing attention to the ways in which growing class stratification, which had accompanied northward migration and urbanization, created new forms of alienation within black communities and new obstacles to erotic and romantic connection. For modernists consciously committed to the anticapitalist struggle (of whom there were a great many more than literary historians have until recently allowed), the crisis of alienation was writ large. For these radicals, the extraordinary political repression of the teens and 1920s marked not only the consolidation of U.S. capitalism against formidable popular opposition. More than that, the Red Scare seemed to demonstrate that a politics of love was impossible in America, that a society could not be constructed here that was founded on solidarity rather than exploitation.

This litany is intended, of course, to be suggestive rather than exhaustive. I mean to propose that we have been right all along to understand U.S. modernism as a literature of loss, though we have not yet understood fully the extent and nature of this loss. The formal experiments that distinguish modern*ist* writing—and it *is* a question of form—were the efforts of American writers to invent strategies of representation that could capture an economic and social transformation that seemed to imperil the most fundamental of human capacities. U.S. modernism was a collective effort to mourn injuries that were experienced at the deepest psychic and libidinal levels, but that were also recognized as shared and as socially induced. These writers, who invented strange new forms to organize a strange new world, struggled in varied ways to understand how their inmost grief and bewilderment had come about. Their stories and poems sought to name—though sometimes also to mystify and disavow—the social forces that had produced such intimate sorrow.

A Divided Tradition

It is my contention that we have, in fact, two modernisms. The early-twentieth-century tradition of experimental writing is deeply divided, containing two very different modes of response to the experiences of loss that accompanied capitalist modernization in the United States. The differences between these two strands must be understood in political and in psychological terms.

Let us begin with politics, at the broadest level. America's most firmly canonized modernism is a literature of pained acquiescence to destructive social forces. The small group of writers who were admitted to the narrow canon of modernism at the height of the cold war had, of course, a rather diverse set of specific (and evolving) political affiliations. But underneath their specific affiliations, most were united by a conviction that the human potentialities they valued most had been imperiled or destroyed by social forces that were irresistible. As a result, they experienced their losses as irrevocable. Much of the irony for which American male modernists are justly famous is, in fact, a defense against the sentimentality, the "prettiness," of thinking that what one had lost (personally and collectively as a culture) could ever be retrieved. Most of America's traditionally canonized modernists—and I will be discussing as emblematic figures of this tradition such diverse writers as Eliot, Hemingway, Fitzgerald, Faulkner, Cather, and Toomer—produced literary works that are structured by the presumption that collective resistance to the damaging forces of modernization was impossible, even unthinkable.

There is, however, another modernism—a sustained tradition of formally experimental writing that is consciously committed to the work of social resistance. This is, equally, a tradition preoccupied with the anguished appreciation of all that a capitalist modernity had imperiled. But it is a tradition whose poetics and forms of storytelling are predicated on the view that the processes of modernization were historically contingent, that the most corrosive forces at work in American life might be altered and ameliorated, and that the human capacities that seemed most constrained might somehow be enabled to flourish in the future. As emblematic figures of this "other" modernism, I will discuss Zora Neale Hurston, H. D., Tillie Olsen, Langston Hughes, and William Carlos Williams. These writers, like those mentioned earlier, had diverse and evolving political affiliations. In their literary works, all were critical of aspects of American capitalism, and four—Hughes, Olsen, and for a time, Williams and H. D.—were directly involved in anticapitalist political formations.[5] Some (H. D., Olsen, Hurston, and to some degree, Hughes) were explicitly concerned with the constraints being placed on women in a modernizing America, and with the revolutionary changes that would be necessary to liberate them—and to liberate love-relations of various kinds in a culture weighed down by misogyny. Two of these writers, Hughes and Hurston, are characteristic of the main line of African American modernism in their effort to delineate the intersection of racism and an evolving capitalist economic order, and to imagine how the dreams of African Americans, so painfully deferred under this regime, might yet be realized. Despite deep differences in political temperament and ideology, then, these authors were all practitioners of a modernism committed to political resistance and to a chastened social hopefulness.

By describing this second group of writers as constituting an "other" modernism, a distinctive current within the modernist movement, I am attempting to extend and integrate the results of two decades of revisionary scholarship. Increasingly referred to as the "new modernism studies," this scholarship has been centrally committed to the project of canon expansion. Critics now widely recognize that modernism was canonized in the 1940s, 1950s, and early 1960s in narrow and parochial ways. Over the last twenty years, scholars have sought to explore the uses and implications of modernist experimentation for women writers, for authors from racially marginalized groups, for working-class writers, and writers on the Left.[6] These various projects of canon expansion have often taken place in relative isolation from one another—and we are, perhaps only now, in a position to understand how, taken together, they have changed our understanding of modernism itself as a large cultural formation whose contours have been substantially redrawn.[7]

I am proposing that many—though not all—of the formally experimental writers who were excluded from the modernist canon because of their subordinate positions in the social hierarchy, or because of their political radicalism, shared a common structure of feeling. Most importantly, they shared the presumption that capitalist modernization was a contingent historical process that might be resisted, controlled, redirected. They imagined that the profound losses that Americans had suffered might somehow be remedied, that the human capacities truncated and proscribed by the processes of modernization might find new forms of realization in a changed social order. These presumptions structured the poems and fictions that they wrote about the experience of their generation. For them, modernist formal experiments were efforts not only to map, but to resist, a painful social transformation. When we read these "other" modernists alongside their more familiar, long-canonized contemporaries, we become newly aware of how deeply the canonized tradition is structured by an opposed presumption: that the process of modernization, however destructive, was irresistible.

I want to emphasize that the difference between these two modernisms is not a difference between condemnation and approval of the social order brought into being by monopoly capitalism. On the contrary, it is one of the remarkable features of American literary modernism that it is nearly uniform in its hostility—often ambivalent, but almost always powerful—to this new socioeconomic order. Eliot's hostility, for example, to the dominant forces of his time, and to consumer capitalism in particular, could hardly be exceeded; Faulkner's critique of America's social pathologies is incisive by any standard. What distinguishes our most firmly canonized modernism is not its affirmation of modernization, then, but its sense of helplessness before it, its acquiescence to a transformation that was perceived to be as irresistible as it was injurious. It is a literature often angry, and usually grief stricken, about the alienating effects of advanced capitalism—but it records these catastrophic developments within literary forms that present a contingent historical process as natural and inexorable.

This naturalizing social vision, with its accompanying posture of anguished resignation, is not gratuitously linked to the process of canonization. Rather, it seems to have functioned within the cultural logic of cold war

America, as its very condition. In the 1940s, 1950s, and 1960s, the United States laid claim for the first time to having produced a globally significant, even dominant, literature, pointing to such celebrated (and Nobel Prize–winning) modernists as Eliot, Hemingway, and Faulkner as the most important evidence of this triumph. This particular strand of literary modernism (like Abstract Expressionism in the visual arts) thus functioned as a cultural bulwark to the assertion of the United States' geopolitical ascendancy in the period after the Second World War.[8] For this literature to have performed this particular cultural work, it needed to be relatively free from explicit suggestions that the emerging economic and political order ought to be resisted—especially from the Left.[9] With hindsight, one can now see the specific ideological utility of equating formal complexity and aesthetic sophistication with political resignation. With the exigencies of the cold war in mind, it is not difficult to perceive why the strand of the modernist tradition that refused such resignation was consigned for decades to obscurity.[10]

Although I am thus proposing a correlation between cold war canonization, social privilege, and a posture of anguished helplessness, such a correlation is not strict or uniform. There were, to be sure, some canonized writers from more privileged backgrounds who should be counted within the "other" modernism. Similarly, some poets and novelists who were excluded from the modernist pantheon and who have been recently reclaimed shared the quiescent structure of feeling that characterizes the established tradition. For this reason, in selecting emblematic figures of the dominant tradition, I have included two—Willa Cather and Jean Toomer—who have had a more tenuous relationship to the canon, and whose less privileged positions in the social hierarchy certainly played a role in their earlier occlusion within a modernist tradition to which they now seem central.[11] Similarly, I have included William Carlos Williams within the ranks of the "other" modernism—and, in Part Two of this book, John Dos Passos in one of his incarnations—in order to make clear that there are more established and more privileged writers who also shared the intuition that the socioeconomic forces breeding a crisis of alienation might, indeed, be resisted, and that Americans might grieve their losses in ways that would enable them to retrieve what seemed everywhere to be imperiled.

The contention that we have two modernisms, then, is not a way of describing the difference between female modernists and male ones, between

African Americans and those identified as white, between working-class and bourgeois writers. It is not even, as the case of Jean Toomer may suggest, a way of distinguishing between conservatives and political radicals within the modernist movement (though this is partly at issue).[12] It is true that the "other" modernism, a tradition of experimental writing committed to the possibility of social resistance, is disproportionately (though not exclusively) a tradition constituted by writers from subordinated social groups. In what follows, I will suggest some of the social, ideological and psychological reasons for this. But the contention that we have two modernisms is an effort, above all, to indicate that American literary modernism is a cultural formation structured by a deep argument about the character of the capitalist transformation of modern life. It is an argument about whether capitalism, and the alienation it has brought, is indeed a second nature, and our ineluctable destiny. And it is an argument about whether it is possible to mourn fully the social injuries that have been inflicted by this economic transformation.

Mourning, Melancholia, and the Problem of Socially Induced Loss

From these preliminary formulations, it should already be clear that the difference between the two modernisms is as much psychological as it is political. They represent two distinct modes of psychic response to collective loss. Using Freudian terms, I will argue that the dominant tradition—the modernism of pained acquiescence—is melancholic. The "other" modernism is a literature engaged in the work of mourning.

I am drawing here, of course, on a distinction initially proposed by Freud in his first sustained essay on the subject of psychic loss, "Mourning and Melancholia" (an essay published in 1917, during the period of literary modernism's burgeoning). The distinction has remained central to subsequent psychoanalytic attempts to understand grieving, and it will help to illuminate the divided structure of feeling that characterizes U.S. modernism. It is also important to note, however, that Freud's model of object-loss was originally developed to analyze private experiences of bereavement. For this reason, it does not adequately capture the complex challenges of mourning collective injuries produced by historically particular social phenomena. In order to develop a fuller and more flexible account of what it means to grieve for social injuries, therefore, I will offer a fundamental theoretical revision of Freud's model of mourning and melancholia.

As those familiar with the essay will recall, Freud distinguishes between two types of grief—or, more precisely, between two psychic strategies for responding to the experience of loss. The first he calls "mourning," and his description draws principally upon the experience of grief that follows the death of a person one has deeply loved. In addition to feelings of sorrow, the main symptom of mourning is the painful withdrawal from life—an incapacity to take "interest in the outside world" (except to the degree that it reminds one of the person one has lost) and an inability to "adopt any new object of love." Freud's account of the work of mourning, although regrettably limited, is highly suggestive. He proposes that mourning involves a particular kind of remembering that is saturated with feeling, a "hyper-cathected" recollection of every aspect of the lost object that bound the mourner to it. This work of memory is performed alongside a process of "reality testing": while the mourner keeps the lost object alive in memory, this remembering takes place always in conjunction with the painful recognition that the object is, in reality, gone. Through this complex work of detailed and loving remembrance in the full knowledge of one's loss, one is able slowly and painfully to bring the process of mourning to an end. This does not mean an end to sorrow, nor does it imply the forgetting of what one has loved. What it means, on Freud's account, is that the mourner is able to regain access to the libidinal energies that have been attached to the lost object, as a result of which "the ego becomes free and uninhibited again." The mourner is, in other words, able to love once more, to engage with interest the world outside.[13]

Melancholia shares most of the features of mourning, but it includes two dire additional symptoms. Most dramatically, the grief of the melancholic is accompanied by acute feelings of self-beratement or self-hatred: large funds of anger and aggression are vented against the self. (As Freud notes in passing—and this will prove significant for my own account of melancholic modernism—this aggression can, in some cases, be directed both at the self and, in a kind of promiscuous and generalized misanthropy, at "everyone else" (246). Hamlet provides Freud with a literary illustration of this phenomenon.) The great danger of melancholia lies in this self-beratement—which, as Freud and subsequent clinicians have emphasized, can lead to suicide. In addition to self-hatred, melancholia differs from mourning mainly in duration. While the work of mourning takes place slowly, it comes to an end after a finite "lapse of time" (244). Melancholia, in contrast, can last indefinitely. Sometimes, after prolonged self-punishment, the melancholic rage can burn itself out. Frequently, it comes to an end only with death itself.[14] Like the mourner but without the promise of liberation, the melancholic is unable to enter into new and dynamic object relations, unable to sustain loving interactions with the world outside.

In the course of a dense, speculative discussion, Freud proposes four possible factors that may contribute to the blockage of mourning and to the development of melancholic symptoms. First, he suggests that melancholia may emerge in response to "ideal" rather than "real" forms of loss—by which he means situations in which a loved person has not actually died, but has nevertheless been lost to the sufferer, as for example in cases of romantic rejection (245, 256). Second, melancholia may be triggered by forms of loss that are, to a substantial degree, unconscious. Freud alludes here to cases in which a patient may well "know *whom* he has lost but not *what* he has lost" in that person—a situation most likely to occur when the loss itself is of an ideal character (245). Third, the process of mourning is often blocked by the presence of strong and unacknowledged ambivalence—conflicted feelings of anger or hatred as well as love—toward the person one has lost (251). (Such ambivalence is likely to be particularly acute in cases of "ideal" loss, especially if one takes rejection or abandonment to be the paradigmatic cause. It should also be evident that a bereaved person is particularly likely to repress, and thus render unconscious, such negative feelings.) Fourth, Freud proposes that melancholia may be especially likely to occur in cases where the original bond of love has been formed on the basis of narcissistic identification. In such circumstances, a person may respond to the experience of loss by a regression from (narcissistic) object love into pure narcissism: because the melancholic takes the object into the ego as an identification, the libidinal energies that had been attached to the loved person may now be withdrawn and redirected toward the ego itself. This regression from object-love to identification provides love with a psychic refuge: "by taking flight into the ego, love escapes extinction" (257). But this retreat into narcissistic identification enables the melancholic, above all else, to displace onto him- or herself the feelings of rage and aggression that were unconsciously felt toward the lost object. It is this displacement of aggression through identification that explains the fierce self-beratement that distinguishes melancholia, including the "tendency to suicide" (252).

In the opening paragraphs of "Mourning and Melancholia," Freud explicitly proposes that more social forms of loss (including quite abstract ones) can give rise to the same psychic responses as the experience of personal loss through death or abandonment. He explains that either mourning or melancholia can emerge in "reaction to the loss of a loved person, *or to the loss of some abstraction which has taken the place of one, such as one's country, liberty, an ideal, and so on*" (243; emphasis added). Having raised this provocative suggestion at the outset of the essay, Freud then immediately moves on to discuss structures of grief and mourning entirely in the private terms of the individual loss of a loved person. Although Freud declined to pursue the matter of collective loss, his comment does suggest how a psychoanalytic inquiry into mourning might be opened onto a social plane. In recent years, historians, sociologists, and cultural critics have pursued this intuition, applying psychoanalytic insights about mourning and melancholia (and about the related phenomenon of trauma) to the varied human experiences of historically particular, collective injury.[15] American modernism provides an exceptionally rich field for studying the psychosocial dynamics of collective loss, because it maps the intimate workings of the psyche in relation to large-scale social transformation. American modernists grieved for the loss of love—and they perceived that the psychic experience of alienation was itself rooted in the pervasive and varied social crises that attended modernization: the loss of established social and cultural hierarchies; the loss of residual ideals of masculinity and femininity; the myriad traumas of working-class life under a regime of intensifying economic exploitation; the ongoing catastrophes entailed by racism; collapsing ideals of the American nation itself, with its constitutive and betrayed promises of political equality and class mobility; the suppression of emancipatory social movements; and so on.

It is important to note that the forms of socially induced loss that concerned U.S. modernists are characterized by the features that Freud identifies as conditions for melancholia. Highly abstract and collective losses, such as the destruction of a political movement or the shattering of a cherished conception of masculinity, are by their very nature "ideal." They will also inevitably involve unconscious elements. Dos Passos knew that he had lost a version of the socialist movement during the Red Scare, as Hemingway knew that he and many of his contemporaries were experiencing a crisis in masculinity—but it should be apparent that what they had lost *in* these things were complex matters of unconscious, as well as conscious, investment. It should be equally clear that the loss of large ideals and social formations will always involve ambivalence: at the very least, there will be anger that these things have allowed themselves to be destroyed, through whatever vulnerability or inadequacy. (This ambivalence will be especially acute in cases where the beloved object is perceived to be actively responsible for its own destruction.)[16] And finally, the social crises that these writers were struggling to mourn entailed the loss of things—ideals, movements, social or cultural formations—to which they were attached through deep bonds of identification. To suffer these losses was to suffer considerable narcissistic injury, and many modernists struggled acutely to understand who they were in the wake of deprivation. In many cases, the rage they felt was directed both at themselves and, misanthropically, at the entire world around them. The conditions for melancholia, then, were abundantly present for writers grieving the psychic injuries that capitalist modernization had produced. Some writers responded melancholically to these conditions, while others were able to find the difficult paths to mourning. These different psychic responses had dramatically different political (as well as literary) implications.

In order to understand the distinctive and politically significant forms of grieving produced by social injury, it is necessary to revise the fundamental model of loss that undergirds Freud's conception of mourning *and* melancholia. In particular, it is necessary to move from a dyadic to a triadic model. Freud's account assumes a scenario in which there are two parties: a subject (the mourner) and an object (that which has been lost). Although the dyadic model may be adequate for analyzing some kinds of private loss, it is insufficient for understanding collective losses produced by ongoing and historically particular social dynamics. In cases of socially induced loss, we need to consider three terms: the subject (which may be an individual or a group), the object (which will generally require a complex definition: an ideal, a social or cultural formation, and so on), and *the social forces* that have destroyed that object or made it unavailable.

The triadic model opens up important questions that remain obscure in Freud's primarily intrapsychic account. The most significant of these asks *why* this object has been lost or rendered inaccessible. Others follow immediately from this: Who or what is *responsible* for my loss? Where ought I to place blame, and what is the proper object of my anger? While these questions are, of course, social (and, in some cases, political), they are also properly psycho-analytic. Freud recognized the decisive importance of anger in the processes of grief, but his dyadic model reduces our capacity to think flexibly about the causes and objects of that anger in a social setting. In Freud's account—and in many psychoanalytic accounts that have succeeded his—the anger of the bereaved is imagined as having only two possible objects: the lost object or the mourner him- or herself. The triadic model demands that we identify the social forces that have produced any particular experience of collective loss, and it holds open the possibility that the bereaved may indeed—and, in some cases, should—feel rage at those social processes or formations. The triadic model does not presume that in cases of socially induced loss, anger will be directed at destructive social forces *instead of* at the mourner or at the lost object. On the contrary, it makes visible the variable relationships that exist between and among those forces, the bereaved, and that which has been lost. In some cases—one might think, for example, of Polish Jews who survived the Holocaust—the bereaved may indeed properly experience the *causes* of their loss (Nazism, organized anti-Semitism) as almost entirely separable from themselves and from what they have lost (loved ones, shtetl communi-ties, a shared Jewish culture). Others—post–Second World War Germans, say, who were children during the Nazi era—may be mourning something (the loss of an idealized image of the German Reich) that is responsible for its own destruction: the cause of loss (and the object of anger) is also that which is loved and grieved for. In other cases—that of a loyal SS officer, for example, grieving the loss of a heroic, imperial Germany after the defeat of Nazism—the mourner is himself inescapably entangled with *both* the object of his loss and that which has destroyed it. The anger accompanying these different scenarios will be variously distributed and will pose different chal-lenges for the work of mourning.

In proposing the triadic model, I have begun with the question of re-sponsibility and anger, because the problem of aggression is so central to the mourning process and to its painfully self-destructive variant, melancholia. For melancholia is, in essence, a form of grieving that is blocked by *uncon-scious* and *displaced* aggression. Freud is clear, and on the whole convincing, about this matter. The melancholic internalizes the lost object, taking it into the ego as an identification. The psychic aim of this internalization is to enable the melancholic to displace onto the self feelings of aggression that are, for whatever reasons, inadmissible to consciousness. I wish to emphasize this point, because some recent critics who have discussed social forms of loss in psychoanalytic terms have failed to honor the full psychic logic of this process of internalization, and they have created confusion about the nature of melancholia and its relation to anger.[17] As we have seen, melancholia is not simply a form of grieving in which anger is present as well as sorrow; and it is certainly not a form of grieving in which anger is more fully acknowledged than it is in mourning. It is a mode of grieving that disavows anger and turns it against the self. When that anger is particularly explosive, and the inability to make it conscious is particularly acute, melancholics may literally destroy themselves because they are unable to name and face the actual objects of their rage. Whether or not melancholia actually leads to suicide, the self-punishment is extreme, as is the depressed cauterization of libido—the indefinite inability to love. The social variants of melancholia are no less painful and no less disastrous: they merely take place on a larger scale.

In cases of socially induced, collective loss—as in purely private instances of bereavement—it is important that sufferers be able to name the causes of their grief and the objects of their anger. If the victims of institutionalized violence and injustice cannot identify the social formations that have harmed them, they too will commonly displace their anger upon themselves—and they will often scapegoat others who may provide convenient substitutes. Canonical works of American modernism amply illustrate the costs of converting unacknowledged or uncomprehended rage into personal and social aggression. The triadic model I have proposed enables us to trace these varied strategies of psychic displacement. It also enables us to grasp the psychic challenges posed by the effort to mourn social losses, particularly in circumstances in which the mourners themselves and the objects for which they are grieving are intimately and variously entangled with the destructive forces that have injured them.

The triadic model also focuses attention on the persistent dynamics that characterize scenarios of social loss. In contrast to the sudden punctuality of losing a beloved person through death, or even of a natural disaster that may kill many people in a community, most socially induced losses are sustained and ongoing. The economic and social pressures that truncate the lives of people in an exploited and impoverished working-class community, for example, do not arrive one day and vanish the next like a tornado. Rather, they will commonly persist throughout a lifetime, even across generations. The effort to grieve these privations (the psychic depletion caused by unrewarding and repetitive jobs, the exclusion from education, the lack of time to nurture families, the denial of opportunities for self-realization, and so on) will take place under the persistent pressure of the very forces that have produced these losses. Similarly, the *objects* being mourned in such instances will not simply vanish, as in the case of a person who has died. When people grieve for relations and human possibilities that are denied by prevailing social structures, they grieve for things that continue to exist in truncated form (their own creativity, familial bonds, and so on)—or that might exist if those ongoing social pressures were diminished.[18] The *duration*, in other words, of such scenarios produces situations in which bereaved people are struggling to grieve for objects that continue to exist in some way and in the presence of destructive forces that continue to impinge upon their lives. As a result, analyses of socially induced loss must be able to describe processes of grieving in which the bereaved must sustain ongoing relations to the objects they are persistently losing and to the social pressures that are persistently injuring them. In such circumstances, neither the objects nor the causes of one's loss are engaged at a purely intrapsychic level—as they may be in the most delimited cases of private mourning. With the triadic model, it is possible to chart such complex grieving processes, taking into account the ongoing relations among the subject of loss, the objects lost, and the social pressures responsible for those losses.

This approach to analyzing social injury reveals the diverse temporalities and variable durations that characterize different historical scenarios. For example, the victims of an urban bombing may mourn an event whose psychic effects are ongoing, but whose causes were punctual—and, perhaps, passing. The victims of the Holocaust must grieve injuries that were inflicted not in the course of a single day, but over a period of years, some of whose causes were immediate (Nazism) and some of which were longstanding and enduring (Western anti-Semitism). For the peoples of the African diaspora, the members of each generation must grieve for immediate personal losses that are directly tied to centuries of slavery—and to the ongoing institutionalized structures of Western racism. For a gay man or woman grieving for years spent in the closet, the process of mourning may require not only the continued daily struggle with a homophobic social order, but also a large act of historical imagination in grasping the scale and duration of such sexual prohibitions in our collective history. Each of these scenarios—and the many others that will differ from them—involves distinct and varied problems of duration, of persistence, of relation to past and ongoing social pressures and formations.

Because the triadic model enables us to account for the duration of experiences of social injury, it provides a valuable context in which to reconceptualize the nature of collective *traumas*. The psychoanalytic concept of trauma has proved fruitful for many scholars concerned with catastrophic social phenomena, but the standard formulations of this concept have limitations as well as strengths. The virtue of the trauma model is its focus on the unassimilability of some forms of social injury. It reminds us that social phenomena can breach our psychic boundaries in ways that we cannot process or tolerate at the moment of their occurrence. This psychic fact can lead not only to intractable forms of suffering, but also to acts of unconscious repetition that can be psychically and socially devastating.[19] In Freud's original formulations, the distinctive unassimilability of traumatic events results most centrally from "the factor of surprise" or "fright."[20] But this focus on sudden punctuality, or "shock," is of limited use in the analysis of ongoing and sustained dynamics of social injury and deprivation. If we are trying to understand the psychic effects of the Holocaust, of capitalist modernization, or of chattel slavery, we are struggling with social phenomena that cannot be said to be experienced indefinitely (for years, decades, centuries) as sudden shocks that take the psyche by surprise.[21] In part, this difficulty may be addressed by noting that these large social processes may produce myriad particular experiences that are suddenly injurious and whose unexpectedness gives them a traumatic character. But the triadic model suggests a fuller explanation of the way in which ongoing social processes can themselves be traumatic. Specifically, I would like to propose that people experience structural social injuries as *traumas* when they do not possess adequate analyses of the processes or formations that have harmed them. In the absence of such social or historical accounts, they will experience these processes not merely as injurious, but as mysteriously and inexplicably so. It is the lack of adequate explanatory social narratives that makes these catastrophic experiences not only painful but psychically unassimilable—and may doom the victims to traumatic symptoms, including the compulsion to repeat. In the case of large-scale social injuries, then, the psyche is "unprepared" (Freud, *PP* 26) and hence traumatized not by the suddenness of its violation, but by an indefinite incomprehensibility of the social process that is wounding it.

By analyzing social traumas within the larger triadic framework, we can also understand more fully what it might mean to remediate them.[22] For those who are experiencing destructive social processes *as traumas*, the psychic task of "working through" must involve not only the painful therapeutic project of raising their injuries to consciousness—but also the work of developing explanatory social narratives that will make the ongoing causes of suffering cognitively intelligible.[23] As victims develop such narratives, they must also confront the rage that will accompany the growing recognition of the nature and causes of their injuries. Although Freud did not focus on the place of anger in the working through of trauma, his passing references to the symptomatic similarities of melancholia and trauma should alert us to the importance of the blockage of aggression in the perpetuation of traumatic suffering (Freud, *PP* 6, 27). The triadic model provides a structure for understanding how the objects of anger can be identified—and what may be at stake in displacing that aggression. As victims gain consciousness of the injuries they have endured (and of their causes), the task of "working through" will become, increasingly, the task of mourning. For traumatic social injuries entail losses: these will commonly include the loss of identifiable external objects (beloved people, communities, social movements, and so on), but they will also include the loss of cherished aspects of the self that has been violated.

An example may be helpful in illustrating the conceptual gains produced by analyzing trauma within the terms of the triadic model. When a woman is raped, this particular event may be (and often is) endured as a trauma: as a violation of the self that is too overwhelming to be psychically assimilated or experienced fully when it takes place. The specifically *traumatic* character of this event may be largely caused by the element of punctual surprise or shock. Such a violation can, to some degree, be worked through on the conventional model of trauma: that which happened but which could not be experienced can, through slow painful therapeutic work, be raised to consciousness. But a woman who survives rape in our society must grieve these injuries, physical and psychic, in the context of a culture that continues to objectify her, to subject her to male predatoriness, and to the misogynist stigma that attaches to sexual violation in a patriarchal culture. These ongoing social pressures must be persistently negotiated in any effort to come to terms with the original injury. The experiences of these pressures, moreover, may themselves be *traumatic*—but in the particular sense I have described: if they are psychically unassimilable, this is not because they are sudden and surprising, but because the woman may possess no adequate explanatory account that makes these continuing impingements comprehensible. In order to work through the trauma she has endured, she will need to bring to consciousness not only the original violation, but also the ongoing social forces that have compounded (and perhaps caused) the individual assault she has suffered. If she can raise these to consciousness, she will be able to identify the objects of her anger, both the individuals and the larger social processes that have harmed her so grievously. If that anger has found adequate expression, she may indeed be able to *mourn* her injury. I do not mean by this that the harm can simply be undone or her sorrow ended. What I mean is that the victim may be able to engage in a psychic process that will enable her to regain access to those libidinal energies that she had attached to things that have been taken from her (feelings of bodily integrity, a sense of social security, and so on).

This brings me, finally, to the dynamics of mourning itself—a psychoanalytic concept that requires fundamental retheorization, especially in a social context. Because Freud was principally concerned with melancholia, his account of mourning is relatively undeveloped. It is also problematic in several respects that have had an enduring influence on psychoanalytic discussions of grieving. Most importantly, Freud suggests that the psychic work of mourning involves a "detachment" of libido, a decathexis, from the object that one has loved and lost. This notion that libido must be "withdrawn" from the lost object in the process of mourning rests upon the so-called "economic" model of the psyche, to which Freud was recurrently drawn. This model presumes that the amount of energy (including libido) in the psyche is limited, contained within a closed system, and that to have this energy available for one object it must be withdrawn from another. For this reason, Freud describes new objects of love or attachment as "replacements" or "substitutes" for objects that have been lost (*MM* 244–245).

These formulations, introduced in "Mourning and Melancholia," have encouraged an unfortunately rigid understanding of the movement from loss to new love. The logic of necessary decathexis in mourning rests on an overly mechanistic understanding of the psyche and implies an unduly constrained conception of our capacity for love. Libido is not infinite, to be sure, but it is not a mechanical closed system either. Freud's implication that the mourner must, as a matter of course, sever affective ties to that which has been loved and lost has appropriately struck some commentators as insensitive to the realities of grieving—and it has prompted a number of recent critics to dismiss the mourning process itself as inherently normative and coercive.[24] We need to refine and expand our conception of mourning in this regard, rather than rejecting what is, in fact, an indispensable psychic process. In particular, I propose that mourning fully for what we have lost involves, not a detachment of libido, but almost its opposite: it involves, above all, the vigorous effort to raise to consciousness one's ongoing libidinal investments in what one has loved and lost.[25] It is the protracted and "hypercathected" recollection of beloved things now lost that enables us to regain access—and to reinforce our ongoing relation—to those aspects of ourselves that were inspired, stimulated, gratified by something still beloved but unavailable to us. This process enables us to hold on, at the deepest affective as well as conscious levels, to those libidinal possibilities in ourselves that were engaged by the object taken from us. The hypercathected activity of mourning thus enables us *both* to sustain our attachment to what we have lost *and* to extend these libidinal energies to new objects.

I want to propose, further, that we should revise—or possibly abandon altogether—the language of "replacement" and "substitution," which rests on the problematic logic of "decathexis" and which has persisted within psychoanalytic discussions of loss. This vocabulary implies that the end of mourning is marked by one's capacity to seek—and find—new objects that take the place, more or less identically, of what one has lost. (It is in this sense that they are "replacements" or "substitutes" and not merely new objects of love.) This is a misleading formulation, for the degree to which one experiences new objects rigidly as replications of the old is, in fact, the degree to which one remains mired in a form of melancholia. It is an indication that one continues to be open to the world only to the extent that it reminds one of that which has been lost. The end of mourning should be understood, rather, as the renewed capacity for dynamic object relation: as the capacity to experience new people and relations with spontaneity, with a receptivity to difference, to newness, to changes in oneself and others. To insist that a full process of mourning leads to such a capacity for dynamic and spontaneous relation is *not* to suggest that new bonds are unrelated to lost objects that have been mourned. For the mourning process, as I have described it, is above all an affirmation of energies in the self that have been engaged and attached to what one has loved and lost. In new love relations, one brings these ongoing and affirmed aspects of the self into contact with different possibilities. The depth and fullness of the mourning process is demonstrated by the dynamism and flexibility with which those libidinal possibilities are extended into the present and the future.[26]

These revisions to the Freudian conception of mourning can be integrated readily into the triadic model, providing us with a richer sense of what it means to mourn socially induced losses. In order for the mourning process to take place at all, those who have suffered injuries at the hands of their society (or by the impositions of others), must be able to name the causes of their loss. Only through some form of social or political consciousness is the anger that accompanies such injuries able to find its proper objects—and only in this way, is the process of grieving free to proceed. Unhindered by self-destructive and displaced aggression, the process of social mourning involves a sustained effort—collective as well as individual—to raise to consciousness the ongoing libidinal attachments of the bereaved to those social possibilities that have been proscribed or imperiled. In social mourning, in other words, we invent or adapt cultural practices that enable us to name our continued yearnings for those forms of social activity and personal realization that have been denied by the social orders in which we live. The literary tradition that I have called the modernism of mourning contains many efforts to perform this imaginative work of grieving. When this particular work of memory can be performed, the victims of systematic social injury are able, not only to recall what they have been denied, but to open themselves to the possibility that those imperiled human capacities might find a way to flourish once again.[27]

To the degree that victims of social injuries seek only to retrieve what they have lost in the mode of rigid replication, the work of mourning remains obstructed. In social, as in private, processes of grieving, the capacity to imagine only replication is a sign that the bereaved can gain access to libidinal energies in themselves only to the degree that they remain exclusively attached to something lost. One can see this phenomenon with particular clarity, for example, in the case of people who are grieving for the disappointment or failure of political movements. In the face of such disappointments, some cauterize their former political aspirations, cutting themselves off entirely from the yearnings they embodied. Others retain access to those desires, but only as a rigid—sometimes nostalgic, sometimes furious—attachment to the precise form of a past political movement: only the return of the slain Dr. King or Malcolm X (or of some imagined precise equivalent) would enable the civil rights movement to regain its momentum, for such people; only a return to the particular socialist movement crushed by the Red Scare would be meaningful; only if young women could imagine feminism in the same terms as those who launched the second wave could the women's movement truly be extended. In such examples, the process of mourning remains significantly impeded.[28] For when the process of social mourning has run its course, when its painful and creative work has been pursued most fully, the bereaved are able to regain access to the aspirations and remembered pleasures attached to lost objects (in this case, disappointed or stalled emancipatory movements)—and to extend those libidinal impulses dynamically in the present, meeting responsively and spontaneously the specificities of an evolving world, scarred but not destroyed by loss.

We know that when private mourning is able to proceed fully, one is able to open oneself to the possibility of new love and attachment. In the case of social mourning, an injured portion of a society is able once again to imagine the possible flourishing of those capacities in themselves that have been denied or imperiled by the social structures in which they live. Political hope is a social form of mourning: indeed, it is the principal form that social mourning takes. (In contrast, political despair—and its ironic variant, political cynicism—are social forms of melancholia.) While some kind of social consciousness is a necessary *condition* for such mourning (something that enables the process, preventing the destructive displacement of anger), political hope is an embodiment and result of the process, its gift. If political hope is not shallow (a form of complacency or ignorance about social injury), it is a remarkable psychic as well as social achievement. It represents the ability to acknowledge the depth of one's loss, to name those aspirations and satisfactions that have been denied, and to imagine how, in some form, they might be dynamically explored and enjoyed in the future.

But like any form of mourning, political hope is an arduous process that poses grave psychic difficulties. For it is not only a relief to recognize that what one has lost might be revived (in the complex and particular sense I have described). Such a recognition can also be a painful burden. If what one has lost—a political movement or the frustrated hopes of an impoverished community, for example—has been crushed by vast social forces, then it is only possible to imagine the revival and extension of such thwarted yearnings if one can also imagine collective resistance and social transformation. To mourn social losses of this kind, to open oneself again to the possible future flourishing of imperiled human possibilities on this scale, is also to accept responsibility for a daunting project of social change. That responsibility is formidable. For many, over the course of the last century, it has been intolerable. Nevertheless, the triadic model should help us to see that the acceptance of social responsibility is not only an ethical or political imperative, but also a psychic necessity. For in mourning socially induced losses, one must find ways to name the causes of one's grief and anger and to imagine how yearnings that have been systematically denied might ultimately find means of realization. Once one recognizes that one's deep needs collide with the social structures in which one lives, one must seek either to deny those needs or to change those structures. This recognition is frightening as well as liberating. As American modernists struggled to mourn all that they and their contemporaries had lost in the process of capitalist modernization, they confronted these choices in varied ways, some mainly through melancholic self-punishments and displacements of rage, others through the chastened hopefulness of more fully realized practices of mourning. All had to negotiate the tantalizing possibility that they might, with others, bring into being a social order in which the human potentialities imperiled by modernization might be revived or made anew, that love itself might somehow be retrieved.

TWO

Melancholic Modernism

During the cold war, American literary critics singled out one strand of experimental writing for canonization and celebrated it as the most sophisticated response to the crises of the early twentieth century. This particular strand of modernist writing—which came to stand for the larger and more varied modernist tradition as a whole—is characterized by a deep social melancholia. These literary texts embody a "structure of feeling," in the sense proposed by Raymond Williams: they enact a systematic pattern of affect and ideology, which shaped a cultural formation that achieved unparalleled cultural prestige over the course of the twentieth century.[1] For several generations, melancholic modernism taught Americans how to understand destructive social transformation and how to organize the tempestuous emotions that accompany it. In this chapter, I will chart that structure of feeling by discussing half a dozen major modernist works. Rather than offering detailed readings of these poems and fictions, I will approach them synthetically, interpreting them in relation to one another in order to reveal the explanatory social gestures and psychological postures they share, despite their many differences. Four of these works are among the most famous in all of American modernism, and I have chosen them because of their emblematic canonical status: Eliot's *The Waste Land*, Hemingway's *The Sun Also Rises*, Fitzgerald's *The Great Gatsby*, and Faulkner's *Absalom, Absalom!* I have also included two other works that have been more recently (and perhaps tenuously) admitted to the modernist pantheon—Jean Toomer's *Cane* and Willa Cather's *A Lost Lady*—in order to suggest the appeal of the melancholic mode for some writers who occupied more subordinate positions in the social hierarchy. Presuming a certain familiarity with these texts, I highlight the representational gestures and psychological dynamics they share. My analysis indicates that many canonical modernists are distinguished by their tendency to naturalize the destructive processes of monopoly capitalism, which they also astutely record. These strategies of naturalization lead to systematic displacements of anger and to an anguished inability to mourn for personal capacities and social possibilities that had been truncated by the emergent social order.

Melancholic modernists are united in their underlying conviction that things of ultimate value to them had been imperiled or destroyed in their own generation. Perceiving their culture to be suffering a deepening crisis of alienation, they imagined that the capacity for human connection in all its forms, from sexual love to social solidarity, was radically endangered. Eros, as Freud describes it—the impulse to form ever-greater unities—had somehow been cauterized or rendered catastrophic. Recognizing that this crisis was collective, they sought historical explanations. In their major works, all tried to identify the social forces that had produced their sense of loss.

The Waste Land stands, of course, as one of the great manifestos of the affective crisis bred by modernization. It is a cry of libidinal despair. Eliot presents us with a world in which love is impossible and sex is a particular nightmare. In his view, rich and poor alike suffer libidinal catastrophe—and though the specific social causes vary, all are rooted in modernization. Material prosperity brings only alienation to the wealthy neurasthenic couple, while the working-class woman has been rendered repellent to her mate (and to Eliot) by the physical depredations and vulgarity of her life. The petit-bourgeois wage-earners fare no better. The typist, reduced to a "human engine" by the economic order, employs popular culture to anaesthetize herself to an "undesired" "assault" that is itself a sexual expression of the "young man carbuncular"'s arriviste aggression (lines 215–256).[2] The horrible failure of erotic love resonates with the collapse of all forms of social cohesion, which are imagined by Eliot to have rested on cultural hierarchies now shattered and confused: in the wasteland of modernity, "you know only / A heap of broken images"; "I can connect / Nothing with nothing" (lines 21–22, 301–302). The dissolution of cultural, like sexual, connection has been brought on by the forces of modernization: materialism, consumerism, a trivializing mass culture, sexually and economically autonomous New Women, the impurity of ethnic intermingling, and of course, hovering in the background, the industrialized carnage of the war.

Within a few years of *The Waste Land*'s publication in 1922, Cather, Fitzgerald, Hemingway, and Toomer all produced texts that confirmed the sense of an underlying affective crisis, while offering varied but related and fragmentary social explanations. In *The Sun Also Rises* (1926), it is not only the literally castrated Jake, but all the novel's male characters who are traumatized by their failed efforts at heterosexual connection—and by the fragility even of male homosocial friendship. Although characters persistently allude to the war in order to explain their wounded psyches and broken relations, Hemingway urges us to perceive broader and more systemic social causes. Like Eliot, he entertains the misogynist explanation that it is the sexually aggressive if anguished New Woman, embodied in Brett, who is to blame for the crisis. But at a deeper level, Hemingway suggests that it is the logic of the market—the requirement that everything must be paid for—that has permeated not only the expatriate metropolis of Paris, but even the remote world of rural Spain, ruining its imagined cultural cohesion, community, and generosity.[3] Although Hemingway's idealized representation of Spain (as the collapsing old world bastion of solidarity and cultural stability) is a historical fantasy that foreshortens the actual process of capitalist transformation, his conceit enables him to register with considerable subtlety the alienating effects of commodification and atomization that he felt so acutely in his own time.[4]

In *A Lost Lady* (1923), Cather seeks similarly (though more self-consciously) to make sense of the disaffection of her own generation by creating a romanticized image of the preceding one. Cather too grieves for the passage of an idealized old order (midwestern, rather than Spanish) in which a harmonious heterosexuality rooted in stable and eroticized gender difference had been mirrored by a stable class hierarchy characterized by loyalty and reciprocity. Cather is deeply ambivalent in her social explanations for this loss. To some degree, she shares the view of her protagonist, Niel, that this beautiful world of gracious connection has been shattered by a resentful and meretricious new elite, embodied in Ivy Peters (Cather's equivalent of "the young man carbuncular") who values only money—and by women like Marian Forrester who (like Brett) are willing to sacrifice loyalty to desire. But Cather also ironizes this view, suggesting that beneath the patina of beauty and loyalty, the actual repressiveness of the old order has torn itself apart. For her, the avarice of the new elite is at bottom the same as the old. The suppressed desires of subordinated women and patronized townspeople will assert themselves with some legitimacy, if also (in Cather's eyes) with a painful ugliness that reveals the absence of love and solidarity.[5]

With a romantic lyricism much like Cather's, and so different from the studied irony of Hemingway and Eliot, Fitzgerald also laments the failure of love in *The Great Gatsby* (1925): the failure of Gatsby's heroic and narcissistic love for Daisy most of all, but also (as in Hemingway) the less explosive but equally unsustainable male homosocial bond between Gatsby and Nick. Like Cather, Fitzgerald strongly associates the most loyal forms of male heterosexual desire with the cherished American capacity for platonic (or algeric) self-invention. (In this shared libidinal structure, Gatsby and Captain Forrester are one.) As a social novelist, Fitzgerald suggests that the affective disasters of the novel are due, in part, to the class character of Gatsby's romantic desire—a form of love so entirely and rigidly structured by a commodified fantasy of class status that it can afford no true recognition to Daisy, no actual relation, no satisfying embodiment.[6] Fitzgerald also indicates that all forms of love are ruined in this novel by the vicious "carelessness" and destructiveness of a class system of which Tom is the "cruel" representative and Gatsby both the would-be victor and one of many victims.

No work from the twenties is more insistent in its concern with erotic disaster and the failure of connection—with the primary libidinal impulse "failed in its function"—than Jean Toomer's *Cane* (1923).[8] Like other African American modernists, Toomer takes a longer view of the historical forces that have produced an unfolding crisis of alienation. (No writer attending seriously to the implications of slavery could imagine that monopoly capitalism had shattered a previously unalienated social order.) In the first section of *Cane,* Toomer introduces a series of characters in rural Georgia who are doomed to erotic and emotional isolation, and he insists that these repeated scenarios of disconnection are part of slavery's legacy. From "Karintha" to "Blood-Burning Moon," the deprivations of slavery have engendered unfulfillable desires and forms of aggression that drive black men and women apart. In the remainder of the work, Toomer emphasizes that the great migration to northern cities has not liberated African Americans from this ongoing disaster. Rather, the encounter with intensifying modernization has compounded the problem, as new forms of alienation, bred by class stratification, materialism, and the constraints of bourgeois respectability, are added to the lingering traumas of slavery.[9]

Faulkner shares Toomer's longer historical vision, similarly emphasizing that the catastrophe of slavery was an integral phase, rather than a precursor, of a capitalist modernization whose hallmark is the instrumentalization of human beings. Carrying the modernist lament into the mid-1930s, *Absalom, Absalom!* offers an extraordinarily ambitious parable in which sexual connection, friendship, and every form of familial love have been cauterized or undermined by intergenerationally transmitted pathologies bred by an interlocking system of racial, gender, and class hierarchies. In Faulkner's account, class humiliation appears as the animating trauma of American society. The novel's primal scene is the moment at which the young Sutpen arrives at the anguished and bewildering recognition that he and his people are no more than beasts of burden, the disregarded agents of a derided labor on which others' status and pleasure depends. Sutpen's "design" is the systematic effort to master this trauma by acquiring precisely that form of power by which he has been humiliated. This effort, which Faulkner represents as both normative and apocalyptic, requires the dehumanization and instrumentalization of everyone who comes within reach: the reduction of black people to chattel slaves, the impossible repudiation of human bonds that makes this racial system an intolerable and unsustainable fiction, the reduction of women to empty tokens of class status and vessels for dynastic reproduction and of one's children to mere markers of the impossible design's accomplishment.

These modernists thus attempted to produce cognitive maps of a historical transformation, "figurations" in Jameson's sense of an emergent social order. All attempted to name the social causes of libidinal catastrophe. But all simultaneously mystified the social forces they had named, producing literary works that naturalized the historically particular developments they identified. Melancholic modernists are naturalists in this general sense, and also in the more specific literary-historical meaning of the term: they are participants in the distinctive U.S. adaptation and intensification of the European (initially French) naturalist literary experiment. They systematically represent contingent forms of historical determination as if they were absolute forms of determinism, and they mainly achieve this effect through figurative and narrative acts of metaphysicalization. First, these writers identify (often with precision) the distinctive, historically particular, and corrosive processes of modernization. Then they portray these phenomena as symptoms of metaphysical inevitabilities, as universal, transhistorical—and irresistible—tendencies of human nature.[10]

We can find an iconic example of this naturalist strategy in one of the most celebrated gestures in U.S. modernism, the concluding paragraphs of *The Great Gatsby*. As I have already suggested, Fitzgerald is, at one level, an insightful social novelist who insists that the libidinal catastrophe recorded in his novel has its cause in a particular set of class relations, and in a particular kind of male heterosexual desire that has been structured by a commodified fantasy of bourgeois life. But in the novel's final paragraphs (as in other passages throughout the text), Fitzgerald devotes his considerable lyric gifts to demonstrating that the disaster that has befallen his characters is, in fact, the result of ineluctable and transhistorical pressures within human nature itself. The process of naturalization follows two main steps. As Nick sits on Gatsby's beach, he imagines that his dead friend's desire for Daisy was itself a mere repetition, an incarnation, of the Europeans' foundational desire for the New World: the "inessential houses" of the Long Island business elite "began to melt away until gradually I became aware of the old island here that flowered once for Dutch sailors' eyes—a fresh, green breast of the new world" (189). There is here an ambitious, incipiently historical intuition at work, as Fitzgerald implies that the particular mingling of libidinal yearnings with dominatory social ambitions that he has illustrated in the early twentieth century may indeed resonate with the animating forces of European imperialism. But this historical association is at once offered and mystified, as Fitzgerald shifts lyrically into a transhistorical meditation on the nature of "wonder."

In the final lines of the novel, he insists that it is not a particular set of class and gender relations that have produced Gatsby's disaster—or the wider disasters of modernity on this continent—but the irresistible workings of desire tout court:

> Gatsby believed in the green light, the orgastic future that year by year recedes before us. It eluded us then, but that's no matter—tomorrow we will run faster, stretch out our arms farther. . . . And one fine morning—
> So we beat on, boats against the current, borne back ceaselessly into the past. (189)

Fitzgerald leaves us here, famously and beautifully, with the impression that it is not a particular social organization of desire that has led to the deaths of Myrtle, Wilson, and Gatsby, and that has consigned most Americans to the valley of ashes. Rather, it is the proleptic nature of desire itself. It is not Gatsby alone, nor the Dutch sailors, but all of "us," who, by pursuing our libidinal yearnings, are carried inevitably backward to our destruction. Fitzgerald offers here an astute insight about psychic life, about the backward-looking nature of many of our deepest wishes. What is notable, and crucial from the standpoint of my argument, however, is the universalization of a particular psychic structure, and its displacement of a concrete social analysis that has been gestured toward and then disavowed. If it is the inherent structure of desire itself that has carried Gatsby to his doom and the Dutch sailors to this continent, then it would appear a kind of naive vulgarity to ask whether a different form of social organization might save the "fresh, green breast of the new world" from the murderous amputation that Myrtle suffers or the great majority of us from lives lived amidst the ashes.[11]

This kind of naturalizing gesture is one of the hallmarks of canonical modernism in the United States, and it is one of the defining features of the melancholic tradition. It is performed throughout *The Waste Land*, as Eliot suggests that the bitter alienation produced by modernization is at once a historically particular crisis and the eternal recurrence of an inescapable existential nightmare: the nightmare of "mixing / Memory and desire," the horror of a sexuality endlessly enacted by bodies doomed to decay and death (lines 2–3).[12] The historical specificity of modernity's crisis is similarly acknowledged and then disavowed in Hemingway's influential early works.[13] In *The Sun Also Rises*, for example, Hemingway records with precision the psychic effects of a particular social transformation in which communal and interpersonal activity (from bullfighting to lovemaking) were becoming increasingly commodified. But his novel metaphysicalizes this emergent social order, suggesting in myriad ways that Jake Barnes's pragmatic philosophy that one "paid for everything" in life is, in fact, a universal matter of psychic and spiritual ontology.[14] Similarly, in *A Lost Lady*, Cather acknowledges that Niel's disillusionment with the "lost lady" is the result of a nostalgic adherence to a particularly untenable patriarchal fantasy. But at the same time, she naturalizes this destructive self-deception, insisting in her own narrative voice, for example, that even nature ineluctably tends to "gild" and "dye" itself: that our most profound experiences of beauty, our deepest yearnings, are illusions "so intense that [they] cannot possibly last . . . must fade, like ecstasy."[15] In *Cane*, Jean Toomer anatomizes the historically particular injuries inflicted by slavery, racism, and rapid urbanization that have produced his characters' erotic and emotional alienation. But in ways that are quite rare among African American modernists, he too relies on naturalist strategies to underscore the universality and inescapability of these traumatic psychic and social dynamics. His characters are uniformly trapped in a set of repetitions that are "uncannily" preordained by "omens." They do not produce their losses, but passively suffer them in a fictive world in which historical causation has somehow been abrogated, as "time and space have no meaning."[16] In *Absalom, Absalom!* and his other mature novels of the 1930s, Faulkner raises this kind of deterministic vision to its apotheosis. Here the discourses of "doom" and "fate" permeate and structure narratives of historical catastrophe, as all of Faulkner's characters (like their creator) at once glimpse and disavow the contingency of social forces experienced as agentless fatalities.[17]

These naturalizing gestures are not peripheral to the prestige or expressive power of these literary works. On the contrary, in cold war cultural discourse, such gestures were celebrated as endowing texts with a "universal" significance that lifted them above any narrow, local frame of reference. Such universalizing acts of historical disavowal enabled critics to assert that a text was not merely an American work, a southern novel, an example of Negro literature, or a specimen of women's fiction. Although these gestures played a crucial role in the canonization process, these authors participated in the tendency to naturalization to varying degrees, of course, within individual works and over the course of their careers. Gestures of mystification and disavowal are often (though not always) enacted in the voices of fictional characters or poetic narrators—by Nick Carraway or Jake Barnes, by Niel Herbert or Rosa Coldfield. In some cases, modernist authors retained an ironic distance from such naturalizing utterances—and the degree of their distance marks the extent to which the structure of melancholia remains incomplete in a particular work.[18] In other cases, the naturalist impulse has been fully embraced by the writer, permeating the texture of the narrative as a whole. In such cases, as we shall see, the process of mourning—and the possibility of imagining social resistance—is blocked. Although there is variation among these works in this regard, gestures of naturalization are central to them all, and these gestures have significant psychological and political effects on this canonized strand of the modernist tradition.

Because destructive social forces are represented as universal tendencies in human nature, or as metaphysical inevitabilities, they appear to be irresistible. As a result, human potentialities that have been imperiled by the forces of modernization are irrevocably foreclosed. All of these writers, from Eliot to Faulkner, lament the failure of erotic and affective connection, but none represents a world in which such connection seems imaginable. All, for example, indicate that violently hierarchical class, gender, and race relations are substantially responsible for alienation, but all manage to represent these catastrophic and historically particular social practices as if they were symptoms of ineluctable, transhistorical impulses in human nature. Similarly, all suggest that experiences of sensuous connection and of social solidarity are vitiated by a process of commodification, but they simultaneously represent the desire for noncommodified versions of these experiences as a doomed tendency to "wonder" or to hanker after illusions. The various forms of modernist irony (including the complex versions of nostalgia that are irony's other face) are deployed precisely in order to defend these authors against the sentimental illusion that these thwarted yearnings could ever be fulfilled.

To understand the psychic effects of these naturalist gestures, we must pay particular attention to the problem of aggression. For some modernist writers, the rage that accompanied traumatic experiences of loss was formidable—but the naturalizing impulse blocks its expression. Precisely to the degree that traumatic social phenomena have been mystified, it becomes impossible for these writers to identify clearly and consciously the actual objects of their anger. Along with their fictional characters, they displace their rage, melancholically, onto themselves—and, misanthropically, onto the world as a whole. Of the authors whom I have mentioned thus far, this dynamic is particularly evident in the cases of Eliot and Hemingway. Like much of Eliot's early verse, *The Waste Land* is a poem of spectacular self-beratement, self-laceration, self-punishment.[19] But the poet's distaste is not only for his own abjection and for that of his fragmentary narrators: his loathing is directed also at all the inhabitants of the waste land, at figures (real and imaginary) throughout Western cultural history, and at the physical and sensuous matter of the world itself.[20] If Hamlet queried, melancholically, "Use every man after his desert, and who shall scape whipping?"[21] Eliot sets out to inflict the punishment. To revise Freud's formulation, we might say that for the melancholic poet, unable to name the actual objects of his rage and lashing out at all around him, it is *both* the ego *and* the world that have become intolerably poor, unbearably vile.

Something similar is true of Hemingway. In *The Sun Also Rises*, Hemingway's narrator and protagonist, Jake Barnes, is notably incapable of expressing his rage about his injury. At the moments when Jake is invited to express this anger, or when he is confronted by the representative of the military establishments that launched and then sought hypocritically to justify the war, he refuses to voice his aggression. Rather, he insists, with hard-boiled irony, that his wound is "a joke."[22] Unable or unwilling to name the social causes of his loss, and indulging instead in the mystifying philosophy that his wound is merely one more instance of "paying" for what one gets in life, Jake's rage (like his grief) is elaborately displaced. There is, of course, the endless round of ritualized self-abuse: the repeated romantic self-abasement, but also the fetishistic and masochistic performance of the rituals of male potency, such as drinking and bullfighting. These rituals are, above all, self-punishing: their goal is to achieve "the maximum of exposure" to psychic or physical harm, while disavowing danger by anesthetizing oneself and maintaining an aesthetic mastery, a "purity of line" (167).[23] In addition to perpetual self-punishment, Jake also displaces his rage misanthropically onto others. The targets of his aggression are sometimes men of comparable social privilege (like Mike) who fail to disavow their pain. More frequently they are figures whose vulnerability in the process of modernization is particularly marked: gay men, Jews, African Americans, women.[24]

The whole of this melancholic structure is, moreover, not only Jake's but Hemingway's. From the novel's opening gesture—it's display of the "lost generation" epigraph—the author clearly seeks to claim for himself the anguished sense of loss experienced by his characters. Hemingway's famous style of omission enacts formally the repression of grief and anger, which are expressed only indirectly through acts of formal mastery and sublimation. And it is not merely Jake but his creator who seeks to mystify and disavow his fitful, partial knowledge of the social forces that have produced these feelings. It is Hemingway too who displaces his rage—at times quite gratuitously—onto the fictional representatives of those victims of modernization who are more vulnerable than he.[25] Lest we underestimate the psychological implications of these melancholic structures of blocked mourning and displaced aggression that are enacted in *The Waste Land* and *The Sun Also Rises*, it is worth remembering the psychic circumstances of these authors. Eliot composed his poem during his hospitalization for severe depression. For Hemingway, the sealed circuit of melancholic self-beratement did, in the end, prove inescapable—and suicide was its ultimate telos.[26]

In other canonical modernists, melancholic structures of feeling are produced by the blockage of more modulated forms of aggression that accompanied deep ambivalence. Cather, Fitzgerald, and Faulkner, for example, are struggling to mourn the loss of social formations to which they were allied through bonds of love and identification. But they were grieving for social formations that they also recognized as toxic and self-destructive. Cather admires and lovingly recreates the old order represented by the Forresters, with its imagined fidelity, loyalty, and respect for beauty untainted by commercial exchange. But her novel simultaneously emphasizes that this old order has destroyed itself, containing beneath its charming surface the same aggression, domination, and materialism that characterizes the new era that has supplanted it. Fitzgerald, like Nick, romanticizes Gatsby's "capacity for wonder" and self-making, though his novel also insists that this class ambition is itself the corrosive force that has destroyed not only Gatsby, but the modern American social order. Similarly, Faulkner shares with Quentin the bitterly conflicted effort to mourn a southern past in which he is libidinally invested and by which his own identity is constituted, but whose violent and institutionalized immoralities have caused incalculable human suffering.

Cather and Fitzgerald attempt to manage their ambivalence through strategies of splitting and displacement. Although Cather's novel clearly reveals that Captain Forrester is implicated in the same structures of power and domination as Ivy Peters, Cather vents authorial aggression almost entirely toward Ivy, shielding Forrester from her anger and distaste through a sustained lyrical nostalgia. In a remarkably similar manner, Fitzgerald directs his aggression fully at Tom (and to some degree, at the devalued Myrtle Wilson), but surrounds Gatsby with a protective aura of affectionate lyricism. Cather and Fitzgerald seem equally aware that these acts of affective splitting are unconvincing and untenable: that Gatsby cannot be distinguished cleanly from Tom, any more than the Forresters can be from Ivy.[27] But the nostalgia persists, a half-conscious practice of disavowal.[28]

Faulkner engages in a different but related strategy for evading the rage he feels at what he has loved and lost. Particularly in *Absalom*, he eschews nostalgia—and this prevents the binarized splitting of aggression and love that Cather and Fitzgerald attempt.[29] In this sense, Faulkner acknowledges and enacts more fully *as ambivalence* his mournful love for something that he insists cannot be separated from what he hates. Like Cather and Fitzgerald, Faulkner does love the American myth of self-making—the dream of overcoming the deprivations and humiliations of working-class youth through herculean efforts, and the projection of oneself into a fantasized domain of aristocratic beauty. But he refuses in *Absalom* to separate that dream, even momentarily, from its toxic realities, from the processes of systematic exploitation and dehumanization on which its achievement rests. Faulkner lays bare with a bitter clarity the especially violent southern variant of this story of modernization, with its central reliance on chattel slavery. But despite the intensity of his critique, Faulkner is unable to proclaim his hatred for that on which he perceives his own identity to rest. In this sense, he shares the predicament of Quentin, who responds to Shreve's question—"Why do you hate the South?"—with the novel's closing words: *"I dont. I dont! I dont hate it! I dont hate it!"* Faulkner calls our attention to the transparency of this disavowal, even as he reenacts it through the very texture of his novel. For Faulkner's anger (like Quentin's—and, for that matter, like Ellen's and Judith's, like Clytie's and Bon's) is both everywhere and nowhere in *Absa-*

lom. It is suppressed and yet it saturates the entire text. It is, moreover, an "impotent and static rage," like Rosa's—and for the same reason.[30] Virtually the only character in the novel whose anger can find a sustained voice, Rosa mystifies the man who has helped to destroy her family as well as his own: she sees Sutpen not as the agent and product of a particular socioeconomic system, but as a "demon." Faulkner has similarly mystified and naturalized the object of his rage. The discourses of doom and fatality, of transhistorical and agentless inevitability, permeate every telling of the story—whether in the voices of his several narrators, or in those gaps where the narration no longer has an identifiable narrator to separate it from its author. These myriad, dispersed acts of naturalization serve Faulkner as they serve Rosa. They make it possible for her to separate the man whom she hates from the lost cause of the southern social order that she has lovingly memorialized. They similarly make it possible for Faulkner to shield what he loved from the direct and violent expression of his anger.[31] Through these naturalist gestures, Faulkner and Rosa succeed in inflating and elevating the catastrophe of southern modernization to the status of a timeless tragedy, a tale to be loved and honored, however harrowing it may be.[32]

As these examples suggest, melancholic modernists invented a range of strategies for protecting lost and beloved objects from direct exposure to their rage. But their acts of repression created a blockage of mourning that entailed a terrible psychic price. That price is paid partly in the suffering that follows from the displacement of anger as self-beratement. When that aggression is redirected misanthropically, moreover, it contributes to the racism, misogyny, and homophobia that are so commonly enacted in melancholic modernism. These forms of displacement have had catastrophic social effects, compounding the human suffering produced by capitalist modernization. Far from diminishing the crisis of alienation that writers were struggling to mourn, they intensify the anguish of that crisis, confirming the hatefulness of a modernity that seemed devoid of love.

The psychic toll taken by melancholia goes well beyond the immediate effects of displaced aggression. For as Freud emphasized, and as subsequent clinicians have confirmed, melancholia signals the incapacity to find new objects of love and to engage in dynamic and vibrant object relations. It is this state of libidinal paralysis to which the protagonists of melancholic modernist works are doomed and which the works themselves formally and substantively enact. All of the texts to which I have alluded, from *The Waste Land* to *Absalom, Absalom!*, are fixated on lost objects—and, ultimately, on the perceived loss of the capacity for human connection. These works insist that lost objects and imperiled human capacities can be neither relinquished nor retrieved. Because they both acknowledge and disavow the nature and causes of traumatic loss, they are fetishistic as well as melancholic.[33] In every case, loss is treated as an experience of unique libidinal value and it is, in effect, substituted for the possibility of love, which is regarded as unrealizable. To employ a formulation from Karl Abraham and Maria Torok, the lost object—and in the case of melancholic modernists, it is the capacity for love itself that has been lost—is not simply internalized: it is has been "encrypted" or "entombed" as an inaccessible presence within the self.[34]

Thus, in *The Waste Land*, Eliot memorializes moments throughout Western culture in which men and women come "home" to emotionally and sexually satisfying love—in references, for example, to Sappho's homecoming sailor or to the steersman's song from Wagner's *Tristan und Isolde* (lines 31–34, 220–221). But these references are embedded within a monumental poem whose chief purpose is to insist that such love is not only threatened in the present because of the contingent historical processes of modernization, but that it is forever inaccessible for transhistorical libidinal and existential reasons. In *The Sun Also Rises*, Brett and Jake continually reinflate the image of what "a damned good time" they "could have had" together, and they cling to this fantasy of an unconsummated but lost and unrealizable love in ways that ruin or foreclose all other meaningful connections. The toll of this melancholic structure is not only erotic and romantic failure, but the effort to evade all affect—an evasion mimicked and reproduced by Hemingway's own style of omission.[35]

Cather's protagonist, Niel, is doomed to a version of the same melancholic structure. Despite his persistent disillusionment with the reality of Marian Forrester, he continually reanimates the fantasy of her ultimate desirability. Refusing any actual connection to Marian by the novel's end, he clings nevertheless to "a bright, impersonal memory" of her. Cather suggests that Niel's own experience of the world remains truncated precisely to the degree that he has entombed an image of what he has lost: in his memory, "Her eyes . . . seemed to promise a wild delight that he has not found in life" (147). Like Niel, Cather herself clings in *A Lost Lady* to a libidinally charged fantasy of an old order that she knows to be an illusion—and she too cherishes this lost illusion, unrelinquishable and unrealizable, beyond any present or future the novel can imagine.

Similarly, Gatsby's rigidly memorialized image of the Daisy he has lost prevents him from relating dynamically to the reality of Daisy in the present, just as Nick's entombed image of Gatsby's failed romantic promise causes him to withdraw from the possibility of love, "close[ing] out" his "interest in the abortive sorrows and short-winded elations of men" (*Gatsby* 7). While Nick expresses the hope that this libidinal withdrawal may be "temporary," Fitzgerald attempts to convince us that "we" are all consigned permanently to this frozen libidinal fate. For him, the libidinal present is no more than "our" futile effort to project into an "orgastic future" thwarted desires that cannot ever be fulfilled because they are, in fact, "behind" us—the forever doomed but forever vibrant traces of what we have lost (*Gatsby* 189).

Like Jake, Niel, and Gatsby, the men of Jean Toomer's *Cane* have entombed their losses in ways that make actual love relations impossible. Toomer repeatedly presents us with male characters who interact with women only as the projections and repositories of all that they have lost as a result of slavery and the toxic social order that followed from it. In the opening story, for example, which sets the tone of the collection as a whole, Karintha is required by all the men around her to "carry," "even as a child," a "beauty, perfect as dusk when the sun goes down." Precisely because she must "carry" the beauty of an afterglow, of something that has already vanished, she (like Daisy and Marian) can never be seen in herself. Unable to shatter this melancholic projection, which is pure misperception, she is doomed to interactions in which even her rage and violence are seen as confirmations that she is "innocently lovely." Unseen, unknown, she feels "contempt" for the men who "will die not having found . . . out" who she is or what she needs (*Cane* 3–4). Perhaps more profoundly than any of his modernist contemporaries, Toomer grasped the paradox that even as melancholia is a condition of grievous libidinal isolation, it is also a condition that can be enacted and transmitted relationally. The women of *Cane*, who are objects of melancholic desire, must also suffer the same psychic and erotic fate as their male contemporaries. They too are doomed either to a state of pure libidinal withdrawal (like Fern or Avey) or to scenarios (like those in "Carma," "Esther," or "Blood-Burning Moon") in which their desires fail to find consummation in satisfying object relations because of the structures of traumatic loss that have defined and contained them.[36] Although Toomer is acutely aware of the anguished outcome of melancholic desire, his text—like the others I have discussed—is a powerful enactment of it. For *Cane* itself fetishizes the beauty of these women who stand as little more than embodiments of grief, "cluster grapes of sorrow" (*Cane* 10). More generally, Toomer's text memorializes a version of African American culture and a structure of personality that are not simply marked by traumatic loss but are almost exclusively reduced to it. *Cane* insists that that which is most beautiful is a culture of grief, which is itself passing away.

In *Absalom, Absalom!*, Faulkner similarly explores and enacts a psychic structure in which love has been vitiated by the rigid entombment of lost objects within the self. Like the protagonists of all the works I have discussed, Sutpen is fixated on the losses produced by systematic social violence—in his case, by the trauma of his own class humiliation. Unlike Jake and Brett, or Niel Herbert, or Nick Carraway, Sutpen does not believe that everything he has lost is irretrievable. In this he resembles Toomer's male protagonists— and, most closely, Jay Gatsby, who famously insists that, "of course you can" "repeat the past" (*Gatsby* 116). Sutpen's dynastic "design," like Gatsby's desire for Daisy, represents an effort to retrieve in every detail that which has traumatized and been denied to him. The melancholic rigidity of this pursuit is responsible for Sutpen's instrumentalization and destruction of all the people in his life. Just as the men in *Cane* are melancholically incapable of recognizing Karintha, just as Gatsby cannot perceive Daisy or Niel Marian, so too Sutpen cannot recognize those whom he might have loved. Perhaps most catastrophically, he cannot recognize his own child, Charles Bon, because a "drop" of black blood distinguishes Bon from Sutpen's entombed memory of his own childhood self and from the projected version of the son who must redeem his loss.[37] Like Gatsby, Sutpen is undone by this incapacity to mourn what he has lost and to retrieve his libidinal investments in a dynamic way that enables new love. And Faulkner insists, with other melancholic modernists, that this condition of psychic immobility is the essence of what it is to be human. He assures us that to be a self is to be, like Quentin Compson, a mausoleum, a "barracks filled with stubborn back-looking ghosts" (*Absalom* 7). As a result, even the most utopian moment in Faulkner's novel—the "marriage of speaking and hearing" between Quentin and Shreve (253)—proves to be for Quentin the masochistic enactment of an identification with an infinitely valued and traumatic past. The promise of intersubjectivity is colonized and ruined by the rigid structure of melancholic grief, and the process leaves Quentin psychically frozen in the end.

Canonical modernism then, which has played so decisive a role in the official narrative of twentieth-century American culture, is a literature in which traumatic collective loss has been grieved melancholically, and which records the consequent cauterization of love—and, indeed, of the capacity to feel. It is the literature of Eliot's traumatized lovers, who are "neither / Living nor dead" (*Waste Land*, lines 39–40). It is the literature of Hemingway's "hard-boiled" expatriates who wish to feel and remember nothing, and who, like *The Waste Land*'s opening narrator, regard with horror the "stirring" of "memory and desire" that threatens to thaw the "forgetful snow" (lines 2–6). It is the literature of Toomer's Fern, whose "sorrow" is buried so deeply that she "desired nothing" and can give in consequence "no joy" to others (*Cane* 16). It is the literature of Rosa Coldfield, through whom Faulkner describes the anesthetized condition of a traumatized melancholia: "There are some things which happen to us [. . .] occurrences which stop us dead as though by some impalpable intervention, like a sheet of glass through which we watch all subsequent events transpire as though in a soundless vacuum, and fade, vanish; are gone, leaving us immobile, impotent, helpless; fixed, until we can die" (*Absalom* 122).

These celebrated works of American modernism have an exceptional expressive power that derives from the intensity of their grief. Their melancholic response to the crises of modernity—with its mystifications, displaced rage, and emotional paralysis—also suited the political exigencies of the cold war. In canonizing these works, the literary establishment could explore the suffering that permeated American life without confronting troubling questions about the social arrangements that had produced such alienation. For several generations, literary critics in the United States insisted that this blocked form of grieving was the most adequate response to the traumas of modernization—and they described this melancholic literature as if it were the whole of modernism. But they had told only half of the story. It was not until the 1960s, 1970s, and 1980s, when the new social movements democratized and radicalized many university English departments, that a new generation of critics became increasingly discontented with this narrow American canon and began to retrieve the tradition's submerged voices. I turn now to some of those reclaimed texts and to the different structure of feeling they embodied.

THREE

The Modernism of Mourning

There is, then, another modernism. It is a literature that emerged along-side the familiar, canonical works—and, like them, developed experimental formal strategies in order to map a process of social transformation so vast that it could be perceived only in fragments. These other modernists also sought to record the traumatic effects of capitalist modernization, and they too recognized that central among these effects was an intensifying crisis of alienation. Like their melancholic contemporaries, they tried to name the socioeconomic forces that had produced experiences of loss that were at once intimate and widely shared. Unlike the writers whom I have just discussed, however, these other modernists did not systematically deploy naturalist literary strategies: they did not mystify the toxic social forces they had named, nor did they disavow or displace the anger that accompanied their grief. In some cases (though not in all), they self-consciously criticized the aesthetic fetishization of loss and the politically obscuring strategies of naturalism. In every case, they sought to direct their anger at the social formations that seemed to vitiate the possibility of love and social solidarity. Their works insist on the historical specificity of the destructive social forces at work in a modernizing America—and, in varied ways, they are committed to resistance. Because of their refusal of naturalism and because of their capacity to acknowledge both the depth of their loss and the targets of their anger, they are capable of performing the work of mourning. These writers invented strategies for naming not only what they had lost, but also the libidinal investments that bound them to these lost objects. Through the work of mourning, they sought—tentatively and cautiously—to imagine how those libidinal investments could flourish in the future.

I will discuss five authors as emblematic of the modernism of mourning: Zora Neale Hurston, H. D. (Hilda Doolittle), Tillie Olsen, Langston Hughes, and William Carlos Williams. I will adopt a different strategy in developing my account of this other modernism than I did in presenting the more familiar, melancholic strand of the tradition. Rather than discussing these texts synthetically in order to emphasize structural similarities, I will offer more detailed individual readings, highlighting the greater degree of variation that exists among these works. The different approach reflects important differences between mourning and melancholia—and between the literary traditions that embody these psychic processes. In my account of melancholic modernism, I demonstrated how, despite their significant variations, a group of canonical texts participate in a rigid psychic structure that derives from the compulsive repetition of negation. This kind of structural analysis is less well suited to texts that are formed through the process of mourning, which is more dynamic, contingent, flexible, and exploratory. Precisely to the degree that the work of mourning marks an effort to reestablish dynamic object relations, to achieve new forms of love based on reciprocity and recognition, its efforts will be as varied as the mourners themselves, the circumstances of their loss, and the new experiences to which they open themselves. While melancholia requires that the bereaved continue to experience the world only so far as it conforms to that which has been lost, the effort to love again is quite a different matter. As the heroine of *Their Eyes Were Watching God* explains, "Love ain't somethin' lak uh grindstone dat's de same thing everywhere and do de same thing tuh everything it touch. Love is lak de sea. It's uh movin' thing, but still and all, it takes its shape from de shore it meets, and it's different with every shore."[1] In discussing the works of these five authors, therefore, I will emphasize the distinctive features of their efforts to mourn, even as I demonstrate how and why they should be seen to constitute a common strand of the U.S. modernist tradition.

It is instructive to begin with Zora Neale Hurston's *Their Eyes Were Watching God* (1937), a novel that—like the works of her melancholic modernist contemporaries—struggles to represent the affective crisis bred by the forces of modernization. Significantly, Hurston insists on naming the forms of love and affective connection that modernity seems to imperil. She represents the quest of her heroine, Janie, as a quest for love. Through Janie, Hurston suggests that the blossoming and flourishing of the self requires dynamic and equitable love relations. In one of the extended metaphors that structure the novel, love is represented as a pollination: a process by which a lover can bring (like "a bee to a blossom") that which will enable one to grow (10–11, 101). Hers is also a highly social vision of love: Janie's yearning for sexual and romantic fulfillment is strongly tied to her desire to be a part of the community in which she lives. For Hurston, love can make us grow and flourish as individuals; it can bring the "ecstatic shiver" of sensuous and libidinal connection (11); and it can bind us more fully and richly to others around us, including those outside the romantic dyad. *Their Eyes* can be understood as a meditation on whether such a love is possible in a rapidly modernizing America—especially for the African American woman, who occupies a position of special vulnerability since she is treated by men, both black and white, as "de mule uh de world" (14).[2]

   Like Toomer and Faulkner, Hurston represents the institution of chattel slavery as a crucial early phase of capitalist modernization, which makes especially evident the human costs of this socioeconomic transformation. Slavery is portrayed as a system in which the effort to extract the greatest possible economic value from labor leads to the instrumentalization of an entire class of people, who are reduced to beasts of burden. As Janie's grandmother, Nanny, explains on the basis of her own experience, this economic system employs racism and sexism to identify those who will be most exploited. Nanny warns Janie that the black woman has been treated not only, like male slaves, as a "work-ox," but also as a "brood-sow" (15): her reproductive labor is exploited as fully as her capacity to produce commodities for exchange. Because Nanny has borne the child of her master, and has watched that daughter raped and forced to bear another vulnerable black girl, she recognizes that the capacity for sex opens the African American woman to an especially painful and intimate exploitation. For this reason, she warns Janie against foolish illusions about love ("de very prong all us black women gits hung on"), and she insists that Janie marry for money, which can alone provide "big protection" against exploitation (22). Like so many figures in American modernist novels, from Sutpen to Gatsby, Nanny hopes that class mobility will provide a defense against the deprivations and humiliations of class subordination.

But like the melancholic modernist works I discussed earlier, *Their Eyes* insists that while class mobility can, indeed, provide protection for a fortunate minority, the achievement of a bourgeois life also entails new forms of alienation. Janie's second husband, Joe ("Jody") Starks, stands as one of American modernism's cautionary figures, demonstrating the intimate disaster that can follow from apparently successful class mobility. As with Sutpen and Gatsby, Captain Forrester and Rhobert, Joe's commitment to patriarchal bourgeois authority leads to bitter isolation for himself and for the woman who must represent and consolidate his success. Because Joe demands that she "class off," Janie finds herself alienated from her community. Because he requires her subordination in their marriage, she loses any sense of emotional or erotic connection even to her husband. Hurston emphasizes that the forces that have deformed Janie's life with Joe are not merely the result of idiosyncratic personal choices or preferences. Rather, the structures of class stratification— which draw upon and offer the false promise of liberation from racial and gender hierarchies—are shown to permeate all relations. The second half of *Their Eyes* famously explores Janie's final marriage to Tea Cake, which is in many respects a utopian relationship of egalitarian and reciprocal love. (Because Tea Cake refuses to separate himself from their working-class peers, their marriage carries Janie into, rather than away from, her community. Because he refuses to separate love from work, Janie discovers that work can indeed be play. Because he refuses to accept the normative gender roles on which bourgeois conceptions of patriarchal authority rest, he can encourage Janie to grow and to discover her abilities, and they are not divided by separate spheres of work and home.) Nevertheless, Hurston's novel emphasizes that no matter how charismatic and intuitively egalitarian Tea Cake may be in some regards, the structures of class hierarchy, interwoven as they are with racism and sexism, permeate Tea Cake's psyche and their marriage. It is Tea Cake's anxiety about his sexual mastery over her—an anxiety rooted in fears about his darker skin color and inferior class position—that cause him to beat Janie and that make him want, in a rabid delirium, to kill her. Even the most ideal of love relations, Hurston suggests, must contend with the alienating effects of modernization, both past and present.[3]

While Hurston's diagnosis of the libidinal crisis produced by modernization is similar to that of the melancholic modernists, she imagines and enacts a different set of responses.[4] Her female protagonist struggles persistently to acknowledge the anger that accompanies her disappointment and to resist the pressures that consign her to isolation. Her resistance takes an individualistic form—and I want to emphasize that the kind of mourning enacted in *Their Eyes* is shaped by this fact. After Janie has endured two unhappy marriages, in which love has been sacrificed on the altar of bourgeois prosperity, she is capable of acknowledging that she does, in fact, "hate" the grandmother whom she also loves. It was she who drove Janie "down a back road after *things*" when Janie had wanted instead to "search" for "*people*" whom she could love (85). Throughout her romantic career, moreover, Janie does indeed resist sacrificing her desire to class ambition and to the forms of patriarchal control that are fused to it. Indifferent to her first husband's property, Janie leaves him when it becomes clear that she cannot love him. Similarly, she recognizes that Joe's determination to be "the biggest voice" in Eatonville has estranged her from him and from her neighbors—and she attempts in various ways to resist his efforts at domination and to end her own isolation. Perhaps most importantly, Hurston structures her novel so that, at its dramatic climax, Janie proves herself capable of killing Tea Cake, the man whom she has loved above all others, rather than allowing him to destroy her.

Janie's capacity to acknowledge anger and enact resistance is directly related to her capacity to mourn. In the middle of the novel, for example, she realizes that her efforts to assert her personality and her desires in her marriage to Jody Starks have failed, and that he would "keep on fighting" until he had "her submission." Having acknowledged both her anger and her sense of loss, Janie commences the work of mourning:

> Janie stood where he left her for unmeasured time and thought. She stood there until something fell off the shelf inside her. Then she went inside there to see what it was. It was her image of Jody tumbled down and shattered. But looking at it she saw that it never was the flesh and blood figure of her dreams. Just something she had grabbed up to drape her dreams over. In a way she turned her back upon the image where it lay and looked further. [. . .] She found that she had a host of thoughts she had never expressed to him, and numerous emotions she had never let Jody know about. Things packed up and put away in parts of her heart where he could never find them. She was saving up feelings for some man she had never seen. (67–68)

What Janie has suffered here is, of course, an "ideal loss" in the Freudian sense: she has not lost Joe himself, but rather, an idealized image of him, the hope that he could be "the flesh and blood figure of her dreams." While there is bitter disappointment in this recognition, Janie is able to look "inside" herself to identify the libidinal investments (mere projections or "dreams," in this case) that had bound her to Joe. Because Janie has acknowledged the anger that she feels toward Joe, she neither displaces it nor repudiates her investments as naive illusions. Rather, she reclaims them as "feelings" that can be "saved up" for future relations, as "dreams" that might yet be realized. In her exploration of Janie's subsequent relationship to Tea Cake, Hurston suggests that, because Janie has acknowledged her anger and her sense of loss, she is able to bring these "saved up" dreams and feelings to a new relationship in a dynamic way, rather than merely projecting them onto her next lover in a melancholic repetition.

Similarly, in the famous concluding paragraph of *Their Eyes*, Hurston seeks again to represent the process of mourning that is enabled by the capacity to acknowledge the aggression that accompanies loss. Hurston has structured her novel to create a situation in which Janie must violently resist the destructive impulses in the man she loves, literally murdering him in order to save herself. It is, one might say, a predicament of maximum ambivalence. In the novel's concluding lines, Hurston insists that it is Janie's capacity to remember the trauma of Tea Cake's aggression and her own violent resistance that enables her also to retrieve her love for Tea Cake, and the investments that bound her to him:

> The day of the gun, and the bloody body, and the courthouse came and commenced to sing a sobbing sigh out of every corner in the room; out of each and every chair and thing. Commenced to sing, commenced to sob and sigh, singing and sobbing. Then Tea Cake came prancing around her where she was and the song of the sigh flew out of the window and lit in the top of the pine trees. Tea Cake, with the sun for a shawl. Of course he wasn't dead. He could never be dead until she herself had finished feeling and thinking. The kiss of his memory made pictures of love and light against the wall. Here was peace. She pulled in her horizon like a great fish-net. Pulled it from around the waist of the world and draped it over her shoulder. So much of life in its meshes! She called in her soul to come and see. (183–184)

In contrast to the desperate effort to forget, which is so evident in melancholic modernism's protagonists, Janie's memory of "the gun, and the bloody body" permeates everything around her in this final scene of the novel. Hurston insists that this memory is a painful "sobbing," but this acknowledgement of grief also entails a liberating expressivity, a kind of "singing." The memory of violence and resistance also enables the recollection of love. Janie painfully reminds herself that Tea Cake is, indeed, irrevocably lost in fact, but this enables her also to identify and retain in memory all that has bound her to him. The image of Janie "pull[ing] in her horizon like a great fish-net" has been widely recognized as an image of the personal agency that she achieves by novel's end: it is also, more specifically, a particularly resonant image of the psychic work of mourning. The external world has been impoverished by Tea Cake's death, but Janie's ego has not. Hurston insists that Janie's acknowledgment of her injuries and her resistance enables a fullness of memory. It is a memory that has the sensitivity of a "kiss" and the muscularity to retrieve all that she has lost and all those aspects of herself that loved and were affirmed by those lost objects.

Hurston's novel thus explores a process of mourning that was inaccessible to her melancholic modernist contemporaries. *Their Eyes* suggests that the acknowledgment of the anger that often accompanies loss enables the work of mourning, which involves a complex combination of letting go and holding on. Janie is, for example, able to relinquish an idealized image of Joe (something that Jay Gatsby and Jake Barnes cannot do), and this letting go enables the retrieval of libidinal capacities in herself that can be explored in future. As a result, Janie is capable, despite persistent disappointment, of a dynamic engagement with the external world. As Hurston explains this paradigm in the opening of the novel, to the degree that women can "remember everything they don't want to forget," they can hold onto the knowledge that in some important psychic respect "the dream is the truth." This capacity to honor deep libidinal yearnings makes it possible to "act and do things accordingly" (1).

It is important to note that while Hurston's fiction provides a strong alternative to the libidinal paralysis and displaced rage of the dominant modernist tradition, it is also an internally divided text. *Their Eyes* contains a strong, subsidiary melancholic impulse as well as the capacity to imagine the work of mourning. To the degree that Janie's losses are personal and private, Hurston can represent her mourning in a rich and largely convincing manner. But to the degree that her losses have been caused by powerful historical forces, and are therefore socially pervasive, Hurston cannot feel or imagine the shape of an adequate mourning. *Their Eyes* is, as I have suggested, a highly social novel, with an ambitious analysis of the ways in which intensifying class stratification was deepening a crisis of alienation that had been produced by class, racial, and gender dynamics already at work during the era of slavery. Hurston's novel insists that Janie's yearning for a reciprocal and egalitarian love is thwarted not merely by the character flaws of her three husbands, but by social forces that ultimately deform all her marriages, including her "love game" with Tea Cake (108). But, like her melancholic contemporaries, Hurston yields to the powerful psychic and ideological pressure to naturalize these forces. This is most evident in the ways she mystifies Tea Cake's aggression toward Janie. Although Hurston has shown that Tea Cake's jealousy is animated by the same insecurities and envies that produce Joe Starks' domineering behavior, the fullest enactment of Tea Cake's aggression is represented as the accidental outcome of his exposure to a rabid dog in the midst of a hurricane. This naturalizing impulse—which makes Tea Cake's violence appear at once accidental and involuntary—enables the kind of splitting that we have seen in Fitzgerald and Cather. Janie (and the reader) can split off the good Tea Cake (who is loving and nondomineering) from the alien force, the "fiend in him," that is instinctively driven to a lethal domination and that must be killed (175). As a result, when Janie mourns at the novel's end, she cannot mourn the patriarchal aggression, fueled by racial and class anxiety, that Tea Cake shares with Joe, nor can she acknowledge the social aspect of the anger that aggression has elicited from her. She struggles to mourn a socially induced injury as if it were a purely private loss. In this sense, Janie's mourning is incomplete and her grief has a melancholic caste that is not present earlier in the text. Janie explains to her friend Phoebe that her desire no longer projects itself into the future, that her libido is now withdrawn, that she means to spend her days in the house she has inherited from Joe "and live by comparisons" (182). There is not merely sadness in the novel's ending, but a kind of melancholic commitment to psychic withdrawal that few critics have wanted to acknowledge. While Janie's final mourning enables her to feel her love for Tea Cake, and the libidinal energies within herself, she can no longer imagine a future in which those energies might find new objects.[5]

The limitation of this structure of mourning is not merely Janie's; it is her creator's as well. Hurston possessed deep intuitions about the possibility of mourning and powerful insights about the social forces deforming the lives of those around her. But she could not bring these fully together. She could imagine Janie's anger at individual men, and she could represent her resistance to them. But she could not give Janie a social consciousness that would enable her to direct that anger at the social processes that Hurston herself was able to recognize. Like her melancholic modernist contemporaries, Hurston could not imagine the shape of a collective resistance that might give a viable social future to Janie's utopian yearnings for love and solidarity.[6] Hurston did enact in *Their Eyes* a form of mourning that could enable one to survive the frustrations of her generation without turning against the libidinal energies that were pervasively being thwarted. There was, perhaps, no writer of her generation who honored those energies more fully. But it would fall to other modernists to explore strategies of mourning that could express more fully the social dimensions of their anger—and the hope for some collective resistance to the forces around them.[7]

Hilda Doolittle might seem a surprising writer to turn to in the effort to identify a modernism engaged in a more fully social form of mourning. For H. D. was, among other things, a lyric poet, the priestess of a sometimes hermetic mystical vision, and a pioneer (like Eliot and Pound) of a revision-ary high-cultural syncretism. But it was precisely the combination of her lyric psychological insight and her ambitious effort to redefine the dominant myths of Western culture that enabled her to imagine one kind of collective resistance to (and collective mourning of) the alienating forces of moderni-zation.[8] By way of illustration, I want to consider *The Flowering of the Rod*, the final cycle of poems in the longer work called *Trilogy*, which H. D. wrote while living in England and struggling to mourn the catastrophic effects of the bombing of London during the Second World War.

Like all the modernist works I have discussed thus far, *The Flowering of the Rod* laments the libidinal crisis precipitated by modernization. For H. D., as for many writers of her generation, the bombing of London (and of other cities throughout Europe) seemed an extension of the industrialized car-nage of the First World War, for now the mass killing and destruction had engulfed the homefront as well as the battlefield. As she explains, the great cities of Europe now "lie broken"; the famed birthplaces of Western culture have been transformed into a vast terrain of death, "The-place-of-a-skull."[9] For H. D., the distinctively modern scale of devastation has produced a psy-chic and affective crisis. In this cycle of poems, she struggles to determine whether she can find in herself and her culture the capacity for love in the face of so much alienation and destruction. *The Flowering of the Rod* is a sus-tained effort to mourn: to find some way to "rise again from death and live," to "mount higher / to love—resurrection" (epigraph 111; [1] 114).

For H. D., the effort to grieve the historically particular injuries of the Second World War was inseparable from the struggle to mourn the much longer catastrophe of patriarchy in the West. *The Flowering of the Rod* rests on the intuition that the persistent denial by men of the fullness and com-plexity of women's humanity has alienated men (and often women) from their own capacity for love and has deprived them of access to the "ecstatic" appreciation of the wholeness and plenitude of the world. H. D. implies that the nearly apocalyptic destructiveness of twentieth-century warfare was a distinctively modern outgrowth of a misogynist culture of self-alienation that stretches back into the founding myths of the West, from Greek and Roman mythology to the Old and New Testaments. In order to mourn the destructiveness of the Blitz, H. D. felt that she had to find the means of mourning the culture of Western misogyny.[10]

Although H. D. suggests that the immediate crisis of the Second World War is rooted in a much longer historical dynamic, *The Flowering of the Rod* does not seek to naturalize the violence of warfare or of misogyny. The comparison with Eliot's *Waste Land* is instructive. As I have argued, Eliot's poem records a distinctively modern crisis of alienation, but simultaneously suggests that this alienation is evident throughout history because it is rooted in inherent, and therefore inescapable, features of the human condition. While the temporal range of H. D.'s poem is comparable (linking events in the present to those of the ancient world), her poem insists on the historical specificity and contingency of even the most longstanding cultural formations—including Western misogyny. *The Flowering of the Rod* contends that a culture of misogyny came into being in the course of human history, that it has been sustained through the actions and choices of individuals in every generation, and that it can be resisted and transformed. H. D.'s ambitious poem proposes that we must intervene in the cultural practices that subordinate and marginalize the female half of humanity if we wish to escape the cataclysmic violence of modern warfare. Her poem does not merely proclaim the possibility of this kind of cultural intervention: it is itself an act of such resistance. In *The Flowering of the Rod*, as we shall see, the work of cultural mourning and the work of resistance are one and the same.

Like Hurston, and unlike her melancholic modernist contemporaries, H. D. enacts in the literary text itself the difficult work of mourning. In the opening section of *The Flowering of the Rod*, the poet experiences the staggering violence of the war—the "bitter fire of destruction" ([1] 114)—as a vast cultural negation of love and social solidarity. But at this moment of painful disappointment and grief, the poet—like Hurston's heroine, Janie—turns inward to identify the persistent libidinal energies that have been denied realization in the external world. She compares her own capacity for love to the "rain" that "would have given life" to those around her. If others refuse this love in the current social configuration, if they "will not grow or ripen," then "the rain will return to the cloud" ([2] 115). Though love may be denied by the social order in which we live, it is a capacity that can be withdrawn and honored in the self, stored up, and given freely in the future.

Like Freud, H. D. emphasizes that this process of identifying and retrieving libidinal energies can only take place when the mourner has given herself over to the protracted project of remembering, in super-charged detail, what she has lost.[11] The poet compares this project of memory to "those migratory flocks" that "hover / over the lost island," the lost "Paradise," of Atlantis. H. D. insists that this "hovering," this remembering, can lead to a retrieval in the self of that which has been lost: "seeking what we once knew, / we know ultimately we will find / happiness" ([3] 116–117).[12] In contrast to the melancholic, who cannot retrieve his libidinal investments, H. D. insists on the productivity of mournful recollection. Through memory, the mourner can retrieve the beloved details of the lost object. Of the birds that hover over their lost paradise, she explains that "what once was—they remember, they remember" ([5] 119); of herself, the poet observes, "what men say is-not, I remember" ([6] 121). And H. D. insists, like Hurston, that mournful recollection enables an active relation to the world, rather than a mere fixation on the past. This kind of memory can lead to "resurrection," as H. D. defines it: "resurrection is a sense of direction, / resurrection is a bee-line, / straight to the horde and plunder, / the treasure, the store room" ([7] 123). "Resurrection" might be described as the end of mourning on H. D.'s model: by dwelling intently on what one has lost, one can ultimately identify past longings and satisfactions, and those psychic investments can function as a compass that directs one into a future in which one can retrieve the "treasure" that has been "plunder[ed]."

The remainder of *The Flowering of the Rod* (poems 12–43) enacts this process of mourning with regard to the misogyny of the foundational myths of Western culture—and of the Christian myth, most centrally. H. D. "hovers" over the Christian story and over the forms of femininity that have been silenced and repudiated in its official versions. In her mournful and revisionary retelling, H. D. focuses on Mary rather than Jesus. In this narrative, "Mary" is a composite figure, containing "Marys a-plenty" ([16] 135). She is the Virgin Mary, a representative not only of maternity, but of the female capacity to give birth to divinity itself (also "bliss" and "ecstasy" in H. D.'s mystical lexicon). She is simultaneously a version of Mary Magdalene, a figure of wayward and condemned female sexuality ("having borne a son in unhallowed fashion" [(16) 135]) and a representative also of the female capacity to perceive and celebrate the divine. She is also Mary-of-Bethany, a woman who refuses her subordinate position in the patriarchal order and is "reviled for having left home / and not caring for house-work" ([12] 129). Through a dense web of symbolic associations, Mary is fused with the Old

Testament Eve and her apocryphal precursor Lilith, as well as with a host of ancient goddesses of fertility, beauty, love, intelligence, and power (Demeter, Aphrodite, Athena; Isis, Astarte, and so on). Through this syncretic vision, H. D. knits together into a single, complex unity the many femininities that have been split off and opposed to one another throughout the Western patriarchal tradition: the virgin and the whore, the maternal and the sexual, the bodily and the intellectual, the reviled and the divine.[13]

The principle drama of H. D.'s story is the drama of recognition. Men persistently attempt to deny, repudiate, silence, or expel Mary: they insist that "it was unseemly that a woman / appear at all" before them; they seek to "eject" her from the presence of divinity, because they imagine that her "Siren-song was fatal" ([22–23] 142–143). When Kaspar, one of the Magi, sees through Mary an ecstatic vision of the wholeness, plenitude, and beauty of the world, he repudiates the vision, and cuts himself off from bliss, rather than abandon his misogyny, which is the "last inner defense" of patriarchal privilege ([34] 158). Through this sustained mythopoetic vision, H. D. attempts to "remember" the dismembered and derided femininities of Western religion and mythology. It is a powerful act of cultural mourning, an effort not only to remember what has been systematically excluded and denied, but to remember as whole that which has been shattered, to honor as divine that which has been defamed. H. D.'s mythopoetic mourning is a form of recollection that is also an offering to the present and the future. At the end of *The Flowering of the Rod*, she represents one more encounter between Kaspar and Mary—an encounter in which he recognizes that it is Mary herself who holds the "most beautiful fragrance, / as of all flowering things together," and he wonders whether or not she can recognize herself as the creator and possessor of beauty, fertility, and divinity ([43] 172). The poet leaves us with this question and with this possibility of affirmation. H. D. suggests that as long as she can remember that which has been forgotten and denied, she can hold it out—to Kaspar, to Mary, to her readers present and future—for recognition. The vast cultural repudiations of many generations can still be undone, she suggests, if we are capable of mourning what we have lost, and of affirming the possibility of its future flourishing.

There is a complex and mutually reinforcing relation between mourning and social resistance in H. D.'s work, as there is in the work of other non-melancholic modernists. The psychic process of mourning that H. D. enacts in *The Flowering of the Rod* is enabled by her capacity to express aggression directly toward the social and cultural formations whose destructiveness she records. Because she has not naturalized these damaging social phenomena, she focuses her criticism on the toxic realities of modern warfare and on the longstanding culture of misogyny in which she believes such warfare is rooted. H. D. is capable, moreover, of distancing herself from these social formations in ways that are alien to melancholic modernism. In the opening section of *The Flowering of the Rod*, for example, the poet insists that it is possible—and imperative—for her to repudiate the entire psychosocial dynamic that has bred modern warfare, and she invites us to join her in detaching ourselves from it. Speaking of the shattered world of wartime Europe, in which modern self-alienation and destructiveness have reached a new apotheosis, she proclaims:

> but this is not our field,
>
> we have not sown this;
> pitiless, pitiless, let us leave
>
> The-place-of-the-skull
> to those who have fashioned it. ([2] 115)

Similarly, when Mary is "snubbed" by Kaspar, who feels that a woman's presence in the male world is "unseemly," H. D. insists that Mary too "knew how to detach herself" from such "insults"—and that she continues to make her presence felt and to refuse patriarchal "dismissal" ([13] 130–131; [18] 137).

H. D. and other nonmelancholic modernists were capable of such acts of disidentification, at least in part, because of their particular positions in the social hierarchy. It is not accidental that most of them occupied positions of racial, class, or gender subordination. Eliot, Hemingway, Fitzgerald, and Faulkner clearly saw themselves as heirs to dominant social and cultural formations, even as they felt hostility toward them. This made disidentification difficult.[14] H. D. (and other modernists of mourning) were also ambivalent, but theirs was a form of ambivalence that proved easier to admit to consciousness. H. D., for example, viewed Christianity as a tradition that was *both* spiritually rich and misogynistic. As a woman and feminist, she did not imagine herself to be an heir to a conventional, patriarchal Christianity. She believed that a profound critique and transformation would be necessary in order for her to claim what was hers in the Christian tradition—and in the Western mythoreligious canon more generally. For her, disidentification and open critique were necessities.

In *The Flowering of the Rod*, H. D. invented one strategy for mourning social injury. The poet identifies what she and others (especially women) have lost in the process of modernization, and she names the social and cultural formations that she perceives to be responsible. More than this, she affirms the persistence of imperiled desires—"the insistent calling" [5] for love and for the full recognition of female complexity—even in the midst of a catastrophic war and a culture of unabated misogyny. She was thus able to express the anger that accompanied loss in ways that were quite different from her melancholic contemporaries. The rage of melancholic modernism is—to use Faulkner's formulation—"impotent and static" because it cannot engage its actual objects and cannot find its part in a dynamic struggle to protect or revive what it loves. In *The Flowering of the Rod*, negativity is fused to hope; aggression is deployed in the cause of preservation or rebirth. However embattled or chastened that hope may be, it enables the mourner of social injury to direct her anger at its actual objects rather than at herself or at those who are still more vulnerable than she.

The modernism of mourning contains varied strategies of resistance. In the case of H. D., social resistance took a particularly high-cultural form because she believed that myth and religion had played so central a role in the development of destructive patriarchal societies in the West. In comparison, Tillie Olsen and Langston Hughes—two working-class modernists—were more focused on the structures of material exploitation at work in modernizing America. Committed activists of the revolutionary Left, they mourned the suffering and deprivations endured by working people as an integral part of their effort to build emancipatory political movements.

In 1932, Tillie Olsen began writing a novel that would subsequently be called *Yonnondio*. She was nineteen years old, a high-school dropout, a young woman of the working class struggling through the early years of the Great Depression. A portion of the novel was published in 1934 in the second issue of *Partisan Review*—an appropriate venue for a work of fiction that was equally influenced by the modernist revolution in the arts and by the revolutionary politics of the Communist Party and the militant wing of the American labor movement. Olsen struggled for five years to complete the novel, but her work was interrupted by the demands of raising four children through "everyday jobs."[15] She ultimately abandoned the manuscript, which was published in its incomplete form only in 1974, after Olsen had achieved literary recognition for her later writing. There is a tragic appropriateness to the truncated state of *Yonnondio*, for the particular difficulties of proletarian motherhood, which ultimately overwhelmed the author's own literary efforts in the 1930s, provide a central subject of her novel.

Offering an exceptionally powerful representation of the human costs of American capitalism, *Yonnondio* stands as one of the great achievements of working-class modernism. Like her more privileged and more famous modernist contemporaries, Olsen was struggling to map the crisis of alienation that permeated every stratum of American life. But she is not concerned with the ways in which that alienation was experienced by a bohemian expatriate like Jake Barnes or by men like Sutpen or Gatsby, with their self-defeating bourgeois strivings. Rather, she focuses on the material and libidinal catastrophe that had befallen those at the bottom of American society. The kind of working-class experience that Eliot approaches from a queasy, voyeuristic distance in *The Waste Land*, or that offers Fitzgerald an abstract symbol in *Gatsby*'s valley of ashes, is explored by Olsen with an intimate and sensuous immediacy. *Yonnondio* focuses on the life of a proletarian family, the Holbrooks, as they pass from the mining towns of Wyoming, to the tenant farms of Nebraska, and on to the slaughterhouses and tenements of a midwestern city. Olsen represents the mind-numbing, body-destroying labor that Jim Holbrook performs as a miner and slaughterhouse worker, dangerous labor that leads to the death of men and women who work alongside him. She emphasizes the frequently ignored, but no less alienating labor of working-class women like Jim's wife Anna, who struggles to raise and feed her children and to keep inhabitable their various squalid homes, while doing what she can to augment her husband's starvation wages.[16] Olsen focuses her reader's attention on the system of economic exploitation that constrains every aspect of her characters' lives: no matter how many hours they work, or how arduous their labors may be, these people remain always at the brink of destitution. *Yonnondio* makes us acutely aware that these are men and women who own nothing but their labor—and who are caught in a system in which nearly all the value that their work can produce goes to the small class that owns the mines, the slaughterhouses, and the tenant farms. [17]

A writer with a materialist orientation, Olsen is also a modernist, who is centrally concerned with the consciousness of her characters.[18] The great accomplishment of *Yonnondio* is its capacity to represent both the material dynamics of exploitation and their psychological effects. Olsen suggests, for example, that the mechanized labor of the industrial workplace—which has its corollary in the repetitive and anxiety-filled domestic labor of working-class women—leads not only to physical injury but also to dreadful forms of self-alienation. The "speed-up" on the slaughterhouse assembly line forces workers to "abandon self": "become component part, geared, meshed, timed, controlled" (114).[19] Olsen emphasizes that without education, these exploited people cannot grasp clearly the enormous system that has caused the traumas and privations of their lives. And without organization, they have no way to express their rage at their employers or at the larger system that eludes their grasp. This anger is often tragically displaced onto those who are most accessible and most vulnerable. Jim beats his wife, and Anna becomes "bitter and brutal" in turn toward the children whom she loves: "Somethin just seems to get into me," she reflects with remorse, "when I have something to hit" (6–7). Love relations of all kinds are damaged, as they are infused with displaced violence and pain. Increasingly exhausted psychically and physically, Anna comes to experience both childrearing and her sexual relations with her husband as unbearable burdens. She becomes emotionally "remote" from her children. As for sex, she "gave herself to Jim, clenching her fists against a pain she had no strength to feel" (56). When she cannot bear this sexual depletion further, she resists—and is raped by her husband and suffers a miscarriage as a result. In the face of these traumas, Anna—like everyone in her family—is "lost in a fog of pain" (57).

Unable to mourn all that they have lost, unable to take in the constant stream of injuries inflicted by social forces that they cannot find a way to resist, the Holbrooks turn away from consciousness. Feeling powerless, Jim attempts "to empty his mind," shutting out both past and future (32). Anna retreats into delirium. Their young daughter, Mazie, seeks to live increasingly in a world of dreams, because "awareness" itself is "pain" (58–59). Olsen suggests that for those who are subject to extreme exploitation, a melancholic self-anesthetization may be experienced as the only avenue of escape from material conditions that assault the psyche as well as the body, imperiling even the capacity for love. Olsen is sympathetic to this melancholic retreat, which she recognizes as a last effort at psychic survival. But she also makes clear that this cauterization of the self is one of the deepest wounds that her characters must suffer.

Olsen is acutely aware of the tendency of modern Americans to naturalize the social forces that have harmed them—and she indicates that this way of understanding the world contributes to melancholia and intensifies the injuries of modernization. In the opening section of *Yonnondio*, for example, she emphasizes that the coal miners and their families cannot understand why so many men must be maimed and killed in performing their work, or why they are all doomed to destitution. On the basis of their immediate experience, and without education, they are unable to understand what forces require such suffering. In the absence of any adequate social account, a collective fantasy has grown up to answer these questions, a kind of gothic naturalism that imagines that the mine itself is a malignant, feminine force of nature that devours men. As Mazie puts it to herself, the mine is the "bowels of earth," "a stummy," "and mebbe she eats the men that come down" (4). Sheen McEvoy, a miner whose face has been torn off in a mining accident, elaborates this idea, thinking that the mine is a voracious woman, "hungry for a child," and that she "takes men 'cause she aint got kids" (11). It is worth noting the psychic self-punishment and displaced aggression implicit in these particular naturalist fantasies: the hungry daughter imagines that her father and other men will be destroyed by a ravenous femininity; the male miner, feeling his own impotence and the misery of the women around him, imagines that men are threatened by a feminine nature frustrated to the point of murderousness. Unable to identify the economic structures that have actually caused their injuries, these battered people direct their aggression and their fear through a misogyny that is, in men, a form of impotent (and guilt-ridden) scapegoating and, in women, a lightly veiled self-beratement. These acts of mystified explanation produce self-destructive outcomes. In an effort to bring the suffering and killing to an end, for example, McEvoy acts on his fantasy by trying to throw Mazie down the mine shaft, hoping to appease the thwarted and murderous femininity of the mine. Unable to name the social dynamics that are crushing them, and resorting to mystifying and naturalizing explanations, these sufferers can only sacrifice their own.[20]

While the naturalism bred of working-class despair is poignant to Olsen, she is harsh in her critique of ruling-class mystifications. She challenges directly the aestheticization of loss that we have seen to be so central to canonical modernism. She forces us to confront the political implications of fetishizing socially induced loss as an inevitability that can be redeemed by the beauty of its representation. Early in *Yonnondio*, for example, Olsen describes the scene of women and children rushing to the mine tipple when they hear the whistle that signals a mine accident. As her characters wait with anxiety to learn the fate of their husbands, sons, and fathers, Olsen interrupts her narrative with a Brechtian interpolation that directly addresses her readers, challenging us to consider our own inclination to aestheticize such catastrophes. Here, at length, is her challenge:

> And could you not make a cameo of this and pin it onto your aesthetic hearts? So sharp it is, so clear, so classic. The shattered dusk, the mountain of culm, the tipple; clean lines, bare beauty—and carved against them, dwarfed by the vastness of night and the towering tipple, these black figures with bowed heads, waiting, waiting.
>
> Surely it is classical enough for you—the Greek marble of the women, the simple, flowing lines of sorrow, carved so rigid and eternal. Surely it is original enough—these grotesques, this thing with the foot missing, this gargoyle with half the face gone and the arm. In the War to Live, the artist, Coal, sculptured them. It was his Master hand that wrought the intricate mosaic on this face—splintered coal inlaid with patches of skin and threads of rock . . . You will have the cameo? Call it Rascoe, Wyoming, any of a thousand mine towns in America, the night of a mine blowup. And inside carve the statement the company already is issuing. "Unavoidable catastrophe . . . (O shrink, super's nephew, fire boss that let the gas collect) . . . rushing equipment . . . bending every effort . . . sparing no expense . . . to save—or recover the bodies . . ."
>
> (*Dear Company. Your men are imprisoned in a tomb of hunger, of death wages. Your men are strangling for breath—the walls of your company town have clamped out the air of freedom. Please issue a statement; quick, or they start to batter through with the fists of strike, with the pickax of revolution.*)
>
> A cameo of this, then. Blood clot of the dying sunset and the hush. No sobs, no word spoken. Sorrow is tongueless. Apprehension tore it out long ago. No sound, only the whimpering of children, blending so beautifully with the far cry of blown birds. And in the smothered light, carved hard,

distinct, against the tipple, they all wait. The wind, pitying, flings coal dust
into their eyes, so almost they could imagine releasing tears are stinging.
(20–21; italics and ellipses in original text)

Here, Olsen confronts us with our desire to have social catastrophe aes-
theticized, to have historically contingent (and preventable) human suffering turned into a commodity that we can cherish for its beauty, a "cameo"
to "pin" onto our "aesthetic hearts." As she makes clear, this desire, this expectation, is trained by a set of aesthetic practices that are deeply rooted in
the culture—and in one strand of U.S. modernism. Many of the representational strategies to which she alludes are those that characterize melancholic
modernism. The death of the miners and the anguish of their families can
be transformed into a suitable aesthetic object, she explains, if the scene is
made to seem timeless and "classical," continuous with the experience of the
Greeks. If we wish to see the shattered face of a miner as an object of tragic
beauty, the causes of this disaster must be naturalized: it must appear that
"Coal" itself, a force of nature, is the "artist" who has created this ghastly
sculpture of "skin" and "rock," in the course of a Darwinian "War to Live."
If we wish to perceive the "bare beauty" of this scene, we must represent the
human sufferers of modernization as small and passive ("with bowed heads,
waiting"), "dwarfed by the vastness" of nature's "night" and of the "tower-
ing" technology that seems elemental in its scale and destructiveness. The
grief of the victims must be represented as a fixed and permanent condition:
"the flowing lines of sorrow" are "carved" so as to appear not only "rigid"
but "eternal." And their silence, their inability to express their grief or anger,
adds crucially to the aesthetic effect: their "sorrow is tongueless," and the
only sound of grief they make—the "whimpering of children"—becomes
itself an indistinguishable part of nature, "blending so beautifully with the
far cry of blown birds."

Olsen makes explicit the political implications of the aestheticization
of social injury. She insists that the naturalism on which it rests serves the
interests of the mine owners, who are in fact responsible. Lofty aesthetic
determinism resonates with the mining company's hypocritical contention
that the blowup is an "unavoidable catastrophe": they are aspects of the same
cultural and ideological formation. As Olsen insists, the company's lie might
as well be carved "inside" the cameo, for the fetishization of socially induced

loss will always serve the interests of those who benefit from exploitative social and economic arrangements.[21]

It is, of course, Olsen's political consciousness that makes this aesthetic critique possible. It is her politics that enables her to recognize that a mining disaster is *not* an "unavoidable catastrophe." Rather, it is the result of individual actions: in this case, as she indicates parenthetically, the mine superintendent has appointed his nephew to a sinecure as "fire boss," and neither of them are concerned enough about the miners' well-being to prevent explosive gas from collecting. More importantly, she insists that an economic structure of exploitation is ultimately responsible for the miners' death and their families' poverty. These injuries are produced neither by a Darwinian "War to Live," nor by a monstrous femininity that devours men, but by a socioeconomic structure that reaches one apotheosis in the "company town," where workers who are paid "death wages" must buy at extortionate company stores and must risk their lives because safety precautions would reduce the company's profit. Olsen offers, in other words, a materialist analysis to counter the naturalisms that persistently obscure the social forces that are responsible for the deprivations of an entire class. Olsen directs her rage—and the reader's—at these social structures, rather than at those who are most vulnerable. She channels the aggression that accompanies collective injury not inward as self-beratement, but outward toward the social formations that have "imprisoned" and "strangl[ed]" so many. The very phrases that are likely to make some readers uncomfortable in this passage[22] —"the fists of strike," "the pickax of revolution"—are the phrases in which Olsen seeks to name forms of collective organization that might enable us to express our anger in ways that could protect the weakest in society from further injury.

Olsen's political militancy enables her to enact a remarkable form of mourning in *Yonnondio*. This may seem surprising—for there are powerful currents in our culture that presume that mourning and political activism are opposed inclinations. In the lore of the American Left, for example, this presumption is famously embodied in Joe Hill's legendary command to his comrades in 1915, before his execution during the Red Scare: "Don't mourn for me: organize!" This presumption has been shared by other political activists, who have similarly feared that the psychic work of mourning, with its consuming focus on the past, will inhibit the forward-looking work of social transformation.[23] For Olsen—as for H. D.—the capacity to acknowledge anger at the social formations that had produced so much suffering allowed her to escape the melancholia characteristic of much canonized modernism. Her political radicalism, in other words, enabled—and was enriched by—the sustained process of mourning enacted in *Yonnondio*.

For *Yonnondio* is not only a militant novel: it is also one of the most sustained expressions of grief in American modernism—indeed, in all of American literature. And *Yonnondio* does not simply grieve: it mourns. I mean by this that the novel performs the complex work that we have seen enacted at an individual level by Janie in *Their Eyes Were Watching God*, and at a more general cultural level by H. D. in *The Flowering of the Rod*. By dwelling on the abyssal losses experienced by the characters in her novel, Olsen seeks to identify the libidinal capacities that existed in the lives of working people in 1930s America, and yet were so pervasively denied. This is an extraordinary feat, precisely because Olsen is so uncompromising in her representation of the hardships experienced by her characters. There is no false optimism in *Yonnondio*: the novel forces us to accept the truncation of her characters' lives, and the unlikelihood of their realizing their aspirations, material, sensual, or affective. But the emphasis on social determination never becomes a pure determinism and it never leads her into the forms of misanthropy that are common in melancholic modernism.[24] Even as the oppression of her characters is relentlessly recorded, Olsen insists on affirming the capacities that lie dormant within them and that are prevented from flourishing. Nothing, for example, could be grimmer than the outlook for the baby, Bess, who is an infant at the time of the Holbrooks' descent into destitution and Anna's psychic and physical collapse. But even as the novel forces us to accept that this child will almost surely be crushed by the environment in which she lives, Olsen assures us that in this baby's play, we can see the "human ecstasy of achievement; satisfaction deeper and more fundamental than sex. *I can do, I use my powers; I! I!*" (132).

Similarly, Olsen emphasizes throughout the novel, that the material hardships of these characters' lives strain their friendships and love relations, and increasingly constrain their expression of emotions that have become ever more painful. But Olsen insists that the *capacity* for expression and connection remains alive within them, no matter how persistently they may be thwarted. In the middle of the novel, for instance, when the Holbrooks visit old friends—who will ultimately prove unable to help them materially, and from whom they will be divided by their ongoing hardships—Olsen seeks to remind us of that which glimmers within her characters. They begin to sing: "They sang and sang, and a longing, a want undefined, for something lost, for something never known, troubled them all. The separate voices chorded into one great full one, their faces into beauty" (53). In their singing, Olsen urges us to hear the sound of a "longing" that persists after it has been denied, after loss, after even the ability to "define" its object has been foreclosed. She insists too that the capacity to express that longing, and to be bound together to others in "beauty," endures.

To take one last example of this work of mourning, Olsen represents late in the novel the kind of mother that Anna might have been—or could yet be—if her life were less constrained by the pressures of economic exploitation. The novel emphasizes in every chapter the way in which these economic pressures produce in Anna a bitter frustration and an alienation from herself that cause her intermittently to harm her children and to withdraw from them. But at the height of the Holbrooks's difficulties, with no money to buy food, Anna goes out scavenging for dandelion greens with her children—and Olsen represents the way in which this brief escape from monotonous toil and a fleeting experience of connection to the natural world return the beleaguered mother to herself and to her children. Anna's momentary experience of the beauty of the flowers, and the sensuous pleasure of their smell, brings a "strange happiness" to her "body," which even her young daughter can perceive. Mazie intuits that this "happiness" is a momentary retrieval of "selfness" in Anna: a brief instant in which her mother has escaped the incessant demands and hardships of her life, and the sense of alienation from the world and from herself (101). This fleeting respite from alienation, this retrieval of "selfness," also enables Anna to connect to Mazie and to provide the love that could heal some of her daughter's suffering: "[Anna's] fingers stroked, spun a web, cocooned Mazie into happiness and intactness and selfness. Soft wove the bliss round hurt and fear and want and shame—the old worn fragile bliss, a new frail selfness bliss, healing, transforming. Up from the grasses, from the earth, from the broad tree trunk at their back, latent life streamed and seeded. The air and self shone boundless" (102). Olsen insists here that, despite the onslaught of poverty, anxiety, and alienation, Anna retains the capacity to feel a connection to herself, to the "latent life" of the natural world, and to the children whom she loves.

I call this description an act of *mourning* on Olsen's part because what she describes here is a libidinal capacity, a potential, something "latent" in Anna that is systematically foreclosed by the social circumstances of her life. As soon as Olsen has reminded us of the libidinal energies that exist in Anna, she reminds us too that these energies cannot flourish in the world in which she lives. Anna's moment of "selfness" and connection lasts only an instant: then "the wind shifted" and brings the stench of the "packing house" to them once again; the children begin to cry for food; the painful material realities of Anna's life return; alienation descends once more. Olsen assures us that "never again, but once, did Mazie see that look [. . .] on her mother's face" (102). What Olsen has recorded here is a possibility in Anna, and in the lives of her children, that will not be realized. It will be lost to them, as it has been and will be to millions of exploited people. Olsen challenges us to acknowledge the reality of its loss—but also, and equally, the reality of its potential. This is not the structure of traditional elegy. Olsen does not represent this moment of connection and love as a recompense for, or a redemption of, her characters' suffering. This is a materialist form of mourning: a mourning that identifies what has been lost, and implies the possible future flourishing of these lost libidinal satisfactions—but not in a domain of religious exaltation or aesthetic transubstantiation, not even through a cycle of natural regeneration, but only—possibly—in an altered society.[25]

The fullness of Olsen's social mourning is signaled by the political hope that emerges in the midst of its enduring grief. *Yonnondio* is not a novel of revolutionary triumphalism. It does not represent—nor did Olsen apparently ever imagine—a successful strike or popular uprising at the novel's end.[26] Olsen did not believe in revolution with any more certainty, for example, than a man who has lost his lover can be certain of finding another person to love. But like the bereaved lover who has passed through the consuming work of mourning, Olsen is psychically open to libidinal possibility—and, in her case, to social transformation. She knows that there can be no redemption or compensation for the suffering produced by American capitalism. But a change in the economic system could bring into being a society in which all might have a chance to live those imperiled capacities—for connection to others and to the beauty of the world, for "selfness" and for "cocooning" those we love. Like H. D., Olsen is aware that one cannot bring mourning to an end through a mere act of will. One cannot simply declare that one is finished "hovering" over loss, any more than one can bring a revolution into being by declaring that its time is now. The revolution that Olsen has in mind is, like the return to love, a dynamic process: by naming what we have lost, we know also what it is in ourselves that we wish to reclaim for future exploration and enjoyment. We find a "bee-line" to "the plunder." But like the renewal of love, the making of revolution is open-ended and improvisatory, not a rigid retrieval-as-replication, but the creation of a space in which people can realize capacities and libidinal possibilities that have previously been thwarted.

The long and painful work of mourning gives content, then, to Olsen's revolutionary politics, even as she believed that politics alone could complete the mourning process. For as we have seen, Olsen suggests that melancholia is one of the ultimate effects of unchecked exploitation. In her view, people's inability to find a means of collective resistance dooms them to silence and to a defensive withdrawal from consciousness.[27] This melancholia can only be undone, she suggests, by collective organization against the social forces that have produced, and continue to produce, such injuries. Only militancy makes possible the kind of mourning that Olsen herself enacts in *Yonnondio*. When the doctor comes to treat Anna after her life-threatening miscarriage, for example, Jim's sense of powerlessness and despair overwhelms him, as he realizes that he cannot afford any of the medicines that Anna must have. He notes that "the doctor says she needs everything she cant get, tells me everything she needs, but not how to get it." Olsen then emphasizes that Jim "could speak no more. [. . .] the things in his mind so vast and formless, so terrible and bitter, cannot be spoken, will never be spoken—till the day that hands will find a way to speak this: hands" (78–79). Olsen suggests here that the "terrible and bitter" things in Jim's mind "will never be spoken" until some practical, material struggle is mounted to alter the social structures that continue to inflict this trauma. Through such struggle, the rage of the exploited can find appropriate expression at its proper objects—and can be expressed in the cause of realizing what has been denied and foreclosed. The "hands" that could make this revolution are also the hands that could weave "bliss round hurt and fear and want and shame." They are, too, the hands of the working-class artist, whose political consciousness enables her to mourn in writing the losses suffered by those around her—and through her mourning, to identify what might yet flourish in the future.

Like Tillie Olsen, Langston Hughes was a working-class modernist seeking to mourn the collective injuries of an exploited people. A lifelong socialist and advocate for racial equality, Hughes also invented an experimental literary practice to conduct the work of mourning and political resistance. Before turning to some of Hughes' explicitly political poetry, I want to begin where Hughes himself began: with the blues. As readers and critics have long recognized, one of Hughes' principal accomplishments was to have created a modernist poetics rooted in the rhythms and idioms of African American vernacular music, especially jazz and the blues.[28] The blues was a wellspring for Hughes's early poetry—and it was decisive for him as a cultural idiom for expressing and managing loss. As Hughes explained, the blues is a cultural practice devoted to grieving, but to grieving in such a way that the bereaved are able to affirm ongoing investments in life. It is not a question of affirmation *replacing* or superseding grief: rather, as Hughes emphasizes, the blues expresses a simultaneity of affect, a dynamic capacity for ambivalence, for registering both grief and love. For Hughes, the humor that runs through the blues is a principal means by which affirmation is expressed in the midst of sorrow: "They are often very sad songs. But there is almost always in the blues something to make you smile." On his account, it is the "ever-present laughter-under-sorrow that indicates a love of life too precious to let it go." Hughes implies, moreover, that the "marching-on syncopation" of the music is the formal trace or expression of this affective dynamism, this capacity for "laughter-under-sorrow," this culturally particular form of mourning.[29]

In the blues poems that he began writing in the early years of his career, Hughes sought persistently to enact this process of mourning—usually in scenarios of personal (most frequently romantic) loss.[30] With their commitment to the expression of ambivalence, these poems commonly grant a central place for aggression alongside love and grief. The speakers (or, more properly, the singers) of Hughes's blues poems often express anger at the objects they have loved and lost, at the men and women who have done them wrong. This capacity to acknowledge the place of aggression in mourning is one of the features that distinguish Hughes—like Hurston, H. D., and Olsen—from their melancholic modernist contemporaries. In Hughes, as in the other modernists of mourning, the expression of anger often leads to a liberation of inhibited libido for the mourner. Consider, for example, "Hard Daddy," a poem first published by Hughes in his second volume of verse, *Fine Clothes to the Jew* (1927):

Hard Daddy
I went to ma daddy,
Says Daddy I have got the blues.
Went to ma daddy,
Says Daddy I have got the blues.
Ma daddy says, Honey,
Can't you bring no better news?

I cried on his shoulder but
He turned his back on me.
Cried on his shoulder but
He turned his back on me.
He said a woman's cryin's
Never gonna bother me.

I wish I had wings to
Fly like the eagle flies.
Wish I had wings to
Fly like the eagle flies.
I'd fly on ma man an'
I'd scratch out both his eyes.[31]

Here, the speaker of the poem sings the blues in an effort to share her sorrow. The principal injury recorded is a private one: the refusal of her "man" to acknowledge and honor her grief. As in the work of Hurston, H. D., and Olsen (and as in so many works of the blues), Hughes sketches the social contours of private loss. For this "hard daddy" relies on a conventional misogyny ("a woman's cryin's / never gonna bother me") as a way of shielding himself from troubles beyond those with which he must already contend as a working-class African American man.[32] But the blues will not be denied. It is a practice of mourning that insists on having its grief acknowledged.

Like Hurston's heroine Janie, and like H. D.'s Mary, Hughes's blues singer refuses to stifle her sorrow and communicates to her listeners the story of her wrongs. In the final stanza, moreover, she gives voice to the anger she feels toward the man whom she has loved and who has callously disappointed her. Crucially, it is a single imaginative gesture, a single fantasy, through which the singer expresses simultaneously her aggression (the wish to "scratch out both his eyes") and her desire for liberation ("to / Fly like the eagle flies"). The libidinal character of this desired liberation is underlined by the fact that she imagines herself, in aggression and freedom, as an "eagle"—with the sexual connotation that this often carries in the blues. ("Eagle rock" was a common blues euphemism for sex during the 1920s). The blues thus provides the singer—and Hughes himself—with an idiom that insistently expresses grief and, by acknowledging the anger that comes with loss, imagines also the possibility of libidinal freedom.

"Hard Daddy" is a poem about individual loss, and the blues enacted here enables a process for mourning personal injury or disappointment. But from the very outset of his career, Hughes also sought to adapt this basic structure of grieving to the challenges of *collective* and socially induced loss endemic to working-class African American life.[33] As in the case of Tillie Olsen, Hughes's effort to mourn the suffering of those most exploited—the poor, and people of color in particular—was fused to his effort to build a revolutionary political movement. Hughes began writing militant political poems (and publishing these in anticapitalist journals) in the earliest years of his career, and these poems reached a crescendo during the 1930s, when Hughes was most optimistic about the possibility of an international socialist revolution.[34] These militant poems (which deserve more attention than they have so far received)[35] express a sustained grief for the forms of suffering and oppression inflicted on millions of people—in the United States and around the world—by the processes of capitalist modernization. It is one of the distinctive features of Hughes's political poetry that it emphasizes the *libidinal* effects of an expanding capitalist economic system that exploits ever more intensively the capacity of human beings to produce and to provide pleasure. Such a system, he suggests, has brought into being a world in which the young are increasingly "too unsure of love to love."[36] Like his blues poems, Hughes's revolutionary verse expresses anger as well as sorrow. While anger usually takes a personal and individual form in the blues, it is expressed in Hughes's revolutionary poems as a call for collective resistance to exploitative economic structures. For Hughes, as for Olsen, the goal of revolutionary struggle is the goal of social mourning. It enables the flourishing of those potentialities that have been denied or foreclosed to the exploited; it enables men and women to retrieve (as H. D. would put it) that which has been "plundered."

During the period of Hughes's greatest militancy, he was particularly self-conscious about the political ramifications of different aesthetic practices and representational strategies. (It was during this period, for example, that he wrote the poem called "Cubes"—which stands as one of the great manifestos of U.S. modernism and offers an exceptionally trenchant political assessment of modernist aesthetic practice.)[37] Like Olsen, Hughes was harshly critical of artistic strategies that fetishize loss. In "Letter to the Academy," for example, a poem published in 1933 during Hughes's sojourn in the Soviet Union, this critique is especially pointed:

Letter to the Academy

The gentlemen who have got to be classics and are now old with beards (or dead and in their graves) will kindly come forward and speak upon the subject

Of the Revolution. I mean the gentlemen who wrote lovely books about the defeat of the flesh and triumph of the spirit that sold in the hundreds of thousands and are studied in the high schools and read by the best people will kindly come forward and

Speak about the Revolution—where the flesh triumphs (as well as the spirit) and the hungry belly eats, and there are no best people, and the poor are mighty and no longer poor, and the young by the hundreds of thousands are free from hunger to grow and study and love and propagate, bodies and souls unchained without My Lord saying a commoner shall never marry my daughter or the Rabbi crying cursed be the mating of Jews and Gentiles or Kipling writing never the twain shall meet—

For the twain have met. But please—all you gentlemen with beards who are so wise and old and who write better than we do and whose souls have triumphed (in spite of hungers and wars and the evils about you) and

whose books have soared in calmness and beauty aloof from the struggle to
the library shelves and the desks of students and who are now classics—
come forward and speak upon

The subject of the Revolution.

We want to know what in the hell you'd say?[38]

This poem stages an angry confrontation between the revolutionary poet
and the celebrated, canonized writers who aestheticize social injuries. Just as
Olsen confronts those who would turn a mining accident into "a cameo" to
pin onto their "aesthetic hearts," so Hughes here condemns those who have
turned "the defeat of the flesh" into "lovely books." Like Olsen, Hughes
emphasizes the political effects of, and the class interests served by, aesthetic
practices that fetishize loss. The authors and books that convert social trauma into "lovely" objects are the ones "studied in the high schools and read
by the best people" precisely because they naturalize and justify the forms of
social hierarchy ("Lord" and "commoner," "Jews and Gentiles," colonizers
and colonized) that facilitate economic exploitation.[39] Hughes is particularly
critical of representational strategies that seek to imply a redemption or consolation of collective suffering by aesthetically elevating these experiences
into a domain of "beauty" or by asserting a "triumph of the spirit" that would
presume to compensate for the "defeat of the flesh." Hughes is no more
interested in aesthetic consolation or in a spiritualized elegiac redemption
than Olsen. Rather, he shares with her a materialist form of mourning that
insists on acknowledging, without evasion or diminution, the bodily reality
of these "defeats"—the "hunger," powerlessness and libidinal constraint that
are produced by economic exploitation.

This materialist mourning acknowledges, like the blues, the anger that
accompanies grief. In revolutionary poems like "Letter to the Academy," that
anger is directed at the socioeconomic structures that are responsible for the
suffering of the poor, and at the cultural formations (literary and academic)
that justify that suffering. For Hughes, as for Olsen, the call to "Revolution" is the alternative to fetishizing collective trauma—and the building
of a movement for social change is the means of fulfilling the work of social mourning. Revolution is imagined here as a process of retrieving that
which has been plundered, of enabling the exploited to realize capacities in

themselves that have been denied and disappointed. Hughes calls for social transformation in the name of libidinal gratification. Through revolution, he wishes to create a world in which "the hungry belly eats"—and because people will be "free from hunger" and material want, their "bodies and souls" can be "unchained." This dream of revolution is not a static, melancholic fantasy of retrieval as replication of a lost past, but a dream of libidinal freedom to realize open-ended potentialities that have been previously truncated. It is a vision that seeks not to fetishize or hypostatize the revolutionary subject as fixed, but a vision of a world in which these subjects can *change*, in which "the poor are mighty and no longer poor." It is a vision in which the full expression of grief, and the articulation of anger at its proper objects, can free us "to *grow*" intellectually, psychically, erotically: to "study and love and propagate, bodies and souls unchained."

After the late 1930s, Hughes's optimism about worldwide anticapitalist revolution waned, and he was personally intimidated by the political repression of McCarthyism—which threatened his tenuous livelihood as a professional writer.[40] As a result, he wrote fewer explicitly revolutionary poems in the latter half of his career, and he largely relinquished the strategy of enacting social mourning through calls for revolutionary resistance. Hughes continued to write about the psychic and material effects of economic exploitation, however, and about the entanglement of capitalism with structures of racial and gender oppression in the United States. He also continued to improvise strategies for social mourning, identifying thwarted human potentialities that struggled to survive in the midst of exploitative and often traumatic social circumstances.

One of Hughes's most distinctive contributions to the modernism of mourning was the invention of an idiom for mourning *political* disappointment. With a special persistence and intensity, Hughes emphasized in his poetry the libidinal power of political ideas and aspirations. He insisted that individuals and groups often express their deepest wishes and most urgent needs through political ideals—and that political disappointments can strike to the very heart of who we are.[41]   Like many African American writers, Hughes struggled especially with the painful betrayal of Enlightenment political ideals in the United States. He deplored the cynical manipulation of the language of "freedom," "democracy," and "equality" to justify a political order that had systematically enslaved, exploited, and disenfranchised

African Americans from the time of the nation's founding. In this regard, Hughes faced a challenge—at once political and psychological—that has been shared by African American writers, artists, intellectuals, and activists from the eighteenth century on. This is the challenge of defining a relationship to Enlightenment political ideals that would enable one to acknowledge the degree to which the vocabulary of democracy had been betrayed and compromised, but that would still allow one to employ this language as a tenable vehicle for expressing the desire for liberation and equality. For Hughes, as for many others, this has been in essence a project of political mourning. It requires the capacity to acknowledge political betrayal, and to register fully the depth of what one has lost, in order to affirm the possibility that disappointed yearnings might yet be realized. The psychological work of political mourning is, in this sense, quite close to the work of recovering from romantic disappointment—the work most commonly performed by the blues: it is the work of remembering in hypercathected detail one's desire (for love, for freedom), in the full knowledge of it's disappointment, so that the desire itself can be affirmed as a lingering impulse that can be projected forward as a future possibility.

As one example of this kind of political mourning, consider a poem first published by Hughes in 1943, and widely reprinted and anthologized under two different titles, "Refugee in America" and "Words Like Freedom."[42] This poem presents with a remarkable directness the psychological ambivalence that lies at the heart of political mourning:

> There are words like *Freedom*
> Sweet and wonderful to say.
> On my heartstrings freedom sings
> All day everyday.
>
> There are words like *Liberty*
> That almost make me cry.
> If you had known what I know
> You would know why.

In the opening lines of the first stanza, Hughes emphasizes the libidinal— even sensuous—pleasure of speaking the language of Enlightenment liberation: "words like *Freedom*," he insists, are "sweet and wonderful to say." In the second half of the stanza, the poet shifts subtly from the outward and punctual act of speaking to the continuous internal impulse that lies beneath it. The (italicized) word, *"Freedom,"* which is pleasurable to say, is revealed to be only the occasional vehicle for a persistent, involuntary drive within the self: the "sing[ing]" of "freedom" "All day everyday."[43] In the second stanza, the poet insists that the same Enlightenment political vocabulary—embodied in the closely related term, *"Liberty"*—has an equal and opposed affective meaning for African Americans. The same words that are "sweet and wonderful to say" also "almost make me cry." In the final sentence, Hughes emphasizes that "words like *Liberty*" produce a feeling of grief in him because he "know[s]" in the present about a painful historical experience (something the reader would have to *have* known in the past in order to understand the poet's grief over the word *"Liberty"*). With exceptional efficiency, the poem expresses an acute ambivalence about the language of Enlightenment political idealism: it asserts that this language is pleasurable because it expresses an enduring impulse in the self, but also painful because of the historical experiences that have belied the promise of these words.

Like the blues, "Words Like Freedom" states its ambivalence starkly and nonreductively. There is no effort to subordinate grief about the betrayal of political ideals to a narrative of affirmation. Nor does grief foster the ironic negation of desire so common in melancholic modernism. Hughes is capable of acknowledging his sorrow and disappointment, while still affirming the yearnings that have been betrayed. While the compromised words of the American Enlightenment are at once "sweet" and sorrowful to the black poet, the libidinal impulse itself, the desire for freedom, "sings / All day every day" in the poet's heart. "Words Like Freedom" does not complete its political mourning with the bold assertion of resistance and the concomitant optimism about libidinal flourishing that we have seen in Hughes's revolutionary verse. There is, instead, a gentler and more tentative gesture enacted in the poem's conclusion. To contemplate the betrayal of *"Liberty"* in the United States arouses anger as well as sorrow in Hughes, but he does not express the explosive anger here that he communicates in "Letter to the Academy." Rather, aggression takes the form of a mild challenge. The poet confronts the reader who has *not* "known what I know" about the betrayal of the American Enlightenment—about the exclusion, exploitation, and subordination of African Americans—and reminds this reader that without such knowledge, he or she cannot understand the grief of those who have suffered this oppression. As so often in the work of mourning, even this mild gesture of aggression brings with it a libidinal opening: for the understated challenge to the reader who does not know is also an invitation to knowledge and connection. The poem's concluding gesture is, in other words, at once a mournful confrontation and an offering. What goes unsaid, but hovers implicitly at the poem's end is that if "you" care to know the reasons for the poet's grief, you might begin to gain the knowledge necessary for helping to realize the failed promise of the American Enlightenment.

I want, finally, to turn to one of Hughes's most famous poems, "Harlem," which was first published in 1951 as part of *Montage of a Dream Deferred*. *Montage* is an exceptionally sustained effort at modernist mourning: in a series of eighty-seven poems, linked formally by the "broken rhythms" of jazz and the blues, Hughes set out to explore the disappointed yet persistent yearnings of an African American "community in transition."[44] "Harlem" is the most philosophical poem in the cycle, a meditation not on particular desires and experiences of loss, but on the very work of mourning itself. The poem attempts, through a series of concrete similes, to explore an exceptionally abstract problem: "What happens to a dream deferred?" This is a remarkable question, for it focuses our attention not on the mourner, not on the person whose dream has been disappointed and postponed, but on the fate of the "dream" itself. When our personal desires or political aspirations are thwarted, for example, what happens to the yearning within us—and to the dream of gratification that we have been able to imagine? The answer offered by Hughes, in a period of political retrenchment but enormous creative productivity, is a complex one, a survey of possible psychic responses.

Here, in its entirety, is "Harlem":

What happens to a dream deferred?
Does it dry up
like a raisin in the sun?
Or fester like a sore—
And then run?
Does it stink like rotten meat?
Or crust and sugar over—
like a syrupy sweet?

Maybe it just sags
like a heavy load.

Or does it explode? (*CP* 426)

In this poem, as in "Words Like Freedom," Hughes emphasizes the ambivalence and uncertainty of mourning, the vicissitudes of an open-ended psychic process whose outcome is variable. The first simile is ambiguous. Most obviously, it suggests that a "dream" is diminished by being "deferred," shrinking and losing its vitality "like a raisin in the sun." At the same time, this image also suggests the possibility that the dream will endure and be intensified over time, just as the sweetness of the raisin is concentrated and its durability enhanced as it dries. (It is this latter possibility that the modernism of mourning typically fosters, seeking through memory to intensify and perpetuate the libidinal investments that have been disappointed through a loss whose diminution of the self is fully acknowledged.) The second simile extends this ambiguous assessment of mourning, elaborating both the potentially negative and positive outcomes of the process. The disappointment of a "dream" is a psychic wound, and the deferral of one's yearnings may, indeed, cause the "sore" to "fester" in ways that threaten the very survival of the self. But for an infected "sore" to "run" may also be a sign that a natural process of healing is taking its course—and by extension, the work of mourning may (as Freud himself proposed)[45] be understood as a painful healing of the wounded self.

Although a "dream deferred" *may* heal and become whole again through the work of mourning, the next simile emphasizes the more dire outcome. This third comparison marks the poem's nadir, it's acknowledgment that a "dream" may indeed be irreversibly ruined by disappointment: that it may die, and become, moreover, poisonous, repellent, noxious to the self and others like the "stink" of "rotten meat." (This is what happens to the yearning for sexual love in Eliot's *Waste Land*: it has become repellent as a result of a particular way of managing its disappointment.) In the final simile of this stanza, Hughes proposes the less dire but still pessimistic possibility that—as in the raisin image—the sweetness of a "dream" may, indeed, be intensified by deferral, but that this intensification entails a kind of cloying rigidity, like the "sugar[ed] over" "crust" of a "syrupy sweet." This is a particularly significant image, for here Hughes emphasizes that some processes of grieving may yield an apparent affirmation that is at once hardened and excessive: one thinks, for example, of Gatsby's entombed fantasy of Daisy or Niel's of Marian—melancholic fantasies in which desire has been precipitated out to form a rigid shell or "crust." The poet extends this litany of grieving's negative outcomes in the poem's penultimate stanza. Longings, he suggests, may be gradually deformed by their own weight (they "sag") when they are denied and deferred—and, "like a heavy load," they can become ever more burdensome to those who carry them.

The direction of Hughes's meditation shifts in the final stanza of "Harlem." This single line, italicized, and coming as it does at the poem's end, seems to mark an emphatic evolution or, perhaps, resolution. Like "Hard Daddy," "Letter to the Academy," and even "Words Like Freedom" (in its mild way), "Harlem" ends with a note of aggression. By leaving us with the question of whether a "dream deferred" might actually "*explode*," Hughes pointedly reminds us that the socially induced losses suffered by the people of Harlem must also breed anger—and a certain pressure of destructiveness. The language of "explosion" suggests not only a sudden, violent eruption—but also the centrifugal movement of that aggression *outward*. There is, in this final line of the poem, an implicit threat—not unlike that at the end of "Hard Daddy" or "Letter to the Academy," though the threat is here more direct if also more abstract. If dreams have been deferred by forces external to the self, the poet suggests, then the libidinal energy of the dream may indeed erupt so as to shatter that which constrains it.[46]

In "Harlem," Hughes acknowledges implicitly that this violent explosion may damage or consume the self, but the emphasis is principally on the shattering of external constraint. The poem evolves clearly toward affirmation of the dream's active libidinal force. In answer to his opening question—"What happens to a dream deferred?"—Hughes proposes, first, a series of comparisons, each of which emphasizes the passive waning and deterioration of desires that have been thwarted: they may "dry up," "fester," "stink like rotten meat," "crust and sugar over," and "sa[g] / like a heavy load." In contrast, the poem's final, italicized question emphasizes the continued activity of the dream, the persistent force of a dynamic, libidinal energy that "explodes." Hughes underlines here not the vanishing or waning of the dream, but rather, its persistent vitality and the release of its energy. This emphasis is intensified by the fact that the possible waning of the dream is sketched by Hughes through a series of comparisons, whereas its explosion is a direct description without need of simile—as if aggression and the concomitant release of energy were a more certain, less mediated property of the dream deferred.[47]

I do not mean to imply that the more pessimistic options explored earlier in "Harlem" are negated by the poem's final line. The blues sensibility in Hughes, as I have suggested, does not insist that love or affirmation supersedes sorrow, but rather that they persist together, in a kind of psychological "syncopation." "Harlem" acknowledges that grieving has multiple modalities and that disappointed yearnings may, indeed, suffer a melancholic fate. A "dream deferred" may become noxious to the bereaved (smelling of death itself, as it does in *The Waste Land*); it may also, in the mode of a nostalgia that disavows its anger, become rigid and cloying as in the fantasies of Gatsby or Niel Herbert; it may become a "heavy load," more burdensome as the years pass, as it appears to be for Jake Barnes or for the Cumaen Sybil who presides over Eliot's melancholic monument. But Hughes insists, along with other modernists of mourning, that there may be persistence, endurance, even healing enabled by the work of grieving. He reminds us at the poem's end that if these possibilities are to be realized, we must attend with particular emphasis to the aggression that comes with socially induced loss, and which—if channeled—might shatter that which has demanded the deferral of our dreams.

By way of concluding this discussion of the modernism of mourning, I want to turn to William Carlos Williams, a writer whose place in the modernist canon is more secure and familiar than the other writers whom I have presented as emblematic of this tradition. Williams's sensibility and his relatively privileged position in the social hierarchy enabled this earlier admission to the narrow precincts of modernist celebrity. But he was a troubling figure for those who framed the cold war version of modernism, and his was a belated and uneasy presence within the established tradition.[48] There are aspects of Williams's poetics that make him assimilable to the dominant, melancholic strand within U.S. modernism.[49] In particular, there is some tendency in his work to aestheticize poverty and other forms of social marginalization. (Among his most widely anthologized poems, for example, consider "The Pure Products of America" or "The Poor" or "Negro Woman").[50] As Olsen and Hughes point out, the inclination to turn social injuries into beautiful objects offering aesthetic consolation can lead to political acquiescence—and there is at times a note of social resignation in Williams, often phrased as a celebration of things as they are. But there is another Williams too: drawn to various anticapitalist political impulses early in life, and to the Social Credit movement in the 1930s; hostile throughout his career to the economic structures that bred poverty and alienation; angered by the complacency and brutality of class privilege; disappointed by the corruption of democratic politics by class elites; committed to a populism that was often substantive (and not merely romanticizing).[51] Williams was, moreover, capable—like other modernists of mourning—of expressing anger directly at the economic and social structures that produced alienation and undermined social solidarity. This current is persistent in Williams's work, and finds expression in such well-known poems as "The Yachts" and "Impromptu: the Suckers," his angry response to the Sacco and Vanzetti executions. The capacity to name the destructive processes of modernization, and to direct his anger at these, also enabled Williams to identify imperiled psychic and affective potentialities, and to gesture toward the forms of their possible flourishing.

In this context, I want to discuss a single poem by Williams, as a coda to my presentation of the modernism of mourning. It is a work from the middle years of his career, first published as a portion of *Paterson II* (1948) and then reprinted separately as "The Descent" in his 1954 collection, *The Desert Music*. "The Descent" does not enact a politicized anger at the destructive aspects of American capitalism, but I have chosen to focus on this poem because it stands as one of Williams's most compelling affirmations of the psychic work of mourning. Williams particularly valued "The Descent" because it was the first poem "that wholly satisfied" him that he had written in what he called "the variable foot." He had experimented for many years with this flexible measure in order to develop a verse form that would speak in "the American idiom," the "new spoken language" of the American vernacular to which Whitman had aspired. For Williams, the variable foot was a contribution to modernism's "profound revolution" against "the cultured patter of the iambic pentameter." But it was a contribution that acknowledged the importance of measure as "the sine qua non of verse," something that the "'free verse' phase" of "modern poetry" had unsatisfactorily relinquished.[52] The variable foot was a formal effort on Williams's part—as the "syncopation" of the blues and the "broken rhythms" of be-bop had been for

Hughes—to find a space for fresh linguistic agency within the constraints of an inherited poetic tradition. For Williams as for Hughes, the richness of the vernacular could only register itself fully in poetry if these constraints could be flexibly negotiated. By rejecting "free verse," Williams insisted that the cultural determination of an inherited tradition could not simply be ignored or abandoned altogether. But the "variable foot" was an effort to demonstrate that this determination was limited rather than absolute.

It was not accidental that Williams felt he had first succeeded in his negotiation with the determinations of inherited poetic form in a poem about mourning. For "The Descent" is, like "Harlem," a philosophical meditation on mourning itself. As Freud emphasizes, the work of mourning is a painful negotiation of external determinations—of the "reality principle." When we mourn, we acknowledge that forces beyond our power have taken from us things that will remain forever lost. But when we mourn fully, we also find a way, simultaneously, to honor the persistence of our yearnings, which may in future find a new and different answer in the world outside. "The Descent" is a bold affirmation of this capacity to mourn, and it may have enabled Williams to accomplish the formal negotiation for which he had long been striving. Relinquishing the "cultured patter of iambic pentameter," which had lost it's vitality, he found a satisfactory measure for the "new spoken language" of the American vernacular. In this sense, the formal accomplishment of "The Descent" is an enactment of the mourning process that the poem celebrates.

The opening stanza of "The Descent" is a paean to the power of memory. For Williams, the "descent" is a name for the psychic experience of "defeat" or disappointment. And memory (as for Hurston and H. D., Olsen and Hughes) is the faculty by which these experiences are negotiated:

> The descent beckons
> as the ascent beckoned.
> Memory is a kind
> of accomplishment,
> a sort of renewal
> even
> an initiation, since the spaces it opens are new places
> inhabited by hordes
> heretofore unrealized,

of new kinds—
           since their movements
                are toward new objectives
(even though formerly they were abandoned). (*CP* 245)

In the first two lines of the stanza, the poet proposes that "the descent" (the experience of disappointment or loss) is a dynamic process, as open-ended and potentially provocative to desire as "the ascent" (the experience of aspiration or anticipation). Disappointment or bereavement can call out to desire, according to Williams, because "memory" holds open before us yearnings that have been thwarted and remain "unrealized." He insists on the *transformative* power of memory, on the forward-looking implications of remembering that which has been lost or disappointed. In this, Williams's formulations are especially resonant with H. D.'s contention that "what men say is-not, I remember" or Hurston's assertion that because women "remember everything they don't want to forget," they can "act" according to their desires and live by the imperative that "[t]he dream is the truth." Like these other modernists of mourning, Williams insists that memory is an active faculty, an agency to be cherished, an "accomplishment." It is transformative and forward looking because the memory for which Williams speaks is not merely a static retrieval of a fixed past, but a recollection of desires, of dynamic possibilities which, though thwarted in the past, might yet unfold in new ways. It is for this reason that memory is not only a "renewal" but "an initiation." To remember that which remains "unrealized" is to remember something that remains "*new.*" Even the recollection of that which one has "abandoned" can be a "movemen[t]" "toward new objectives."[53]

    Williams elaborates on the dynamics of mourning in the second stanza, emphasizing in particular his concern not merely with loss, but with "defeat":

No defeat is made up entirely of defeat—since
the world it opens is always a place
           formerly
                unsuspected. A
world lost,
        a world unsuspected,
                beckons to new places
and no whiteness (lost) is so white as the memory
of whiteness   .

The poet makes clear that when he speaks of "the descent," he has "*defeat*" in mind—the disappointment that follows from external constraint or opposition. He insists that even "defeat," the enforced abandonment of objects or aspirations, can be mourned. The ground for Williams's optimism is, again, the dynamism and open-endedness of this grieving process. If we can hold onto the knowledge that what we have lost is not only a fixed object in the past, but also a potentiality or yearning in the self, then we may appreciate that it is always "a world unsuspected." "No defeat is made up entirely of defeat," on Williams's account, because defeat brings us into contact with desires that remain "unrealized," and we can see that the thing we have lost is an object of discovery and surprise, a "new place" that "beckons" to us. It is, for Williams, "always" something "unsuspected."

As the poet reaches for an illustration of loss in this highly philosophical poem, he chooses the abstraction "whiteness": "no whiteness (lost) is so white as the memory / of whiteness   ." This example enables Williams to emphasize still further the potentiality of the lost object. What is lost is always an "open" "space," a "whiteness," like the white space on the page before the period, a space that can be filled with the unfolding, "unsuspected" shape of one's desire. In this regard, the tendency of memory to idealize what has been lost (the "memory of whiteness" is always greater than the "whiteness (lost)") does not disturb Williams, because it is the openness, unsuspectedness, potentiality of the object that he intensifies in memory. This stands in stark contrast to the vision of melancholic modernists who, when they are able to idealize what they have lost (as in the nostalgic moments in Cather and Fitzgerald), feel an accompanying need to negate their affirmation as mere illusion. It is the rigidity of melancholic idealization (its "sugary" "crust," as Hughes might put it) that produces, at least in part, the need for denigration. In Williams—as in the other modernists of mourning—the flexibility of memory makes a particular form of idealization psychically tenable. For he describes an idealization that facilitates a dynamic relation to an "open" and "unsuspected" "world," rather than an idealization that traps one within the confines of a rigidly fetishized past, cutting one off from new object relations, from love.

In stanzas three and four, Williams explicitly associates this activity of memory in the work of mourning with the reawakening of love and the shedding of that which inhibits libido.

With evening, love wakens
        though its shadows
                which are alive by reason
of the sun shining—
        grow sleepy now and drop away
                from desire   .

Love without shadows stirs now
        beginning to awaken
                as night
advances.

Here, Williams compares "the descent" of mourning—the psychic journey down into the self—with the descent of "evening." The poet suggests that this "descent" into memory shields the self psychologically from the external forces that veil or obscure "desire," just as the descent of "evening" liberates objects from the "shadows" produced by "the sun."[54] Through mourning, "love wakens" and sheds the "shadows" that inhibit "desire."[55] We have seen this psychic dynamic, presented abstractly by Williams, enacted in concrete social circumstances throughout the modernism of mourning. In *Their Eyes*, Janie remembers the death of Tea Cake and retrieves her love for him ("the kiss of his memory") from amidst the shadow of his aggression and her necessary act of self-defense. H. D. remembers the violence of war in *Flowering of the Rod* in order to "mount higher to love—resurrection," just as she remembers the long history of Western misogyny in order to affirm the wholeness of a libidinally alive femininity. Olsen dwells on the painful deprivations of her characters in order to retrieve their capacity for love, which floats free (however briefly) from the shadows of exploitation that inhibit its full expression. Hughes's blues singer remembers the callousness of her "hard daddy" in order to revive in herself the desire to "fly like the eagle flies," just as the poet must recall that "words like *Liberty*" "almost make me cry" in order to affirm the fact that "On my heart-strings freedom sings / All day everyday."

In the final stanza of "The Descent," Williams pulls together the themes of the poem, insisting on the power of mourning to work through the "despair" that follows acute loss:

The descent
            made up of despairs
                        and without accomplishment
realizes a new awakening:
                        which is a reversal
of despair.
            For what we cannot accomplish, what
is denied to love,
            what we have lost in the anticipation—
                        a descent follows,
endless and indestructible   .

Like other nonmelancholic modernists, Williams emphasizes that mourning's ultimate affirmation arrives through the acknowledgment, rather than
the denial, of loss. The work of mourning is not a disavowal of defeat or
hopelessness. It is, indeed, "made up" of these experiences. What Williams
affirms is the psychic possibility of a "new awakening" and a "reversal / of
despair" precisely through the memory of what has been "denied to love." As
in the case of Hughes, the process of mourning is a kind of psychic syncopation: a "despair" that, through the work of memory, can lead to an "awakening" of desire, and to despair's "reversal." Williams thus offers an especially
bold affirmation of mourning's power. For he recognizes quite fully the fragility of love relations in a culture in which desire is cast in shadow by the
powerful forces that revolve around us. He recognizes too that our efforts at
"accomplishment" (including resistance) will, like our efforts at love, often
meet with "defeat." What is "indestructible" on his account is the capacity
to mourn: the capacity of the self, through memory, to regain access to the
open-endedness of desire.

PART TWO

The Two Modernisms at War

Dos Passos's USA *Trilogy*

American modernism is a cultural formation structured by an argument about modern capitalism and the alienation it has produced. Intellectually, modernist writers struggled to understand whether the emerging economic order was an irresistible fact of life, the condition and horizon of all social possibilities, a second nature. Psychologically, they grieved for the injuries that this economic transformation had inflicted. The two modernisms represent different affective and formal responses to these challenges, two sides of an evolving argument. The dominant strand of the tradition, privileged during the cold war, naturalized the social causes of the crisis of alienation—and grieved, as a result, melancholically. The "other" modernism deployed experimental techniques in order to map the historical forces that divided

Americans from one another and from themselves. Disputing the claim that modern alienation was an expression of ineluctable human nature, writers in this tradition mourned for denied forms of intimacy, solidarity, and expressivity. They invented strategies of resistance—and the most ambitious among them insisted that a social order could be created in which imperiled human capacities would be realized.

In previous chapters, I have drawn a map of the two modernisms with broad strokes, revealing the contours of the literary field. For heuristic reasons, I have discussed the traditions as if they were separate, and I have assigned major works to one or the other. Such a division is justified by the fact that, in most texts, one structure of feeling predominates—and my aim, thus far, has been to reveal the distinctive features of each structure of feeling. But this heuristic strategy has also entailed a simplification. As some of my earlier readings indicate, the conflict between the two modernisms is enacted *within* individual texts as well as between them. In their efforts at cognitive mapping, many works oscillate between the hope for political transformation and the conviction that the alienating forces of modernization were finally irresistible. Sustained social analysis frequently gives way to universalizing mystification, while the protracted expression of a naturalizing vision is often disrupted by bursts of acute social insight. Psychologically, most texts contain both mournful and melancholic impulses, in complex and varied tension. In works that are predominantly melancholic there are moments of fuller mourning, while in texts that typify the modernism of mourning there are bouts of melancholic withdrawal, self-beratement, numbness.

In order to reveal the complex and dynamic interplay of the two modernisms, I will devote the following chapters to a detailed exploration of a single major work. The case-study approach makes several things possible. It will allow me to provide a social and biographical account of a particular experience of the crisis of modernization and to analyze the personal and cultural obstacles to grieving faced by one writer in a specific social setting. This focus will also enable me to analyze the formal strategies through which the oscillating impulses of mourning and melancholia are enacted and to reveal their concrete political implications.

John Dos Passos's *U.S.A.* trilogy provides an exceptionally rich subject for such a case study. Although widely misunderstood and increasingly ignored during the cold war era, *U.S.A.* is a quintessential work of American

modernism. A formally ambitious text, *U.S.A.* contains multiple representational modes that enable the trilogy to embody—perhaps more fully than
any work in the tradition—*both* the modernism of mourning *and* its melancholic counterimpulse. In the biographical prose poems that constitute one
strand of the trilogy, for example, Dos Passos created an idiom for political
mourning that is virtually without peer in American letters. Here he grieved
for the suppression of an entire political movement in ways that reveal how
decisively collective efforts at social change require the capacity to mourn.
In another strand of the trilogy—the fictional storylines—he grieved with
a fierce, obsessively elaborated and unremitting melancholia, developing a
fully realized naturalism that mystifies the social causes of loss in ways that
rival even his most depoliticized contemporaries. Because of the unusual
formal separation of *U.S.A.*'s representational modes, the oscillations between mourning and melancholia are uniquely visible. At the same time,
neither mode is pure, and the balance between them shifted over the decade
of the trilogy's composition, revealing with exceptional clarity the dynamic
interplay of the two modernisms.

Experimental in form, *U.S.A.* is also quintessentially modernist in its social preoccupations. Like his contemporaries, Dos Passos was centrally concerned with the problem of alienation and with other corrosive effects of the
burgeoning economic order. As a sophisticated intellectual and a committed
man of the Left, however, he was more politically self-conscious than most
of his literary peers and had more developed analyses of social and historical dynamics. He insisted that the ambitious project of *U.S.A.* was to chart
the changes wrought in American life by the shift from "competitive" to
"monopoly capitalism,"[1] and he sought to explain the systemic causes of the
crisis of modernization. More than this, *U.S.A.* explores in detail the popular
mass movement that arose to challenge the new economic order. Grieving
the injuries inflicted by American capitalism, it also assesses the possibility of building an alternative social order in which those injuries might be
remedied.

From the mid-teens through the mid-1930s, Dos Passos actively allied
himself with anticapitalist political movements, and in *U.S.A.* he represented
the material and libidinal aspirations that had been expressed by hundreds of
thousands of Americans through anarchist, syndicalist, socialist, and communist political formations. He explored the difficulty of sustaining faith in the

possibility of such fundamental social change and examined the crises and disappointments that early-twentieth-century American radicals had faced. In particular, he was concerned with the external repression of the American Left during the Red Scare of the teens and 1920s—and with what he viewed as the radical movement's self-destruction during the 1930s, as a result of the rise of Stalinism. Written over the course of a decade, the trilogy was Dos Passos's sustained attempt to mourn for these two very different kinds of political disappointment. In this effort, he and his work were deeply conflicted. In the biographical prose poems (and in some of the Camera Eye segments), Dos Passos is able to mourn with remarkable fullness, identifying his investments in a political movement that was being eviscerated—and defining those investments as a living tradition that his readers might embrace. In the fictional storylines of *U.S.A.*, he grieves melancholically, turning the full force of his rage against his own radical aspirations and insisting that the effort to imagine a nonexploitative and nonalienated society was itself a naïve delusion doomed inevitably to failure

U.S.A.'s preoccupation with the fate of anticapitalist radicalism in the United States was largely responsible for its early fame—and for its subsequent marginalization. In the 1930s and 1940s, many of America's most prominent literary critics were themselves political radicals or were left-liberals anxious to define their relation to the anticapitalist movement. Lionel Trilling and Edmund Wilson, Malcolm Cowley, Granville Hicks, and Alfred Kazin all wrote passionately about *U.S.A.*, which they viewed as central to, even definitive of, the daring new literature of their generation. From across the Atlantic, Sartre famously declared that Dos Passos was "the greatest writer of our time," and Leavis too wanted to have his say.[2] With the onset of the cold war, the praise came abruptly to an end, especially in the United States. The anticapitalist urgencies of the trilogy became increasingly disturbing, as the climate of McCarthyism permeated the culture, including the universities. As the cold war version of modernism was consolidated during the 1950s and 1960s, with its privileging of melancholia and political quiescence, *U.S.A.* posed a peculiar problem. Its undeniable formal ambition and its melancholic dimension made it appear to belong to the emerging modernist canon. But its explicit condemnation of capitalism and its lyrical celebration of the revolutionary Left seemed to place it beyond the pale—along with other works that were now dismissed as propaganda. Dos Passos's own rapid transformation from icon of the literary Left to anti-Communist supporter of McCarthy compounded the confusion. In this charged political climate, leading scholars of U.S. modernism chose increasingly to ignore *U.S.A.* By the seventies, the trilogy had come to occupy its anomalous status as a kind of modernist black sheep, a disavowed central text, at once widely recognized and studiously neglected.

As I suggested in Chapter One, the processes of cold war canonization worked not only to marginalize politically threatening texts, but also to incorporate them when it was possible to neutralize or obscure their disturbing elements. The critical fate of *U.S.A.* is emblematic in both regards. For even as most scholars of modernism ignored it, there were some critics who sought to save the trilogy from obscurity. Many of these attempted, implausibly but with considerable ingenuity, to separate the author and his trilogy from the taint of anticapitalism. They insisted, to cite merely a few examples, that *U.S.A.* was not "socialist," "the very opposite of Marxism," not opposed to "capitalism," and "not informed by any intellectual commitment to the left."[3] Scholars influenced by consensus-school historiography argued that Dos Passos only *appeared* to have been "a radical activist who became a conservative apologist," when in fact he was "a conservative who became what he always was."[4] Literary critics promulgated accounts of the trilogy that exclusively emphasized its melancholic dimension and made it appear to conform to the politically quiescent norm that had been imposed on the modernist tradition. Arthur Mizener set the tone in 1951, when he asserted that *U.S.A.* is an "ironic" work of "satire" concerned with the "permanent defects of humanity" and with "defeats" that are "beyond social or political redress." In succeeding decades, this critical line flourished. Claude-Edmonde Magny, for example, insisted that Dos Passos's "attack" was not principally directed at "the capitalist system" but "ultimately against Being." Iain Colley similarly warned that "to read [*U.S.A.*'s] main intention as directly political is to miss the essence of Dos Passos' work": a concern with "entropy" and "chaos," with the "absurd" character of "human society," which cannot be "rationally understood" because it is shaped by "mysterious forces," and for which Dos Passos had no "hope for radical improvement."[5]

The trilogy's political preoccupation with capitalism and its alternatives thus led to its marginalization and misrecognition during the cold war. For decades, *U.S.A.*'s self-proclaimed champions obscured that which made it most significant for American culture. Seeking to fit it to the pattern of a truncated modernist canon, they obscured that which made it, in fact, quintessential: its anguished—and fully enacted—conflict between mourning and melancholia, between the political hope for radical social change and the despairing conviction that capitalism was the grim truth of human nature. To retrieve *U.S.A.*'s actual political concerns, and its full psychic and formal complexity, is thus to retrieve American modernism's central argument.[6]

Toward this end, I will begin my case study by offering a detailed biographical account of Dos Passos's political evolution, attempting to clear away misconceptions that proliferated in cold war accounts of the author and of the American Left more generally. Tracing one man's highly self-conscious encounter with the crisis of modernization, I will emphasize in particular the ways in which Dos Passos was drawn into radical political movements because of his growing conviction that capitalism was inimical to social solidarity, democracy, and individual self-realization. In subsequent chapters, I will turn to the *U.S.A.* trilogy itself in order to trace the interplay of the two modernisms in Dos Passos's effort to grieve the losses endured by American radicals and to sustain his faith in the possibility of social transformation.

FOUR

John Dos Passos and the Crises of American Radicalism, 1916–1936

John Dos Passos did not have the sort of upbringing that one might expect of a man who went on to become a prominent figure of the literary Left. He did not have a working-class childhood; nor did he inherit radical political ideas from his family or immediate community. His father was a wealthy lawyer who had built a highly successful practice in finance and corporation law. The younger Dos Passos received an elite education: he went to prep school at Choate, did the Grand Tour of Europe with a private tutor, and then spent four years at Harvard. He perceived himself appropriately as a member of the nation's elite.[1] When his political radicalism first emerged at Harvard in the teens, it was accordingly a rebellion against the arrangements of American society from the standpoint of the privileged, not the dispossessed.

This rebellion first took the form of a bohemian revolt against the constraints, repressions, and alienations of conventional bourgeois life. In letters written from Harvard in 1915 and 1916, for example, Dos Passos persistently condemned the education he was receiving and the narrow, exclusionary culture of which it was a part. He derided his elite education as "nothing but a wall that keeps [people] from seeing the world." He insisted that the intellectual and social habits of his class prevented young people from having a rich and intense experience of life, from forming a full range of social connections, from actively appreciating and understanding the world in which they lived. The mixture of "petty snobberies," crass materialism, and a prudish genteel morality seemed to him "an abomination" "so blinding to the human beauty that everything is warm with." Dos Passos comes through in these early letters as an ardent young man, eager for intellectual and sensual vitality, longing for a breadth of experience that seemed foreclosed by a bourgeois world that he perceived as "corsetted" by its own mores,[2] and swathed in the "cotton-wool" of conventional thought and elitist prohibitions. (Fifteen years later, in *U.S.A.*, he would describe his time at Harvard as "four years under the ethercone.") He expressed a wide range of desires as organically connected to one another, and as equally proscribed: he wanted forms of intellectual and aesthetic stimulation that seemed to have no place in the university; he wanted to know and feel connected to people, without regard for class divisions or for genteel society's fussy attempt to separate "decent people" from "life's meaner things"; he wanted sexual experience in a prudish world that seemed committed to repression. ("Eros is a great god," he proclaimed—but then quickly lamented "how few votaries he has.") If he were to pursue his own exuberant, youthful desires, Dos Passos felt that he would have to revolt against the staid world of alienating privilege and constraint. As he put it to his close friend and primary correspondent, Rumsey Marvin, he was inclined to divide the world into two sorts of people—"[t]he people who are free, who are in revolt, and the people who are shackled by all convention." The young bohemian knew which side of that divide he meant to be on.[3]

While still at Harvard, Dos Passos tried to place his own personal revolt within a larger historical context and to give it a recognizable political shape. In his most ambitious piece of undergraduate journalism, for example, an essay entitled "A Humble Protest," he argued that the central problem of his time (and of modern history more generally) was the conflict between "humanism" and "industrialism." With its roots in ancient Greece and its modern flowering in the French Revolution, the humanist tradition sought, in broad terms, the "realization of the fullness of man." Dos Passos elaborated this humanist ideal in aesthetic terms. The two primary "aims" of human life, he suggested, were "the desire to create" and "the desire to fathom," both of which were "intangibly mixed up" with the "sense of beauty." He went on to argue that industrialization prevented men and women from realizing their capacities for creativity and understanding. His case had two main components. On the one hand, the great majority of people "grind their lives away" in "degrading, never-ending labor" "without ever a chance of self-expression." On the other, the small, privileged elite did not even benefit from this "narrowing and stultifying" labor of the majority: in fact—and here he spoke from his own frustration as a member of the upper class—the cultural and material results of the "Industrial system" seemed to him "actually destructive of the capacity of men for living, for the fathoming of life, for the expression of life." In short, industrialization had brought different forms of slavery for the rich and the poor: "Under industrialism [. . .] three-fourths of the world are bound in economic slavery that the other fourth may in turn be enslaved by the tentacular inessentials of civilization."[4]

This early statement of principle and protest reveals a good deal, both about the young Dos Passos's intellectual formation and about the values and sensibility that would continue to drive his mature political commitments. His relationship to aesthetic humanism would certainly evolve over the decades. But in the course of his long and contradictory career, he would never abandon the basic intuition he expressed here: that a good and just society was one in which all individuals were as free (and as materially able) as possible to find means of creative self-expression and to perceive the beauty of their world and of the people around them. His aestheticism was a call not only for the appreciation of formal art, but also more generally for the direct sensual enjoyment of the world—a call not merely for the "expression of life," as he put it in his essay, but also for "living" itself.[5] With an adolescent's intellectual daring, Dos Passos was trying to name the "aims" of human life, to define the very content of freedom, according to his own ebullient intuition. In the idiom of a humanist aestheticism, he found a relatively respectable vocabulary for his burgeoning bohemian belief: that an idealistic social criticism could be founded on a commitment to maximizing the capacity of individuals to take aesthetic and sensual pleasure and to find the fullest possible range of social connections, unimpeded by class divisions.

This first sustained articulation of Dos Passos's aesthetic humanism was already fused in 1916 to an incipiently anticapitalist critique of American society. In "A Humble Protest," he identified "the Industrial system" as the primary obstacle to the humanist "realization of the fullness of man." Although he did not use this particular vocabulary at the time, he effectively argued that it was *economic exploitation* on the one hand ("three-fourths of the world are bound in economic slavery") and *alienation* on the other (alienation of rich and poor alike from their own creative capacities and from one another) that thwarted individual self-realization and community in industrial society. Dos Passos's ideas about politics and economics would evolve a good deal over the next two decades, but this basic concern with exploitation and alienation would provide an enduring element of his radical critique.[6] I call this early analysis *incipiently* anticapitalist, however, because he was still relying upon a Romantic conceptual framework that identified "industrialism" (rather than capitalism) as the central object of his criticism.[7] Moreover, to the degree that he had any attitude at all toward anticapitalist political movements per se in 1916, it appears to have been casually dismissive.[8] Within a year, however, Dos Passos would be identifying himself as a "revolutionist" and he would embrace the radical movement for the very reasons he laid out in "A Humble Protest."

This alignment with the anticapitalist Left was enabled, above all else, by Dos Passos's encounter in the spring and summer of 1917 with the bohemian radical milieu that had been thriving in New York City for almost a decade. With its geographical focus in Greenwich Village, this left-wing bohemia brought together a wide array of political and cultural radicals— socialists and anarchists, trade union militants, radical artists, writers and intellectuals, campaigners for a host of political causes from women's suffrage to pacifism. The desire for individual freedom and the revolt against gentility that Dos Passos had expressed privately in his correspondence were being defiantly and energetically expressed in the pages of the bohemian radicals' heterodox journal, *The Masses*. Here writers were championing free love and birth control; they were calling for a "new paganism"; they were debating innovative developments in modern art that defied genteel aesthetic (as well as moral) conventions. And this bohemianism was fused to an explicit commitment to revolution. Writers in *The Masses* were condemning capitalism for its "puritanism"—and arguing that only a revolution in the economic order would create a society in which all individuals would have an opportunity for self-fulfillment and self-expression, for pleasure and beauty in their own lives. (As Emma Goldman phrased an anarchist version of this argument in a speech reprinted in *The Masses*, the revolution to overthrow capitalism was to be "a war for a seat at the table of life, a war for well-being, for beauty, for liberty."[9]) While Dos Passos had been offering a vaguely defined Romantic criticism of the "Industrial system," the editors of *The Masses* were openly allying themselves with the revolutionary wing of the anticapitalist movement—with figures like Big Bill Haywood and Emma Goldman, Mother Jones and Eugene Debs. (They were particularly drawn to the "direct action" tactics of the anarchists, and the anarcho-syndicalists of the Industrial Workers of the World [IWW]).[10] This fusion of a revolutionary anticapitalism with an expansive commitment to individual liberation of all kinds, and with an interest in the liberating potential of new forms of modern art, was exhilarating to Dos Passos. He came now to feel that it was capitalism that was responsible for the forms of alienation and exploitation that he deplored. And he began to believe that the radical movement offered a more fully political extension of his own aesthetic-humanist commitments. Here was a revolutionary movement explicitly committed to the attack on class divisions, on exploitation and alienation, on genteel hypocrisy and constraint. It was, he believed, a mass movement committed to enabling all members of society to find the fullest degree of personal freedom and the greatest opportunity for self-expression.[11]

If Dos Passos's experience in New York drew him, then, from a Romantic humanism into the anticapitalist Left, his direct experience of the First World War the following year intensified the process of his radicalization. Although he considered himself a pacifist by 1917, he was nevertheless eager to see the war first-hand as a noncombatant, and he went to France as a member of the Norton-Harjes Ambulance Service. The war affected him deeply. In his letters and diary entries written at the front, Dos Passos expressed some of the despair so common among those who encountered the carnage directly. Echoing the now-famous comments of other literary contemporaries who served in the military or in the ambulance corps, he wrote about his bewilderment that centuries of European culture should have led to this frenzy of self-destruction, and about his feelings of futility and personal paralysis.[12]

But he also brought with him to France a more searching political critique of his society than most of the "gentlemen volunteers" with whom he served—and his emerging radicalism both shaped, and was in turn shaped by, his wartime experience.[13] The war confirmed and magnified the self-destructiveness of industrial capitalism, as Dos Passos was beginning to understand it. While he wrote persistently about the "decency" of the young men he met at the front, he also perceived the ways in which the military replicated and enforced the class hierarchies that divided and set people against one another in civilian society. As he looked at the organization of the army, he saw a grim vision of the capitalist future: "[t]he spectacle of the whole world lashed to war in dirty greyish uniforms—ordered about by the middle classes [in] the shape of petty officers, by the high financier spheres in the shape of generals & such canaille." In "A Humble Protest," Dos Passos had already written of industrialism as a "ponderous suicidal machine," but it was only at the front that he realized the full significance of this idea. It was not simply that the bloodshed on the battlefields was itself so fully mechanized, but also that the war—and all the social machinery that was driving it—seemed to him to spell the destruction of everything he valued. "For all the things of the mind," Dos Passos wrote to the Spanish intellectual Jose Giner Pantoja, "for art, and for everything that is needed in the world, war [. . .] is death."[14]

As he struggled to identify the causes of this "suicidal madness," Dos Passos persistently blamed the economic competition among wealthy industrialized countries and the nationalist ideologies with which they attempted to cover their mercenary interests. Because he had spent much of his childhood abroad, Dos Passos always had a tendency toward cosmopolitanism—and even before leaving for France this tendency was intensified and politicized by his encounter in New York with socialist internationalism and with the anarchist opposition to nation-states and governments of all kinds. "One thing comes out clear," he wrote in his diary in January 1918: "the one thing that enslaves people more than any other to the servitude of war is nationalism" and he went on to explain that "the patriotic cant" was "the mask of all the trade-greed." A few months later, he wrote in a similar vein that "At the bottom of all our nationalities—under the royal robes and the polished imperial helmets and the abstract talk of domination—are hidden the murky factory chimneys that are our world's God." As he grew ever more disgusted by the continuing bloodshed, Dos Passos also began to make more explicit in his own mind the connections between the economic forces fueling the war and those that were deforming people's lives at home. He had the foolhardiness to express these opinions to Jose Giner Pantoja in a letter in which he said not merely that the war was being fought "for greedy nations in a world drunk on commercialism" but also that in all the allied nations "there is nothing, either for the rich or the poor, but slavery; to industry, to money, to the mammon of business." Most flagrantly, he suggested that only in neutral Spain and in Bolshevik Russia was "the conquest not quite complete." The letter ran foul of the censors, and Dos Passos was dismissed from the ambulance corps and sent back to the United States in the summer of 1918.[15]

Perhaps the most important effect of the war on Dos Passos's political thinking was his emerging conviction that the dominant economic forces shaping Europe and America were fundamentally incompatible with the rights and values of democracy. In his ill-fated letter to Pantoja, he had written that "it seems to me that with the war, with the military service law, liberty [in my own poor country] is extinguished for a long time to come, and the day of triumph for plutocracy has arrived." The same month, he noted in his diary that a man in the United States had been sentenced to death for refusing to serve after he had been drafted and assigned to a military unit—and Dos Passos asked himself "Won't it be strange if it comes to that in my case?"[16] Although it didn't "come to that," his expulsion from the ambulance corps for the sentiments expressed in his letter did confirm, in an immediately personal way, that the interests of the "plutocracy" had indeed superseded the most fundamental democratic liberties, including the right to free expression. This growing sense of the collision between capitalism and democracy marked an important evolution in Dos Passos' political outlook. Before his experience of the war, his radicalism largely rested on the recognition that capitalism constrained expressivity—and this recognition was now being extended into a wider political domain. In the next few years, his commitment to a participatory conception of democracy would grow—as would his sense of the danger that capitalism represented.

By 1918, his recognition of this danger was already acute. He knew that his own experience in the ambulance corps was only the mildest reflection of the wartime assault on democracy in the United States. The Espionage Act, passed by Congress in 1917 in order to enable the government to respond to any political activity that might weaken the war effort, led to one of the most intense phases of political repression in American history. The Red Scare of the late teens and early 1920s caused a great many to agree that "plutocracy" had triumphed over democratic liberties, and it had decisive effects on the political development of the young writer.

Before turning to these postwar developments, however, it is important to emphasize the psychological implications of Dos Passos's embrace of radical politics in 1917 and 1918. In these years, he registered at an intimate personal level the intensifying crisis of alienation that seemed to permeate American society. He was horrified by the war's carnage and fearful of the rising tide of political repression. While he felt the injuries inflicted by these toxic social developments, he did not experience them as unnamable traumas—as did many of his contemporaries. The anticapitalist Left provided him with social and historical explanations for these destructive phenomena. As a result, the young writer perceived the losses endured by millions on the battlefields of Europe and throughout capitalist societies not as mysterious inevitabilities, but as the effects of an economic order that might be challenged through collective action. By participating in a political movement, Dos Passos was able to direct his anger at what he understood to be the systemic causes of these injuries, while also imagining an alternative future. His political commitment over the next two decades was animated by the force of these losses and by the strength of the hopes that the Left helped him to sustain. By 1918, Dos Passos understood himself to be a participant in a revolutionary mass movement that was international in scope. In the years ahead, he would carefully scrutinize the political formations of the anticapitalist Left, seeking to understand his place in this movement that aimed to bring into being a less alienated, more democratic society—even in the face of mounting political repression.

The period between 1918 and 1925 was a time of intensive political and literary self-definition for Dos Passos. During these years of apprenticeship, he published four novels, two of which—*Three Soldiers* (1921) and *Manhattan Transfer* (1925)—established him as an important young figure on the American literary scene. In *Three Soldiers*, he sought to record the destructiveness of the war, but in contrast to many novels of the period that are more familiar to readers today, Dos Passos focused his attention on the repressiveness of military life. Like his wartime letters and diaries, the novel represents the army as a catastrophic encapsulation of a society whose mindless discipline, violence, and conformity destroy all that might have flourished in the individuals who compose it. In *Manhattan Transfer*, Dos Passos began to develop the experimental formal techniques that would enable him to represent the libidinal alienations and personal isolation bred by monopoly capitalism—a literary project that would find its fullest flowering in the later *U.S.A.* trilogy. During these years, he was also searching and experimenting politically, trying to define his radicalism in relation to the varied formations of the anticapitalist Left—both to those that he had first encountered in New York in 1917 and to emergent formations in the United States and around the world. This process of political self-definition and evaluation is recorded in his letters and dairies—and in a growing number of published political essays, through which he was beginning to establish himself in the postwar years as a political journalist as well as a novelist.[17]

Perhaps the most striking feature of his political outlook at this time is the remarkably wide range of his sympathies, which extended across the entire anticapitalist spectrum. He continued to be interested in the forms of anarchism, syndicalism, and social democracy that he had first encountered in New York. In the months before his service in the ambulance corps, Dos Passos was strongly influenced by the anarchists' commitment to solidaristic free association and by their repudiation of the state and all forms of institutionalized hierarchy. He found in the IWW (the primary expression of revolutionary syndicalism in the United States) an enduring model of radical free association in action. And he was (despite his antistatist inclinations) strongly drawn to the Debsian Socialist Party's pursuit of a democratic strategy for socialist transformation.[18] In the years after his return from the European war, Dos Passos consolidated his relationship to each of these formations—and to others on the anticapitalist Left that he now encountered for the first time. Developing an increasingly internationalist frame of reference, he wrote with admiration about Spanish anarchists and about the revolutionary syndicalist movement in Portugal. He showed an increasing interest in the activities of European social democratic parties—particularly the British Labor Party. And, like anticapitalist radicals around the world, he was exhilarated by the successful Bolshevik revolution of 1917. Although his strong anarcho-syndicalist inclinations made him skeptical and balanced in his evaluations of Soviet Communism, he was nevertheless enthusiastic about the promise of the burgeoning international Communist movement.[19]

In part, the catholicity of these sympathies reflected the fact that Dos Passos was, after all, an intellectual—and a young, institutionally unaligned, intellectual at that. Had he been an active participant in party politics or a labor organizer, he would have been forced to make clearer choices between strategic alternatives. But as a novelist and political journalist, Dos Passos was freed of the burden (and perhaps also deprived of the discipline) imposed by such practical responsibilities. Struggling to define his own commitments, and believing passionately in his intellectual vocation, he recognized that there were many impulses within the radical movement, that different strategies might be more appropriate at different moments and in different places, that there were no scientific certainties about how best to build a liberatory alternative to capitalism. He believed that the movement was an ongoing experiment in which many things must be tried—and in which errors, as well as achievements, must be named. For almost two decades after his return from the battlefields of Europe, he wrote explicitly from an anticapitalist position, but he wrote as a moral and cultural critic of a political movement that he understood to be large, variegated, and evolving, rather than as an advocate for a single program or party.

Dos Passos had been radicalized during a particular moment of heterodoxy and fluidity in the American Left, and he carried this sensibility with him into the postwar period, retaining a relation to all the formations, new and old, that seemed congenial to his ideals.[20] To say that he was open in this way to many tendencies is not, however, to say that he indiscriminately or uncritically embraced all the organizations and impulses within the anticapitalist Left. On the contrary, during the years after the First World War, he carefully evaluated the political formations around him on the basis of consistent criteria. His evaluations rested, above all, upon the humanist and democratic commitments that had animated his radicalism from the outset. His nuanced assessment of the Soviet Union in the early 1920s is emblematic in this regard: while he celebrated the promise of "pure democracy" in the soviets as well as the massive expansion of education and popular access to the arts, he also warned against the "new tyranny" threatened by the Tcheka and by the unbridled power of the Bolshevik state.[21] Whether he was writing about the soviets in the Caucasus or the Portuguese Syndicalists, about Wobblies in Seattle or Communist miners in Kentucky, he wanted to know whether opportunities for self-expression and for participatory democracy were being maximized as a constitutive part of the struggle for socialism.

Dos Passos thus evaluated the anticapitalist movements around him during the postwar years on the basis of the humanist and democratic commitments that were embryonically present in his Harvard aestheticism, were then strongly influenced by the First World War, and were decisively shaped by the anticapitalist formations that he encountered in the United States from the time of his Greenwich Village sojourn. In the months and years after his return from the European war, these commitments increased in intensity for Dos Passos. But a major political crisis was at hand. At the very moment when the radical formations that had fostered Dos Passos's anticapitalism had reached their fullest flowering, they were also being threatened by two separate events. The first of these was the Red Scare of the late teens and 1920s—a phase of political repression that was far more destructive than the later Red Scare of the 1950s. Within a few years of the war's end, this assault had effectively destroyed the radical movement as Dos Passos had known it. The second blow came from within the movement itself. The founding of the Communist Third International in 1919 split the movement internally, precipitating a process of factional division and internecine conflict. This internal fragmentation compounded the damage done by the fierce repression of the Red Scare.

The Red Scare reached its peak in the years between 1917 and 1920. This campaign of political repression was waged (both overtly and covertly) by virtually every branch of government, from President Wilson and the Congress to state legislatures and city councils; it was endorsed and prosecuted by the entire judicial system of the nation up to the Supreme Court; and it was enforced not only by the police and the army, but also by extralegal vigilante activity on a vast scale. This systematic repression was precipitated and ideologically justified by the U.S. entry into the First World War in the spring of 1917. Most American radicals opposed U.S. participation in a war that they viewed as serving imperialist and capitalist ends—and this opposition brought down upon them the full weight of wartime jingoism and hysteria.[22]

The wartime assault on the Left was massive in scale and devastating in effect. Under powers granted by the Espionage Act of 1917, the Postmaster General led a systematic national campaign to silence the anticapitalist press, denying second-class mailing privileges to those radical newspapers and magazines that were not suspended or banned outright. By the end of the war, virtually every one of the hundreds of radical periodicals in the United States had been interfered with, and most of the papers that served rural radicals (the backbone of the prewar anticapitalist movement) were driven out of business. Meanwhile, federal prosecutors set out to cripple both the Socialist Party and the IWW by arresting national and regional leaders. It is an indication of the climate in which these prosecutions were conducted that one jury required less than an hour to bring back guilty verdicts against 113 Wobblies, accused of ten thousand separate crimes, during a single mass trial in 1917. Rank-and-file members of the Socialist Party and the IWW were also being arrested, jailed—and violently attacked by vigilantes around the country. Communists and anarchists, as well as Socialists and Wobblies, were beaten, tarred and feathered, lynched, forcibly deported; radicals were prevented from holding meetings; editors were forced to change their editorial policies or have their presses destroyed. During the last year of the war alone, the mixture of vigilante activity and official prosecution led to the destruction of some fifteen hundred of the Socialist Party's five thousand locals.[23]

Fueled by burgeoning anxieties about the Russian Revolution, the postwar assault was even more intense.[24] By the end of 1919, the anticapitalist formations that had inspired Dos Passos had been crushed under the weight of external repression. Of his radical "heroes," Debs and Haywood had been sentenced to ten- and thirty-year prison terms, respectively; Emma Goldman had been deported; and Max Eastman had been tried twice for sedition. *The Masses* had been banned altogether in 1917. The IWW had been destroyed as a functional labor organization by 1918. The Socialist Party, with so many locals crushed, so many papers destroyed, so much of its first-rank leadership in jail, was a weakened and reduced shell of its prewar incarnation.

Of all the acts of repression perpetrated during the Red Scare, the one that touched Dos Passos most personally was the protracted prosecution and ultimate execution of two working-class immigrant anarchists, Nicola Sacco and Bartolomeo Vanzetti.[25] Like many other American radicals and civil libertarians, Dos Passos believed that Sacco and Vanzetti were the innocent scapegoats of anti-Red hysteria—that they had been falsely accused, convicted, and ultimately sentenced to death because of their anticapitalist convictions, and that their political persecution was further fueled by ethnic and class hatred. He started working for the Sacco and Vanzetti Defense Committee in 1925, and in the year and a half during which their final legal appeals were presented and rejected, he devoted his skills and his growing prestige as a writer to the effort to save their lives. During these months of advocacy work, he came to see their case as crystallizing the meaning of the Red Scare as a whole. Sacco and Vanzetti, he wrote in the summer of 1927, had become "huge symbols" and their "case has become part of the world struggle between the capitalist class and the working class, between those who have power and those who are struggling to get it."[26] In the course of this struggle, the "capitalist class" was apparently willing to destroy the fragile institutions of democracy upon which the United States had ostensibly been founded if this was necessary to maintain its hold on power. This perception of the corrosive effects of capitalism on American democracy was not, of course, new for Dos Passos. But the "judicial murder" (as he called it) of Sacco and Vanzetti came to stand for all the antidemocratic repression of the Red Scare. When Sacco and Vanzetti were finally electrocuted in August 1927, Dos Passos experienced their execution as a personal as well as collective defeat. He had committed his own energies and talents to their cause and he now shared, more immediately than before, the feelings of anger and disappointment, fear and failure, that so many activists on the Left had endured in the preceding years.[27]

At the very moment when the radical movement was subjected to this extraordinary external repression, it was also shattering from within. The founding of the Communist Third International in January 1919—an event that fanned the flames of the Red Scare in the United States—had the additional effect of precipitating a process of internal fragmentation and bitter factionalization within the ranks of the American Left. Although most American radicals enthusiastically supported the Russian Revolution, they were deeply divided about its relevance as a model for the anticapitalist movement in the United States. More specifically, they disagreed about how to respond to the Comintern's insistence that those wishing to join the Third International should adopt Leninist (democratic-centralist) party organization and should pursue an immediate revolutionary strategy aimed at the seizure of state power. With the founding of two competing American Communist parties in September 1919, these debates led to institutional as well as ideological splits. The Socialist Party, for example, was torn apart in

1919—and would never again regain its strength or its unifying centrality for the radical movement.[28] The Wobblies, reduced to virtual organizational chaos during the Red Scare, were similarly divided between those holding the old syndicalist commitments and strategic priorities and those who believed that Communism had replaced syndicalism as the leading edge of the revolutionary movement. Of equal importance to Dos Passos, these conflicts were also being enacted in the organs of the radical press, where the former spirit of tolerance and heterodoxy was giving way by the early 1920s to the internecine factionalism and vituperation that would characterize anticapitalist politics and intellectual life, to varying degrees, for several decades.[29] None of the institutions that had shaped Dos Passos's radicalism escaped these internal conflicts, which severely compounded the damage being done to the movement by the external repression of the Red Scare.

These complex events had two practical effects on Dos Passos in the late 1920s and early 1930s. First, the outrage he felt about the government-sponsored persecution of the Left—culminating in the executions of Sacco and Vanzetti—propelled him into the period of his greatest creative productivity and his most active and militant political engagement. In the months immediately following the executions, he began working on a new literary project—the most ambitious and influential work of his career. *U.S.A.* (as that project came to be called) was a direct response to this decade of political repression. The Sacco and Vanzetti case is its primal scene: not only the catalyst that led to the trilogy's production, it is also *U.S.A.*'s climactic event, the devastating telos toward which its disparate narratives travel. This literary productivity was, moreover, matched by the most intense commitment to political activism that Dos Passos would ever make. During most of the decade he spent writing *U.S.A.* (1927–36), he embraced the role of committed radical intellectual, establishing himself as one of the most prominent literary voices of the American anticapitalist Left.

The second effect was that Dos Passos's intensified radical activity in the late 1920s and early 1930s took place primarily in organizations affiliated with the Communist Party. This reflected a profound change—not in Dos Passos's political outlook, but in the nature of the American Left. The writer himself remained committed in these years to essentially the same anticapitalist vision to which he had subscribed during the teens. But the particular institutions and organizations that had shaped his radicalism had collapsed—and during this period, the Communist Party emerged as the preeminent (and indeed, in the minds of many, the only viable) formation of the American Left.[30] From the point of view of Dos Passos's personal political development, there was an irony in this history—and it would prove, by the mid-1930s, to be a tragic one. At the very moment when he had arrived at a degree of political maturity, and had acquired the reputation that enabled him to function as a prominent public intellectual, the political subculture and movement that had inspired him, and for which he could have spoken most eloquently, had been destroyed. He would continue to feel closer in sensibility and vision to Debs, Haywood, and Max Eastman than he did to William Z. Foster and Mike Gold. But middle-class idealist though he was, Dos Passos also had a surprisingly strong streak of political pragmatism. If the Left had any future in the United States it seemed to him to lie with the Communist movement—and so, like most of those who survived the Red Scare with their radical commitment intact, he tried to find his place in the orbit of the Communist Party (CP).[31]

The psychological difficulty and significance of this political transition should not be underestimated. Like hundreds of thousands of Americans, Dos Passos had to grieve for a profound political loss in these years—the loss of a complex mass-movement of anticapitalist political aspiration. For Dos Passos, as for many others, this was a deeply personal injury, a psychic wound as well as a political one. The radical formations that had embodied his own aspirations were now in ruins; the leaders whom he admired, and with whom he identified, had been suppressed; the inadequacy of his own powers had been made painfully evident to him by the execution of Sacco and Vanzetti. Many of his contemporaries were unable to mourn such injuries, and they abandoned the Left in despair—as many have in the wake of other moments of political repression. Dos Passos was, however, able to find a way to mourn, and the *U.S.A.* trilogy enacts that strenuous process, as I will show in subsequent chapters. For now, I want to emphasize that his political and literary productivity during this period is itself a testament to Dos Passos's ability to work through the injuries inflicted by the Red Scare. In his political journalism of the 1920s and early 1930s, and in *U.S.A.*, he identified the social causes of his loss, and directed his anger at the social formations that he perceived to be responsible. Particularly in his literary work, he dwelled at length on the radical movement he had admired, raising to consciousness what he had lost. As a result, he was able to find in the movement associated with the Communist Party a new political formation through which he might explore and extend his thwarted hopes. The subsequent history of his relations with the CP was heavily affected by this prior experience of loss. On the one hand, there remained always in him a certain rigidity, a suspicion, a lingering sense that the Communist Left did not possess the virtues of the earlier radical movement, which he continued to idealize. (It is this rigidity that explains, in part, Dos Passos's surprising incapacity to appreciate some of the most appealing features of the revolutionary politics of the 1930s.) But on the other, Dos Passos was able to reclaim access to libidinal energies and political aspirations that had been aligned with the Left since his days at Harvard—and he projected them into a more liberated future that he believed American radicals, in the orbit of the Communist Party, could still bring into being.

From the outset, Dos Passos's relationship to Communism was complex and highly ambivalent. Despite his active participation in Communist-affiliated organizations, he was never a member of the Communist Party.[32] This was in part, as he explained to the readers of *Modern Quarterly*, simply a "matter of temperament": he was by political sensibility more of a "scavenger and campfollower" than he was a "natural party [man]." Of course, this "matter of temperament" was also intimately connected to Dos Passos's long-standing and deep-seated reservations about Communism as a particular strategy for building a socialist society.[33] Perhaps most fundamentally, he remained suspicious of statist versions of socialism, and he continued to prefer the anarcho-syndicalist dream of a decentralized economic transformation brought about by practical labor struggles through which workers would take democratic control of their workplaces and establish an equitable distribution of the wealth produced by their labor. In 1931 for example, at the height of his Communist-front activity, he confessed to Edmund Wilson that "I can't make up my mind to swallow political methods. Most of the time I think the IWW theory was right—Build a new society in the shell of the old."[34]

As a writer and intellectual, Dos Passos was also persistently antagonized by the ideological orthodoxy and alienating linguistic rigidity that he felt pervaded Communist intellectual life and cultural initiatives. In the same letter to Wilson, for example, he complained that, while Left intellectuals in America needed "a new phraseology" that would make it possible to "organize mentally what is really happening now," Communist organs like the *Daily Worker* seemed to be comprised of nothing but "clippings from Bukharin's scrapbasket." He was particularly concerned that the ideological inflexibility of some Communists made them deaf to the democratic and egalitarian idioms that were deeply rooted in American political life and which, he believed, offered invaluable resources for the anticapitalist movement. When Wilson sent him a Party-influenced manifesto in the Spring of 1932, Dos Passos objected that "it smells too strong of Thirteenth Street [that is, CP headquarters in Manhattan] for my taste," and reiterated that the most "useful" task for left intellectuals ("people like us") was to "introduce a more native lingo into the business." It was this perception of intellectual rigidity that caused Dos Passos to tell the editors of *Modern Quarterly* that "I don't see how a novelist or historian could be a party member under present conditions." And it was his commitment to expressive freedom and democracy—as strategic priorities and as ultimate objectives for the movement—that caused him, at the very peak of his Communist-front work, to exclaim in a letter to Wilson: "Goddamn it, I havent enough confidence in the CP to give it a blanket endorsement."[35]

But despite his criticisms and reservations, Dos Passos was willing to support the Communists because he believed that they alone were plausibly "fighting for socialism" in the United States. When the editors of *Modern Quarterly* asked him, for example, whether becoming a "socialist" would have the same "effect" as becoming a "communist," Dos Passos replied: "I personally think the socialists, and all other radicals have their usefulness, but I should think that becoming a socialist right now would have just about the same effect on anybody as drinking a bottle of near-beer."[36] Because he perceived other left formations as ineffectual,[37] he committed himself to working in the orbit of the CP. He felt a strong enough sympathy for the Party's leadership in 1932 to sign a public endorsement of their presidential and vice-presidential candidates.[38] He worked actively with—and was willing to identify himself publicly as an officer of—a substantial number of Communist-led organizations.[39] And he felt close enough to the Party's revolutionary anticapitalism that he was eager to participate, as an activist journalist and independent intellectual, in a substantial number of Communist-led campaigns—including important labor conflicts, civil rights struggles, and radical resistance to ongoing state repression.[40] Many of these campaigns attracted him precisely because they involved civil libertarian as well as economic and labor issues, but Dos Passos wrote about them from an explicitly anticapitalist perspective. It is especially significant in this regard that, while some of these causes were also championed by the recently founded American Civil Liberties Union, Dos Passos affiliated himself instead with the Communist-led International Labor Defense, which organized the media campaigns as well as the legal support for many civil rights and labor struggles in the late 1920s and 1930s.[41]

Perceiving a steady escalation of class conflict throughout the 1920s, Dos Passos came increasingly to believe that Americans would have to choose between two outcomes: either the working-class movement would bring about a positive socialist transformation of society, or else the American "owning class" would turn ultimately to fascism in its desperation to retain power. In a 1932 article about the rise of German fascism, for example, he warned his compatriots that "what's happening in Germany is neither fantastic nor incredible. It is the norm of the world of industrial war, strikes, repression of labor unions, Scottsboro, Harlan, Boston of the Sacco-Vanzetti case, Washington of the Centralia massacre, California of the Southern Pacific, the Los Angeles of Inspector Hines." He went on to insist that in the United States, as throughout the capitalist world, "[t]he men on top have minds geared only for profit, for their own power and easy money" and, if threatened, "they'll wreck the works to save themselves as light-heartedly as the German industrialists and landowners set the fire of Hitlerism."[42]

In the context of this intensifying class conflict, and the threat of fascism if "the men on top" prevailed, Dos Passos was clearly committed to making a contribution to the success of "working class radicalism." While he always insisted that middle-class intellectuals like himself were not likely to affect the outcome of "the class war" in any decisive way, he did believe that the politics of his time would be determined by the outcome of this struggle. And he was eminently clear about which side of the conflict he was on, as a member of "the radical fringe of the middle class." He commonly referred to writers and intellectuals as members of the "producing class" or "white collar workers"—and he persistently promoted the formation of a radical alliance of such intellectual "producers" and manual workers.[43] As early as 1927, for example, explaining the purpose of the New Playwrights Theatre, which he had just launched with several radical colleagues, he asserted that this "revolutionary" theater would "draw its life and ideas from the conscious sections of the industrial and white collar working classes which are out to get control of the great flabby mass of capitalist society and mould it to their own purpose." In a similar vein, in his 1933 essay about the rise of fascism, he argued that it was "the workers and producers, manual and intellectual" who alone (and "from underneath") could save the democratic features of American "civilization" from the destructive behavior of "the men on top." As a writer, activist journalist, and public intellectual, Dos Passos was thus explicitly committed to what he liked to call the "radical movement" to build "a workers' and producers' commonwealth." He was strongly ambivalent about the Communist Party—but throughout the late 1920s and early 1930s, and in the wake of internal fragmentation and external repression, he perceived the Party as "the most advanced outpost" of that movement and developed a pragmatic and constructive relationship to it.[44]

In 1934, Dos Passos's productive, if ambivalent, alliance with the Communist Left collapsed. As a result of further developments within the international Communist movement, his attitude toward the Communist Party shifted from wary alliance to intense hostility, and his relationship of pragmatic compromise with the Party was suddenly transformed into one of explosive and irresolvable conflict. Two events catalyzed this transformation.

First, on February 16, 1934, a group of Communist activists disrupted, and managed to break up, an antifascist rally at Madison Square Garden organized by the Socialist Party and a group of radical labor unions.[45] Dos Passos joined two dozen other Left intellectuals and writers in publicly condemning this divisive, factional behavior on the part of the Communist Party. The letter of protest appeared in the *New Masses*—and the editors (some of whom were Party members) responded with an editorial condemning the signers and appealing to Dos Passos ("the revolutionary writer, the comrade") to separate himself from their company. Dos Passos had been angered by this kind of Communist factional activity for years[46]—but because of more general developments within the international movement, the Madison Square Garden riot had a particularly ominous significance. During its Third Period (1929–1934), the Comintern had been directing Communist Parties around the world to attack, rather than support, other parties and organizations of the anticapitalist Left: Social Democratic and Labor Parties, as well as non-Communist labor unions, were branded as the allies of capitalism and as "social fascists" who were effectively indistinguishable from the actual fascists of the far Right. This Communist attack on other left groups, and the destruction of any joint resistance, contributed to the fascist seizure of power and the subsequent liquidation of the Left in a number of European countries, including Germany, Italy, Spain, and Austria.[47] In this context, Dos Passos viewed the Madison Square Garden riot as the domestic enactment of an international strategy of internecine factionalism that would destroy the anticapitalist movement in the United States, as it had done elsewhere, and would ultimately encourage the forces of economic exploitation and political repression.

For the next nine months, Dos Passos struggled with the practical quandary that he expressed in a published letter to the *New Masses'* editorial board. He believed that the Comintern's policy threatened to destroy not only the CP, but the entire anticapitalist movement, "ruin[ing] for our time [. . .] the effort towards a sanely organized society."[48] While he was publicly urging the Party to reform its factional outlook before it was too late, a personal letter to Edmund Wilson written the same week reveals the depth of his pessimism more frankly. "[T]he whole Marxian radical movement is in a moment of intense disintegration," he insisted. The "situation," he feared, might already be "hopeless." By the autumn, Dos Passos had become even more apprehensive about the self-destructive behavior of the Communists in particular, and of the revolutionary Left as a whole, during what seemed to him to be an era of intensifying right-wing "reaction." In October, for example, he wrote to John Howard Lawson that, given the waning power of the revolutionary movement ("just think back to 1919 [. . .] and figure out how much bigger the chance of socialism by revolution was then"), radicals needed to adopt a "psychology of defense" and a strategy of "retreat" rather than pursuing their current policy of divisive and ultimately suicidal "advances." Dos Passos expressed his angry impatience with the Communists, whose "shrill vituperative heroism" he still couldn't "help admiring," but who seemed now to be merely "frittering away into vicious and childish nonsense."[49]

At the same time, however, and in the very same letters in which he was expressing these misgivings, Dos Passos also continued to assert the strategic evaluation he had made in the 1920s: that there was simply no viable alternative to the Communist Party. Even as he was communicating his anger and mounting despair to Wilson, for example, he warily reiterated that "if you don't put your money on the Communists—it's no use putting it on anybody else until they've proved something." Similarly, no matter how much he criticized the CP in his letter to Lawson, he still insisted that he saw no alternative formations on the anticapitalist Left with which he felt he could align himself. He acknowledged that A. J. Muste's American Workers Party, whose anti-Stalinism had attracted other radical intellectuals, held some appeal—but he insisted that they were practically powerless, "just emasculated communists."[50] He also noted that he'd been reading "the Industrial Worker weekly with considerable pleasure" and he went on to observe nostalgically, as he had for years, that "I still feel more in common with the wobbly line of talk than any other." But he was under no more illusions about the Wobblies' viability than he had been in the mid-1920s: they were part of the movement's past, not its future.

Attempting to hold fast, then, both to his principles and his pragmatism, Dos Passos was politically baffled in the winter of 1934. He could neither continue to align himself with the Communist Party, whose "vicious and childish nonsense" seemed to him to threaten the entire radical movement, nor was he willing to embrace other organizations that were closer to his own principles and sensibility but that seemed incapable of mounting a credible challenge to American capitalism.

The second catalytic development took place in the final weeks of the year, when a disastrous turn of events in the Soviet Union shattered completely Dos Passos's hardened relationship to the Communist movement and plunged him into a deeper political crisis. On December 1, 1934, a member of the Politburo of the USSR, Sergei Kirov, was assassinated—and Stalin's response to the murder (which he may or may not have ordered) ushered in the era of the Great Purges.[51] Dos Passos recognized that the fierce repression following Kirov's murder marked a dramatic new stage of antidemocratic deterioration within the Soviet regime. By late December, Dos Passos was already writing to Edmund Wilson that "[t]his business about Kirov [. . .] has completely destroyed my benefit-of-the-doubt attitude towards the Stalinists." He insisted that the Russian Revolution had "gone into its Napoleonic stage," that the "progressive tendencies in the Soviet Government" had been destroyed by the "self-protective tendencies" of an established elite willing to do anything to "perpetuate" its "power." "From now on," Dos Passos lamented, "events in Russia have no more interest—except as a terrible example—for world socialism."[52]

In response to this new phase of repression in the USSR, Dos Passos repudiated in sweeping and emphatic terms both the Soviet regime and the international Communist movement. The post-Kirov terror was the final outrage that shattered Dos Passos's precarious compromise and drove him from ambivalence into outright hostility.[53] He made clear to Edmund Wilson that it was not merely the Soviet regime, but the international Communist movement as a whole, that had been fatally discredited by "the vicious rubbish" of sectarianism and by "the new terror" in the Soviet Union. He explained that, as far as the factional wars went, he was inclined to side "with the American orthodox" in the Party over their reformist detractors because of their greater practical activity—but he insisted emphatically that "the time has passed to be with any of the Marxist parties." He argued that the self-immolating "Stalinist performances" were now irrevocably "alienating the working class movement of the world." "What's the use of losing your 'chains,'" he asked Wilson, with a characteristic mixture of sorrow and rage, "if you get a firing squad instead?"[54]

Dos Passos's encounter with Stalinism in 1934–35 was the decisive political turning point of his life. It precipitated a crisis of political self-definition that went beyond questions of pragmatic affiliation. On the one hand, he was as deeply critical of capitalism and as convinced of his own radical analysis as he had ever been. Insisting that "any movement towards ousting the bosses has got to mobilize" the "basic trend" toward democracy, he was still able, for example, in the fall of 1934, to express the faltering hope that "reds" in America might yet reclaim their radical democratic project: "I'd like to see 'em hang red ribbons on the liberty bell and take it away from Chase National Bank."[55] But on the other hand, in the face of Stalinism, Dos Passos felt for the first time a strong impulse to distance himself from all forms of left politics.

This new inclination to repudiate the radical movement as a whole is an indication of the severity of the psychological and political crisis that Dos Passos now faced. Indeed, the catastrophe of Stalinism posed a more severe challenge than had even the Red Scare—and the task of grieving for this disillusionment was far more difficult. Now the leading formation of the Left seemed to be responsible for its own destruction. Dos Passos was enraged at the very movement that had carried his most passionate political hopes and whose self-immolation now seemed imminent. In political as in private circumstances of loss, such explosive ambivalence poses the greatest obstacle to the work of grieving.[56] For Dos Passos to have mourned this second political crisis would have required that he be able to understand what exactly had caused "the vicious rubbish" of sectarianism and the "new terror" in the Soviet regime—to have understood, in short, what he hated and condemned within the Left itself—even as he affirmed those impulses within the movement that he had loved and admired for two decades. This is easily enough stated, but the intellectual and psychic challenge of working through such ambivalence is formidable. For Dos Passos (as for many radicals of his and successive generations), it proved impossible.

What Dos Passos did, instead, was to evade this burden of ambivalent grief by turning against the Left entirely. In letters and articles from 1934 and 1935, he invented a range of tortured strategies for repudiating the movement he had long loved, for demonstrating that American radicalism was unambiguously and irretrievably toxic, for separating himself from the political aspirations of his whole adulthood.

The first of these strategies entailed the mystification of the actual destructiveness that Dos Passos rightly saw in Stalinism. Although his historical and political sophistication enabled him to identify with some clarity the "steps" of the Soviet regime's "Napoleonic" deterioration, Dos Passos obscured his own social analysis by inventing naturalistic arguments that suggested that the disasters of Stalinism and capitalism alike were the result of inevitable tendencies in human nature and human society.[57] Thus, in February 1935, he wrote to Edmund Wilson that left-wing middle-class "intellectuals who wallow in communist hatreds are just exhibiting the same sort of disease"—a "middle-class neurosis," he called it—displayed during the First World War by American civilians who had embraced the "behind the lines war psychology" of "hun hating." In an essay written the same year, he asserted that if writers remained true to their vocation, they would "find more and more that [they] are on the side of the men, women and children alive right now against all the contraptions and organizations, however magnificent their aims may be, that bedevil them." In both examples, Dos Passos was attempting to find a formulation that could encompass the quite different evils of Stalinism and of American capitalism and somehow assimilate them to a common, and nonpolitical, problem. In the first instance, both "hun hating" and left sectarianism are reduced to a peculiar "neurosis"; in the second, the murderous hypocrisies of both capitalist and Stalinist institutions are seen as embodiments of a mysterious dynamic by which "contraptions and organizations" with "magnificent aims" come inevitably to "bedevil" the people they are intended to serve.[58] Such formulations obscure social causes and, as a result, place these phenomena beyond the reach of practical intervention. Capitalism and the movement that sought to challenge it are subject to the same inexorable dynamics. Internecine hatred and the betrayal of ideals become axiomatic human tendencies, not political problems to be understood and addressed.

Even as he thus sought to make the Stalinist corruption of an emancipatory movement appear inevitable, Dos Passos also invented phobic strategies to brand that movement as essentially alien. Abandoning the internationalism that he had embraced for decades, he began in the months after the Madison Square Garden riot to apply racist, nationalist, and nativist epithets to political tendencies. For the first time, he wrote habitually not simply of "democracy" but of "Anglo Saxon democracy" as the tradition that must be extended and revitalized.[59] Simultaneously and conversely, he began to dismiss the corrupted formations of the revolutionary Left in frankly anti-Semitic terms. In a demoralized letter to John Howard Lawson from October 1934, for example, Dos Passos condemned at length the failings of the Marxist Left as a function of the "neo-ghetto ignorance" of "typical jewish New Yorkers." He then went on to blame the self-destructive behavior of the American Communist Party on its "New York jewish leadership," and he ended the letter by insisting that the "New York rebellious mentality is a jewish European import and [. . .] it is dying out now that the sources have been bottled up. Now it's the creation of an american mentality or death."[60] This nativist strain in Dos Passos's political outlook registered itself particularly strongly, as we will see, in the last volume of *U.S.A.*—and it became an increasingly central component of his politics in succeeding decades. For now, it is important to point out that the *function* served by these racial terms was to provide an external ideological means for separating two values that had been systematically intertwined in Dos Passos's thought for years—democracy (here associated with the valued "Anglo Saxon") and socialism (which could now be rejected, if for no other reason, because of its association with a foreign and unsavory Jewishness). At a psychological level, Dos Passos drew here on a culturally sanctioned racism in order to evade his own painful ambivalence through a process of splitting. Unable to sustain his identification with a political movement that was betraying its own democratic commitments, Dos Passos resorted to a vulgar racial essentialism in an effort to fix a firm boundary between what he valued and what he sought now to revile.

This attempt to split off the value of "democracy" from the tarnished idea of socialism increasingly pervaded Dos Passos's political thinking. Having thought of the anticapitalist movement for two decades as the best possible *means of achieving* democracy, Dos Passos began in 1934 to speak of democracy as an "*alternative*" to socialism. Immediately after the Madison Square Garden riot, for example, he suggested to Edmund Wilson that the "only alternative" to the self-destructive Marxian Left might be a "passionate unmarxian revival of AngloSaxon democracy." Similarly, as he tried to make sense of his political position in the wake of the Kirov affair in January 1935, he told Wilson that "some entirely new attack on the problem of human freedom under monopolized industry has got to be worked out."[61] Whether he projected democracy backward into a racially distinct past or into an undefined future associated with something "entirely new," he attempted now to place his central political ideals in simple opposition to the movement whose failures he could not grieve.

Dos Passos was himself aware that these strategies for separating himself from the Left were intellectually and psychologically untenable. Mystifying the causes of his political disappointments could not bring understanding. The rigid repudiation of what he also loved would not enable him to imagine a future in which thwarted hopes could find fruition. His letters from these years reveal a pained self-consciousness about the futility of his efforts to respond to the crisis of Stalinism through nativist and racist negations.

The letter to Lawson from which I have quoted, for example, is punctuated with self-ironizing asides acknowledging the anti-Semitism of his own remarks: "[A. Hitler please copy]"; "(me and Adolph just anti-semite buddies)." Dos Passos communicated a similar discomfort when he concluded a letter to Wilson by saying that, given his newfound nativism, "it would be funny" if he "ended up an Anglo Saxon chauvinist" like his father. And his letters display an acute awareness that the "[A]merican mentality" for which he was calling might take "dirty nationalist forms" if left to domestic fascists, though the letters do not offer any substantive account of how his own brand of nativism was less "dirty." These anxious remarks make clear that, for a man who had been horrified by the rise of fascism in Europe and who had been warning against its plausibility in the United States, there could be little relief in the kind of racist and nationalistic solutions he was now advancing. Even as he turned to anti-Semitism in order to help him manage his ambivalence, he felt the structure of his own disavowal crumbling.[62]

Unable to name clearly the causes of the anticapitalist movement's corruption, or to acknowledge directly his mixed feelings of loyalty and anger, Dos Passos was incapable of expressing coherently his political hopes. His new attempt to champion a democratic "alternative" to socialism was repeatedly thwarted by his continued conviction that anticapitalist politics was itself the route to democracy. As soon as he proposed to Edmund Wilson that an "unmarxian revival of AngloSaxon democracy" constituted the best "alternative" to socialism, he immediately acknowledged the naive futility of the proposal, which in no way addressed the economic impediments to popular self-government. "I don't see," he insisted, "How you can coordinate Fourth of July democracy with the present industrial-financial setup." "Maybe Roosevelt is already as far as we can go in that direction," he mused. But Dos Passos did not believe in 1934 that Roosevelt was anywhere near "far" enough, and the mere thought of accepting that compromise led him to end his letter with the baffled observation, quoted earlier, that "if you dont put your money on the Communists—it's no use putting it on anybody else until they've proved something." Seeking to repudiate the anticapitalist movement, even as he shared its underlying principles, he was indeed confused about where to place his thwarted political investments. Unable to acknowledge and work through his ambivalence, he oscillated between momentary affirmations and swift repudiations. Reasserting the need for a democratic anticapitalism, he would then insist on the inevitability of its betrayal. Calling for "an entirely new attack on the problem of human freedom under monopolized industry," he would then pessimistically assert his skepticism that "the coming period of wars and dictatorships" produced by the economic order would "giv[e] anybody a chance to work anything out."[63] Unable to mourn the injuries of Stalinism, Dos Passos was drawn into a deepening political melancholia.

This state of political turmoil, confusion, and internal conflict continued through the months and years during which Dos Passos struggled to finish the last volume of *U.S.A.* The melancholic beratement of the movement that had expressed his own political aspirations continued with a mounting intensity over the next decade, until the author had succeeded in separating himself completely from his own anticapitalist ideals. The ferocity of that repudiation carried Dos Passos through a remarkably brief moment as a New Deal Democrat, transforming him into a vehement opponent not only of Communism, but also of social democratic and labor parties, of labor unions, and ultimately of all forms of welfare-state liberalism. For the radical yearnings he had harbored in his youth, he increasingly substituted a nostalgic fantasy of a lost democratic American past. One of the leading figures of the literary Left, Dos Passos rapidly became an icon of that most melancholic of American political phenomena: the God-That-Failed syndrome. Unable to acknowledge what he had long loved and admired in an emancipatory movement now compromised by Stalinism, Dos Passos repudiated the whole tradition of radical aspiration. That task of mourning proved too difficult.

The *U.S.A.* trilogy enacts the process of Dos Passos's political grieving. He launched this work—the greatest of his career—explicitly and self-consciously as a response to the external repression of the Red Scare. In some portions of the trilogy, especially in the biographical prose poems, Dos Passos produced an exceptionally rich version of the modernism of mourning. Here he identified with loving precision what he and hundreds of thousands of American radicals had lost, and he projected forward those thwarted aspirations for future affirmation and extension. But this effort to mourn was complicated, and ultimately derailed, by Dos Passos's fiercely melancholic response to the emerging crisis of Stalinism and to the specter of the Left's self-destruction. That conflict between political mourning and melancholia is enacted with remarkable intensity and unparalleled visibility in the trilogy. Nowhere in the American literary tradition can we see with greater clarity the political implications of the two modernisms.

FIVE

The Modernism of Mourning in *U.S.A.*

"Writing So Fiery and Accurate"

The executions of Sacco and Vanzetti in the summer of 1927 constituted a turning point in John Dos Passos's life, an emotional and political watershed. It was not—as some critics have mistakenly asserted—the moment at which he entered the radical Left. It was, rather, the moment at which he registered, with an inescapably personal urgency, the political loss entailed by the Red Scare. In the years that passed between the immigrant anarchists' initial arrests in 1920, at the height of the Palmer Raids, and their executions in 1927, Dos Passos had evolved from admiring observer of the anticapitalist movement to committed activist. During these years, he had established himself not only as a prominent young novelist, but also as a radical journalist in the tradition of John Reed. In 1926 and 1927, he worked for the Sacco and Vanzetti Defense Committee, devoting his prestige and talent as a writer to the campaign to save their lives. He had met both men, had sat next to them in the jails at Dedham and Charlestown, had heard them describe their dreams of an egalitarian society. When they died in the electric chair, he experienced their executions in an acutely personal way. He identified with their idealism and their vulnerability. Having placed his own energy and resources in the balance, he now felt the slightness of his own agency and the power of the interests he had presumed to oppose.

Sacco and Vanzetti became, for Dos Passos, the symbolic representatives of the entire anticapitalist movement that had been crushed in the course of a repressive decade. These men, he wrote, had become "huge symbols" and "part of the world struggle between the capitalist class and the working class." He called the period of their prosecution and executions "seven years of agony of the working class." In an essay written before their deaths, he described them as representative figures of the anticapitalist continuum that he so much admired: a continuum of disparate political institutions and formations, with differing strategic emphases, but unified by a shared commitment to building an economic and political alternative to capitalism. He explained that they were participants in a political community comprised of "anarchists, syndicalists, socialists of various colors. The Russian Revolution had fired them with new hopes." In rendering their political outlook, Dos Passos emphasized not particular sectarian or institutional loyalties, but the underlying emotional and moral impulses that motivated their radicalism—the yearning for forms of freedom made impossible by the capitalist economic system, the desire for a less alienated way of life. He described Sacco's "anarchism" this way: "He loved the earth and people, he wanted them to walk straight over the free hills, not to stagger bowed under the ordained machinery of industry." Vanzetti's "anarchist-communist" politics—which was "less a matter of labels than of feeling, of gentle philosophic brooding"—stemmed from "the hope [. . .] that somehow men's predatory instincts, incarnate in the capitalist system, can be canalized into other channels, leaving free communities of artisans and farmers and fishermen and cattlebreeders who would work for their livelihood with pleasure, because the work was itself enjoyable in the serene white light of a reasonable world."[1] When they were put to death in the Charlestown jail, Dos Passos experienced it as the literal and symbolic culmination of an entire radical generation's suppression; it was this vulnerable, utopian aspiration that the "capitalist class" was systematically, and effectively, destroying.

In the weeks following the executions, Dos Passos felt that writers on the Left had a responsibility to respond to this repression. "It is up to the writers now to see to it that America does not forget Sacco and Vanzetti so soon as it would like to." He went on to insist that:

> Sacco and Vanzetti must not have died in vain. We must have writing so fiery and accurate that it will sear through the pall of numb imbecility that we are again swaddled in after the few moments of sane awakening that followed the shock of the executions. America must not be allowed to forget. All the elements on the public stage who consider themselves alive and who are considered alive, college professors, writers, labor leaders, prominent liberals, protested that they were mighty shocked and that *if* the state of Massachusetts went ahead with the executions. . . . Workers all over the country felt their blood curdle at the thought. Well, it has come to pass. Well, we have protested. Our blood has curdled. What are we going to do now?[2]

Dos Passos's personal answer to this question was to do what he did best: he began work on a new novel. This literary enterprise, which evolved over the next ten years into the *U.S.A.* trilogy, was an explicit response to the Sacco and Vanzetti executions—and to the decade of anti-Red hysteria and repression. It was an attempt to mourn a political loss. That work of political mourning was complicated (as such work usually is), because Dos Passos's grief was accompanied by much anger and bitterness. He hoped to extend into the future the traditions for which Sacco and Vanzetti stood, but his hope was alloyed by stirrings of despair. *U.S.A.* would enact this difficult effort to grieve. From the outset, he set himself the task of producing that writing—"so fiery and accurate"—that would prevent Americans from forgetting the suppressed traditions of democratic anticapitalism.

He undertook this task of political memory most directly in the biographical prose poems dispersed throughout *U.S.A.* More than half of the biographies in the trilogy's first two volumes are devoted to American anticapitalist radicals who suffered the repression of the Red Scare. These radical biographies are among the richest and most ambitious expressions of the modernism of mourning. Here, Dos Passos reflects on the losses suffered by the American Left during these years—and mourns in a way that facilitates an ongoing political commitment and a forward-looking project of radical tradition building. In order to pursue this project, Dos Passos developed a new literary form, the modernist biographical prose poem. These brief, poetic sketches, as we will see, document the hard facts of political repression during the Red Scare and enabled Dos Passos to identify the social causes of his loss and the objects of his anger. They also provided a means for making conscious what he had lost in the destruction of this political movement. Through these memorials, he sought to name the libidinal sources of anti-capitalist aspiration in America: the fundamental psychic and emotional impulses that had animated the radical movement—and that might yet be taken up by all those seeking to reduce the alienation of modern life.

I . The Method of Dos Passos's Biographies: Modernist Mourning as Political Tradition Building

Taken together, the ten radical biographies of *U.S.A.* constitute a collective portrait of the anticapitalist movement of the teens as Dos Passos saw it. In *The 42nd Parallel*, he celebrates Eugene Debs, the leader of the Socialist Party; Big Bill Haywood, the standard-bearer of the IWW; Charles Steinmetz, the immigrant socialist inventor; and Robert La Follette, the radical senator from Wisconsin. Dos Passos's *1919* contains biographies of two Wobbly martyrs—Joe Hill, the famed organizer and songwriter who was executed by the State of Utah, and Wesley Everest who was lynched during the Centralia Massacre of 1919. It also includes the biographies of three socialist intellectuals—John Reed, the revolutionary journalist; Randolph Bourne, anticapitalist cultural critic; and Paxton Hibben, a little-known diplomat and writer. The last of the radical biographies appears in *The Big Money* and treats Thorstein Veblen, whose writings had a formative influence on Dos Passos's own socialist vision.

   The particular figures whom Dos Passos chose to include in this pantheon of early-twentieth-century radicalism reflect the breadth—and the narrowness—of the author's own political identifications. Dos Passos was clearly concerned to include figures who would represent the ideological heterogeneity and fluidity of the anticapitalist continuum before and during the First World War. Toward this end, the biographies include anarchists, syndicalists, communists, and socialists of various kinds. Many of these figures were Marxists, but many were also rooted in indigenous, non-Marxist, anticapitalist traditions, from Populism to Edward Bellamy's Nationalism to the Single Tax movement of Henry George. The portraits reflect certain kinds of sociological diversity, which Dos Passos clearly valued in the movement. He includes foreign- as well as native-born radicals: two of the ten are immigrants, and two more are the children of immigrants. Although most of these figures were born to the working class, several were middle-class radicals like Dos Passos himself. Most rose to prominence, either as labor organizers, radical political figures, or intellectuals, but Dos Passos was concerned also to include the obscure rank-and-file Wobbly martyr, Wesley Everest, and the relatively unknown Paxton Hibben.

The exclusions enforced by this pantheon are as significant as its inclusions. The complete omission of women from the tradition is particularly striking, as is the "whiteness" of Dos Passos's portrait of the Left—which excludes not only African Americans and non-European immigrants, but also Jews and emigrants from southern and eastern Europe. Although it is true that most American radicals of the teens were, in fact, native born—and that the movement did not have the racial and ethnic diversity of the Popular Front Left of the 1930s—Dos Passos presented a narrower picture of the movement than his own experience warranted.[3] It is, for example, remarkable that Dos Passos did not write a biography of Emma Goldman, who had been one of his radical "heroes" in the teens—and a more direct influence on his political vision than many of those whom he did include. Clearly, he sought to canonize those figures with whom he felt most deeply identified, in whom his libidinal investments (conscious and unconscious) were most intense and whose loss for him was most acute. He focused on men who, in some respects, resembled himself (intellectuals are represented, for example, in disproportionately large numbers)—and women tend to be objects in their stories: occasions for male action and the focus of male desires and fears. The gender and ethnic narrowness of his selections embodies a constriction of identification characteristic of many white male radicals of his generation.

Considered together, these ten biographies constitute a personalized memorial to the victims of the Red Scare. They delineate the social processes by which the disparate formations of the anticapitalist Left were destroyed. All of these radicals are crushed under the weight of external repression. Each of the prose poems tells a story of constraint, disappointment, frustration, failure, and defeat. Generally following a two-part trajectory, each traces the rise and fall of a single figure. In the first part, Dos Passos describes the path that brought each man into the movement, the material and emotional sources of his radicalism, and the context in which his aspirations achieved political embodiment. In the second part, he describes the ways in which these aspirations were thwarted, the careers destroyed, the hopes defeated. Most dramatically, the biographies of Joe Hill and Wesley Everest recount the tales of men who, like Sacco and Vanzetti a decade later, were murdered for their radical commitments.[4] In the case of the political and labor leaders—Debs, Haywood, and La Follette—Dos Passos was concerned to show that men who successfully articulated the interests and dreams of millions of working-class Americans were ultimately silenced, marginalized, and separated from their constituencies: all are vilified by the press and by mainstream political forces; Debs and Haywood are isolated and broken by incarceration; Big Bill is ultimately driven into exile and death in the Soviet Union.

The fate of the intellectuals is less dramatic, but while their repression is more subtle, it is no less effective. John Reed is repeatedly prosecuted and jailed. Bourne too is harassed by spies, sees his manuscripts confiscated, and has increasing difficulty finding publishers for his work. Veblen, despite the international prestige of his anticapitalist economic analysis, is driven into increasingly obscure university posts and ever greater isolation. While Steinmetz is cynically celebrated by the publicity men at General Electric as the "magician" who invented the electrical transformer (the vast profits of which make him General Electric's "most valuable piece of apparatus"), his commitment to building a socialist society is patronized, contained, thwarted. Whether these men are actually murdered, simply jailed, or ground down by harassment, whether they are actively censored and silenced, or merely marginalized institutionally and isolated personally, they are all defeated. As a group, these biographies illustrate the destruction of a large and varied political movement. Taken separately, each indicates, in microcosm, the price paid by individuals for this repression.

Dos Passos was attempting in these biographies not simply to record, but also to mourn, this history of political defeat. This required, in the first place, a clear acknowledgment of what had been lost. Dos Passos wanted his readers to remember what America's "governors and owners" wanted the nation to forget: the democratic and egalitarian anticapitalist movement that the Red Scare had systematically destroyed. After the Sacco and Vanzetti executions, he had insisted that it was "up to the writers" to prevent such a forgetting, and these biographies were among his principle acts of memorialization. This commemoration was imperative because, as Dos Passos emphasizes throughout these sketches, one of the central ideological tasks of the Red Scare was to obscure and erase the memory of the defeated radicals, particularly after their deaths. So, for example, he notes at the end of Wesley Everest's biography that the coroner lied about the cause of the Wobbly's grisly death, and that while the government had "buried" his comrades in "Walla Walla Penitentiary," Everest's corpse was buried "nobody knows where" by the vigilantes who murdered him. If Everest lies in an unmarked grave, other radicals die abroad, either in exile like Haywood, or in revolutionary service like Reed, equally forgotten in their own nation. The official record of Hibben's life in *Who's Who* (which Dos Passos juxtaposes, in ironic counterpoint, with his own account),[5] makes no more mention of his politics than do the public relations men who control the public image and legacy of Steinmetz. There is a particular pathos for his biographer in the fact that Veblen is so bitterly isolated and despairing by the end of his life that he does the work of censorship and suppression himself, asking in his own will that "no tombstone, slab, epitaph, effigy, tablet, inscription or monument of any name or nature, be set up to my memory or name in any place or at any time." Dos Passos's biographies explicitly set out to mark these unmarked graves, to remember the forgotten men. "But we will remember," he says of La Follette; "but his memorial remains," he insists of Veblen.

Like all works in the modernism of mourning, these biographies enact a process of grieving that is forward as well as backward looking. Through them, Dos Passos seeks to identify what he has lost so that disappointed yearnings can be renewed. Like H. D. "hovering" over the forms of femininity derided by a patriarchal culture, or like Langston Hughes meditating on the many "dreams deferred" by African Americans, Dos Passos here returns repeatedly to political aspirations that were crushed during the Red Scare. And like them, he recollects so that (to use H. D.'s formulation) he can make a "bee line" for that which has been "plundered." Above all, he marks individual experiences of failure and loss so that he can reconstitute them within an ongoing tradition of emancipatory aspiration. As these biographies suggest, the work of mourning takes a particular form when the object of grieving is a political movement. Under these circumstances, the thing that has been killed need not remain dead. A collective tradition that has been destroyed in a particular manifestation can be renewed through the agency and memory of those who are still living. Dos Passos figures this renewal in various ways. At times, he represents it quite literally as a project of reanimating the dead. After describing Randolph Bourne's premature death, for example, Dos Passos assures us that "If any man has a ghost / Bourne has a ghost." At other moments he reminds us of unfinished work left behind by these defeated radicals: of the "undelivered speech" left on La Follette's desk when the Senate had become "a lynching party" and "wouldn't let him speak"; of the fact that when Bourne died, he was "planning an essay on the foundations of future radicalism in America." The unspoken words are there for us to hear, he suggests; the work remains for us to take up in the present.

In his modernist, biographical prose poem, Dos Passos developed a literary form that enacted this complex work of political mourning and tradition building. In appealing at the time of the Sacco and Vanzetti executions for a writing at once "fiery and accurate," Dos Passos gestured toward the duality that he went on to cultivate in these biographies. Impelled by a powerful documentary impulse, they provide an "accurate" representation of actual lives and historical events. By recording painful facts that the nation's dominant "myths" sought to hide from view, Dos Passos hoped that he might "sear through the pall of numb imbecility" in which the American people were "swaddled" by the capitalist-controlled mass media. The prose poems are works of nonfiction, resting upon Dos Passos's substantial biographical and historical reading.[6] But they are not conventional works of documentary history. Refusing the detached tone of scholarly objectivity, they are "fiery" in the sense that they are saturated with the passionate, subjective investments of their author.[7] Nowhere in the trilogy does Dos Passos communicate more explicitly his own political sympathies and moral judgments: his admiration for the traditions of American radicalism and his contempt for the violent hypocrisy of government-sponsored repression conducted in the name of democracy and freedom. The biographies are also suffused with the author's feelings of loss, betrayal, and rage. Even as they are accurate documentary accounts, then, they are also polemical, partisan, and intensely personal. This fusion of accuracy and emotional expressivity is responsible for their success in performing the work of social mourning. Identifying for

Dos Passos the nature of his loss and the social forces that had produced it, they allowed him to direct his grief and anger at their respective objects.

The representational method of the biographies operates simultaneously at two levels. On the simplest and most readily apparent plane, they offer highly compressed factual narratives of the lives and political careers of these figures. We are generally told, for example, where and into what sort of family each man is born and when he dies. The milestones and turning points of his political development, as well as the nature of his successes are recorded, as are the kinds of repression to which he is subjected, and the circumstances of his political defeat. These narratives are studded with facts: the date on which the Centralia Massacre took place; where Steinmetz attended school; the names of the magazines that would and wouldn't publish Bourne's articles. The recording of historical details contributes to Dos Passos's project of mourning and political memory: as he said after Sacco's and Vanzetti's executions, "Every detail must be told and retold."[8] But the factual accounts are also subject to extraordinary compression. Because an entire life is told in two or three pages, every detail has been carefully selected. The resulting logic is essentially poetic: virtually every fact or detail takes on the status of a metaphor, and the metaphors have been arranged so as to constitute a small number of expressively potent gestures. On this second level, through the dense pattern of fact-based metaphors, Dos Passos struggles to reveal the libidinal roots of anticapitalist aspiration. He attempts to represent the ways in which his figures' political commitments originated in certain primary impulses—toward social connection, toward aesthetic and sensual pleasure, and toward self-expression—all of which he saw as thwarted in capitalist society. This strategy marks a persistent effort to humanize the radical experience: to make his reader feel the pulse of socialist and anarchist aspirations, to capture the underlying forms of desire and pleasure, vulnerability and pain, from which they spring. In these prose poems, Dos Passos attempts to identify what is at once most fundamental and most enduring in the radical impulse: to represent the idealistic resistance to capitalism, and the longing for a more egalitarian, more solidaristic, and more liberatory form of social organization. Because of his method, Dos Passos's own desires and motivations are often fused with those of his biographical subjects and political predecessors. This blending of subjectivities lies at the very heart of the tradition-building project: it is the literary enactment of an aspiration that is thwarted in one life, but continues to live in another, and is extended to the reader for affirmation.

II. *"Lover of Mankind": Socialism as Brotherhood*

The first of *U.S.A.*'s biographies offers a portrait of Eugene Debs—a man whom Dos Passos saw as a symbol of the anticapitalist political continuum of the teens, and who had been one of his heroes from the time Dos Passos first entered the movement in the summer of 1917. A careful analysis of this biography will enable us to see Dos Passos's "fiery and accurate" method at work and to identify elements of his libidinal account of the sources of radical aspiration.

Like most of the prose poems, the biography of Debs has a two-part narrative structure—describing the rise, and then the fall, of a radical career and personality. As in many of the sketches, the first part of this biography begins with what might be described as a brief "introduction": a few opening lines that seek to place Debs's origins according to a set of geographical, sociological, historical, and cultural-psychological coordinates.

> Debs was a railroadman, born in a weatherboarded shack at Terre Haute.
> He was one of ten children.
> His father had come to America in a sailingship in '49,
> an Alsatian from Colmar; not much of a moneymaker, fond of music and reading,
> he gave his children a chance to finish public school and that was about all he could do.[9]

These introductory sentences—apparently simple, declarative, and factual—are already operating on two levels, unfolding two distinct but related stories. On the first level, Dos Passos is laying the historical groundwork for a factual tale about Debs's political career. The opening sentence tells us Debs's occupation and enough about the circumstances of his birth to fix his sociological position as a member of the midwestern working class: a manual laborer, born in a "shack." This first gesture also participates in the conventional radical iconography of Debs as the quintessentially American, native-born socialist leader. In the early 1930s, when anticapitalist radicalism was being denounced as "foreign" and "un-American" (as it had been earlier, and would be later), Dos Passos and others found it strategically valuable to emphasize that the Socialist Party—and its leader—had emerged from American soil and experiences. But Dos Passos immediately qualifies and complicates this familiar radical-from-Terre Haute image by emphasizing the immigrant origins of Debs's father. More specifically, he goes out of his way to place Debs's familial origins within the history of European Enlightenment revolutions, by implying (somewhat deceptively) that Debs's father was part of the wave of refugee revolutionaries who fled Alsace and other strongholds of radical Republicanism after the suppression of the revolution of 1848.[10] Dos Passos thus seeks to draw simultaneously on nationalist and internationalist impulses within the American Left: to reinforce the image of Debs as the standard-bearer of an indigenous American socialism, and to remind us that the American Left was enriched by, and was inseparable from, international and multigenerational radical movements.[11]

On a second level, these terse opening sentences begin to lay down the fact-based metaphors through which Dos Passos will unfold his account of the sources of Debs's socialist aspirations. The first sentence sets up a symbolic tension that will prove significant between the "railroad" and the "shack"—between the expansive energy and mobility associated with the male world of work on the one hand and the constrained space of domesticity on the other. The second sentence tells us that the decisive psychofamilial fact of Debs's childhood is that he is one among many siblings. Identified as a brother first, and only secondarily as a son, Debs will, on Dos Passos's account, prove to be the visionary of brotherhood—a man who seeks to bring into being a society founded upon fraternity and solidarity, and who tragically confronts the obstacles (both psychological and material) to such a bonded community of peers and equals. In the third sentence, characterizing Debs's father, Dos Passos begins to establish a central opposition between the economic realities of capitalist society and the yearning for full self-expression. Telling us that Debs's father was "fond of music and reading" and that he was "not much of a moneymaker," Dos Passos suggests that while this preference for aesthetic fulfillment over "moneymaking" may have been a matter of temperament or choice, the father has bequeathed the conflict to his children, since his lack of money means that it was "all he could do" to let them "finish public school" before the imperative of work put an end to the opportunity for education. The rest of the biography will interweave these three metaphorical strands, exploring Debs's dream of fraternity as a means of achieving the material conditions for universal self-realization—and exploring the failure of that dream in the face of fears embedded in, and symbolized by, a conventional domesticity.

After these opening lines, Dos Passos proceeds to tell the story of Debs's rise from teenage railroad worker to Socialist candidate for president of the United States. I will quote here the remainder of the prose poem's first half, because I want to offer the kind of detailed close analysis that Dos Passos's biographies deserve but rarely receive.[12]

> At fifteen Gene Debs was already working as a machinist on the Indianapolis and Terre Haute Railway.
> He worked as a locomotive fireman,
> clerked in a store
> joined the local of the Brotherhood of Locomotive Firemen, was elected secretary, traveled all over the country as organizer.
> He was a tall shamblefooted man, had a sort of gusty rhetoric that set on fire the railroad workers in their pineboarded halls
> made them want the world he wanted,
> a world brothers might own
> where everybody would split even:
> *I am not a labor leader. I don't want you to follow me or anyone else. If you are looking for a Moses to lead you out of the capitalist wilderness you will stay right where you are. I would not lead you into this promised land if I could, because if I could lead you in, someone else would lead you out.*
> That was how he talked to freighthandlers and gandywalkers, to firemen and switchmen and engineers, telling them it wasn't enough to organize the railroadmen, that all workers must be organized, that all workers must be organized in the workers' co-operative commonwealth.
> Locomotive fireman on many a long night's run,
> under the smoke a fire burned him up, burned in gusty words that beat in pineboarded halls; he wanted his brothers to be free men.
> That was what he saw in the crowd that met him at the Old Wells Street Depot when he came out of jail after the Pullman strike,

those were the men that chalked up nine hundred thousand votes for him in nineteen-twelve and scared the frockcoats and the tophats and diamonded hostesses at Saratoga Springs, Bar Harbor, Lake Geneva with the bogy of a Socialist president. (*42P 25–26*)

At the factual or documentary level, this passage is characteristically efficient in its production of a clear and highly selective portrait of Debs's career. Leaving aside facts that might impede the basic gesture (such as Debs's early service as a mainstream state representative), Dos Passos tells the story as the evolution of a working-class radical's vocation: from machinist, to rank-and-file member of the Brotherhood of Locomotive Firemen, to secretary of the local, to traveling organizer, to the leader of the famous Pullman strike (a landmark event, of course, in the history of American labor, which made Debs a national figure), and finally to the presidential candidate of the Socialist Party who won nearly a million votes in 1912.

Alongside this factual narrative, Dos Passos also offers a libidinal account of Debs's socialism as rooted in his commitment to brotherhood. His vision, according to Dos Passos, is of "a world brothers might own / where everybody would split even." This is a more complex proposition than it might first appear. Dos Passos is not simply suggesting that Debs's feeling of fraternity leads to the desire for a general social solidarity. More specifically, he implies that, for Debs, the bond to other men leads to the desire for *collective ownership* ("a world brothers might own") and for *material equality* ("where everybody would split even"). A few lines later, the ramifications of this basic fraternal impulse are elaborated further, as Dos Passos insists that Debs "wanted his brothers to be free men." To acknowledge a man as one's brother, that is to say, is also to want him to be free. What emerges here is Dos Passos's intuition that, at least for Debs, the feeling of fraternity was itself the root of the commitment to freedom, equality, and collectivity. Although these formulations are so deceptively simple that one might well read past them as obvious, they are in fact remarkable. They refute in the simplest terms a dominant strand of liberalism (in which freedom is commonly understood to be opposed to the values of equality and community), as well as the American tendency to assume that a more or less atomized individualism is the foundation of freedom. I do not mean to suggest by this that Dos Passos is offering an argument in political theory: he is attempting not so much to prove a necessary relation among abstract political values, as to provide an evocative account of the emotional and temperamental proclivities that enabled socialists like Debs to experience liberty, equality, and collectivity as a unified social ideal. It is for this reason that Dos Passos entitled the biography "Lover of Mankind": for it is, indeed, an exploration of a particular kind of love—a libidinally charged connection to others—that, according to Dos Passos, inspired Debs to believe in the desirability of a more solidaristic and egalitarian form of social organization that would enable "brothers to be free men."

The passage I have quoted insists that Debs's fraternal impulse—his "love of mankind"—also expresses itself through an intensely, and irreducibly, democratic politics. Initially, Dos Passos emphasizes that Debs is a great orator whose "gusty rhetoric" inspires his working-class listeners with his own vision of brotherhood: "he made them want the world he wanted." Coming from Dos Passos, who was always fearful of and hostile toward demagogues, there is something potentially ominous about this formulation, suggesting as it does the disturbing capacity of a speaker to impose his will, to "make" others want what he wants.[13] Raising this possibility in order to dispel it, however, Dos Passos hastens to distinguish Debs's capacity for inspiration from the desire for manipulative power or hierarchical authority. Significantly, the only words actually quoted from Debs in the first half of the biography are his explicit rejection of hierarchical leadership. Debs declares that he is "not a labor leader" in the sense that he does not want his brothers "to follow [him] or anyone else." He warns that "If you are looking for a Moses to lead you out of the capitalist wilderness you will stay right where you are. I would not lead you into this promised land if I could, because if I could lead you in, someone else would lead you out." These words articulate the conviction (deeply shared by Dos Passos) that, as a matter both of principle and practical strategy, the labor movement (and the socialist movement that had grown from it) must not reproduce the pervasive model of hierarchical leadership and passive "followers." If the goal was to build "a world brothers might own," then the movement must be one of "brothers" and "free men" not "leaders" and "followers." While this model places a premium on active agency and individual responsibility, these values are not articulated at the expense of solidarity or community. In the next sentence, Dos Passos emphasizes that Debs's fraternal impulse entails an appeal to both: "That was

how he talked to freighthandlers and gandywalkers, to firemen and switch-
men and engineers, telling them it wasn't enough to organize the railroadmen, that all workers must be organized [. . .] in the workers' co-operative
commonwealth." Even as Debs addresses the railroad workers as men capable of rejecting the role of "followers," he also calls upon them to reject all
narrow constraints on their spirit of solidarity. He urges them, for example,
to reject the craft unionism that separated skilled workers (firemen, switch-
men, engineers) from one another and from the unskilled (freighthandlers,
gandywalkers). He calls upon them to embrace the expansive socialist vision
of a "co-operative commonwealth" in which *all* workers (not merely railroadmen) would join together in building a solidaristic society committed
to economic equality. As Dos Passos imagines it, the impulse of fraternity in
Debs is outward moving, seeking ever-larger and more inclusive community,
even as it insists always upon the agency and autonomy of individuals. This
is not merely a way of talking ("That was how he talked to freighthandlers"),
but also a way of *seeing* others as "brothers" who might be "free men" ("That
was what he saw in the crowd that met him . . . after the Pullman strike").
And Dos Passos ends the first half of the biography by asserting that it is precisely Debs's capacity to see and to address men in this way that accounts for
his degree of popularity: for "the men that chalked up nine hundred thousand votes for him in nineteen-twelve" are precisely the "crowd" in whom
Debs saw his "brothers."[14]

To say that Debs's fraternal vision leads to a simultaneous insistence upon
individual agency and an expansive solidarity is not to say that Dos Passos
simply ignores the tension between these ideals. He is, in fact, centrally concerned with the problem of how to imagine a form of individual agency
(a form of nonhierarchical leadership, in effect) that will not deform a democratic and collaborative community of equals. This problem is registered
in a representational tension between the emphasis on Debs's exceptional
capacity to inspire and the fraternal nature of his ideal. Through an evolving
metaphor drawn from Debs's work as a locomotive fireman,[15] Dos Passos
both explores this tension and figures a utopian resolution. Immediately before the first invocation of Debs's vision, Dos Passos compares the socialist's
oratory to the ignition of a fire: his language is "a sort of gusty rhetoric that
set on fire the railroad workers in their pineboarded halls." This initial metaphorical rendering of Debs's inspirational power poses two problems. First,

it emphasizes a certain distance and difference between Debs and the other workers, representing the socialist's "gusty rhetoric" as the external enabling cause or agent (the wind) that produces the "fire" of fraternity in the other men. Second, the image implies an ambiguous tension between the "fire" Debs creates and the flammable "pineboarded halls" in which the inspirational gathering takes place. The transmission of the fraternal impulse, in other words, threatens figuratively to destroy the context, or space, in which that fraternity is enacted.

When Dos Passos redeploys the metaphor a few lines later, this problem of an inequality (or a form of self-assertion) that threatens to destroy the fraternal project is resolved through a more complex version of the same figure: "Locomotive fireman on many a long night's run, / under the smoke a fire burned him up, burned in gusty words that beat in pineboarded halls." Several things are important about this revision of the metaphor. First, Debs's vision of fraternity is now represented as stemming directly from the practical work that he shares with the other railroadmen: the "fire" of fraternity that "burned him up" is a metaphorical extension of Debs's actual work "on many a long nights' run," "under" the literal "smoke" of the locomotive. Second, Debs himself now "burn[s]" with the same fire that (in the first metaphor) has been lit in the other workers.[16] This suggests a rejection of the hierarchical difference previously implied between orator and listener, external agent of inspiration and object of that inspiration. In an inventive twist, it democratizes the Romantic trope of the exceptional artist's unique blaze of inspiration, making Debs's oratory now the expression of the fire produced by a common experience. That fire—that vision of fraternity—is no longer something that Debs simply gives to others with his "gusty words"; rather, the words themselves issue from a blaze that arises from the workers' common activity. The fire "burns in" Debs's rhetoric because his words are themselves the roar of a fraternal blaze that the men build together, an expression of the utopian potential of their shared labor.

Finally, the fire (and the "gusty words" that are now, in effect, its flame) no longer threatens to destroy the "pineboarded halls." Rather, as Dos Passos builds more explicitly on the locomotive image, Debs's "gusty words" and the shared fire of fraternity now "beat" in the union halls just as the fire beats in the locomotive, carrying the train forward "on many a long night's run." Debs's inspiring language is an animating force, its potentially destructive power now productively controlled by a collective enterprise that need not be threatened by energies that it can harness toward its own ends. The "pine-boarded halls" (which echo that earlier enclosure, the "weatherboarded shack" in which Debs was born) are no longer the fixed, fragile, flammable containers of a fraternity endangered by the eloquence of its own spokesman: rather, they are figuratively transformed into the locomotive itself, hurtling through the night, impelled forward and outward by the explosive libidinal energies of the individuals who make up a revolutionary, fraternal movement.

The first half of the biography thus offers a documentary account of Debs's career as a labor organizer and political spokesman; and it explores Debs's socialism as rooted, above all, in a powerful fraternal impulse. The second half of the prose poem tells the story of Debs's suppression during the Red Scare, and it explores the libidinal as well as historical causes of that suppression. The remainder of the biography reads as follows:

> But where were Gene Debs's brothers in nineteen eighteen when
> Woodrow Wilson had him locked up in Atlanta for speaking against war,
> where were the big men fond of whiskey and fond of each other, gentle
> rambling tellers of stories over bars in small towns in the Middle West,
> quiet men who wanted a house with a porch to putter around and a fat
> wife to cook for them, a few drinks and cigars, a garden to dig in, cronies to
> chew the rag with
> and wanted to work for it
> and others to work for it;
> where were the locomotive firemen and engineers when they hustled him
> off to Atlanta Penitentiary?
> And they brought him back to die in Terre Haute
> to sit on his porch in a rocker with a cigar in his mouth,
> beside him American Beauty roses his wife fixed in a bowl;
> and the people of Terre Haute and the people in Indiana and the people
> of the Middle West were fond of him and afraid of him and thought of him
> as an old kindly uncle who loved them, and wanted to be with him and
> to have him give them candy,
> but they were afraid of him as if he had contracted a social disease,
> syphilis or leprosy, and thought it was too bad,
> but on account of the flag
> and prosperity

and making the world safe for democracy,
they were afraid to be with him,
or to think much about him for fear they might believe him;
for he said:
While there is a lower class I am of it, while there is a criminal class I am of it,
while there is a soul in prison I am not free. (*42P* 26–27)

The documentary content of this passage has been organized, once again, to produce an efficient singularity of effect: that at the very height of his popularity, Debs was arrested for his public opposition to U.S. participation in the First World War; that his prosecution and imprisonment were part of the massive government-directed assault on American radicalism (led by President Wilson), which also involved a sustained official campaign of jingoistic, anti-Red propaganda; and that, by the time Debs was released from prison, he had been effectively isolated from much of his working-class constituency, was broken in health, and never regained a significant political role in the years before his death.[17] At this documentary level, Dos Passos offers a compressed and nuanced account of the social *causes* of Debs's political defeat and of the American Left's loss of its preeminent spokesman. Dos Passos thus directs his own anger—and that of his readers—at President Wilson, at the government's systematic policy of incarcerating dissenters, and at the ideological apparatus that successfully deployed a militarist nationalism to intimidate all those seeking economic change in the name of a more just and less alienated society.

But Dos Passos's task of mourning runs deeper than this. For he recognized that the suppression of Debs and other radicals was made possible not only by the actions of the government, but also by weaknesses within the Left itself, which failed adequately to resist the onslaught. In order to mourn the destruction of American radicalism, in other words, Dos Passos also had to come to terms with his anger at the movement he had loved and lost. While the documentary strand of the Debs biography identifies the structures of government-sponsored repression, the libidinal strand that accompanies it focuses its attention—and its anger—on these deeper (psychocultural) failings within the movement itself. Facing this kind of ambivalence is, as we have seen, one of the deepest obstacles to mourning—and the second half of the Debs biography seeks to meet this challenge. Having acknowledged the structures of external repression, Dos Passos seeks most strenuously to understand the fears that caused Debs's "brothers" to abandon him.

The second half of the biography is largely organized around the angry question, "But where were Gene Debs's brothers in nineteen eighteen. . .?" and the implicit, polemical argument that the incarceration of Debs, and the destruction of the mass movement for which he was a spokesman, were enabled by a fear of solidarity within the working class. For Dos Passos asserts that the very people whom Debs saw and addressed as "brothers" were ultimately "fond of him and afraid of him and thought of him as an old kindly uncle who loved them, and wanted to be with him and to have him give them candy." This sentence makes no pretense of objective dispassion: it is saturated with a sarcasm that expresses Dos Passos's own anger, disappointment, and judgment. It argues that the working people of the Midwest feel a deep ambivalence about Debs (that they are at once "fond of him and afraid of him")—and, more specifically, that underneath their fear lies a continuing desire for benign paternalism. Debs has seen and addressed them as brothers, but they "thought of him," in return, as an "old kindly uncle." He has offered them a vision of fraternity, but they want him "to give them candy." This last phrase is especially damning, for it suggests that Debs's "brothers" have more than accepted the passive role of "followers," wanting him not only to "lead" but simply to "give them" the good things they desire. Debs has warned them that if they "are looking for a Moses to lead [them]," they will "stay right where [they] are"—and Dos Passos suggests that the warning, unheeded, has come true. Yearning still for a hierarchical figure who will deliver the things they want, they have forsaken the promise of brotherhood and have declined the challenge of active individual commitment to collectivity and equality. As a result, the movement that might have enabled "brothers to be free men" has been broken. Having hardly glimpsed the "promised land," they have remained in "the capitalist wilderness."

The fate of socialism, according to this account, is the fate of a certain kind of desire. Dos Passos imagines socialism, as I have already suggested, as rooted in a fraternal impulse that is active, explosive, always outward moving, seeking ever-expanding community, connection, and solidarity. Its figure is a fire that does not consume or quench itself, that does not destroy the conditions of its possibility, whose burning is an animation, an expression of self and an invitation to others. The fear of socialism is imagined as a deformation of this desire, or a substitution for it of another kind of want: a yearning, instead, for a passive gratification that brings desire to an end, a yearning that Dos Passos associates not with mobility and social expansiveness, but with fixity, social limitation, and a cessation of energy.[18] The desire for hierarchy is the principal form that this fear of fraternal libido takes: a desire not for active democracy but to "follow" where another "leads"; a desire not for the reciprocities of love, but simply to be "loved"; a desire for an avuncular dispensation of the kind of sweet, compensatory treats that pacify a child.

Even as Dos Passos marshals this incisive critique of the socialist movement he loved and mourned, he also succumbs to the temptation to displace his anger—and at least partially to obscure the object of his condemnation. This displacement takes the form of a misogyny that provides a different name for American radicals' fear of solidarity. The writer suggests, in short, that his comrades have evaded Debs's fraternal love because they have chosen to embrace a conventional, feminized domesticity. In response to the angry question, "But where were Gene Debs's brothers in nineteen eighteen[?]" Dos Passos replies, in effect, that they are at home with their wives. The ominous significance of this misogynistic logic evolves slowly over the course of the prose poem's second half, as Dos Passos charts the deformation of an expansive, solidaristic desire (figured by him, and many others in his generation, as fraternal and therefore male) into a constrained domesticity, marked female. Speaking of Debs's "brothers," Dos Passos begins by asking: "where were the big men fond of whiskey and fond of each other, gentle rambling tellers of stories over bars in small towns in the Middle West [?]" This initial characterization offers a kind of homosocial male pastoral that gives a specific metaphorical form to the idealized fraternity evoked in the first half of the biography. It is an image of working men together, enjoying simple pleasures (they are "fond of whiskey"), reciprocally exchanging affection (they are "fond of each other"), and sharing experiences through acts of self-expression (they are "rambling tellers of stories"). The second characterization is far more ambivalent. It metaphorically suggests the deformation and constriction of the fraternal impulse: they are now "quiet men who wanted a house with a porch to putter around and a fat wife to cook for them, a few drinks and cigars, a garden to dig in, cronies to chew the rag with / and wanted to work for it / and others to work for it." This second image is by no means wholly negative, for it contains many of the original impulses: these are still ordinary men, enjoying the simple pleasures of drink and "chewing the rag" with their "cronies"—and Dos Passos still insists on their inclination to "work" for their pleasures alongside "others." But as the scene has shifted from the public space of the "bar" to the private space of the "house," a new constraint and passivity emerge: the "big men" who were "rambling tellers of stories" have now become "quiet men" who, with an implicit aimlessness, "putter around." Moreover, and more importantly, as soon as a woman is introduced as a necessary presence within this domestic scene, male desire takes on a supine hierarchical character that notably collides with the assertion that these men "want to work for it." The role of this "fat wife" is simply to "cook for them," to perform the work that enables men to have their appetite sated without any exertion of their own. The characterization of the wife as "fat" is crucial to the symbolic structure Dos Passos is creating here: the woman in the domestic space is explicitly desexualized; she is represented not as an equal partner who shares and stimulates an active libidinal desire, but as a functionalized, quasi-maternal figure who (like the "old kindly uncle") brings a certain hunger to an end. Through this image, Dos Passos suggests that the same men who want brotherhood also want a domesticity that discourages the active, expansive, reciprocal, and self-sustaining desire associated with fraternity, eliciting (and satisfying) in its place a yearning for passive gratification.

The full significance of this embrace of domesticity is only revealed in the following sentence, where Debs's own homecoming is described:

And they brought him back to die in Terre Haute
to sit on his porch in a rocker with a cigar in his mouth
beside him American Beauty roses his wife fixed in a bowl.

Because the preceding sentence has ended, "where were the locomotive firemen and engineers when *they* [emphasis added] hustled him off to Atlanta Penitentiary," the pronoun at the beginning of this new sentence is disturbingly ambiguous: its implied reference is to "the locomotive firemen and engineers"—but the grammatical referent is the unspecified official "they" who have "hustled him off" to jail. As a result, Debs's "brothers," who have turned fearfully from the expansive fraternity of socialism to the passivity of a feminine domesticity, are now ambiguously associated with the very men who have taken Debs to jail. The domestic retreat to which they bring him is figured, in turn, as an affective equivalent of the jail itself. Home is where he is brought, explicitly, "to die." It is the end and antithesis of mobility, energy, and the movement outward to new connection. The "railroad-man" who "traveled all over the country as organizer" is now relegated to a "rocker" on the domestic "porch." The unquenchable fire of fraternity that "burned" in his "gusty words" and that "set on fire the railroad workers" is now parodically reduced to the cigar that silences him. The presiding spirit of domesticity, the desexualized wife, now tellingly "fixe[s]" flowers "in a bowl," just as Debs himself is fixed, stationary and silent, in the domestic space. Heaping up the ironic signifiers, Dos Passos insists that these flowers, which decorate Debs's confinement, are "American Beauty" roses—an emblem and reflection of the jingoistic patriotism in the name of which Debs has been incarcerated.

Through these images, Dos Passos thus explores and expresses a deep anger at the socialist movement he had loved and lost. He condemns, above all, the willingness of American radicals to turn away from the difficult and exciting challenge of equality and solidarity. He partially displaces this anger through a conventional (if peculiarly socialist) misogyny, implying that his male comrades' embrace of hierarchy is somehow, to some degree, the fault of women: that a desexualized, feminized domesticity (and the "fat wife" who embodies it) has lured them away from the promise of fraternity and socialism. The importance of this misogyny must not be underestimated. For Dos Passos, as for many male radicals of his generation, the socialist promise of a "fraternal" solidarity often rested (unconsciously as well as consciously) on the exclusion of women—an exclusion that had devastating consequences for a movement that imagined itself as forging an inclusive solidarity. In this particular context, as Dos Passos sought to mourn the failures of the Left, he deployed that misogyny in ways that shielded male radicals from the full force of his anger, shifting blame in part onto women who were constructed as seductive outsiders.

This misogyny creates, however, only a *partial* displacement—for it does not wholly obscure the central object of Dos Passos's critique. He focuses his anger most directly and persistently at male radicals and at their fear, which has made Debs's imprisonment possible. It is they who have consigned him to the passivity, constraint, and isolation of a libidinal condition whose end is death. Above all, Dos Passos condemns their continued yearning for hierarchy. For here lies one of the most remarkable insights of the Debs biography, and of Dos Passos's political mourning: that hierarchy (including patriarchal authority) leads to a libidinal diminution, a weakening, of all—leaders as well as followers, those raised to dominance as well as those who accept their own subordination. Because his brothers fear fraternity, they have placed Debs in a hierarchical position of authority (as "leader," "uncle," father figure)—and yet this elevation does *not* make Debs more powerful. Rather, it reduces him to precisely the same state of passivity, silence, and constraint to which the "brothers" have fearfully reduced themselves. By making him the "kindly uncle" who "give[s] them candy," they also make him the childlike figure on the porch who is tended by his maternal wife. The same ambiguous effect is also present in the treatment of the wives themselves, who are at once made into subordinates (servants) and into superiors (maternal figures who have the power to satisfy the passive men who wait for their service). Dos Passos insists here on a deeply egalitarian insight, even as he himself partially evades and vitiates it by his own uneasy misogyny: that hierarchy weakens. When people fear the challenge and the emotional intensities of equality, and turn instead to the apparent safety and ease of hierarchical relationships imagined as benign, they thwart the libidinal possibilities of their own lives and of those whom they have constructed as "leader," "uncle," father, mother.[19]

Dos Passos goes on to suggest that, in the grip of this fear, Debs's "brothers" can no longer remain open to the expansive, egalitarian impulse for which he speaks. They must close themselves off to "the gusty rhetoric" that formerly "set [them] on fire." The fraternal vision that Dos Passos has described as an animating, self-renewing blaze that "burned" in all the men, they now perceive as a contagion that threatens to stigmatize and destroy them: "they were afraid of him as if he had contracted a social disease, syphilis or leprosy." Again, the metaphor is more complex than it looks. It contains, to begin with, an erotic component, in that the fear of socialism is now imagined as analogous to the fear of a sexually transmitted disease: syphilis. The sexuality purged from the domestic space suddenly reappears here in the fears of Debs's "brothers." Having turned to a desexualized domesticity as an alternative to a threateningly intense form of solidaristic desire, they now perceive that desire to be a "social disease" like those transmitted through illicit sexual connections.[20] The relationship implied here between socialist aspiration and sexuality deepens Dos Passos's libidinal account of socialism. For this fearful fantasy mirrors, through its negation, a positive intuition that pervades *U.S.A.*: that a socialist politics might be rooted not only in the desire for an expansive homosociality, but also in the longing for nonalienated sexual connections. (There are, of course, at least two kinds of sexuality repressed in this prose poem: the heterosexuality purged from the bourgeois domestic space and the homosexuality toward which Dos Passos's representation of these passionate, exciting male bonds tends but that it never openly acknowledges.)[21] Dos Passos insists here that Debs's comrades fear his invitation to socialism just as they fear the dangers of sexuality.

The imagined destructiveness of unfettered, undomesticated relations is fantasized most concretely in the reference to leprosy: a disease that, in literally eating away at the body, destroys and reduces individuals rather than augmenting them through connection. The metaphor dramatically distorts and reverses the initial utopian image of the locomotive fire, which animates without destroying and carries the men outward to new connections. Through a monstrous inversion, the logic of disease does indeed resemble the logic of solidarity. Both are transmitted to an ever-widening population through intimate contact and expressions of desire. To see socialism as a lethal and contagious disease is to see it as a force not of life but of death. From this fearful perspective, it appears not as the promise of equality, collectivity, and freedom, but as the threat of destruction. To describe this impulse as a "social disease" is to capture the fear of stigma that surrounded socialism during the intimidating ideological campaign of the Red Scare ("on account of the flag / and prosperity/ and making the world safe for democracy / they were afraid to be with him"). Engaged in the strenuous work of mourning, Dos Passos here again reminds us that the losses suffered by American radicals were, indeed, the result of a vast ideological campaign—but burrowing deeper, in his grief and anger, he insists that these losses stemmed also from American radicals' fear of their own desires.

Enveloped in these fears—which were at once deeply psychological and eminently material—"the people of the Middle West" seek to separate themselves from the danger that Debs now represents. Like a sexual transgressor in a puritanical society, he must be cast out (especially by those who feel his transgressive desire in themselves). The bearer of a deadly disease, he must be quarantined. And because it is his words that carry the promise—or threat—of fraternity, the people are not merely "afraid to be with him," but even "to think much about him for fear they might believe him." To hear the words would be to open themselves again to the possibilities of a repressed desire; to "think about him" is to risk "believing" in the potentialities, political and personal, that have burned in all of them.

In the second half of the prose poem, then, Dos Passos identifies with considerable subtlety the causes of his political loss and the objects of his anger. He sketches in brief strokes the political and ideological formations of the Red Scare that crushed leaders such as Debs. He had the courage to acknowledge also that the movement he had lost must share some blame for its own demise: that the hundreds of thousands who were active Socialists, and the millions who had sympathized with the movement ("the people of the Middle West" among them), had failed to resist the government's suppression of a democratic movement for social change. While there is some displacement of this anger through a conventional misogyny, Dos Passos insists that if the Left was to grieve for its losses fully, it must acknowledge most centrally its fear of its own desires—for equality, for solidarity, for unfettered and expansive connection.

Having acknowledged the depth and the objects of his anger, Dos Passos was able in the concluding lines of the prose poem to fulfill the work of mourning, to perform rhetorically and substantively the quintessential gesture of the radical biographies. Here he regains access to his own psychic and political investments in a movement whose defeat he has factually documented and libidinally anatomized. He reminds the reader that the human possibilities that Debs embodied persist into the present, despite their past negation. Having insisted that Debs's contemporaries are afraid to "think much about him for fear they might believe him," Dos Passos proceeds to reassert precisely what they are too fearful even to think about: "for he said: *While there is a lower class I am of it, while there is a criminal class I am of it, while there is a soul in prison I am not free.*" This famous statement enacts one last time, now in Debs's own words, the solidaristic impulse—the "love of mankind"—that Dos Passos has identified as the affective root of his socialism. It is, above all, a declaration of solidarity, an assertion that he stands with all those who are vulnerable—to economic exploitation in particular, and to the forms of criminalization that follow from economic vulnerability in a class society. Much of its power derives from the idealistic and performative character of the statement: from Debs's assertion not simply that he *is* a member of the lower class, but that as a matter of principle, of loyalty—of fraternal "love"—he *will always be* a member of that class, as long as one exists. The expansive and utopian character of the utterance is intensified by our knowledge that Debs's identification with "the criminal class" is rooted in his own experience of imprisonment. This lends a particular pathos, and an aura of indomitability, to his lingering, perpetual promise that "while there is a soul in prison I am not free." Just as the persistence of this declaration of solidarity survives his own incarceration, so too the expansive, outward-moving character of the solidaristic impulse survives the libidinal constraint imposed upon him by his comrades' fearfulness. For at the heart of his declaration lies an identification, an empathy, that refuses to be limited—by geography, nation, ethnicity, or gender; even by time.[22] It expresses a love that perpetually seeks, and finds, new objects, new comrades.

The rhetorical structure here is as important as the content of the words. The entire second half of the biography consists of two complex, lengthy sentences. The first is an impassioned question—"But where were Gene Debs's brothers[?]"—which creates a direct appeal to the reader, demanding that we establish an active relationship to the story being told, and assume the responsibility to reply. The second sentence ends by confronting the reader with the very words that Debs's own contemporaries have refused to hear. Having evoked the expansive, utopian potential of Debs's fraternal vision in the first half of the biography, and having insisted in the second that Debs's comrades betrayed that vision because they feared (as well as shared) it, Dos Passos then concludes by placing us in their position, reconstituting once again the crucial moment of personal and political decision. (The structure of this situation is remarkably similar to the end of *Flowering of the Rod*, composed a decade later, but which I described in Chapter 3. There, H. D. similarly confronts Kaspar and the reader once again with Mary's presence, calling out to us to affirm that which has been previously denied.) Here, Dos Passos says, are Debs's words: it is up to you, as it was up to them, to listen or not, to embrace or reject this possibility as your own. Depriving us of the luxury of not thinking or not hearing—of not remembering—he offers the opportunity of deciding anew. The eerie temporal-linguistic shift from the historical past tense of the biography to the present tense of Debs's utterance enacts in language the essential, difficult work of tradition-building: that something crushed in the past—an idea, a feeling, a libidinal impulse, a political aspiration—continues to exist in the present. Debs speaks, now, again: to us. It is the hopeful gesture, the gift, of a robust mourning. That which had been embodied in the dead socialist is reanimated, the betrayed ideal is recalled, the words remembered. A writer in political mourning over the Red Scare, Dos Passos recalls the lost hero and the betrayed ideal, not merely as a private memory, as a retreat from new relationships and new possibilities. Rather, the memory is proffered here as a means of reaching out from past to present, from author to reader, in the hope of extending and renewing a shared aspiration.

III. "Appetite for Everything": Socialism, Pleasure, and Self-Expression

"Lover of Mankind" is emblematic of the radical biographies of *U.S.A.* in its enactment of this rich process of political mourning. In it, we can see Dos Passos's effort to identify the causes of his loss and the objects of his anger. We see also his effort to name the libidinal energies embodied in the suppressed traditions of American radicalism—and to offer these for future affirmation. The Debs biography emphasizes most centrally the solidaristic impulse, the effort of American socialists to reassert the "love of mankind" starkly denied by a social order predicated on class exploitation. In other biographies, Dos Passos explores other aspects of the revolt against alienation, other libidinal impulses expressed by the radical movements crushed during the Red Scare. With particular persistence, he focuses on American radicals' yearning for self-expression and on the desire for sensual and aesthetic pleasures that were proscribed by the repressiveness of bourgeois culture and by the privations of working-class life. As I have emphasized in the first half of this book, American modernists were surprisingly united in their perception that the capacity to experience such pleasures and to express such desires had been imperiled by the processes of modernization. In the radical biographies of *U.S.A.*, Dos Passos insisted that the effort to retrieve and realize these human possibilities had found expression in a mass movement. The Red Scare was a particularly alarming—and lethal—demonstration that those who held political and economic power in the United States would not tolerate such a movement or the social changes that it demanded. But in mourning the suppression of these idealistic radicals, Dos Passos sought to extend into another generation an awareness of the pleasures and human possibilities that might yet exist.

A number of the prose poems explore the ways in which a commitment to revolution could evolve out of—and remain rooted in—the yearning for aesthetic and sensual pleasure. This is especially marked, for example, in the biographies of John Reed and Paxton Hibben, the two radicals in Dos Passos's pantheon who most resemble the author in background and trajectory. Raised like Dos Passos in well-to-do families, and educated at Ivy League colleges, Reed and Hibben are initially represented as aesthetes and hedonists. Reed "was husky greedy had appetite for everything"; "he liked men he liked women he liked eating and writing and foggy nights and drinking and foggy nights and swimming and football and rhymed verse and being cheerleader ivy orator making clubs" (*1919* 10–11). In a similar vein, Hibben "drank a lot, didn't deny that he ran around after girls, made a brilliant scholastic record" and "wanted / travel and romance [. . .] wellgroomed adventures in foreign lands" (*1919* 155). What is most striking in these descriptions is Dos Passos's characteristic fusion of a range of desires as continuous with one another, and expressive of a single, but multifaceted "appetite": the desire for sexual experience and for many forms of social connection; for intellectual as well as physical pleasures; for aesthetic enjoyment—of the external world ("foggy nights") and of expressive culture ("rhymed verse"); a desire to make as well as to appreciate; to have "adventures"; to experience and take pleasure in "everything."

While emphasizing the elite character of their privilege, and even of some of the pleasures to which they aspire ("*ivy* orator," "*wellgroomed* adventure"), Dos Passos rapidly moves on to suggest that the expansiveness of their desires soon collides with the constraints of their class position. Reed (like Dos Passos himself) rejects Harvard and the bourgeois conventionality that it embodies precisely because he hears "the deans and the instructors all crying in thin voices refrain." Dos Passos emphasizes that their desire for diverse social connections and experiences leads them to feelings of affection and sympathy for people outside their class. The conviviality and sociability that are an organic feature of their pleasure seeking, in other words, lead to a sense of solidarity with many kinds of people, including those who are exploited by an inequitable economic system. Dos Passos explains that "Jack Reed wanted to live in a tub and write verses; / but he kept meeting bums workingmen husky guys he liked out of luck out of work"—and these encounters lead him to ask, "why not revolution?" Reed sympathizes with "bums" and "workingmen" "out of work" not because he feels pity or guilt, but because he "*liked*" them, and sees them as "husky guys"—vital, energetic, full of desire, like himself. (Hibben, similarly, is "always standing up for his *friends*, for people out of luck.") Solidarity with those who are "out of luck" is thus represented as an expression or extension of the pleasure-seeking impulse: the same "appetite" that makes Reed want to "live in a tub and write verses" also makes him eager for new connections—and forces him to reject the restricted "tub" of elite society and class privilege. The pursuit of sensual and aesthetic pleasure leads to an expansive social solidarity, which leads, in turn, to the revolt against economic exploitation and a class-divided society. It is Reed's generous affection and enjoyment—the "Playboy" sensibility from which his biography takes its title—that causes him to refuse to take sides during the First World War, and to identify instead with all "the boys who were being blown to hell, / with the Germans the French the Russians the Bulgarians." It is the same "appetite" that draws Reed and Hibben into the Communist movement—that makes Reed stand "with the soldiers and peasants in Petrograd in October," that causes Hibben to "wal[k] the streets all night with the revolutionists."[23]

Dos Passos draws an equally strong connection between radical politics and the desire for aesthetic and sensual pleasure in the biography of Randolph Bourne. The trajectory is slightly different, as Bourne's capacity for enjoyment is represented not as the easy flowering of a privileged life, but as the triumph of yearning and receptivity over class disadvantage and physical deformity:

> weak health and being poor and twisted in body and on bad terms with his people hadn't spoiled the world for Randolph Bourne; he was a happy man, loved die Meistersinger and playing Bach with his long hands that stretched so easily over the keys and pretty girls and good food and evenings of talk. When he was dying of pneumonia a friend brought him an eggnog; Look at the yellow, it's beautiful, he kept saying as his life ebbed into delirium and fever. He was a happy man. (*1919* 90)

Here again, Dos Passos describes a wide continuum of desires: Bourne takes pleasure in hearing and in making music; he is drawn erotically to "pretty girls"; he enjoys the sensual pleasure of "good food" and the intellectual pleasure of conversation. Even at the point of death, as the rigidities of personality dissolve into "delirium and fever," he remains fully receptive to the aesthetic and sensual intensity of color.

Dos Passos goes on to suggest that this capacity for pleasure also provides the wellspring of Bourne's political commitments. Initially, he "seizes" (with the same "feverish intensity") on an optimistic version of John Dewey's pragmatism and embraces the politics of Woodrow Wilson's "New Freedom." But then, "in the crazy spring of 1917," Bourne begins to see through the venal hypocrisies that were offered as justification for U.S. participation in the First World War. As if his capacity for aesthetic and sensual pleasure were an intellectual and political touchstone—an intimate personal knowledge of a world organized for pleasure and use rather than profit and exploitation—Bourne now decodes the self-serving ideological lies of the class society in which he lives:

> for *New Freedom* read *Conscription*, for *Democracy*, *Win the War*, for *Reform*, *Safeguard the Morgan Loans*
> for Progress Civilization Education Service,
> Buy a Liberty Bond,
> Strafe the Hun,
> Jail the Objectors. (*1919* 90)

Bourne is one of the great truth-tellers: this man, who is represented (perhaps uniquely in *U.S.A.*) as "happy" and as committed even in his own dying to the pleasures of life, is also peculiarly equipped to reveal his society's commitment to death and destruction. It is Bourne who can see clearly that the very terms that should function as political equivalents to a psychic state of openness, flexibility, and receptivity ("Freedom," "Democracy," "Reform") are themselves being used as a cynical screen for killing ("Win the War"), for murderous racism and nationalism ("Strafe the Hun"), for domestic constraint and repression ("Conscription," "Jail the Objectors")—all in the financial interests of an oligarchy ("Safeguard the Morgan Loans"). It is the capacity for pleasure that enables him to see the death drive that impels the capitalist nations—to see, according to his famous dictum, that *"War is the health of the state."*

Dos Passos's prose-poems suggest that anticapitalist radicalism is rooted in a drive for self-expression as much as it is in the yearning for pleasure. He repeatedly emphasizes that the radical movement has afforded opportunities for individual creativity. More specifically, he is concerned to show (as in the case of Debs's oratory) that self-expression need not be incompatible with a commitment to solidarity. Rather, he suggests that in the very process of realizing their own expressive capacities, these radicals were also giving voice to the needs and desires of their comrades. He tells us, for example, that Bill Haywood "was an organizer, a speaker, an exhorter, the wants of all the miners were his wants" (*42P* 86). Dos Passos suggests here that in taking on the role of "organizer," Haywood exercises his own expressive talents (as "speaker" and "exhorter")—and also that this act of creative agency is predicated upon his capacity to empathize with the "wants" of others and to speak for them as well as for himself. In "Playboy," Dos Passos similarly emphasizes John Reed's exceptional creative gift (he "was the best American writer of his time")—and then goes on to insist that Reed's talent is inseparable from his receptivity to others. When Reed is sent "to Paterson to write up the strike" of textile workers, for example, it is in the end from "the strikers in jail" that he "learned the hope of a new society where nobody would be out of luck." Or again, when a magazine sends him "to write up Pancho Villa," it is "Pancho Villa [who] taught him to write [. . .] and the brown quietvoiced peons dying starving killing for liberty / for land for water for schools. / Mexico taught him to write" (*1919* 12). Reed's greatness as a writer, on this account, stems from his capacity to relinquish the arrogant detachment of presuming to "write up" the experience of others and to "learn" instead from them—to integrate their experiences and aspirations into himself. Like Haywood, he makes their "wants" his own.

In other biographies, Dos Passos emphasizes that through acts of creative self-realization, radicals were able not only to speak *for* others, but also to enable comrades to find their own means of self-expression. He suggests, for example, that in taking up the role of political orator crusading against the elite-financed political "machines" of the day, La Follette was simultaneously realizing his own creative aspirations (initially embodied in the desire to be "an actor") and also expanding the expressive opportunities of others.

According to Dos Passos, "he worked all his life making long speeches full of statistics, struggling to save democratic government, to make a farmers' and small-businessmen's commonwealth" (*42P* 325). La Follette's own acts of self-expression (his "long speeches") are animated by a desire to extend a democratic process that will enable widespread political self-expression (to create a "democratic" "commonwealth" in which ordinary "farmers and small businessmen" would have their say).

Dos Passos offers a similar, but more fully utopian, version of this dynamic in the biography of Joe Hill. Hill has an exceptional talent for giving expressive form to ideas circulating in the revolutionary movement, ideas that he has heard and learned from others. He had, as Dos Passos puts it, "a knack for setting rebel words to tunes." But this particular form of self-expression (already a collaboration) is represented by Dos Passos as opening up dramatic political and expressive possibilities for many others:

> Along the coast in cookshacks flophouses jungles wobblies hoboes
> bindlestiffs began singing Joe Hill's songs. They sang 'em in the county
> jails of the State of Washington, Oregon, California, Nevada, Idaho, in the
> bullpens in Montana and Arizona, sang 'em in Walla Walla, San Quentin,
> and Leavenworth,
>   forming the structure of the new society within the jails of the old. (*1919* 368)

Through this characteristically Whitmanian description that strings together lists of jails and states and worksites, Dos Passos captures the expansive, outward-moving, enabling potential of expressive culture, which can be passed—like the "fire" of Debs's "gusty rhetoric"—from one person to another: an anthem of collective possibility. Because Joe Hill has found the music, working people all over the country can express their discontents and their dreams of a different society. One man's songs provide a vehicle through which others can transmit the content of a working-class radicalism ("*And the union makes us strong*"). More than this, the very activity of singing prefigures the egalitarian "new society" of which they dream. Drawing on the Wobblies' syndicalist motto, "building the new society in the shell of the old," Dos Passos suggests that the achievement of individual self-expression, and its widespread dissemination, makes it possible even "within the jails of the old" exploitative society to begin "*forming*" (not merely imagining) the "*structure* of the new." The solidaristic sharing of expressive possibilities is thus imagined not merely as a goal of the revolution, and a means of achieving it—but as a living enactment of a liberated social order.[24]

Dos Passos understood the impulse to self-expression and the pursuit of pleasure to be intertwined, and their relation to one another is clearly explored in the biography of Charles Steinmetz, the immigrant socialist inventor of the electrical transformer. After telling us that "Steinmetz was a hunchback," Dos Passos goes on to explain that:

> mathematics to Steinmetz was muscular strength and long walks over the hills and the kiss of a girl in love and big evenings spent swilling beer with your friends;
> on his broken back he felt the topheavy weight of society the way workingmen felt it on their straight backs, the way poor students felt it, was a member of a Socialist club, editor of a paper called *The People's Voice.*
> (*42P* 290)

In the first part of this description, Dos Passos again provides a portrait of the expansive continuum of a man's pleasures—in physical agency ("muscular strength"), in the sensuous experience of the external world ("long walks over the hills"), in romantic and sexual connection ("the kiss of a girl in love"), in convivial social relations ("evenings spent swilling beer with your friends"). All of these pleasures are associated, through a single metaphorical assertion, with "mathematics"—Steinmetz's great intellectual passion and his principle form of self-expression. The metaphor here is in one sense ambiguous, for it is not clear whether the yearning for these pleasures is unsatisfied in Steinmetz (perhaps because of his physical disability) and, therefore, that mathematics is a compensatory means of self-realization; or whether all these pleasures are echoed, or additionally gratified, through his intellectual project. In either case, Dos Passos clearly suggests that the force of those yearnings animates his work in mathematics. The extraordinary scale and impact of Steinmetz's electrical invention ("electricity that is mathematics made power") reflects the power released when a person finds a means of fully expressing libidinal energies. "Steinmetz jotted a formula on his cuff," Dos Passos explains later, "and next morning a thousand new powerplants had sprung up" (*42P* 291).

If the first half of the description proposes that Steinmetz's mathematics is associated with fundamental desires for pleasure, the second half suggests that his socialism is a form of political self-expression animated by an equally significant experience of vulnerability. The inventor's "broken back" becomes a metaphor for the sensitivity with which he registers the burden of society's "topheavy weight"—for the pain that he feels as a "poor student" in an inequitable society, a pain that he shares with the "workingmen" whose physical, productive capacities (their "straight backs") are exploited. Not an abstract ideology, socialism is a direct response to a pain as concrete as a "broken back" (as concrete, too, as the pleasure of "the kiss of a girl in love").[25] Like Dos Passos's other radicals, Steinmetz responds to this pain by reaching out to others in solidarity (he joins "a Socialist club") and by expressing his own vulnerability in a way that enables others to do the same (he becomes the "*editor* of a paper" significantly called "The People's Voice").

In this single complex sentence, then, socialism and mathematics are represented as related expressions of desire and vulnerability. Dos Passos implies that Steinmetz's political and intellectual impulses, rooted in the same depths of personality, are inseparable. Later, he explains explicitly that Steinmetz "believe[d] that human society could be improved the way you can improve a dynamo" (*42P* 291–292). Socialism, like electrical invention, is an act of creative agency, an imaginative reorganization of the world to make it conform more fully to his desires. A rebellion against the exploitation of his vulnerability, it is also an act of faith, a "belief" that through his own creative activity he might "improve society." Unlike Dos Passos's other radicals, Steinmetz devotes his life's work principally to mathematical invention, not to social revolution. But Dos Passos is at pains to show that the two impulses are animated by the same cluster of desires, vulnerabilities, hopes, and capacities.

As a group, then, the biographies explore Dos Passos's intuition that the anticapitalist movement was animated by desires for expressivity and for forms of aesthetic and sensual gratification that were foreclosed by the alienated social order produced by monopoly capitalism. He represents these yearnings as inseparable from the solidaristic impulse (the "love of mankind") so central to the Debs biography. At one level, unfettered connection to others (both social and erotic) is represented as one of the principle pleasures that these men seek. More generally, they are united by the intuition that a more solidaristic form of economic organization will enable them to realize their expressive, sensual, and social desires. These three impulses—for solidarity, for self-expression, for aesthetic and sensual pleasure—are woven by Dos Passos into varied but consistent patterns of radical personality.

As in the case of Debs, Dos Passos represents the suppression of these radicals as the violent repudiation of these underlying aspirations. Having focused on their impulse to self-expression, Dos Passos then emphasizes how these men are silenced by external repression. Under the assault of the Red Scare, John Reed, for example, has no more opportunity to write or to learn from the experiences of others: "no more chance to write verses now, no more warm chats with every guy you met up with" (*1919* 13). Magazines no longer "had the nerve to publish [Bourne's] articles" and "a trunk full of manuscript and letters was stolen from him in Connecticut" by government agents (*1919* 90–91). While Joe Hill "went on making up songs" even when "[h]e was in jail," the authorities finally bring his singing to an end by executing him, "up against the wall in the jail yard in Salt Lake City" (*1919* 368). La Follette is ultimately silenced by the very people whose right to political expression he has championed: "The press pumped hatred into its readers against La Follette [. . .]; in Wheeling they refused to let him speak" (*42P* 325).

The Red Scare is depicted as the negation of all those pleasures that the radical movement has set out to realize: the libidinal impulses in each man's life are crushed by the organized destructiveness of a repressive society. ("Force to the utmost, thundered Schoolmaster Wilson" (*1919* 91).) Reed, the man who "liked everything," now finds that "[t]he world's no fun anymore"; "this was grim" (*1919* 13). Over and over, incarceration separates these men from the pleasures of the world. Bourne, for example, was "taking a walk with two girl friends" by the sea "at Wood's Hole" when "he was arrested" (*1919* 91). Having emphasized the continuity between political radicalism and the yearning for sensual pleasures, Dos Passos persistently dwells on the ways in which the repression of the Red Scare registered itself in forms of physical assault on the bodies of these radicals. Big Bill, for example, "was sick with diabetes, [. . .] prison had broken down his health" (*42P* 87). At his twentieth reunion, Paxton Hibben's Princeton classmates "started to lynch him" (*1919* 158). Most graphically, the anti-Red vigilantes who capture Wesley Everest "bashed his teeth in with the butt of a shotgun" and, later, as he "lay stunned in the bottom of the car, a Centralia businessman cut his penis and testicles off with a razor. . . . Then they hanged him from the bridge in the glare of the headlights" (*1919* 401–402). The maiming and murder of Everest stands as a gruesome symbolic climax toward which all the violence of the biographies tends. Within Dos Passos's masculinist idiom, castration functions as a quintessential image for political repression. It captures the murderous aggression of the Red Scare and the attempt to deny the potency of the radical movement that Everest represents. It indicates also the peculiarly antisexual character of this assault, the enraged attempt to negate a political movement that was, at its heart, a libidinal revolt against alienation. It is not enough for the vigilantes to murder the Wobbly; not enough even to "bas[h] his teeth in," rendering him nearly mute before his death: they must also practically and symbolically destroy his capacity for sexual pleasure before they display the mangled corpse, impotent and desexualized, before them "in the glare of the headlights."[26]

In their varied scenarios, then, the radical biographies all enact a politicized version of American modernism's most fundamental story: the triumph of alienation; the persistent thwarting of libidinal vitality and of the desire for human connection. But like other works in the modernism of mourning, these prose poems map the particular social causes of these catastrophic experiences of loss. Although Dos Passos represents the systematic and repetitive character of these stories of defeat, he does not naturalize the social phenomenon he has recorded. He keeps clearly before us the organized and contingent social processes that constituted the Red Scare: the actions of President Wilson, the repressive laws passed by Congress, the biased behavior of the courts, the incarceration of political leaders, the legally sanctioned executions and the vigilante murders, the Palmer Raids and the deportations, the ideological manipulation and intimidation that led to the censorship of a generation. Dos Passos charts the complexity of this repressive apparatus, which was informal as well as institutionalized, cultural and psychological as well as political and judicial. But he continually emphasizes the economic interests that were, beneath it all, served by the Red Scare. It was "the frockcoats and the tophats and diamonded hostesses at Saratoga Springs, Bar Harbor, Lake Geneva" who most feared "the bogy of a Socialist president" (*42P* 26). It was "the businessmen" who recognized that "it was worth money to make the eagle scream" during the First World War— and who demanded the suppression of those who opposed a capitalist war

(*42P* 86). It was, after all, "the Morgan Loans" that needed to be "Safeguard[ed]" (*1919* 90). It was General Electric that regarded Steinmetz as "a piece of apparatus" and insisted that he must not tinker with "human relations that affect the stockholders' money and the directors' salaries" (*42P* 291–2). It was the railroad magnates who first learned to fear Debs and the Brotherhood of Locomotive Fireman, the mineowners who were first alarmed by Big Bill and the Western Federation of Miners. It was the "ten monopoly groups" who controlled all the timber of the Pacific Northwest who were most threatened by the Wobblies in Washington State. It was men from "the Chamber of Commerce" who led the lynch mob and "a Centralia businessman" who castrated Wesley Everest (*1919* 399–402).

Dos Passos here directs his anger, and the reader's, at the economic formations that had produced an inequitable, exploitative, and alienated social order—and that violently destroyed the democratic mass movement that emerged to challenge it. As my analysis of the Debs biography has indicated, Dos Passos also acknowledged and explored the anger that he felt toward the failings of American radicalism itself. But that self-criticism does not supplant or obscure Dos Passos's rage at the economic order that was ultimately responsible for the injuries suffered by Americans in the course of modernization and for the particular losses endured by the American Left during the Red Scare. Dos Passos succeeds, remarkably, in directing anger at an entire economic and social formation. For he is able to recognize that the losses of the Left had been caused by individuals (from Woodrow Wilson to the unnamed businessman with the razor) and by institutions (from the Chamber of Commerce and the American Legion to the *New Republic* and the Supreme Court); by an economic class and by the political system over which that class had gained control; by corporations like General Electric and the vast railroad conglomerates; and by an economic order that had shaped them all and that was constituted by them.

Because Dos Passos was able to identify the nature and objects of his anger in these prose poems, he was able also to mourn the losses of the Red Scare. Through that mourning, he identified in detail what he had lost in the suppressed formations of American radicalism—and he wove these stories of defeat and disappointment into an ongoing tradition of aspiration. He adopted a range of strategies, as I have suggested, to represent the persistence of that which had been lost: the marking of unmarked graves; the reanimation of lost comrades through narrative retellings; the reinvocation of words and ideas as resources for the present; the description of unfinished work as still available for extension. In some of the biographies, Dos Passos also emphasizes the ways in which these defeated men attempted to transmit their aspirations into the future. He mentions, for example, one of the most famous gestures in the history of the American Left—Joe Hill's "last word [...] to the workingstiffs of the I.W.W." before his execution: "'Don't mourn for me organize'" (*1919* 368). Dos Passos's prose poems honor and repeat Hill's intergenerational tradition-building gesture, although their own mode of procedure suggests a significantly revised version of Hill's epitaph: mourn for me, remember me, organize. While the Wobbly himself seems to have thought that time spent mourning was time lost from the movement, Dos Passos engaged in this modernist mourning as itself a means of organizing, a strategy to rebuild a movement that had suffered so many catastrophic losses.[27]

IV. "The Bitter Drink" of Stalinism and the Abandonment of the Radical Biographies

Although Dos Passos mourned the radicals suppressed during the Red Scare in the biographies distributed through the first two volumes of *U.S.A.*, he was unable to sustain that process of mourning, and the political hope that it expressed, in the trilogy's final volume. In the years during which he wrote *The Big Money*, his relationship to Left politics was transformed by the rise of Stalinism. In 1934, his growing ambivalence toward the Communist Party exploded into fierce and outright hostility. As I have shown, Dos Passos turned not only against the CP, as a particular, flawed incarnation of anticapitalist politics, but against the political ideals he had himself been struggling to sustain since the time of the Red Scare. The work of political mourning became far more difficult—indeed, for Dos Passos, it proved impossible. In grieving for the earlier crisis of the Red Scare, he had had to face ambivalence: he felt anger at the failings of that earlier generation of American radicals (and in particular, as we have seen, at their fear of their own egalitarian desires)—but the bulk of his anger was directed at the external forces that had destroyed the lyrical Left he loved. Now, as he struggled with great difficulty to write the last volume of *U.S.A.*, Dos Passos was filled with rage at the Left itself, whose leading institution seemed to him to be destroying all that he valued in the movement. Most importantly, he proved unable to name clearly the nature of that anger—and to distinguish between what he had long loved and what he now hated in American radicalism. The strategies that he had invented for mourning the Red Scare proved inadequate for meeting this second political and psychological crisis.

The Big Money contains only one biography of an American radical, the sketch of Thorstein Veblen, significantly entitled "The Bitter Drink." In this prose poem, Dos Passos struggled one last time to grieve the traditions of American radicalism suppressed during the Red Scare. But the author's ambivalences were now so explosive, and increasingly so mystified, that he could no longer perform the full work of mourning. Confronted with an anger he could not fully name, he began to displace his rage onto impulses within the Left that he had most admired and believed in. Grieving becomes transfixed, self-immolating. In "The Bitter Drink," mourning becomes melancholia.

The Veblen portrait attempts to follow the literary structure and psychological strategies of the earlier radical biographies. At the documentary level, it traces the rise and fall of one of Dos Passos's political heroes. The biography sketches Veblen's evolution from the son of a Norwegian immigrant farmer to the intellectual iconoclast and internationally recognized author of books such as *The Theory of the Leisure Class*, *The Theory of Business Enterprise* and *The Vested Interests and the Common Man*. There was no intellectual or theoretician of the Left who had influenced Dos Passos's own economic analysis more deeply. He celebrated Veblen as the person who had most clearly revealed the nature of modern America, "a society dominated by monopoly capital." Veblen had been able to map, to "establish" a "diagram," of a socioeconomic order characterized by "the sabotage of production by business, / the sabotage of life by blind need for money profits" (*TBM* 89). While describing Veblen's intellectual achievement, Dos Passos also traces his increasing isolation in an academic world permeated by anti-Red hysteria, which consigns him to ever-more obscure university posts, "all the good jobs kept for yesmen, never enough money, every broadening hope thwarted" (*TBM* 84). The personal disappointments of Veblen's career run parallel to his political disappointment: initially inspired (like Dos Passos himself) by "Debs's speeches, growing laborunions, the I.W.W. talk about industrial democracy" and hopeful that "the workingclass would take over the machine of production," Veblen is demoralized when "the monopolies cracked down" and "American democracy was crushed" (*TBM* 89). He ends his life, on Dos Passos's account, "lonely" and deprived of hope.

As in the earlier biographies, Dos Passos seeks to identify the libidinal sources of Veblen's radicalism. His lifelong identification "with the working-class instead of with the profittakers" (*TBM* 88) stems from a multigenerational family history of productive farmers being pushed off their land—first, in early-nineteenth-century Norway (as the "townsmen" learned to extract "profit" from the farmers), and then again in Veblen's own generation as his immigrant family was losing its hard-won foothold in America along with all the other "farmers of the Northwest [who] were starting their long losing fight against the parasite businessmen who were sucking them dry" (*TBM* 84, 87). As an intellectual, Veblen sustains this solidarity with the working class against those who exploit them and he condemns an economic system that values profit over all else. (Despite the economic and professional rewards he would reap, he refuses to "settle down to the business of the day, which was to buttress property and profits with anything usable in the debris of Christian ethics and eighteenthcentury economics" (*TBM* 86).) Veblen's radicalism, like that of Dos Passos's other militants, is animated by a solidaristic impulse, then, and also by a commitment to the unalienated creativity and sensuous gratification that were "sabotaged" in modern America by the "blind need for money profits" (*TBM* 89). Like so many of Dos Passos's radicals, Veblen's militancy is associated with a bohemian yearning for a liberated, sensuous life: with sexual vitality, in particular, and with creative receptivity to the world. When Veblen first marries, for example, "the young couple [. . .] did everything but earn a living. They read Latin and Greek and botanized in the woods and along the fences and in the roadside scrub. They boated on the river and Veblen started his translation of the *Laxdaelasaga*" (*TBM* 87). Resisting the imperative to "earn a living" (and to acquire the class status that his wife's family expects), the two indulge a wide range of intellectual and sensuous pleasures, exploring equally the world of ideas and of nature. Veblen joins the ranks of Dos Passos's other radicals who seem determined to realize what Marx liked to call "species being." As he works to name the social conditions that make productivity possible, his intellectual creativity dovetails with his continued physical invention (he writes "with a pen of his own designing"; he likes "carpentering" and makes bookshelves from "packingcases"). His political and intellectual radicalism is, moreover, associated throughout the biography with his sexual waywardness and attractiveness to women (when he gives lectures on economics, "the girls fell for him so") (*TBM* 85, 88–89). In Veblen, as in his predecessors, we see the same pattern of aspiration, in which the solidaristic impulse is fused to yearnings for self-expression and sensuous gratification.

Seeking to mourn Veblen's disappointed strivings as he had mourned those of his comrades in the earlier biographies, Dos Passos concludes "The Bitter Drink" with a familiar forward-looking gesture. While Veblen's demoralization at the end of his life has become so complete that he wishes to prevent any act of memorialization, Dos Passos insists on marking his life and death, his yearnings and disappointments—and on declaring the persistence of what Veblen sought to express. In the final lines of the last of the radical biographies, Dos Passos proclaims: "but his memorial remains / riveted into the language: the sharp clear prism of his mind" (*TBM* 91).

In all these ways, then, "The Bitter Drink" attempts to enact the strategies of mourning discovered and elaborated in the earlier radical biographies. But these strategies cannot run freely; they are blocked and tangled in a new way. In the first instance, they are obstructed because Dos Passos confuses and mystifies the causes of his subject's failure and disappointment. The prose poem's organizing metaphor, "the bitter drink," exemplifies the problem. The biography centrally compares Veblen to Socrates, who was condemned by his contemporaries to swallow poison in punishment for his persistent, critical questioning. At one level, the comparison provides a social account of Veblen's tragedy: like its ancient Athenian precursor, the American ruling class during the era of the Red Scare has destroyed its preeminent philosopher, its discomfiting truth teller. On this account, the tragedy of Veblen's life is a story about a man's destruction by the social order he has questioned. But as he elaborates the metaphor, Dos Passos also emphasizes that Socrates's death—and Veblen's failure—should be recognized as a kind of suicide, a self-destruction. Just as Socrates voluntarily "drank down the bitter drink one night when the first cock crowed," so too does Veblen deliberately destroy himself, though in a process that is more systematic and prolonged: "Veblen drank it in little sips through a long life" (*TBM* 84). The author not only metaphorically shifts responsibility for Veblen's political and personal loss onto the injured man himself, but also and more importantly, he naturalizes this suicidal behavior.

In one of the prose poem's recurring phrases, Dos Passos insists that Veblen "suffered from a constitutional inability to say yes" (*TBM* 84). His injuries and disappointments are the result of a mysterious temperamental incapacity for affirmation, an innate negativity.

Significantly, the corrosive negativity from which Veblen "suffers" is indistinguishable from his radicalism. It is precisely the uncompromising moral faculty that Dos Passos also admires in him and wishes to celebrate. In the earlier radical biographies, Dos Passos represents socialist and anarchist aspirations as animated by a libidinal openness to the world—and, as we have seen, he also describes Veblen's radicalism in this way at some moments in the prose poem. But in "The Bitter Drink," Dos Passos introduces a far darker intuition that arrests the work of political mourning: that Veblen's radicalism—and the larger movement for which he stands—is animated by a shutting out of the world. The opening lines of the prose poem, for example, introduce Veblen as "a grayfaced, shambling man lolling resentful at his desk with his cheek on his hand, in a low sarcastic mumble of intricate phrases subtly paying out the logical inescapable rope of matter-of-fact for a society to hang itself by" (*TBM* 83). Veblen's radical critique appears here, from the outset, as animated by a "resentful" temperament that expresses its aggression through a "sarcastic" invitation to society to destroy itself. Dos Passos did, truly, admire Veblen's sarcastic idiom (a critique he later describes as "etched in irony")—which resonated with the author's own inclination to satire, and with what Dos Passos saw as the Marxist project of "rigging the countinghouse's own logic to destroy the countinghouse" (*TBM* 89, 86). But in representing Veblen's anticapitalism as an expression of resentment and a wish for social self-destruction, Dos Passos has come a long way from his emphasis on Debs's socialist "love of mankind" or John Reed's communist "appetite for everything." Political radicalism appears here as an expression not of eros, but of the death drive. Dos Passos further elaborates this naturalized account of anticapitalism by suggesting that Veblen's radical resentment and hostility toward the American social order should be understood as an inborn trait inherited from his Norwegian forebears. These clannish and parochial Scandinavians, from their "narrow valleys" and "narrow farms," "had always been scornful of outlanders' ways," Dos Passos repeatedly explains: they are a people characterized by their "suspicion and stubborn dislike of townsmen's ways" (*TBM* 84–85). Veblen's anticapitalism appears, in this light, as an expression of a "stubborn" "suspicion" of the new, the urban, the modern; it wells up from the provincial's temperamental "scorn" for outsiders.

Dos Passos suggests, further, that because Veblen's radicalism emerges from this kind of resentment, from the "constitutional inability to say yes," it has an inherently self-defeating and self-destructive quality. In contrast to the men memorialized in *The 42nd Parallel* and *1919*, who were libidinally energized and enlivened by the practice of their revolutionary politics, Veblen appears from the outset of the biography to be rendered passive and sluggish by his "resentful" "lolling." As he "mumbles" his radical critique, vitality seems to drain away from the "grayfaced, shambling man" (*TBM* 83). Most importantly, the practice of radical politics never draws Veblen closer to others in a solidaristic community of love and shared aspiration—as was the case in the earlier biographies. Veblen's politics only isolates him. At the very height of his productivity and fame as an anticapitalist intellectual, Veblen already "lived like a hermit," a "bitter" man (*TBM* 88). Increasingly, "his friends found him harder than ever to talk to, harder than ever to interest in anything" (*TBM* 91). In "The Bitter Drink," Veblen's radicalism appears at times to be a self-imposed version of those "narrow farms" of his forebears, a self-created version of the solitary confinement to which the earlier radicals of *U.S.A.* had been doomed by external repression.

This dark vision of political radicalism as animated not by solidarity but by a self-isolating negativity is fused, in "The Bitter Drink," to a still deeper, more primary libidinal pessimism. Dos Passos represents Veblen's sexuality (which is associated with his radicalism) as fundamentally destructive—of Veblen himself and of the women in his life. His intellectual and political charisma draws women to him, and his sexual waywardness seems, at one level, to be an embrace of unalienated and gratifying libidinal possibilities. But Veblen's philandering destroys his idealized first marriage with Ellen Rolfe, whom he drives away with his infidelity. His second wife ends up in a sanitarium, "suffering from delusions of persecution" (*TBM* 88, 90). In this formulation, Dos Passos seems to glimpse momentarily a *social* cause for the destructiveness of Veblen's sexuality, implying an incipiently feminist analysis of male sexual privilege and its cost to women. But the author evades this social insight, by indulging in a Left misogyny that associates Veblen's second wife's "delusions of persecution" with the capitalist economy's tendency to take on "the systematized delusions of dementia praecox" (*TBM* 90–91).

This comparison implies that the injured wife's rage and sense of victimization, prompted by her husband's infidelity, resembles the capitalist system's irrational self-destructiveness. This misogynist formulation does not exonerate Veblen's behavior, but rather, serves to mystify what Dos Passos represents as an involuntary destructiveness in his sexual impulses. Veblen experiences his sexuality as a passive fatality, and his liaisons as something that merely happen to him. "He suffered from woman trouble," Dos Passos explains: "the girls fell for him so" (*TBM* 88). The biography records Veblen's comic, if hapless query, "What is one to do if the woman moves in on you?"—and his ironic observation that Stanford's "president doesn't approve of my domestic arrangements; nor do I" (*TBM* 88). Despite the humor of these remarks, Dos Passos represents Veblen's sexual desire, like his political yearnings, as catastrophically and inherently self-defeating: through each new act of sexual connection, Veblen destroys the bonds of love he has already formed and dooms himself to isolation.

The structure of naturalization that organizes "The Bitter Drink" is familiar: it is, indeed, the central move of melancholic modernism. It resembles, for example, the way in which Fitzgerald produces a subtle social account of Gatsby's tragedy as the outcome of a particular class and gender order, but then seeks to recast it as an illustration of the universal and transhistorical dynamics of "wonder." It resembles Eliot's indictment of a modernizing social order, which seeks simultaneously to insist that modern alienation is a timeless condition, the outcome of the existentially inevitable mixing of "memory and desire." For the first time in the radical biographies, Dos Passos seeks to explain the desperate disappointments of early-twentieth-century American radicals by joining the ranks of those who insist that the desire for social solidarity and libidinal connection leads ineluctably to its own failure, to alienation.

"The Bitter Drink" is thus a complex, psychically divided text, struggling to mourn the Red Scare in the manner of the earlier biographies, but plunging into the painfully conflicted dynamics of a social melancholia. As he composed the final volume of *U.S.A.*, Dos Passos's ongoing effort to grieve for the political repression of the teens and 1920s was complicated by a growing ambivalence about the anticapitalist Left. He was acutely concerned that the radical movement was destroying itself after 1934, and "The Bitter Drink" registers a conflict between the author's admiration of the movement and his intensifying anger. But the biography of Veblen does not concern itself with the real, destructive dynamics that Dos Passos discerned in Stalinism. The author was unable here, as later, to identify the specific causes of the movement's internal failings. Instead, he entertains in "The Bitter Drink"—as in his letters and nonfiction writings of the period—a nebulous, naturalized fantasy that a politics of solidarity (like sexuality) inevitably destroys itself. Because he displaces his anger and mystifies its actual objects through this gesture of naturalization, Dos Passos cannot pursue the work of mourning fully. He cannot extend persuasively into the future those things he cherishes in the disappointed radical. Although the prose poem ends with the familiar forward-looking gesture—"but his memorial remains / riveted into the language"—this act of transmission is unconvincing. Since Veblen's politics have brought him only isolation, since his radical questioning has been revealed to be "an incapacity to say yes," then this final memorialization must be a melancholic one. That which Dos Passos has loved and lost in Veblen has also been represented as inherently incapable of realization, and not merely denied fulfillment by historical contingencies. That which he admires, and for which he grieves, dooms itself to failure. Like the lost objects grieved by other melancholic modernists, Veblen's political yearnings become here a beautiful illusion, to be cherished despite its impossibility and self-destructiveness. The promise of a less alienated and more equitable society has come to resemble the green light at the end of Daisy's dock.

Although "The Bitter Drink" thus represents a more unconsciously conflicted, more obstructed, more melancholic work of grieving than the earlier radical biographies, the difference is not absolute. For the libidinal pessimism, the naturalizing impulse, present in the Veblen biography can be seen—as an occasional, peripheral tendency—as early as "Lover of Mankind." We should recall, for example, that in describing Debs's passion for fraternity, his "desire for his brothers to be free men," Dos Passos insists even in his most positive formulation that the "fire" of this vision "burned him up" (*42P* 26). From the very outset of *U.S.A.*—in the wake of all the losses endured by the Left during the Red Scare, and in the context of his own ambivalences about the Communist Party even in the late 1920s—Dos Passos struggled with the fear that the anticapitalist dream was, at its root, self-destructive. He feared that the "fire" of American radicalism always threatened to "burn up" its champions.

But when he wrote "Lover of Mankind" (and the other radical biographies in the trilogy's first two volumes), he believed that the movement could contain and transform the potentially destructive impulses that arose within it. By the mid-1930s, however, as he struggled to write the trilogy's last volume, his fear of American radicalism's self-destructiveness had become overwhelming. As his fear and anger crested, the tendency to mystify and naturalize that destructiveness increased. Dos Passos had relied on misogyny, from the outset, as a way of managing ambivalences toward the movement that were not fully conscious, as a way of displacing some of the anger he felt toward his male comrades. As the trilogy evolved, that tendency persisted—and, in some respects, increased. These peripheral impulses in the earlier biographies become more central in the last: a literary project that had been remarkably full in its mourning, now becomes quite significantly melancholic.

In this sense, "The Bitter Drink" differs from the earlier radical biographies as a matter of degree—and this should remind us that mourning and melancholia are not, in truth, binary opposites. They are divergent tendencies on a continuum of grieving. In any complex process of grieving—and most are complex—there can be movement across this continuum, as the bereaved struggle with the negativity that accompanies loss, as they acknowledge or disavow aggression to a greater or lesser extent. When the situation of grieving is dynamic, when the experience of loss is ongoing, and one's relation to the lost object undergoes dramatic change—as was the case in Dos Passos's experience of American radicalism—mourning may, indeed, become more (or less) melancholic. "The Bitter Drink" enacts such a change within the dynamics of one man's political grieving, as it shifted in the direction of intensifying melancholia.

Although it is important to acknowledge the continuities between mourning and melancholia, it is equally important to recognize their different implications. "The Bitter Drink" shares many features of the earlier radical biographies, but its rising melancholia expressed a profound psychic crisis in Dos Passos's life—and the end of a political hope. In this prose poem, he tried to grieve the losses inflicted by the Red Scare and, through that mourning, to extend anew the possibility of a socialist transformation of America. But in the writing itself, mourning grinds to a halt. Naturalizing the causes of a generation's political loss, Dos Passos replaces a concrete analysis of failures within the Left with a mystified libidinal pessimism. The bereaved author can no longer imagine a future for these thwarted political aspirations. "The Bitter Drink" is the only biography of an American radical in *U.S.A.*'s final volume. After this painfully conflicted effort, he abandoned the project of memorialization and Left tradition building altogether.

The absence of any other radical biographies leaves a striking void in *The Big Money*, just as the relinquishing of his own anticapitalist aspirations left a void in Dos Passos himself. The author attempted to fill the structural gap in the trilogy's final volume with the portraits of technocratic heroes—the Wright brothers and Frank Lloyd Wright, in particular—who provide at least some positive cultural counterweight to the negative portraits of profiteering industrialists, financiers, and media moguls like Ford, Insull, and Hearst. The inclusion of positively represented inventors had some precedent in the earlier volumes—as, for example, in the biography of Luther Burbank ("The Plant Wizard") in *The 42nd Parallel*—but Dos Passos attempts to make them bear a greater symbolic weight in *The Big Money*. His substitution replicates the fallback position that he attributes to Veblen in "The Bitter Drink." As Veblen's optimism about revolution wanes, he retains one final "hope": "that the engineers, the technicians, the non-profiteers whose hands were on the switchboard might take up the fight where the workingclass had failed" (*TBM* 90). This substitution proves inadequate for Veblen, who descends further into bitterness and disappointment—as, indeed, it proved inadequate for the author of *U.S.A.* Dos Passos can make the Wright brothers and Frank Lloyd Wright resemble the martyrs of the Red Scare only to a limited degree. He celebrates their visionary, world-transforming creativity, and he reveals that creativity to be ultimately constrained and manipulated by a business-dominated society that concerns itself with profit above all. But however much Dos Passos admired the great modern architect and the inventors of the airplane, they cannot provide an adequate substitute for the political revolutionaries whose loss he continued to grieve. They produce and invent in order to satisfy human needs rather than to increase profits, but even Frank Lloyd Wright (the "preacher, prophet, exhorter" of "clean construction [. . .] based on uses and needs") cannot imagine a revolution against a corrosive economic order. In celebrating these technological inventors, Dos

Passos continued to memorialize the persistent but imperiled capacity for human creativity, but he was no longer holding out to a new generation the promise of a more solidaristic society.

After completing *The Big Money*, Dos Passos revised some of the radical biographies that had appeared earlier in the trilogy before they were reprinted in a new edition of *The 42nd Parallel* and in subsequent editions of *U.S.A.* The revisions were relatively modest, but they suggest the complex psychic and political adjustments that the author struggled to make as his mourning for the Left gave way to melancholia.[28]

Dos Passos rewrote the final sentences of the biography of Big Bill Haywood, for example, in order to depict the USSR more negatively and to undercut any implication that Soviet Communism might provide a future for anticapitalist aspirations that had been crushed in the United States during the Red Scare. The original version of "Big Bill" describes Haywood's final persecution in the United States—the courts' refusal to retry him or to reconsider his twenty-year jail sentence—and ends with his flight to the Soviet Union as a place of sympathetic exile for a man whose political vision made him an enemy in his own country: "He was sick with diabetes, he had had a rough life, prison had broken down his health. Russia was a worker's republic; he went to Russia and was in Moscow a couple of years and died there and they burned his big broken hulk of a body and buried the ashes under the Kremlin wall."[29] Russia stands here as a place of retreat and respite for a man "broken" by political persecution in the United States. There seems to be little or no irony in Dos Passos's claim that the USSR was "a worker's republic"—the very thing he hoped the United States might one day become.[30] The final image of Haywood's ashes being buried "under the Kremlin wall" suggests, moreover, that at least in the Soviet Union, this champion of the American Left, this spokesman for "the wants of all the workers," has received a meaningful memorialization. While Haywood's acts and words remain either unremembered or vilified in America, the Soviet Union marks his grave, keeping alive the memory of his efforts and symbolically celebrating them as part of the foundation of a living and ongoing movement. His burial at the Kremlin, in other words, stands here as one of the forward-looking gestures offered by the radical biographies, an insistence that the Red Scare has not succeeded in entirely obliterating the libidinal impulses of American radicalism. This final image does, of course, contain ambivalence. There is a bitter poignance to the fact that Big Bill has been forced into exile, has died so far from home, and is honored only in a foreign land. The burning of "his big broken hulk of a body" completes the destruction of this political hero, and his burial "under" a "wall" marks the emphatic, tragic end of a thwarted life. Dos Passos thus figures the Communist state as a graveyard of American radicalism, in the full ambivalence of the trope: it is in some sense the telos of the Red Scare's destruction of the democratic Left—but it is also the repository that honors the past and gestures toward a future for that suppressed tradition.

In revision, Dos Passos heightened the negativity of this final image, undermining its potentially redemptive, forward-looking dimension. His altered and expanded version, which has been reprinted in all editions of *U.S.A.*, reads this way: "Russia was a workers' republic; he went to Russia and was in Moscow a couple of years but he wasn't happy there, that world was too strange for him. He died there and they burned his big broken hulk of a body and buried the ashes under the Kremlin wall" (*42P*, 87). By adding that Big Bill "wasn't happy there," Dos Passos suggests that Haywood himself did not perceive the Soviet Union as a satisfying embodiment of his lifelong radical aspirations. Nor, by implication, should we. This revision casts an ironic shadow on the initial claim that "Russia was a worker's republic." Given Haywood's own experience, this assertion now appears to be a false illusion, which we may have shared with Haywood, and which we should now relinquish. All of this, of course, alters the tenor of the final image as well, for now Big Bill's burial at the Kremlin no longer seems an appropriate memorialization. Rather, he appears to be buried, trapped in perpetuity, in a place that has made him unhappy: his corpse and his memory have been appropriated by a state "too strange" for him to call home, too alien to extend the impulses for which he lived and sacrificed. A fearful nativist sensibility replaces Dos Passos's more expansive and hopeful internationalism. Of course, the need to revise the "Big Bill" biography in this way clearly expresses the emergence of an anti-Communism so powerful that Dos Passos could not even allow his earlier work to stand. But what is crucial for my current purpose is the *psychological* meaning of this ideological revision. Dos Passos has reworked the conclusion of this biography in a way that fundamentally thwarts the final, forward-looking gesture of political mourning that had been so central to the radical biographies. He now insists that no meaningful memorial to Big Bill resonates in the present. Condemning the existing memorial as a perverse appropriation, Dos Passos himself can no longer imagine a gesture toward the future that might stand in its place.

The revisions to the Haywood biography thus starkly reveal the way in which Dos Passos's anger and grief over Stalinism caused him to foreclose the structure of mourning he had previously developed. Unable to visualize a future for the radical tradition, Dos Passos turned melancholically to the past in a new way. The revision of the biography of Robert La Follette indicates that the author sought now, in classically melancholic fashion, to transfer his love for an internationalist movement for social change to a nostalgic fantasy of a vanished and inaccessible American past.[31]

In the original version of "Fighting Bob," Dos Passos had included in the prose poem's final section two emphatic denunciations of the illusion of democracy in the United States. When La Follette opposed U.S. involvement in the First World War, the press and his colleagues in the Senate attacked him harshly and sought to silence him. Dos Passos insists that the jingoism and anti-Red hysteria organized against the radical senator marked a clear repudiation of democracy—and, more than this, the author questions whether democracy had ever been a reality in America at all: "With the death of the 65th Congress representative government died in this country, if it had ever been alive." A few lines later, Dos Passos moves from questioning the reality of "representative government" in the United States, to insisting emphatically that it had never been anything but an illusion. He describes La Follette as "an orator haranguing from the capitol of a lost republic that had never existed."[32] On this account, the radical senator speaks for a democratic possibility, for a true republicanism, that had "never existed" in the United States and that had been denied with special virulence during and after the First World War. These formulations reflected Dos Passos's chastened and mournful radicalism in the period before the crisis of Stalinism: they insist that America had never realized the democratic values upon which it purportedly rested, and that only a radical movement against its dominant economic arrangements would make the illusion of democracy a reality.

As Dos Passos turned away from the possibility of such a future realization, he sought to resuscitate the fantasy that America had, indeed, at one time fulfilled its democratic promise. From "Fighting Bob," he excised the claim that during the teens "representative government died in this country, if it had ever been alive"—and he eliminated the still more unequivocal assertion that the American republic "had never existed." Instead, Dos Passos resorts to the classically melancholic formulation that La Follette was "an orator haranguing from the capitol of a *lost republic*" (*42P* 325, emphasis added). In this version, reprinted in every edition of *U.S.A.*, Dos Passos insists that American democracy exists neither in the present or future, but in an irrevocable past. The "republic" that Dos Passos cherishes is beautiful and worthy, but "lost" to us all—not something that we might realize through an ongoing political movement. Clutching to a fantasy of past plenitude that he himself had long recognized as an illusion, Dos Passos has become—like F. Scott Fitzgerald's melancholic subject—fixated on an object of desire that is now "already behind him," as he himself is "borne back ceaselessly into the past" (*Gatsby* 189). The grieving but forward-looking internationalist has become a nostalgic American patriot.

There is a special poignance to the blocked mourning of "The Bitter Drink," to Dos Passos's abandonment of the radical biographies, and to his melancholic revision of the works of mourning he had accomplished a few years earlier. For the radical biographies constitute the one strand of *U.S.A.* in which Dos Passos successfully created a sustained psychological space in which the Red Scare could be mourned. In these biographies, he produced that "writing so fiery and accurate" for which he had called in 1927—a writing that could record the hard facts of repression and that could identify and extend the aspirations of a crushed American radicalism. From the very outset, there were other modes of *U.S.A.* in which Dos Passos grieved melancholically, venting his aggression at the failed movement itself and seeking to distance himself from the lyrical Left he had lost. The rise of a pronounced melancholic tendency in "The Bitter Drink" (and in the revisions of "Big Bill" and "Fighting Bob") does not, therefore, mark the emergence of something dramatically new in *U.S.A.*, but rather, the collapse of the one genre in which mourning had been sustained. There would only be one last, brief moment of mourning in the remainder of *U.S.A.* For the rest, a far more bitter, self-punishing, socially quiescent mode of political grieving would prevail.

SIX

Melancholic Modernism in *U.S.A.*

Naturalism and the "Torment Of Hope"

In the summer of 1926, a year before he began work on the *U.S.A.* trilogy, Dos Passos went to visit the convicted immigrant anarchists Nicola Sacco and Bartolomeo Vanzetti in prison. In his account of these meetings—one of his many contributions to the effort to save their lives—the young writer describes the witch hunt that had led the state to sentence these men to death, and he attempts to record the prisoners' experience of this political nightmare. In one of the article's most remarkable passages, Dos Passos tries to describe Sacco's state of mind as he waits to learn whether his final appeal will result in a reprieve or in his execution: "by this time the nagging torment of hope has almost stopped, not even the thought of his wife and children out there in the world, unreachable, can torture him now. He is numb now, can laugh and look quizzically at the ponderous machine that has caught and mangled him. Now it hardly matters to him if they do manage to pull him out from between the cogs."[1] However accurate this description may have been as an account of the doomed man's actual state of mind, these sentences articulate a particular strategy for managing traumatic personal and political loss—a strategy that Dos Passos clearly wanted to believe the young anarchist had successfully adopted in his moment of greatest vulnerability.

In this account, Dos Passos presents Sacco as the victim of a sustained social injury. Sacco's political persecution leads here, above all, to deprivation and isolation. He has already lost all that he loves: his "wife and children" are "unreachable," along with the rest of "the world" he has inhabited with them. But Sacco's loss is not merely punctual. Even in his deprivation, he must endure the knowledge that this loss may become permanent, beyond reclamation. He may lose his future altogether, his life. For Dos Passos, the "torture" of this situation lies in the fact that Sacco must contend with "the torment of hope"—with the possibility that he might actually escape death and retrieve some part of that which has been taken from him. As the novelist sought imaginatively to identify with the incarcerated anarchist, he found the prospect of sustained desire so tormenting that he wanted to believe that Sacco had found a way to cauterize it. He claims that Sacco has made himself "numb" to his deprivations and to any hope for the future. Dos Passos proposes, moreover, that this capacity to anesthetize himself accompanies a particular way of viewing the world. Perceiving the social forces that have "mangled" him as "a ponderous machine"—iron, inhuman, beyond his control—he can relinquish all hope and can cease to feel his pain. By adopting an ironic vision of destructive social formations as an inexorable machine, the victim can achieve emotional detachment: he can "laugh" at that which grinds him up and separates him from all he loves; he can feel that his own fate "hardly matters." By naturalizing the social causes of his loss, in other words, Sacco can free himself from "the torment of hope."

It is my contention that in the fictional narratives of *U.S.A.*, Dos Passos sought to manage his own complex, ongoing experience of political loss by enacting precisely this strategy, which he attributed in 1926 to the condemned anarchist. The twelve story lines of *U.S.A.* are naturalistic fictions that represent the destructive social formations produced by monopoly capitalism as a "ponderous machine," irresistible and catastrophic, in which millions of lives are being "mangled." I will focus my analysis, in particular, on the three narratives that follow the lives of fictional anticapitalist radicals: "Mac" in *The 42nd Parallel*, "Ben Compton" in *1919*, and "Mary French" in *The Big Money*. These narratives are neither more nor less naturalistic than the trilogy's other story lines, but they reveal most clearly the psychological and political effects of Dos Passos's deterministic fictions. In these stories, the author employed narrative strategies that naturalized the social forces that had produced the pervasive condition of alienation in American life, as well as the specific catastrophe of the Red Scare. Through these narratives, Dos Passos numbed himself to the political losses he had endured and invented an ironic technique for mocking the destruction of the political movement he had held so dear. In the radical story lines of *U.S.A.*, Dos Passos crushed his aspiration that the anticapitalist Left might flourish in the future. He wrote and grieved melancholically, in an effort to still "the torment of hope."

In this way, the fictional narratives of *U.S.A.* provide a remarkable psychological and political counterpoint to the biographical prose poems. In the fictions, Dos Passos naturalized what he historicized in the biographies. Here, he directed his anger misanthropically at the entire world—including the movement he had loved. He disavowed the grief enacted in the biographies, seeking to protect himself from the pain of his own disappointment. I turn now to an exploration of the melancholic mode of *U.S.A.*

I. Documentary Determinism: Radical Politics in the Fictional Story Lines of U.S.A.

In "Mac," "Ben Compton," and "Mary French," Dos Passos struggles with the history of political loss that he was simultaneously recording in the radical biographies. In these fictions, he represents once again the political formations he had admired in the early years of his radicalization, as well as those in which he actively participated in the late 1920s and 1930s. Mac stands as the fictional representative of the IWW—the movement that Dos Passos persistently viewed as the most promising incarnation of American anticapitalism. Ben Compton functions as a bridge figure: his political career spans the prewar IWW politics that Dos Passos nostalgically idealized, the wartime radicalism he saw suppressed during the Red Scare, and the Communist-front politics of the late 1920s and early 1930s in which Dos Passos himself actively participated. Ben is radicalized by anarchists, joins the IWW and receives his political baptism by fire in a particularly infamous instance of anti-Wobbly repression. By the end of his narrative, Ben has become an outspoken opponent of the First World War and a champion of the Russian Revolution.

Finally, in the "Mary French" narrative of *The Big Money*, Dos Passos represents the postwar political campaigns in which he himself invested so much energy and hope. In this last of the radical story lines, we enter the orbit of Communist-led politics in the 1920s and 1930s through Ben Compton, who reemerges as a Party member and labor organizer. We encounter it also through Mary herself, whose radicalism evolves from the genteel social reformism of Hull House through union militancy and finally into the committed political campaigning of a Communist-front organizer (albeit one who remains independent of the CP). For all the ways in which Ben and Mary differ from their creator, their campaigns are his campaigns. Through them, Dos Passos rehearses the major activist engagements of his own career on the Left: the 1926 Passaic textile strike, the Sacco and Vanzetti Defense Committee, the coal strike in Harlan County, Kentucky.[2] All of these were formative experiences for Dos Passos. Mac, Ben, and Mary are, thus, the imaginary bearers of Dos Passos's own political yearnings and experiences. They represent the political formations with which he most identified and for which he grieved throughout the trilogy.

In these fictions, Dos Passos seeks once again to record the libidinal roots of political radicalism—though his technique for doing so is strikingly different from the one he deployed in the biographical prose poems. Although the author systematically drains his fictional characters of consciousness and feeling, he nevertheless sketches with considerable acuity the structure of personal relationships that brings each into the movement. Here, as in the biographies, Dos Passos insists that political investments are personal responses to large-scale social phenomena. Political commitments reflect both the particular ways in which social formations scar the lives of individuals and the particular outlets that men and women can discover for expressing thwarted desires.

In his representations of Mac, Ben, and Mary, Dos Passos highlights two main sources for the emergence of revolutionary personalities. First, he emphasizes the ways in which the pressures of a capitalist economy tear families apart. In his masculinist idiom, Dos Passos emphasizes, in particular, that male and female children alike must live with an acute sense of their fathers' incapacity to live up to prescribed patriarchal roles. For all three of these characters, radical politics provides a means of understanding and systemically addressing deeply personal, familial injuries—including those produced by paternal vulnerability. Second, each of these characters seeks to find within the radical movement itself forms of solidarity that are denied within the larger society. Each yearns for intimate affective and sexual connection as well as for larger, collective expressions of comradeship. These two libidinal strands—the healing of familial wounds and the realization of solidaristic desires—are persistent in the lives of all Dos Passos's radical characters, though they are interwoven in various ways that reflect their particular gender and class positions.

In the first of these narratives, for example, Mac's father, crippled on the job, loses his meager employment as a watchman in the course of a strike and can neither provide for his family nor protect his wife from the overwork that contributes to her premature death. Unable to meet the expense of her medical bills and funeral, he sneaks out of town with Mac and his sister, feeling "like a whipped cur."[3] Mac's maternal uncle Tim, a socialist, explains to them all that they are not responsible for the loss and shame they must endure and that their anger should be directed instead at "the system" (*42P* 13). As Mac grows into adolescence in uncle Tim's household, he holds with increasing tenacity to a socialist politics that provides him with an account of working people's suffering that does not blame the victims and with some means of imagining a transformed future. This attachment to an anticapitalist politics is then solidified by the charged homosocial bonds that Mac forges with a series of male comrades. Although economic pressures tear apart all of Mac's families (those in which he is a child, spouse, and father), the movement promises—and fleetingly provides—experiences of connection. These affective experiences are powerful enough to cause Mac to struggle throughout his narrative (with varying degrees of success) against the pressures of consumerism and the lure of class mobility, in the name of working-class solidarity and revolutionary politics. As he explains to his wife and brother-in-law, he wants to follow Debs's advice to "rise with the ranks, not from the ranks" (*42P* 108).

In "Ben Compton," Dos Passos elaborates a similar portrait of the radical as a young man. The son of working-class Jewish immigrants, Ben undergoes a less extreme but nevertheless decisive experience of familial vulnerability and paternal inadequacy. A skilled worker, Ben's father succeeds in paying the mortgage on a modest house for decades, but then loses everything when he cannot continue to make his payments: "he was a failure: thirty years he had worked in America and now he was a sick old man all used up and couldn't provide for his children" (*1919* 371). Ben initially responds to the specter of his father's failure in normative fashion, planning to redeem his family's loss through his own upward mobility. In Ben's case, the embrace of radical politics does not precede the experience of male homosocial comradeship, but is effected through it. When he meets the handsome proletarian anarchist, Nick Gigli, Ben is drawn simultaneously into a charged personal relationship and into a political vision of solidarity that provides him with an alternate way of understanding, and redressing, the vulnerabilities of his family life. Ben's commitment to the revolutionary Left is sorely tested by political repression and by the temptations of class mobility that his education makes possible. But his libidinal attachments are sufficiently deep for him to sustain (with more constancy than Mac) his commitment to the movement, for which he makes enormous personal sacrifices.

In "Mary French," Dos Passos finally provides the portrait of a *female* radical, something that is notably absent from the biographical prose poems. The author imagines Mary's radicalism as libidinally rooted in a politically inflected oedipal drama. Mary's sensitive and affectionate father devotes his energies as a doctor to serving the poor—and he is derided by Mary's socially ambitious and materialistic mother, who views him with contempt and anger for his failure to provide. Mary loves and identifies with her father, and she wishes to become the socially and personally compassionate woman her mother is not. Dos Passos suggests that Mary's subsequent political radicalism stems both from her identification with her father's solidaristic social vision and from her desire for the affective connection that her mother denies her. Mary wishes, in short, both to *be* (like) her father and to become the woman who could fully love and be loved by (a man like) him. Despite their relative class privilege, Mary's family is represented as another casualty of the economic order: her mother's class ambition corrodes her marriage; her father's worthy commitment to the poor brands him as an inadequate husband, and leads ultimately to his death from overwork. Mary's middle-class radicalism is thus both an attempt to keep faith with her father's sense of social responsibility and also an effort to find a less alienated way of living than her parents'. She sometimes describes this (as the adolescent Dos Passos had in his letters and diaries) as a search for something more "real" than the sheltered but deadened world of bourgeois privilege—which is embodied for Mary in her mother's socialite existence and in her own experience as a Vassar student. The radical movement provides her with the promise of this more "real" existence—and Mary is drawn from social reformism into labor militancy both by her ideals and by the intense personal bonds she forms with male radicals. Significantly, Dos Passos cannot imagine Mary forming powerful bonds to other female radicals. All of her experiences of libidinal connection within the movement are to men—and the pattern of sublimated male homosocial connection that shapes Mac's and Ben Compton's narratives are echoed with a difference in Mary's heterosexual relationships with male comrades. Despite these important variations in gender and class configuration, Mary shares with Mac and Ben a set of libidinal investments that enable her to sustain her political commitments in the face of considerable material and personal hardship.

In these three stories, then, Dos Passos represents the radical political formations that he most admired and identified with—and he schematically but revealingly explores the libidinal roots of rank-and-file activists' commitments. As a result, the crushing of these political formations—and of the characters themselves—takes on a pathos in some ways reminiscent of the radical biographies. In these fictions, the political movement destroyed by the Red Scare is given once more a human face. Political repression appears, once again, as the violent thwarting of primary libidinal impulses shared by many particular individuals. It is the longing for social solidarity and for charged personal connection that has been denied; it is the search for an alternative to economic exploitation and alienation that has been crushed. Like the biographical prose poems, these are narratives of loss. They tell the story of a vast collective injury that was experienced by hundreds of thousands of Americans as an intimate personal desolation.

It is significant, then, that Dos Passos tells this story of defeat in a way that deadens the feeling of loss—in his characters, in his own narration, in his readers. He achieves this anesthetization, perhaps most obviously, through a particular kind of deterministic plotting. He represents the destruction of the American Left just as he imagined Sacco would have figured his own destruction: as the mechanical, irresistible effect of "a ponderous machine."

Dos Passos's story lines are prolifically plotted, presenting the reader with a dazzling stream of incident and event. In "Mac," "Ben Compton," and "Mary French," the plots involve a remarkable array of political acts and conflicts. In no other work of American literature does one encounter such a panoply of strikes, demonstrations, protests, and struggles. Anarchists, syndicalists, socialists, communists, right-wing labor bureaucrats, and revolutionary union militants write, speak, address demonstrations, challenge the bosses, strike for better conditions, chain themselves to lampposts in free-speech fights, organize rallies, devote themselves to struggle individually and en masse. But all of these plots, all of these individual resolutions and collective actions, end the same way. All are doomed to failure.

Political defeat is uniform, continuous, unremitting in *U.S.A.*'s story lines. Every effort made by these fictional radicals leads to the telos of disappointment. No strike is ever won and no protest succeeds in any way. The employers—assisted by the police, the army, and the courts—invariably crush the unions, jail the demonstrators, silence the dissenters. Mac and Ben each participate in unsuccessful IWW-led strikes and free-speech fights. Ben is brutally beaten by anti-Wobbly vigilantes, is later jailed for speaking in support of the Russian Revolution, and still later organizes a series of failed miners' and textile workers' strikes before finally being purged from the Communist Party. Mary works selflessly for strikes in Pennsylvania and New Jersey, all of which fail, and she throws herself feverishly into the futile campaign to save Sacco and Vanzetti. Dos Passos represents political defeat exclusively and with a numbing repetitiveness. Political failure is a structural principle of this storytelling, a compositional axiom. The fictional narratives refuse, for example, the two-part structure of the biographies, which record success before suppression, and which mourn fully by weighing accomplishment in order to measure loss. In contrast, the fictions insist on losses that precede and preempt accomplishment.

Because every political effort ends in failure, the reader of Dos Passos's story lines is trained in a certain expectation. By the time we have reached the "Ben Compton" narrative, as soon as the author introduces any radical initiative into the plot, we know what its outcome will be. Although these are stories of political struggle, we can hardly doubt their denouements. Dos Passos eliminates nearly all sense of contingency: these narratives enact myriad particular conflicts, and a wider political and class struggle that contains them all, but the outcomes small and large appear determined in advance.

This kind of deterministic plotting is, of course, one of the defining features of the naturalist literary tradition. Realist writing—of which naturalism is a distinct variant—concerns itself most centrally with the phenomena of social determination: the characters in realist works wrestle, individually and sometimes collectively, with the social and economic forces shaping their lives. Naturalism is that strand of the realist tradition in which writers represent historically particular (and thus limited and contingent) forms of social determination as if they were absolute. Naturalist fictions represent individual agency as insignificant. Although their protagonists make choices and take actions, these only drive them further into the destructive social mechanisms that constrain and mangle their lives. This is true of the major European naturalists, from Zola to Hardy—as it is of their American contemporaries and followers, from Crane and Norris onward. Both in Europe and the United States, naturalist fiction concerns itself with many forms of social determination, but the pressures exerted by industrial capitalism and its accompanying gender and racial orders are the tradition's abiding preoccupation. Stephen Crane's *Maggie: A Girl of the Streets*, for example, launches its heroine into a world of modern urban poverty and misogyny— and Maggie's efforts to liberate herself serve only to ensure her degradation and destruction. The more of the novel we read, the more certain we are of the inexorability of her fate. The same is true of the characters of Norris's *McTeague*, who will be ineluctably destroyed by greed (in its economic and sexual variants)—as the protagonists of *The Octopus* will be crushed by the economic might of the railroads. Once Hurstwood begins his decline into poverty in Dreiser's *Sister Carrie*, we cannot doubt where he will end.

In the fictions of *U.S.A.*, Dos Passos works assiduously and self-consciously in this idiom. Like his naturalist precursors, Dos Passos sets the protagonists of the radical story lines in a fictional environment in which every effort to challenge American capitalism fails with the same certainty. The multiplicity of Dos Passos's radical plots—one of his distinctive contributions to the naturalist tradition—serve to convince us that not merely one type of radical activity or another, one political ideology or organizational strategy, will fail, but that all are equally doomed. The educated and the uneducated, the cynical and the sincere, the revolutionary and the reformist, all are slated for disappointment and defeat. Halfway through the trilogy, we are as convinced of their demise as we are when we read of Maggie, McTeague, or Hurstwood.

Because political defeat is universal in *U.S.A.*, the crushing of anticapitalist initiatives ceases to feel like a contingent historical phenomenon. This may seem a peculiar claim since Dos Passos's fiction appears to be so distinctively—and so radically—"historical." Most of the setbacks that his anticapitalist characters endure are, after all, actual historical events: IWW strikes and free-speech campaigns were indeed crushed in the teens in Nevada, Washington, and California; Wobblies were beaten and murdered during the Everett massacre; thousands of American radicals were imprisoned, like Ben Compton, for speaking against the First World War and in support of the Bolshevik revolution; the strikes at the Pittsburgh steel plants and the Passaic textile mills are matters of the historical record, as are the violence and political cynicism with which they were broken; Sacco and Vanzetti died in the electric chair. These are facts. Indeed, as Barbara Foley has observed, *U.S.A.* marks an important stage in the evolution of the historical novel precisely to the degree that this "documentary" fiction is structured by "externally verifiable historical events" to which his fictional characters are "subordinated."[4] But it is equally true that Dos Passos subordinates these historical events to a strict narrative determinism. Because of their selectivity, these fictions exaggerate the real and formidable forms of social determination constituted by the Red Scare, representing them as absolute and irresistible. Dos Passos practices here, in short, a documentary determinism.

This fusion of documentary history with a pure narrative determinism marks a distinctive contribution to the evolving tradition of American literary naturalism. From the very outset, naturalist writers in the United States had been drawn to documentary effects. Norris, for example, provides a good deal of documentary detail in describing the late-nineteenth-century San Francisco scene in which McTeague and Trina enact their destructive drama. Dreiser similarly seeks to record with factual accuracy many aspects of the Chicago and New York social milieux in which the fictional characters of *Sister Carrie* function. Dos Passos's narrative practice differs from earlier naturalist representations, in part, in the sheer scale of documentary material that he subsumes within a strict determinism. More importantly, his focus is different. Earlier writers such as Crane, Norris, and Dreiser drew on documentary effects principally to describe with a heightened verisimilitude the social formations crushing the lives of their protagonists. In the radical story lines of *U.S.A.*, Dos Passos documents not merely the destructive social formations accompanying monopoly capitalism, but also the largest social movement of his time—a vast collective effort of resistance. Although Hurstwood, for example, participates in the Brooklyn streetcar strike of 1895, Dreiser does not seek to convince his reader that Hurstwood's experience of the strike embodies the truth of the American labor movement. Dos Passos aims for precisely such an effect. The multiplicity and pessimistic repetitiveness of the radical plots, and the weight of documentary material they contain, mark an effort to narrate not merely a story of individual failure but the history of the entire American Left as a tale of irresistible destruction.

The strict determinism of these narratives has the further effect of emptying the characters' political struggles and aspirations of meaning. To the degree that Dos Passos makes political failure inevitable, his protagonists can learn nothing from their setbacks. Any character's adaptation or improvisation, any change in course, simply yields another proof of futility. Mary French, for example, evolves from genteel social reformer to revolutionary socialist—but her growing radicalism does not alter her effectiveness in any way. It merely marks another path to failure. Indeed, there are only two possible plot trajectories for these fictional radicals and they are, in their different ways, equally grim. Either they abandon their political principles in order to survive or they are destroyed by the system they oppose. Mac follows the first of these paths, gradually relinquishing his commitment to building "the workers' cooperative commonwealth" in order to achieve a comfortable petit-bourgeois place within the system. In contrast, Ben and Mary refuse to compromise their principles, and they are gradually destroyed by their resistance to the inevitable. Refusing to bestow upon them the potential glamour of violent death, and the eschatology of martyrdom this might entail, Dos Passos represents them as merely ground down and worn out. Their passion is used up, their energy depleted. As in many naturalist fictions, the narrative of their defeat is, in essence, one of exhaustion. (In this regard, these characters resonate, for example, with Hurstwood in Dreiser's *Sister Carrie*, or Lily Bart in Wharton's *House of Mirth*, or Edna in Chopin's *The Awakening*—though Dos Passos has deprived these exhausted protagonists of even the pathos and final self-determination of suicide.) As the trilogy ends, Ben and Mary continue in the path of futile commitment: Ben is seeking a job doing "reliefwork" despite having been purged from the Communist Party, while Mary continues to sacrifice herself to the doomed cause of the Pennsylvania miners. What lies ahead is only the further waning of energy, rising desperation, and increasing isolation. Because their failure is certain, they are not tragic, but pathetic in their dogged self-destruction.[5] Inevitability breeds banality. In this way, the strategies invented by Dos Passos to give potential future significance to a suppressed radical movement in the biographical prose poems are undone by the strict determinism of the fictions. Where failure has become an axiomatic certainty, the effort to mourn and to hope can only appear as a stubborn, masochistic illusion.

This cultivation of hopelessness is, indeed, one of the principal psychic and expressive effects of Dos Passos's deterministic narratives. In "Mac," "Ben Compton," and "Mary French," the despairing radical novelist returns to the scenes of his own political activism and aspiration in order to tell them as stories of inevitable defeat. He reviews all the political formations of the Left he admired, all the strategies and practical efforts he had joined, all the ideals he had shared, in order to convince himself and his readers that the project of resisting monopoly capitalism was doomed—not contingently, but absolutely—to failure. He resembles the political prisoner sentenced to death who returns obsessively to all the conceivable strategies of escape and appeal in order to convince himself that there is, indeed, no liberation possible. In this way, he struggles to accommodate himself to his terrible fate. The sheer multiplicity of the radical plots, with their monotonously repetitive failures, are a testament to the psychic difficulty of such an enterprise. This is not the work of mourning, which finds new release and new objects for disappointed yearnings. It is, rather, a melancholic storytelling that seeks to kill a desire that perpetually reasserts itself. It is a storytelling that seeks to convince the grieving mind, through repetition, that desire will meet only disappointment and should cease.[6]

II. From Determinism to Misanthropy: Self-Expression as Self-Alienation

Dos Passos's fictions are misanthropic as well as deterministic. In this misanthropy, the author follows one of the main lines of American naturalism—a line that marks an important adaptation of the European tradition. European naturalists such as Zola and Hardy represent the systematic ways in which individual lives are crushed by the destructive forces of modernity. In *Jude the Obscure* (1895), for example, Hardy's protagonists are desperately undone by the workings of the English class system and its gender mores, which thwart Jude and Sue's strenuous efforts at upward mobility and personal liberation. Similarly, Etienne Lantier and the impoverished miners of northern France cannot—despite their ingenuity, solidarity, and sacrifice—successfully overcome the power of the exploitative mine owners in Zola's *Germinale* (1885). The forces of social determination are as powerful, as nearly absolute, in Hardy and Zola as they are in Dos Passos's fictional narratives. But in the European tradition, even the harshest recognition of social determination rarely leads to a novelistic repudiation of human beings' capacity for love, self-reflection, and higher aspiration. Zola and Hardy are centrally concerned to represent the yearnings and abilities that a brutal social order prevents from flourishing. The pathos of their novels derives precisely from the collision between the richly explored aspirations of Jude and Etienne and the forms of social organization that deny them.

In contrast, the dominant strand of U.S. naturalism, represented by such canonized figures as Crane and Norris, insists not merely on a strict social determinism, but on a reductive representation of modernity's victims. It is not simply that destructive social formations inhibit the growth of emotional and intellectual capacities: these American novels tend to deny the existence of those capacities altogether. In *Maggie*, for example, Crane not only represents the material inescapability of urban poverty: he depicts the poor as driven by timeless brutal instincts, as incapable of imagining for themselves anything beyond the violence of their surroundings and the empty platitudes of their culture. In *McTeague*, Norris criticizes a social order structured by avarice, but his account slides into a misanthropic representation of human beings as *innately* greedy, driven by *instincts* of brutal possessiveness, and naturally incapable of affective sexuality or moral reflection. In this dominant version of U.S. naturalism, in other words, the most destructive features of modernization are represented not merely as having *effects* on the modern subject, but as stemming from the timeless brutal impulses and inabilities of those subjects. This slide from determinism to misanthropy characterizes only *one* strand of the U.S. tradition, although it is the strand most firmly canonized. The versions of naturalism produced by writers from subordinated positions in the social hierarchy—works like Chesnutt's *The Marrow of Tradition*, Chopin's *The Awakening* and, later, Richard Wright's *Uncle Tom's Children*—are far closer to the European tradition in offering explorations of harsh social determination that nevertheless eschew misanthropy. But it is the naturalism of the Crane and Norris tradition that Dos Passos extends in the fictional story lines of *U.S.A.*

Finally, it is Dos Passos's misanthropy that enables him to complete the naturalization of the American Left's defeat. In the fictional narratives, he seeks to convince us that the anticapitalist movement was doomed to failure not simply because of an imbalance of power (which might, conceivably, change), but because human beings are *inherently* incapable of realizing the libidinal impulses that American radicalism sought to fulfill. In particular, the men and women who populate the fictional world of *U.S.A.* are unable to express (or to understand) their own aspirations in any meaningful way—and, perhaps most pessimistically of all, they are uniformly incapable of sustaining libidinal connections. If socialism, for Dos Passos, was a politics of liberated expressivity—and, in the deepest sense, a politics of love—there could be no fuller or more fundamental repudiation of his radical aspirations than the linguistic and affective misanthropy of his fiction.

Although Dos Passos thus extends the misanthropic impulse in U.S. naturalism, the formal techniques of his negation differ from those of his literary precursors. American naturalists of the late nineteenth and early twentieth centuries rely mainly on figurative and expository practices in order to produce naturalizing effects. Crane and Norris, for example, persistently compare the stupid brutality and violence of their characters to that of animals. They further reinforce the ahistorical (or transhistorical) character of these behaviors through editorial interventions proclaiming, for instance, that schoolboys fight "in the modes of four thousand years ago" or that a nineteenth-century sexual assault is the welling up of "hereditary evil" which passes through "an entire race," stretching back to the "fourth and five hundredth generation."[7] Dreiser draws less frequently on systematic animal and natural metaphors to describe the destructive behaviors of his characters, but he retains and elaborates the expository practices of naturalization. (When Dreiser editorially explains to us in *Sister Carrie*, for example, that modern celebrity acts like opium on the unprepared consciousness, or that fortunes wax and wane like bodily powers, he makes sociological phenomena appear to follow biological dynamics.)[8] Melancholic modernists continue to draw heavily on both the figurative and expository practices of the nineteenth-century naturalists. When Hemingway develops at length the comparison between the behavior of the bulls and of his human protagonists in *The Sun Also Rises*, he draws on the figurative naturalizing idiom of Crane and Norris. When Fitzgerald expositorily revises the tragedy of Gatsby as an illustration of the inevitable tendencies of human "wonder," he takes a page from Dreiser's book. In the fictional narratives of *U.S.A.*, Dos Passos is equally committed to representing social destructiveness as an expression of an ineluctable human nature—but he does not rely on these figurative or expository techniques. Rather, as we shall see, he achieves a similar end through the systematic reductiveness of his characterizations. By representing a remarkable array of characters—varied in class and subculture, in gender and ethnicity, in educational attainment and moral sincerity—as invariably subject to the same set of cognitive and affective incapacities, Dos Passos seeks to convince us that the lyrical visions of the American Left were doomed to failure not merely by a contingent balance of power, but by the very stuff of our shared humanity.

At the broadest and most fundamental level, Dos Passos famously drains his fictional characters of subjectivity. His protagonists act; they are often acutely alive to sensory experience; they have fragmentary thoughts; but they cannot meaningfully reflect on what they do or on what happens to them. They form and end relationships, change jobs, move from place to place, participate in political activity—and they endure all manner of loss. But they can hardly be said to register their experiences, emotionally or intellectually. Although Dos Passos writes melancholically, his characters are not dimensioned enough to grieve at all—even to be melancholics. Here, for example, is Dos Passos' representation of the death of Mac's father: "Pop puttered round on his crutch for several years, always looking for a job. Evenings he smoked his pipe and cursed his luck on the back stoop of Uncle Tim's house and occasionally threatened to go back to Middletown. Then one day he got pneumonia and died quietly at the Sacred Heart Hospital. It was about the same time that Uncle Tim bought a linotype machine" (*42P* 16). This account is then followed by a paragraph about the linotype machine, and Dos Passos never again alludes to Mac's loss of his father. The death is recorded as a piece of data, given roughly the same attention as the fact that Mac's father smokes a pipe. And so it goes in Dos Passos's fictional narratives: abortions, failed marriages, lost friendships, crushed political campaigns take place and pass away without emotional response or substantive reflection. This is, as Alfred Kazin memorably put it, "a machine prose for a machine world": characters are carried along by Dos Passos's sentences, like unsentient commodities upon a conveyor belt, stamped by one event and then another and another, but registering virtually nothing.[9]

This elision of subjectivity in the fiction is a controlled and intentional effect, which Dos Passos insisted was the very heart of his representational method. When Edmund Wilson objected to this "straight naturalistic" representation of characters without consciousness, Dos Passos demanded that Wilson at the very least acknowledge that he was developing a consistent and coherent literary technique. The author called it a "behavioristic method" designed to "generat[e] the insides of the characters by external description."[10] There may be some truth to this claim—which resembles Hemingway's account of his own style of "omission" and Cather's rationale for "the novel démeublé"—but there is also a strong element of disavowal (or at least misdescription) in Dos Passos's contention. For as one reads the fictional component of *U.S.A.*, one does not feel the omitted intellectual or emotional "insides" of these characters: these are simply characters who appear to have no "insides." This is a fictive world populated by human beings who lack even rudimentary forms of consciousness.

It would be wrong, however, to suggest that the impoverishment of subjectivity is produced in *U.S.A.*'s story lines solely by narrative omissions. Dos Passos also employs a more active—indeed aggressive—representational strategy to insist upon his characters' inability to relate meaningfully to their own experience. Everyone in the fictional story lines speaks and thinks in clichés. The educated and the uneducated alike, the rich and the poor, the sincere and the hypocritical: they all use language in ways that trivialize their feelings and ideas. Nearly every effort to communicate empties experience of its meaning. Language is an entirely reified medium in this fictional world, at once rigid and reductive. As a result, acts of self-expression or reflection are acts of self-alienation. And because they cannot control or adapt the language through which they express themselves, these characters cannot communicate meaningfully about anything—including, of course, their political aspirations.

At least in part, Dos Passos was representing what he believed to be a real crisis of language that had emerged in early-twentieth-century American life. He wrote persistently, and with considerable astuteness, about this crisis in his published journalism, in his letters, and in other portions of the trilogy. In the story lines of *U.S.A.*, he naturalizes and mystifies a social phenomenon whose historical causes he elsewhere recorded.

Dos Passos recognized that the burgeoning mass media (radio, newsreels, and the increasingly centralized popular print media) had an unparalleled capacity to manipulate the social consciousness of millions of Americans. When Sacco and Vanzetti were executed, for example, he was painfully aware that this ominous political event could be almost instantaneously trivialized and erased from popular memory by the press. He pointed out, in this context, that: "One of the most extraordinary things about industrial society of the present day is its idiot lack of memory. Tabloids and movies take the place of mental processes, and revolts, crimes, despairs pass off in a dribble of vague words and rubber stamp phrases without leaving a scratch on the mind."[11] Dos Passos here deftly indicates the way in which the emergent media ("tabloids and movies") of a particular historical moment (the "industrial society of the present day") *caused* a particular loss of "memory" in individual subjects. And the writer emphasizes the distinctive role of language in this process: it is the "vague words and rubber stamp phrases" of the new media that simultaneously drain off the affect of outrage and despair in the populace, even as they reduce important events to numbing clichés that cannot be meaningfully retained. Throughout his journalism of this period, Dos Passos emphasized that this was not a mysterious formal characteristic of the media themselves, but an expression of the political and economic interests that they served. Language was as brazenly manipulated in the Hearst press as images were by William Hayes—head of the film industry's infamous Hays Office—who cynically ordered "all news films" dealing with the Sacco and Vanzetti executions to be "taken from the vaults and burned" (*MNP* 99).[12]

While he was particularly concerned with the ways in which the media manipulated and trivialized language, Dos Passos also recognized similarly destructive practices on the part of intellectual and cultural elites seeking to protect their class privilege. In the autobiographical Camera Eye segments appearing at the end of *U.S.A.*, for example, the author famously lamented the ways in which the "old words" of the nation's founders (those mythic "haters of oppression") had been "ruined" and "worn slimy in the mouths of lawyers districtattorneys collegepresidents judges," "politicians and news-papereditors."[13] In his political writings, Dos Passos emphasized that such elites had cynically manipulated political language in fueling the fires of the Red Scare. He condemned, for example, the President of Harvard and oth-ers who had officially urged the Governor of Massachusetts to allow the executions of Sacco and Vanzetti to proceed, charging them with a willfully misleading and incendiary abuse of political language. He deplored Presi-dent Lowell's "loose use of the words 'socialistic' and 'communistic'" in such an explosive political context, contending that it would have been "franker" for these Boston Brahmins "to admit that as anarchists and agitators you hate these men and disapprove of their ideas."[14] As a result of such partisan manipulation of language, important political phenomena were reduced to words that had been made meaningless.

Dos Passos perceived a related kind of linguistic rigidity within Communist-front campaigns of the early 1930s—and he insisted upon the damaging po-litical consequences of this form of rhetorical ossification. As early as January 1931, Dos Passos was complaining to Edmund Wilson that the "antihokum phrases" of the Left seemed "about as poisonous as the hokum phrases" of the establishment Right. He went on to insist that "this question of lan-guage is pretty important," since as long as publications like the *Daily Worker* sounded like "clippings from Bukharin's scrapbasket," people on the Left would never be able "to organize mentally what is really happening now."[15] Over the next few years, he persistently expressed his impatience with Left rhetoric that seemed so petrified that it couldn't possibly "influence other people" and with the "communist veneer of phrases" and "mindclosing la-bels" that could only corrupt the "high standards of accuracy" that would enable writers to describe "reality."[16]

Clearly, Dos Passos believed that the reification of language was a wide-spread phenomenon of his time—one that operated across the political spec-trum, influencing the educated elite as well as the mass-culture-consuming public. But in his nonfiction writing (and in some portions of the trilogy), Dos Passos emphasized the historically contingent character of this syn-drome. He analyzed the particular class interests that motivated the abuse of language in the case of the mass media and Red-baiting elites, and he identi-fied the particular political strategies and formations that had produced such practices within the Left.

In a more positive spirit, Dos Passos insisted that trivializing language could be refused, that the "idiot lack of memory" could be overcome. At the very height of his outrage about the media's manipulative reporting of the Sacco and Vanzetti executions, he still proclaimed the possibility of "writing so fiery and accurate" that it would "sear through the pall of numb imbecility"—and he produced such writing in the biographies of *U.S.A.* Throughout the 1930s, he affirmed the special role of professional writers in this rhetorical struggle. In his contribution to the radical American Writers' Congress in 1935, for example, he expressed his continued faith in the writer's capacity, and responsibility, to go on trying "to discover the deep currents of historical change under the surface of opinions, orthodoxies, heresies, gossip and the journalistic garbage of the day." He acknowledged that words like "liberty, fraternity and humanity" had become "old and dusty and hung with the dirty bunting of a thousand crooked orations," but he went on to assert that "underneath they are all still sound. What men once meant by these words needs defenders today." Two years later, in the preface to a 1937 edition of *The 42nd Parallel*, the author similarly praised the persistent determination of writers "to test continually slogans, creeds and commonplaces in the light of freshly felt experience."[17] As an activist as well as a writer, Dos Passos invited his comrades on the Left to join him in this project of linguistic renewal, which he saw as a condition for political change. He struggled actively to liberate radical ideas and aspiration from their hackneyed expression in an inert and alienating jargon. He called for (and tried to formulate) "a more native lingo" that would speak to American conditions and sensibilities.[18]

Throughout the period of *U.S.A.*'s composition, then, Dos Passos *mourned* the social consequences of linguistic reification. Identifying the systemic causes of this abuse and expressing his anger accordingly, he was able to affirm his faith in the possibility of meaningful expression. But this work of social mourning was difficult and conflicted. Even in his political writing and his letters, one can hear the occasional tendency to displace his anger, to blame those who had been most victimized, to condemn the Left as a whole, to insist that his writer's faith in language was a naive indulgence. To give merely one example, in the *New Masses* article written immediately after the Sacco and Vanzetti executions in which Dos Passos called for "a writing so fiery and accurate," the full statement of his condemnation of the media teeters on the very edge of a misanthropy that he was also struggling to keep at bay: "Tabloids and movies," he wrote, "take the place of mental processes, and revolts, crimes, despairs pass off in a dribble of vague words and rubber stamp phrases without leaving a scratch on the mind *of the driven installment-paying subway-packing mass*" (*MNP*, 99; emphasis added). Even as he offered here a social analysis of the syndrome he lamented, Dos Passos began to direct his anger and contempt at those who suffered from it. There is an entire history of failed social movements enacted in this sentence: for one can hear the angry and disappointed radical begin to turn, in a familiar elitist gesture, on those with whom he hoped to build a freer and more just society. Perhaps, the sentence suggests, it is not merely the media but the "subway packing mass" who are at fault; perhaps it is the great mass of human beings themselves who are impermeable, who cannot control or even register the meaning of words.

In the fictional story lines of *U.S.A.*, Dos Passos enacts this misanthropy on a vast scale, and with a numbing, unleashed repetitiveness. Here, he mystifies and universalizes the phenomenon whose historical contingency and social causes he analyzes in his journalism. It is not merely the Hearst press that seeks to produce "an idiot lack of memory"; it is not certain elites who manipulate the shibboleths of the Red Scare; it is not some within the Left who speak entirely in "mindclosing labels": it is *everyone* in the fictional universe of *U.S.A.* who has lost control of language and is doomed to self-trivialization. In this world, everyone is part of the intellectually vacuous "subway-packing mass"—and, as a result, political transformation is doomed to failure. Dos Passos persistently presents us with scenarios in which his fictional radicals attempt to share political ideas or reflect on their own commitments and these efforts only demonstrate their vacuity. As the clichés spill from their mouths, they make a mockery of the movement's emancipatory aims. These narratives thus enact a bitter melancholic grieving, for here Dos Passos smears his anger over the entire fictional world, making his own faith in language and liberation appear to be a laughable delusion.

Consider, for example, the scene in "Mac" in which two working-class men meet and discover with exhilaration that they share a socialist commitment. At the level of plot, this is a highly positive scenario, rich with political significance. Two young men who have experienced the corrosive and exploitative effects of the economic order exchange ideas in an effort to imagine a liberated future of solidarity and justice. Dos Passos celebrates such moments of political expression throughout his activist journalism and in the radical biographies. And there is no moment in "Mac" at which Dos Passos's hero feels a greater sense of pleasure, solidarity, personal agency, and political possibility.

But in this dialogue, as in dozens of similar scenes, Dos Passos's characters speak in reductive clichés. Describing to Mac the political meaning of Edward Bellamy's *Looking Backward*, the book that "made me a socialist," Ike Hall explains:

> "It's about a galoot that goes to sleep an' wakes up in the year two thousand and the social revolution's all happened and everything's socialistic an' there's no jails or poverty and nobody works for themselves an' there's no way anybody can get to be a rich bondholder or capitalist and life's pretty slick for the workingclass."
>
> "That's what I always thought . . . It's the workers who create wealth and they ought to have it instead of a lot of drones."
>
> "If you could do away with the capitalist system and the big trusts and Wall Street things'ud be like that."
>
> "Gee." (*42P* 55; ellipsis in original)

The trivializing effect of this dialogue derives from its disturbing mixture of sincerity and vacuity. Mac and Ike are expressing ideas that we know to be responsive to their experience and aspirations. But their speech is comprised of mystifying tautologies and simplistic formulations. Ike focuses, for example, on the Rip Van Winkle-like framing conceit of *Looking Backward*, which obscures any sense of how "the social revolution" might come about, and he reduces his own vision of a better future to the cloying phrase that "life's pretty slick for the workingclass." Mac, in turn, expresses the foundational anticapitalist intuition—available to virtually anyone who has felt deprived of the product of his or her labor—that "It's the workers who create wealth and they ought to have it." But Dos Passos undermines the integrity of this assertion by adding a hollow fragment of political boilerplate as a final qualifying phrase—"instead of a lot of drones." Communication founders, as Mac's language coagulates into cliché. Ike replies with a vague tautology ("If you could do away with capitalism," then its problems would go away), to which Mac responds with the insipidly affirmative "Gee"—which Dos Passos dangles, for maximum effect, on a line by itself.

Through hackneyed dialogue of this kind—hundreds upon hundreds of pages of it—Dos Passos insists that even at the very moments of maximum sincerity and investment, his characters are incapable of substantive communication. And this is true not merely of the uneducated working class: the regime of linguistic reification applies with the same intensity to the articulate and the purportedly eloquent, to the leaders as well as the followers. Only five pages after he offers a celebratory biography of Big Bill Haywood, for example, Dos Passos introduces the legendary orator and Wobbly organizer into Mac's narrative. Haywood delivers one of his famous speeches about class solidarity and the "one big union"—and he delivers it in the context of the iconic Wobbly struggle at Goldfield, Nevada. Between 1905 and 1907, the IWW succeeded in organizing virtually all the workers in this remote Nevada mining town, across many divisions of race, ethnicity, and language, and across a wide array of skilled and unskilled trades.[19] In this scene, then, Dos Passos represents one of the American radicals he most admired, engaged in a historic struggle in the saga of American labor.

But here, as in the exchange between Mac and Ike, communication fails, even as it appears to take place:

> Big Bill talked about solidarity and sticking together in the face of the masterclass . . . Big Bill was saying the day had come to start building a new society in the shell of the old and for the workers to get ready to assume control of the industries they'd created out of their sweat and blood. [. . .] The exploiting classes would be helpless against the solidarity of the whole workingclass. The militia and the yellowlegs were workingstiffs too. Once they realized the historic mission of solidarity the masterclass couldn't use them to shoot down their brothers any more. The workers must realize that every small fight, for higher wages, for free speech, for decent living conditions, was only significant as part of the big fight for the revolution and the co-operative commonwealth. [. . .] By the time Big Bill had finished speaking [Mac's] mind had run ahead of the speech so that he'd forgotten just what he said, but Mac was in a glow all over and was cheering to beat hell. He and Fred Hoff were cheering and the stocky Bohemian miner that smelt so bad next them was clapping and the oneeyed Pole on the other side was clapping and the bunch of Wops were clapping and the little Jap who

was waiter at the Montezuma Club was clapping and the sixfoot ranchman who'd come in in hopes of seeing a fight was clapping. (*42P* 92–93)

At the level of plot, this passage describes a legendary orator realizing the full promise of political language: by describing their common cause, Big Bill enables his diverse working-class audience to feel and enact a revolutionary solidarity. But the details of Dos Passos's representation undermine such a positive reading of this scene. The celebrated orator has no eloquence and offers an almost unbroken string of clichés. Although his hackneyed words still carry some weight of meaning and argument, before Big Bill's speech is finished, Mac has "forgotten just what he said" but is nevertheless "in a glow all over and [. . .] cheering to beat hell." Dos Passos seems to imply that these clichés produce a kind of involuntary emotional response (he is "in a glow all over") that replaces intellectual understanding altogether. And it is not only Mac who experiences political speech in this spontaneously enthusiastic but vacuous manner: it is, by implication, the entire audience that responds as he does. Dos Passos emphasizes their shared incomprehension through his characteristic use of free indirect discourse, which suffuses the third-person narration with the implied verbal mannerisms of those who are being described. Those in the hall who are "cheering" Big Bill's message of class solidarity view one another derogatorily as an assemblage of racial and ethnic stereotypes: as a mass of Wops, Japs, and smelly Bohemians.

In this scene, as in the exchange between Mac and Ike, Dos Passos simultaneously depicts a positive moment of political communication and insists that such a scenario is ruined by the linguistic and cognitive incapacities of all those present. One can feel here—as in his reference to the "subway-packing mass"—the force of a painful ambivalence: the impulse to idealize is countered by the determination to hold up to ridicule the object of his own idealization. Mocking that which he had long believed in, he struggles to liberate himself from "the torment of hope." As he pursues this enterprise, page upon page, through a thousand acts of ambivalent denigration, he attempts to convince his readers that it is not only speaking and listening that are impossible: self-reflection itself is also ruined. The very process of thinking, even for the most educated and thoughtful, is self-trivializing.

Dos Passos represents Ben Compton, for example, in precisely this way. At one level, he offers us in Ben a model of the much-romanticized working-class intellectual. He emphasizes the young man's commitment to the movement and the sacrifices he makes for his own education: Ben works evenings to make money to support his studies; he reads Marx at the public library in his free time; he joins the Socialist Party and attends lectures at the Rand School. But at the end of the paragraph that describes these efforts, Dos Passos vitiates their positive implications by employing a bit of Marxist boilerplate: "He was working to be a wellsharpened instrument" (*1919* 376).[20] Through free indirection, this trite formulation is attributed to Ben himself. He understands his own creative and expressive project through the mechanical repetition of a petrified phrase that bears no mark of his particular experience. And that phrase, moreover, enacts a grim self-objectification, as Ben imagines that to learn and to act is to become merely the "instrument" of others. As it turns out, greater education and intellectual power lead only to a more active form of self-reification.

Dos Passos deploys similar techniques to belittle the politics of Mary French, the character whom he admires most and represents most sympathetically of all those who populate the trilogy. Mary's political sincerity is never questioned by Dos Passos, and her politics express an emotional depth and range that the author allows to no other figure.[21] She is also in crucial respects the radical character most like Dos Passos himself. She too is a college-educated middle-class radical whose socialism is a moral choice, stemming not from the personal experience of exploitation, but from an emotional and intellectual identification with those who suffer from material inequalities. Perhaps for this very reason, Dos Passos treats Mary's commitment both with more respect than that of his other fictional radicals, and at times with a greater hostility and condescension. Consider, for example, his description of the moment at which Mary makes the solitary decision, on a sleepless nighttime train ride back to Vassar, to dedicate herself to political work:

> [Mary] lay in the Pullman berth that night too excited to sleep [...] thinking of the work there was to be done to make the country what it ought to be, the social conditions, the slums, the shanties with filthy tottering backhouses, the miners' children in grimy coats too big for them, the overworked women stooping over stoves, the youngsters struggling for an education in nightschools, hunger and unemployment and drink, and the police and the lawyers and the judges always ready to take it out on the weak; if the

people in the Pullman cars could only be made to understand how it was;
if she sacrificed her life, like Daddy taking care of his patients night and day,
maybe she, like Miss Adams . . .
      She couldn't wait to begin. (*TBM* 101)

At one level, Dos Passos uses Mary here, as he has used Mac and Ben, as a vehicle for expressing positive components of his own political vision. She (like Dos Passos himself) condemns the injustice of the economic order and the class bias of a political and judicial system controlled by the rich and "always ready to take it out on the weak." She, like her creator, seeks to use her own class privilege and education to make "the people in the Pullman cars" aware of the darker realities of American life.

But like the rest of the fictional radicals, Mary can think only in clichés, and Dos Passos holds up for ridicule her deepest aspirations. In Mary's case, it is not the self-reifying orthodoxy of a vulgar Marxism that Dos Passos mocks, but the sentimentality that the author disdained in genteel social reformers. Mary's litany of the "social conditions"—which categorizes "drink" as a comparable evil to "hunger"—exudes a genteel moralizing sensibility that Dos Passos scorned. In the same spirit, he goes on in the final phrases of this passage to reduce Mary's aspirations for social change to a sentimental narrative of saintly self-sacrifice for the poor. He drives home this point by beginning the next paragraph with the assertion that "she couldn't wait to begin." Emphasizing Mary's impatient longing to martyr herself as soon as possible, Dos Passos implies that the self-sacrificing impulse that drives her political fantasy is masochistically self-serving. What makes this scenario all the more disturbing is that self-sacrifice is no mere abstraction for Mary, but a familiar and concrete phenomenon: her father has, indeed, lost his prosperity, his marriage, and his health in his selfless service of the poor. And so Dos Passos forces us once again to encounter the disturbing combination of sincerity and vacuity.

In all these passages, then, Dos Passos implies that, with or without the Red Scare, the project of American radicalism was doomed to failure from within. Unable to control language, these radicals trivialize their own commitments, as they speak and listen—even as they think. Dos Passos was wrestling here with a real phenomenon, whose historical causes he himself identified in the economic order of monopoly capitalism and, in particular, in the new communications media it had spawned. But throughout the fictional storylines of *U.S.A.*, Dos Passos represents this phenomenon of linguistic reification as if it were an indelible aspect of human nature itself.[22]

The linguistic pessimism of these stories expresses an acute melancholia. Through these representations, Dos Passos systematically displaces the anger that accompanied his sense of personal and political loss. His sustained aggression should be understood, in part, as a version of the scapegoating so persistent in the work of other melancholic modernists. Dos Passos's representation of the intellectual vacuity of his working-class characters resonates, for example, with the elitism on display in Eliot's *Waste Land*. And the specifically linguistic denigration of working-class people has strong roots in canonized bourgeois naturalism—as, for example, in Crane's representation of working-class speech in *Maggie* or Norris's in *McTeague*.[23] But the element of self-beratement is still more pronounced. These narratives do not merely try to direct aggression outward at figures who lie safely at a distance from their maker. Dos Passos loads his radical characters with his own qualities, his own hopes, his own experience—and he then ridicules them systematically. While earlier critics have described this authorial aggression in other ways, I want to emphasize its *self-punitive* element.[24] There is "satire" here, to be sure, and a particular species of humor. Dos Passos adopts an ironic distance from his own political hopes and the movement that embodied them. As in his account of Sacco facing the electric chair, Dos Passos attempts in these fictions to "laugh" at the "ponderous machine" of monopoly capitalism, and also at those "mangled" by it—including those, like himself, who had sought to resist it. His stories suggest that, in an important sense, his characters have involuntarily brought their fate upon themselves—and, given its inevitability, the outcome perhaps "no longer matters." This is a bitter mode of grieving, in which the disappointed radical bewilders himself about the causes of his loss, and treats the objects of his love with an undifferentiating contempt.

III. Melancholic Misogyny and Homophobia: The Impossibility of Love

There is a second aspect of Dos Passos's misanthropic naturalization of the Left's failure in the radical story lines. Even as he suggests that an emancipatory anticapitalist politics was doomed by the pervasive tendency to linguistic self-trivialization, Dos Passos elaborates another pessimistic view of human nature that was perhaps still more painful to him: that men and women were ultimately incapable of sustaining love. As we have seen, Dos Passos's anticapitalist politics was rooted, from the very beginning, in a personal revolt against the alienation that he perceived to be endemic in American life. He yearned for a more solidaristic social order—and for a society that would enable the flourishing of love relations of all kinds, sexual and affective. Throughout *U.S.A.*, Dos Passos associates radical politics with sexual freedom and gratification and with libidinally charged experiences of comradeship. He pursues this association as strongly and systematically in the fictional story lines as in the biographical prose poems. Mac, Ben, and Mary all join the radical movement in an effort to repair the alienations and intimate injuries inflicted by a capitalist society, and they are bound to the movement by the libidinal connections they forge to other radicals. But in these, as in all the fictional narratives, Dos Passos insists on the uniform failure of every effort at affective, romantic, and sexual connection. In these stories, with their myriad variations, love always founders. As with his representation of political repression and linguistic reification, Dos Passos exaggerates and universalizes the libidinal alienation of his world, transforming a social phenomenon into an undeviating condition that appears to be fundamental to human nature itself. This libidinal pessimism, like its linguistic counterpart, plays a central role in the melancholic grieving of these fictions. By insisting on the invariable failure of love, Dos Passos attempts to harden himself and his readers against the apparently childish hope for a more solidaristic society. In order to effect this harsh negation of human bonding—and to secure the repudiation of any future realization of disappointed desire—Dos Passos draws heavily on the forms of misogyny that were pervasive in his culture and on the homophobia entangled with it.

For male radicals in *U.S.A.*, the most valued and most intensely charged relations within the movement are, by and large, those with other men. Female radicals play a larger role in the fictions than in the biographical prose poems, but Dos Passos nevertheless emphasizes the centrality of male homosocial bonds within the cultures of the American Left. For Mac and Ben, as for Eugene Debs in "Lover of Mankind," radicalism is deeply rooted in the impulse of brotherhood, in the love of men for one another. Mac first acquires socialist ideas from his Uncle Tim, and his conscious embrace of a radical identity takes place in and through his fraternal relationship with Ike

Hall—a relationship that he reproduces with a long chain of male comrades. Ben Compton similarly enters the culture of American radicalism through his friendship with the attractive immigrant anarchist, Nick Gigli. Dos Passos represents these fraternal bonds as loyal, unselfish, and reciprocal in a fictional world otherwise dominated by grasping self-interest and manipulation. Male comrades buy one another meals with their last dollar; they sacrifice for one another; they share work and drink and political ideals. Ben happily gives up his own job to join Nick when he goes out on strike, just as Mac leaps at the chance to join his brothers in any number of strikes and free-speech campaigns. Their commitment to a politics of solidarity is rooted in, and made real by, their actual experience of libidinal connection. Dos Passos strongly suggests that the intensities of these bonds between men who share barracks and boxcars as well as ideals and affection are erotically charged. When Mac and Ben ride the rails together ("It's the cat's nuts, Ike"), they "lay down to sleep side by side" (*42P* 58–59). When Ben announces that he will go out on strike alongside Nick, his moment of entry into the radical movement, Nick "hauled off and kissed him on both cheeks" (*1919* 373).

While Dos Passos celebrates these intense friendships, he also represents them as peculiarly fleeting. Their power seems to require a concomitant disavowal. However strong and inspiring they may appear to be, they prove incapable of sustaining themselves. Male comrades are invariably torn apart in the radical story lines; they separate as suddenly as they come together, usually with no comment on the part of the author and no lasting sentiment on the part of the characters. After Mac and Ike have passed through many adventures together, for example—working and tramping, sharing aspirations and (like most male characters in *U.S.A.*) whoring together—they are suddenly and irrevocably separated one night when Mac loses his footing and misses a freight train that Ike has successfully hopped. Dos Passos notes with characteristic blankness that "[t]hat was the last he saw of Ike Hall" (*42P* 70). The narrative never again mentions Ike or Mac's feelings about him. The image of Mac standing on the tracks watching as Ike vanishes forever, "the two lights on the end of the train fading into the November haze," may be taken as emblematic of the fate of male friendships in the radical story lines. However intense fraternal relations may be, they are severed by chance and by the exigencies of modern life, and they disappear into a haze of invisibility at the moment of their rupture. Men do not resist separation;

they do not protect or sustain established bonds; they do not seek to retrieve them in the face of loss.

The narratives capture a familiar conundrum in modern America: that most men experience a peculiar difficulty in consciously acknowledging and sustaining the strength of their relations to one another. Dos Passos himself delineates this phenomenon, yet he also enacts the disavowal at its heart. For it is he who emphasizes the power and pleasure of these bonds, only to insist unwaveringly that they must dissolve. The social phenomenon is naturalized through countless repetitions. Although we meet many male radicals, and see them forge bonds of sympathy, affection, solidarity, and shared commitment, we see them invariably lose one another, without a moment's resistance or afterthought. Here, Dos Passos seems to say, are the much-vaunted bonds of revolutionary solidarity: so apparently deep, but in truth so shallow.

In "Lover of Mankind," Dos Passos had accused an earlier generation of American radicals of turning away from the intensities of fraternal love—and of having thus weakened the movement in ways that made the repression of the Red Scare possible. In the radical story lines, he himself naturalizes this phenomenon, representing it not as a culturally particular fear that might be surmounted, but as a universal, mechanical, emotional vacuity. Male bonds appear to dissolve neither because of fear nor because of the social arrangements that produce it, but because of a mysterious and uniform incapacity. These stories deny the ability of men to embrace their love for one another, just as they deny the human capacity to speak or think meaningfully about the yearning for solidarity. The narratives themselves insist on the inherent unsustainability of a love whose importance they melancholically record.

In the name of this repudiation of revolutionary comradeship, Dos Passos draws on the psychically underlying, culturally pervasive, melancholic structure of homophobia. Having suggested that American radicalism had drawn much of its libidinal intensity from homoerotically charged male bonds, Dos Passos seems determined to disavow the power and durability of such relations. As Judith Butler has cogently argued, normative modern gender identities rest on the repudiation of same-sex attachments from the time of our earliest experience—and on the melancholic burial of desires and lost love relations whose very existence must be denied.[25] The embrace of normative gender identity, in other words, creates a vast reservoir of ungrievable, because disavowed, loss. In the pessimistic mode of the radical story lines, as

Dos Passos struggles to harden himself against his painful political losses, he draws on this culturally pervasive homophobia and on the reservoir of melancholic grief it creates in every subject. The deployment of homophobia in this way, as a libidinal prop for the melancholic grieving of other social injuries, is not unique to Dos Passos. It stands, in fact, as a persistent feature of melancholic modernism, especially among male writers. Hemingway, for example, secures and intensifies the libidinal pessimism of *The Sun Also Rises* through Jake's violent homophobia, and through Bill's anxious insistence that at home in New York he would have to deny his love for Jake ("I'm fonder of you than anybody on Earth") because "It'd mean I was a faggot" (*Sun* 116). Eliot similarly, if more glancingly, forecloses the possibility of a same-sex outlet for male love in *The Waste Land* through his phobic rendering of Mr. Eugenides's homosexual proposition (*Waste Land* lines 208–214). Dos Passos occasionally indulges in this kind of explicit homophobic negation in *U.S.A.*—as in his representation of Margo Dowling's first husband, Tony, for example, or in the spectacular scene of Dick Savage's humiliating hold-up by two black male prostitutes (*TBM* 246–248). But the pessimistic repudiation of fraternal love in the radical story lines is a far more persistent and eloquently melancholic disavowal of a libidinal bond that Dos Passos celebrates and then repeatedly denies.

If homosocial and homoerotic bonds are thus doomed to a hazy but inescapable dissolution in the radical narratives, heterosexual relations suffer a harsher (and more openly explored) fate. In these, as in all the fictions of *U.S.A.*, Dos Passos insists on the uniform failure of heterosexual love. We should remember in this context that the author's personal hostility to capitalist society had, from the very beginning, stemmed in part from a perception of its repressive deformation of heterosexual relations. Like many radicals influenced by the bohemian socialism and anarchism of the teens, he strongly associated anticapitalist politics with the cause of sexual liberation. In the biographical prose poems, he represents solidaristic political commitments as an expression of the same libidinal impulses that seek realization in sexual connection. The same is true for the fictional radicals in "Mac," "Ben Compton," and "Mary French," in whom the yearning for social solidarity and for sexual love are fused. Dos Passos emphasizes, for example, that Mac's sexual desires and his political passions (engaged by his support for a printer's strike) emerge simultaneously, and mix together in his adolescent fantasies: "The girls looked terribly pretty and their skirts blew in the wind and [Mac] felt the spring blood pumping hot in him, he wanted to kiss and to roll on the ground and to run out across the icecakes and to make speeches from the tops of telegraph poles" (*42P* 17). Similarly, Mary French discovers Left politics and her own sexual desires simultaneously, as she falls in love with the labor militant Gus Muscowski and with the steelworkers' strike in which he participates (*TBM* 116–119). In all three narratives, Dos Passos traces his protagonists' sexual and political careers in tandem, suggesting that these yearnings spring from a common source and share a related fate.

And what a grim fate it is. In all the fictional narratives, including those focused on radicals, Dos Passos insists that heterosexual love is doomed. His representation of this failure—like his portrayal of linguistic reification and of the repression of the Red Scare—draws on an astute social analysis of a historically particular phenomenon. In this case, Dos Passos traces with harsh insight, and with as much persistence as any writer of his generation, a set of disastrous cultural contradictions in the shifting sexual mores of early-twentieth-century America. These contradictions represent, in essence, a distinctive new variant of the longstanding, patriarchal, sexual double-standard that comes into being with the modern sex-gender system.

In *U.S.A.*, male characters want sex—which they generally experience and openly acknowledge as an instinctual urge. (Ike characteristically tells Mac: "God damn it, I need a woman . . . wet dreams weakens a guy" [*42P* 62].) Women are the normative objects of these involuntary urges, but men experience their physical "need" as detached from any interest in individual women or from any desire for emotional connection. Men fear marriage, which is the only fully condoned context for sexuality but which men perceive as a painful constraint on their freedom in a society that values and requires mobility. As a result, men in the trilogy are forever struggling to "get" sex from women outside of marriage. Either they seek out prostitutes or they cajole or force themselves upon women to whom they are not married or engaged, or from whom they are about to run off. They commonly deride women who resist sex as old-fashioned prudes—but, adhering themselves to the vestiges of an older code, they also stigmatize sexually compliant women as whores. Dos Passos's female characters must, for their part, play their assigned roles within this grisly drama. Whether these women have repressed their sexual desires in accordance with a Victorian morality, or wish to acknowledge their sexuality as a modern woman's entitlement, they usually resist having sex outside of marriage. Dos Passos emphasizes, time and again, the good reasons for this resistance: both the devastating implications of pregnancy for the unmarried woman and the risk of stigmatization if they comply with their lovers' sexual demands.

This historically particular cultural arrangement leads to a pitched battle between the sexes. Single men experience perpetual sexual frustration at the hands of women, whom they generally resent because of their resistance. Single women, on their side, must forever fight off the sexual advances of men, often denying their own sexual desires in the process. When women do give in to their own desires or to those of their lovers, they suffer the consequences—facing the reality of stigmatized and financially untenable single motherhood or risking the psychic and physical dangers of illegal abortion. For precisely these reasons, women do, indeed, seek to draw men into marriage, often manipulatively, in ways that men predictably experience as entrapment. Dos Passos represents conventional marriage as alienating and sterile—and men seek to evade this fate by attempting to satisfy their sexual desires with prostitutes, whom they generally fear, revile, and find disappointing. Dos Passos represents these dynamics repeatedly, across scores of fictional relationships of all kinds, from adolescent dates and one-night stands to established marriages, affecting characters from a wide array of social, economic, and ethnic backgrounds. Through the repetition of these scenarios, in varied environments, he demonstrates to quite devastating effect the persistence of these destructive and contradictory social formations.

Although this toxic and unsatisfying sexual regime prevails in all the narratives, Dos Passos reveals its distinctive inflection within the subcultures of American radicalism. In particular, the usual male resistance to marriage takes on a political cast in the radical story lines. Male union militants and revolutionaries warn one another to avoid marrying, insisting that the financial obligation to support a wife and children inevitably undermines a man's ability to go on strike, to risk going to jail, or to accept the other uncertainties of participation in a radical movement. An IWW leader, Fred Hoff, characteristically explains to Mac that "A man's first duty's to the workin' class. [. . .] A wobbly oughtn't to have any wife or children, not till after the revolution" (*42P* 93). This purportedly pragmatic logic, expressed by many men in the pages of *U.S.A.*, easily devolves into a distinctive anticapitalist form of misogyny that vilifies women as a danger to male radicals. Uncle Tim, for example, admonishes Mac: "dont ever sell out to the sonsofbitches, son; it's women'll make you sell out every time" (*42P* 33). Nick Gigli similarly warns Ben that "a revolutionist ought to be careful about the girls he went with, women took a classconscious workingman's mind off his aims, they were the main seduction of capitalist society" (*1919* 373). Male radicals thus phobically identify women with capitalist society itself—and they seek to manage their own ambivalences about heterosexuality (the desire for connection to women colliding with the fear of marriage) by deriding women as the seductive instruments of an economic order that wants them to "sell out." This radical variant of misogyny leads to the same set of dysfunctional behaviors endemic in all the fictional narratives—but these behaviors take on an additionally ruinous meaning, as the twinned yearnings for social solidarity and for sexual connection collide with one another.

In the fictional story lines, then, Dos Passos offers a socially substantive representation of this historically particular system of sexual mores and gender relations. His representation is, moreover, informed by the feminist analyses that circulated widely in left intellectual subcultures of the teens, 1920s, and 1930s.[26] Focusing five of the twelve narratives (including one of the radical story lines) on female protagonists, Dos Passos reveals sympathetically the ways in which women are placed in an impossible sexual double bind: resented if they withhold sex outside of marriage, but reviled if they comply; feared as potential wives, but usually derided on any other terms. These narratives also emphasize the real and inequitable vulnerability to which women are subject because of pregnancy within this social order. Dos Passos's story lines perceptively explore the cost of female sexual repression and frustration, and they reveal the larger corrosive effects of misogyny in American culture—including the subcultures of the Left. He focuses attention on the way in which male radicals' political wariness of marriage fuels predatory sexual behavior and the callous evasion of responsibility. (It is the otherwise sympathetic Ben Evans, for example, who pithily explains to Mac that he shouldn't worry about his pregnant girlfriend, since "if a girl wasn't a goddam whore she wouldn't let you, would she" [*42P* 94].) Dos Passos also astutely emphasizes the misogynist presumptions that prevent Mary French's male comrades from perceiving or reciprocating the noncoercive, egalitarian love relations, based on shared political commitment, that she desires and offers to them. Gus Muscovsky, for example, remains so entrenched in his view that "a woikin'man ain't got no right to have a wife and family," and that casual affairs with "free and easy, Polish girls" provide his only alternative, that he cannot recognize Mary as an intelligent and committed comrade who wants also to be his lover (*TBM* 123–124). Don Stevens and Ben Compton, educated radicals who pay lip service to the ideology of free love, prove equally unable to conduct egalitarian love affairs. They treat Mary as subordinate amanuensis if also lover, and they refuse her a sustained emotional connection even though she shares their revolutionary commitments and their wariness of marriage. In all these ways, Dos Passos's narratives offer an astute and incipiently feminist analysis of a dysfunctional, because misogynist, sex-gender system. At the same time, however, Dos Passos systematically naturalizes these sexual dynamics, indulging in the very misogyny that he also reveals in his characters. In this domain, as in others, he universalizes, through myriad repetitions, the real social phenomenon he has represented.

While Dos Passos calls attention to the destructive tendency of male radicals to perceive women as "the main seduction of capitalist society," the author himself gives literary weight and body to this phobic fantasy. He persistently represents female characters as materialistic harpies, incapable of understanding or sympathizing with Left politics, determined to make the radical men in their lives "sell out" their commitments. Uncle Tim refers to his wife as "that terrible forktongued virago I'm married to" (*42P* 33)—and Dos Passos himself urges us to see her in precisely this way. While the narrative enables us to see that Uncle Tim's political commitments have imperiled the financial viability of his family, Dos Passos encourages us to sympathize with Tim's generous spirit of solidarity in supporting the printers' strike and to view with an amused contempt his wife's shrewish condemnation of "godless labor unions" and her punishing assertion that it "serve[s] you right too, Tim O'Hara" that the strike-breaking master printers have driven him to bankruptcy. Similarly, Dos Passos enables us to recognize the extreme vulnerability of Mac's fiancée, Maisie, when Mac runs off without explanation to join the Wobblies at Goldfield, betraying his promise to marry her after she has finally capitulated to his sexual advances. But Dos Passos also vilifies Maisie as another virago, who condemns Mac's "ungodly socialistic talk" (111), whose "eyes shone" and who feels "drunk" when her brother talks about "money" (108), and who is indeed determined to make Mac sell out his politics in order to gain a bourgeois life. Mary French's mother stands as yet another avatar of the shrewish materialist. She condemns her noble husband for having "ruined" her life by taking on "miserable foreigners and miners" as patients, when he could have become "a rich man" by serving the wealthy (*TBM* 93, 95). She belittles and emasculates him at every turn, significantly refusing even to sleep with him. When he will not repudiate his commitment to the poor, she leaves him in order to pursue the materialistic life she values above all else.

In these situations and many others, Dos Passos offers at one level a socially perceptive account of the ways in which the privileging of solidarity over prosperity creates strain within marriages—and in which women, traditionally responsible for the stability of the home, may feel disproportionately the material price of such efforts at social change. But he never represents this as a struggle or conflict shared by the partners in a marriage. Rather, male characters manage this tension by vilifying their wives as "viragos"—and Dos Passos himself, quite remarkably, indulges in precisely this misogynist structure of feeling. Even as he suggests the real vulnerabilities faced by these wives and mothers, he turns his readers against them, demonizing them, and implying that these heartless, materialistic shrews are the cause of male radicals' domestic troubles. Dos Passos himself persistently deploys this phobic Left stereotype, reenacting and elaborating it across a wide range of social situations. These representations echo the depiction of Debs's "fat wife" in "Lover of Mankind," who presides over the Socialist leader's domestic incarceration, functioning as a displaced misogynist stand-in for the fraternal abandonment and political repression that have actually harmed him. While that gendered displacement is only momentary, a single move in the prose poem, Dos Passos inflates it throughout the radical story lines, in which misogyny becomes a dominant part of the narrative structure of feeling. The viragos take the blame for the collision between revolutionary politics and domestic stability.

The peculiar, unstable mingling of feminist insight and misogyny is one of the most striking features of Dos Passos's fiction—as is the collision of his occasionally sympathetic attention to gay sexual desire with his indulgence in a conventional homophobia. In a letter to Ernest Hemingway, written as he struggled to compose the last volume of *U.S.A.*, Dos Passos lamented that the "[w]hole trouble with the opus is too many drawing room bitches—never again—it's like fairies getting into a bar—ruin it in no time" (*14C* 408). This is a revealing comment, coming from an author who was personally uncomfortable with, and even hostile to, normative, heterosexually predatory masculinity—but who was nevertheless willing to join Hemingway in his macho posturing. It is entirely characteristic of Dos Passos that he wrote a trilogy so significantly concerned with the experience of women (and into whose fictional universe he had admitted gay men), but then reviled them as "drawing room bitches" (and ruinous "fairies").[27] The misogyny and homophobia of the fictional narratives contribute substantially to the melancholic dimension of Dos Passos's vision. They enable the systematic foreclosure of human connection, which is essential to the bitter repudiation of solidarity as an impossible (if lovely) fantasy. For who is left to love once a man has reviled both women and those men who might love him in return? This normative posture can only doom the straight man to a well of libidinal isolation and despair. As Dos Passos sought in the radical story lines to depict the impossibility of the solidarity to which American radicalism had committed itself, he drew deeply on this well of negativity—which was, as his letter to Hemingway suggests, an aspect of himself.

Just as Dos Passos naturalizes the failures of the Left by exaggerating the iron-clad determinism of political repression, and by exaggerating the universality of linguistic reification, so too he exaggerates the inescapability of the libidinal dead-end to which the sex-gender system dooms his fictional radicals. It is not simply that Dos Passos misogynistically pairs off his male radicals with viragos who demand the abandonment of social solidarity as the price of heterosexual love. Beyond that, the author brings an equally grim libidinal determinism to bear on sexual relationships between male and female radicals who share the same political passions—and who might thus be expected to find a better romantic fate. Dos Passos introduces into his narratives a number of women who are committed to the movement, who criticize bourgeois marriage, and who embrace an ideology of free love and sexual equality—but their romantic relationships are doomed to failure with the same inevitability. This requires a good deal of authorial manipulation and, in particular, the deployment of forms of misogyny that stand outside the materialist virago stereotype.

In the male-centered radical narratives, "Mac" and "Ben Compton," Dos Passos introduces several female characters who seem to provide promising romantic alternatives to heartless and castrating female materialists. These women are comrades in the movement, committed to free love as well as revolution. But Dos Passos refuses to allow such relations to flourish. In some cases, he subjects them to the same hazy imperative of libidinal disso-lution that characterizes male homosocial bonds within the Left. After Mac leaves his shrewish wife Maisie, for example, he travels to Mexico to regain a life of revolutionary male mobility, adventure, and solidarity. Once he ar-rives, his Mexican comrades immediately welcome him, take him to a politi-cal meeting and to a party—and provide him with a lover. In this peculiar scene, which has the air of a cartoon fantasy of male sexual and political ad-venture, a Mexican male comrade introduces Mac to his new lover, explain-ing that Encarnacion is "nice girl . . . Not goddam whore . . . not pay, she nice workinggirl . . . comrade" (115; ellipses in original). The chain of signifiers implies an escape from the repeated double binds of Mac's previous sexual history: here is a woman who is neither a "whore" whom he must "pay," nor a prudish would-be wife, nor a virago who will seduce him from his revolu-tionary commitment. The unreality of this scene is, of course, marked by the fact that Encarnacion stands as no more than a passive, racially eroticized fantasy object, who has simply been given to Mac, with no volition on her part—but who nevertheless willingly joins him in this apparently easygoing heterosexual extension of revolutionary comradeship. Most importantly, Dos Passos insists on the ultimate insignificance of this relationship, dismissing Encarnacion from the text as abruptly—and with as little explanation—as he does the male comrades who come and go from Mac's life.

In Ben Compton's narrative, Dos Passos introduces two female comrades who, while also peripheral, are explored in somewhat greater detail. At first, they seem similarly to promise a way out of the libidinal conflict between heterosexuality and political commitment. In contrast to the passive fantasy object, Encarnacion, these two women are active sexual subjects, who con-sciously assert their desires for a heterosexual bond between comrades. In both cases, however, Dos Passos provides a phobic representation of this sexual agency, transforming the possibility of heterosexual comradeship into a frightening specter of predatory femininity. Ben and the passionate young syndicalist Helen Mauer decide to "live in free union together," as they oppose bourgeois marriage and agree that they should not have children so that they can "give all their strength to the movement" (*1919* 378–379). Dos Passos provides them with a few paragraphs of romantic happiness (more than usual in *U.S.A.*) in order to open a window onto this possibility of an egalitarian sexual love rooted in shared political activism. But he then rapidly destroys the idyll. Ben goes briefly to jail for union activity and discovers on his release that Helen has taken another lover. Although she assures him that "we're all comrades" and that "Billy doesn't mean anything to me," Ben cannot accept her demand that he "oughtn't to be so conventional" and possessive (*1919* 380). Dos Passos urges us to sympathize with Ben, who declares bitterly that "you mighta waited till I got outa jail," thus implying that by following her code of free love, Helen has sexually and politically betrayed her imprisoned comrade.

In the pages that follow, Dos Passos pursues this association further, increasingly identifying Ben's experience of female comrades with his experience of political repression. Although Helen lingers at the periphery of Ben's narrative, the romantic promise of their relationship does not recover from the implication of betrayal. As Ben comes under increasing scrutiny (and is ultimately imprisoned) for his revolutionary opposition to the war, he not only withdraws from Helen but comes to experience another female comrade as a threatening figure, preying upon his vulnerability. A wealthy radical and the sister of Ben's lawyer, Fanya Stein desires Ben as a lover and as a political ally (she too is an "an ardent pacifist" and urges Ben to "read Tolstoy and Kropotkin"). Ben, however, experiences this combination of active sexual and political interest as disturbing. And it is Dos Passos himself, and not merely Ben, who codes Fanya Stein as a frightening figure, whose various strengths—her sexual assertiveness, her intellectual and material assets, her desire to participate in the movement—are represented as manipulative and self-serving. At one of the low points of Ben's vulnerability, for example, as the appeal of his prison-sentence drags on and he feels a desperate sense of his own powerlessness in the face of wartime jingoism and repression, Fanya offers her love and assistance—which Dos Passos represents this way:

> She'd pulled him down on her bed and was stroking his forehead. "Poor boy
> . . . I love you so, Benny, couldn't you think of me a little bit . . . just a little

teeny bit . . . I could help you so much in the movement . . . Tomorrow we'll talk about it . . . I want to help you, Benny." He let her untie his necktie. (*1919* 391; ellipses in original)

Here, Dos Passos transforms the sexual female comrade into an invasive, quasimaternal figure, who infantilizes her "poor boy" "Benny" and whose power to offer material assistance appears ominously tied to a sexual demand ("couldn't you think of me a little bit") that Ben does not want to meet but to which he submits.

Fanya Stein, like Helen Mauer, thus appears as the misogynist flip side of Encarnacion. Within the male-centered radical narratives, Dos Passos imagines the female comrade and lover in one of two principal modes. Either she exists as a passive, unthreatening fantasy object, whose active libidinal power has been erased and disavowed by the text or, when her power is acknowledged, she appears as threatening and manipulative, reducing the male radical to impotence. Dos Passos draws on these two misogynist constructs in order to create a sense of the impossibility of a sexual flourishing between comrades. In these representations, we can also see the ways in which this melancholic negation of human connection draws on the equally deep wells of exclusionary racial ideology and feeling. For each vision of femininity draws on a corresponding racial fantasy: the compliant, docile, sexually available (but disposable) Mexican girl, and the aggressive, invasive, threatening Jewish woman.[28]

In Mary French, Dos Passos allows himself to pursue in greater detail, and with more sympathy, the female radical as political and sexual subject. Mary stands neither as an empty token nor as a threat. In her, Dos Passos went as far as he ever would in imagining a female radical endowed with many of his own qualities, a female version of himself, worthy of identification. He represents her as a thoughtful, educated, middle-class anticapitalist; he grants the integrity of her radical commitments, as he honors the affective as well as sexual dimension of her romantic desires. But even as he idealizes Mary, he dooms her to erotic and political failure.

Mary offers a series of male radicals the possibility of a noncoercive, egalitarian sexual love, rooted in a shared life of political activism. In part, as I have already suggested, Dos Passos indicates that such a love cannot flourish because her male lovers cannot perceive or accept it, mired as they are in misogynist presumptions that Dos Passos sketches quite powerfully. With marriage off-limits, Gus can see only the "free and easy," disposable, proletarian girls of the neighborhood as lovers. Don and Ben accept Mary as a lover, but only as a subordinate in the movement, not as an equal. But Dos Passos also naturalizes the forces that cause Mary's serial romantic failure. As in the partly melancholic biography of Thorstein Veblen, "The Bitter Drink," Dos Passos implies that the basic libidinal impulse at work in Mary's life—the twinned sexual and political yearning—is fundamentally masochistic and self-destructive. The man to whom Mary develops the closest attachment, Ben Compton, stands as the purest embodiment in *U.S.A.* of radical political commitment as death drive. Ben appears masochistically determined to suffer as much as possible, to martyr himself to the cause: he works himself to exhaustion and collapse; he courts repression at every turn, characteristically declaring, for example, that "I'd as soon go to jail as not" (*TBM*, 402). Dos Passos implies that this willful impulse to self-destruction also causes him to deny the human substance of his relation to Mary. Despite the fact that they "loved each other," when Mary tells Ben that she is pregnant, he callously insists that "it would distract him from his work" and that "it would spoil her usefulness in the struggle for several months." Like an automaton, he declares that "they had to sacrifice their personal feelings for the workingclass" (*TBM* 398, 400). Although Mary is enraged at Ben as she goes off to have an abortion, Dos Passos also depicts her own commitment to the cause as animated by a similar spirit of self-destructiveness and self-sacrifice. This is true from the very moment of Mary's decision to devote her life to activism, as I have noted earlier, and this only intensifies as she grinds herself down physically and psychically in the course of her narrative.

More than this, Dos Passos emphasizes that Mary's attachment to Ben—and later to Don—expresses an erotic version of the masochistic impulse that is enacted in her politics. For Mary actively chooses men characterized by a mode of political commitment that is both self-destructive and guaranteed to erase her needs. Dos Passos implies, in other words, that Ben's callous denial of her as well as himself is not an accidental feature of his personality, but the very thing that has drawn Mary to him, the very object of her desire. Dos Passos drives home this point by having Mary repeat precisely this relational structure with Don Stevens immediately after she has been painfully thwarted by Ben. Despite Mary's apparent autonomy, her intellectual accomplishment and political discipline, she instantly embraces the role of subordinate acolyte to the male radicals whom she eroticizes. Even after Ben has denied her needs, Mary still "thrilled to him the way the workers did at meetings when he'd come to the platform in a tumult of stamping and applause" (*TBM* 401). She remains libidinally bound to him in the very dynamic of her mistreatment: "if he'd give her one smile just for her before he bawled her out before the whole office because the leaflets weren't ready, she'd feel happy all day" (*TBM* 402). Mary follows the same well-worn libidinal path with Don Stevens, being drawn virtually instantaneously into a role of subordination, passively following in the wake of his activity: "Mary had lost all her initiative. Suddenly she'd become Donald Stevens's secretary. She was least unhappy when she was running small errands for him" (*TBM* 409). Dos Passos emphasizes, moreover, that Mary is drawn precisely to a man whose passion is directed elsewhere. Watching Don deliver political speeches (as she had watched Ben), she recognizes afterwards "the shine in his eye [. . .] the look, Mary used to tell herself, of a man who had just come from a date with his best girl" (*TBM* 469). In this libidinal configuration, Mary's romantic relationship with Don is not strengthened by their shared political commitment, but is rather undermined by it: Mary desires men whose political passions do not bring them closer to her, but keep her always at a distance—as if politics (and the narcissistic pleasure of addressing the crowd) were really their "best girl."

Although Mary appears to hunger for sexual equality and a shared activist life, Dos Passos thus implies that she is ultimately driven by a self-denying libidinal impulse to subordinate and sacrifice herself, to participate in love affairs and political movements that will deny the satisfaction of her own needs. Even as he traces the gender arrangements that marginalize Mary in her personal and political life, Dos Passos naturalizes her disappointment as the result of her own self-defeating impulses. Mary stands, in the end, as a masochistic feminine version of Thorstein Veblen in "The Bitter Drink": Dos Passos melancholically recasts her radicalism, like his, as a "constitutional inability to say yes," as a negativity rooted in her very nature (*TBM* 84).

To complete the picture of Mary's libidinal isolation, it remains only to emphasize Dos Passos's refusal to provide his heroine with any female comrades at all. While heterosexuality uniformly fails, female homosocial or homoerotic bonds have been erased entirely from Dos Passos's account of the Left. While the author persistently emphasizes that fraternal love constitutes a libidinal foundation for the movement, he cannot imagine or acknowledge that the love of women for one another might be an equally indispensable wellspring for American radicalism's solidaristic enterprise. Mary has no sisters in arms. Her only female friend, Ada Cohn, stands as a tamer incarnation of the female materialist: while she provides some forms of emotional and material support to Mary, her individualist indifference to politics (and her investment in the alienating superficialities of the drawing room) makes her incapable of sharing the deepest impulses in Mary's personality. As Dos Passos has arranged her narrative, Mary's desire to live in a less alienated world can only conceivably find realization through her relations, romantic and political, with male radicals. And those relations fail not only because of the repressive social structures within which Mary lives but also, Dos Passos suggests, because the underlying libidinal impulse is self-destructive at its root.

In his own experience, and in the stories he told about the movement in *U.S.A.*, Dos Passos imagined that American radicalism was at the deepest level a revolt against alienation. His fictional radicals long for libidinally charged experiences of comradeship and for a solidaristic mass movement that could challenge an alienating and exploitative economic order. Their yearnings for emotional and sexual connection are, on Dos Passos's account, inseparable from their political aspirations: they are twinned impulses, with a common source. In the radical storylines, Dos Passos insists that all efforts at connection are doomed to failure—and that the larger aspirations of American radicalism must be acknowledged accordingly as a laughable illusion. In order to demonstrate the inevitability of love's disappointment, Dos Passos drew on the deep reservoirs of misogyny and homophobia (and on the exclusionary racial ideologies that feed and draw on them). He insists on the mysterious weakness, the disavowed intensity, of the male homosocial bonds on which radical movements had so relied, and he denies entirely their female equivalents. He enacts myriad heterosexual relations in order to demonstrate their varied but undeviating failure. Even as he identifies the forms of misogyny that contribute so decisively to these failures, he indulges in misogynist constructions in ways that make them appear to be our very nature. Marriages cannot succeed because wives are materialist viragos; free love fails because female comrades are either passive, substanceless, fantasy objects or frightening sexual aggressors; even the ideal female radical is revealed to be driven by a masochistic commitment to her own subordination and denial.

Reeling from the violent repression of the Red Scare, and increasingly alarmed by the toxic self-destructiveness of Stalinism, the disappointed radical sought in these fictions to harden himself against any faith that the aspirations of American radicalism could still be realized. He sought to still the "torment of hope," to enable himself and his readers to "laugh and look quizzically at the ponderous machine" of alienation that had "caught and mangled" a generation. Struggling to tell a melancholic story of the inevitable failure of beautiful but unrealizable yearnings, he drew on the most pessimistic visions of humanity contained within his own psyche and culture. Misogyny and homophobia, mingled with a commonplace racism, provided powerful resources for such a vision—in the radical story lines of *U.S.A.*, as in other works of melancholic modernism. The melancholic gesture of negation must, however, be indefinitely repeated, for its work can never be complete. The story lines enact a grim, compulsive repetition; they rehearse over and over again the same misanthropic and misogynistic scenarios. For the very persistence of Dos Passos's own yearnings for solidarity and libidinal connection requires the constant reassertion of a fierce denial that promises, but never delivers, the "numb" anesthetization of a pervasive and ongoing social injury.

"The Language of the Beaten Nation Is Not Forgotten"

Dos Passos's Camera Eye and the Unfinished Work of Mourning

The *U.S.A.* trilogy enacts a remarkably sustained and visible struggle between the two modernisms. In the radical biographies, Dos Passos mourned the suppression of a mass movement that had arisen to challenge monopoly capitalism. Identifying the systemic causes of the Red Scare, and directing his anger accordingly, Dos Passos was able to measure what the Left had lost, even as he retrieved the movement's ideals for affirmation and extension. But this work of mourning was countered, from the very outset of the trilogy, by the fierce melancholia of *U.S.A.*'s naturalist fictions. Seeking to still the "torment of hope," to escape from the burden of political disappointment, Dos Passos naturalized the causes of the Left's failures in these fictions and vented a torrential, mocking anger at the movement he had loved. The two modes of response were at war with one another from the start, but the balance between them shifted over the decade of the trilogy's composition. As Dos Passos encountered the crisis of Stalinism, and experienced an intolerable ambivalence toward the radical movement itself, the work of political mourning ground to a halt in the final volume. In *The Big Money*, even the radical biographies become melancholic—and are then abandoned altogether. Melancholia prevails.

But it is a testament to the depth of Dos Passos's continued attachment to American radicalism, and to the dynamic complexity of his grieving, that *The Big Money* contains one final, lyrical burst of political mourning. In the trilogy's penultimate Camera Eye segments, Dos Passos represented his failed effort to save the lives of Sacco and Vanzetti—and his psychological response to their execution. With impressive fidelity to the logic of grief, the autobiographical Camera Eye (like all the components of the trilogy) suddenly converges on the political loss that had crystallized a decade of repression in the author's mind and had prompted the writing of *U.S.A.* itself. It is not surprising that in the most intimate and personal strand of the trilogy, Dos Passos was able, one last time, to pierce the melancholic shell of displaced, self-consuming rage and to feel once more the grief of American radicalism's suppression. As he felt the contours of what he had lost, he was able to revive, with momentary brightness, the promise of solidarity.

In the fifty-one Camera Eye segments, dispersed throughout the trilogy, Dos Passos traces the development of his own subjectivity, placing particular emphasis on the familial, social, and psychosexual influences that had shaped his evolving political consciousness. In the Camera Eye, he offers fragmentary, stream-of-consciousness representations of decisive moments in his psychic life, from early childhood to his emergence as a radical writer and activist in the late 1920s and early 1930s. The twenty-seven segments that appear in *The 42nd Parallel* subtly render the intimate processes by which a bourgeois white male subjectivity is formed. The largely autobiographical persona of the Camera Eye learns to place himself in a privileged position within racial and class hierarchies by internalizing the patronizing racism of his father and the more violent prejudice of his southern mother; by learning to distinguish between the "clean young American Rover Boys" who attend prep school like himself and the local "Bohunk and Polack" "muckers" who "do dirty things" (CE 7); by attending church with the patrician "Pennypackers," even as he wonders "who were the Molly Maguires" (CE 11); by learning about the working-class, immigrant household of his father's childhood (CE 15), even as he prepares to go to Harvard, where he will be taught that to "remain a gentleman," one must not "be seen with Jews or Socialists" (CE 25).[1] Similarly, an eroticized, hierarchical gender difference is internalized through the oedipal drama with his parents—and, despite the homoerotic attractions of a working-class boy (CE 9), the narrator grows into an apparently normative heterosexuality through a titillating early initiation by a servant girl (CE 12) and through adolescent desires for sexual contact that he nevertheless lacks the "nerve" to act on because of his bourgeois upbringing (CE 19, 24). The Camera Eye segments of *1919* explore the disillusionment of the World War One years, during which the narrator suffers the personal loss of both parents, and then the growing awareness that the war's destructiveness, class hypocrisy, and toxic sexual politics seem to make a mockery of the genteel social vision that he has internalized. As he grows into an adult creative and political identity in *The Big Money*, the narrator struggles with the painful contradictions of his own personality. Increasingly critical of a social order of which he is a privileged beneficiary, he feels like an "imposter" (CE 44), placed in a "pigeonhole" he abhors (CE 45), "peeling the onion of doubt" (CE 46), wearing "the old raincoat of incertitude," wondering "has he any? face" (CE 47). He enacts his ambivalence about the economic order, in part, according to the libidinal structure of a left misogyny, which causes him to view women of his own class as alluring yet repellant embodiments of capitalism itself: "dollars are silky in her hair soft in her dress sprout in the elaborately contrived rosepetals that you kiss" (CE 46). But he simultaneously struggles to develop a conscious political analysis, embracing anticapitalist radicalism, even as he fears that a committed politics requires the acceptance of "slogans" and the abandonment of an honest intellectual skepticism (CE 46). The Camera Eye, in short, traces the emergence of a radical political consciousness that remains precarious and conflicted because the abhorred structures of social inequality have been internalized so deeply that political commitment feels, to some degree, false and self-indicting.[2]

The penultimate Camera Eye segments (numbers 49 and 50), which appear nearly at the trilogy's end, enact the final consolidation of radical consciousness, in the face of self-doubt and political disappointment. These late Camera Eyes are among the most famous portions of *U.S.A.* In a work that defies easy excerpting, they are often anthologized as representative of the trilogy as a whole. For many readers, they remain the most memorable feature of the work, often vivid decades after first reading. Their lasting power derives from the intensity with which they enact political mourning. During a period of growing despair and ambivalence, as he was struggling to relinquish the political commitments of two decades, Dos Passos was able to express one last time his faith in American radicalism—and in the possibility that a defeated nation might yet find words to express and retrieve what it was losing.

In the first of these segments, Dos Passos describes his internal meditations during a trip, undertaken partly on foot, from Plymouth to North Plymouth, Massachusetts. He has gone to Plymouth for the purpose of interviewing Bartolomeo Vanzetti's neighbors as part of his work on the Sacco and Vanzetti Defense Committee. With a compressed, poetic efficiency that resembles that of the biographical prose poems, Dos Passos sketches a parable of historical deterioration, betrayal, and loss. Modern capitalism has reduced the iconic place of the Pilgrims' landing to the grim ugliness and alienating standardization of a working-class slum: "company-houses all the same size all grimed the same color" and all appended to the "huge sheds" and factories of the Plymouth Cordage. Dos Passos mourns, above all, the political loss that has accompanied this toxic economic order. The nation founded and persistently renewed by immigrant "haters of oppression" has betrayed its central emancipatory impulse: in the era of the Red Scare, the Palmer Raids, and the impending executions of Sacco and Vanzetti, those who still "wanted a world unfenced" have been persecuted and intimidated into silence. Vanzetti's neighbors are afraid even to speak of the anarchist fish peddler from whom they bought eels on the day he was accused of committing murder elsewhere, and they are afraid to acknowledge that they "listened to his talk" of a free society.[3]

As in the radical biographies, Dos Passos refuses the strategies of naturalization, and he directs his anger at the economic order that has deformed the nation and at those responsible for the ideological justification of political repression. Rejecting the universalizing linguistic misanthropy of the fictional story lines, Dos Passos here identifies more specifically those responsible for having "ruined" the "old words the immigrant haters of oppression brought to Plymouth." They are the "lawyers districtattorneys collegepresidents judges" who have manipulated and falsified the language of democracy in order to protect the economic interests of a ruling elite and in order to persecute and silence working-class dissenters. Because Dos Passos's anger is not misanthropically directed at all humanity, it is possible for him to mourn what has been imperiled in America—and to affirm the power of language through which that mourning might take place. In stark contrast to the fictional story lines, he insists on the writer's capacity to use words flexibly and meaningfully in order to recollect truths that the ruling elite seeks to obscure and falsify. Working with "pencil scrawls in my notebook the scraps of recollection the broken halfphrases," Dos Passos affirms his own "effort to intersect word with word to dovetail clause with clause to rebuild out of mangled memories unshakably (Old Pontius Pilate) the truth." Registering the depth of the nation's betrayal, Dos Passos insists that it is still possible to "rebuild the ruined words," to renew the compromised promise of democracy, and to extend a long tradition of resisting "oppression." It should be emphasized that Dos Passos's mourning here is not simply a nostalgic clinging to a fixed tradition located in the past. Rather, he urges his readers to be open to the dynamic, changing face of America's emancipatory tradition: "this fishpeddler you have in Charlestown jail," he explains, "is one of your founders Massachusetts" (*TBM* 391). In this final transvaluation, Dos Passos resists a rigid and exclusionary nativism. He calls upon his contemporaries to recognize that what is best in the United States, what is now imperiled and betrayed by the most powerful, remains alive in the incarcerated immigrant anarchist.[4]

Dos Passos' capacity for political mourning is then challenged by still further disappointment, when Sacco and Vanzetti are actually executed. The next segment of the Camera Eye (50) records that disillusioning event and Dos Passos's remarkable attempt to grieve for it. Once again, the writer insists that there can be no coming to terms with the executions without identifying social causes and directing anger accordingly—without enabling his readers to "feel who are your oppressors America." Dos Passos offers an angry, forceful analysis of the way in which a structure of intensifying economic exploitation has produced an owning class with such power that it can manipulate political discourse, control the electoral process and the judicial system, and wield the violent authority of the state to destroy those who resist. This class has "sweated the wealth out of our people"—and with that wealth, "they hire and fire the politicians the newspapereditors the old judges the small men with reputations the collegepresidents the wardheelers." Because they have "the dollars," they have also "the guns the armed forces the powerplants / they have built the electricchair and hired the executioner to throw the switch." The economic order has produced not merely class conflict, but a class war, waged (through its paid surrogates) by the most wealthy: "all right," he declares, "we are two nations." And Dos Passos acknowledges that the owning class is, at the moment, clearly "stronger" than the rest of the country: "all right you have won"; "we stand defeated America" (*TBM* 413–414).

Having registered the depth of this political loss and having identified the objects of his anger, Dos Passos is able to mourn with remarkable fullness. Even as he insists that "we stand defeated," he affirms the persistence of those aspirations that have been thwarted and of the egalitarian social possibilities that have been so violently truncated. Dos Passos wonders whether the master class, the "conquering nation," can understand that—even as they execute Sacco and Vanzetti:

> the old words of the immigrants are being renewed in blood and agony tonight do they know that the old American speech of the haters of oppression is new tonight in the mouth of an old woman from Pittsburgh of a husky boilermaker from Frisco who hopped freights clear from the Coast to come here in the mouth of a Back Bay socialworker in the mouth of an Italian printer of a hobo from Arkansas the language of the beaten nation is not forgotten in our ears tonight
> the men in the deathhouse made the old words new before they died.
> (*TBM* 414)

In these lines, among the most famous in the *U.S.A.* trilogy, Dos Passos retrieves with great intensity the tradition-building idiom of the radical biographies. Here once again he insists that even in the face of extreme political repression, the egalitarian and solidaristic vision of American radicalism endures. Although these men have been incarcerated like Debs and Haywood, although they have been murdered like Joe Hill and Wesley Everest, the desire that animated their lives—for an end to "oppression"—is not dead. It is a yearning and a potentiality shared by all the radicals left behind, who have struggled to save the lives of Sacco and Vanzetti and who must now endure their loss. In the "agony" of grief, these many angry and disappointed comrades can feel and name that which they are losing—that for which they continue still to yearn. In Dos Passos's formulation, it is the "hat[red] of oppression" that is the vibrant kernel of the American political tradition—an impulse persistently compromised in the nation's history, and now betrayed most fiercely by the beneficiaries of an exploitative economic order. But that impulse persists because it is shared and extended within an ongoing political movement. Dos Passos emphasizes, moreover, that that impulse is not merely conserved in a static repetition but is dynamically "renewed" through a collective engagement with the urgent particularities of the present.

Nowhere in *U.S.A.*, not even in the radical biographies, does Dos Passos affirm so strongly the power of political community to respond to loss at the very moment of its occurrence. He insists here that all those who have protested the incarceration and execution of the anarchists—the young and the old, the women and the men, the immigrants and the native born, the skilled workers and the jobless hobos, from every part of the country—are bound together in grief and anger, and in renewal of a betrayed tradition of aspiration. Such an affirmation on Dos Passos's part requires a shedding of the defensive misanthropy of the story lines: he acknowledges that the educated and uneducated alike can find a way to make "the old words new" as they give voice to that which has been denied. Perhaps most strikingly of all, the Camera Eye narrator is able at last to shed the sense of falsity and detachment that has separated him from the movement he has wanted also to embrace. Affirming the power of language and memory, he is able to experience himself as part of an ongoing community of wounded idealists: "the language of the beaten nation is not forgotten in *our* ears tonight" (*TBM* 414, emphasis added).

It should be emphasized that this affirmation of mourning's power entails no denial of the depth and reality of loss itself. The enactment of political mourning *does* enable the Camera Eye narrator to perceive that the oppressed retain some latent power: he recognizes that during Sacco and Vanzetti's funeral, "the streets belong to the beaten nation"—and the "conquering" class is "scared" as well as those whom they have conquered. But the Camera Eye ends with its clear-eyed acknowledgment of failure and disappointment: "we stand defeated America." The work of mourning is never a denial or repudiation of loss: for Dos Passos here, as for all the writers who constitute the "other" modernism, it is the full acknowledgment of social injury and its accompanying anger that enables one to experience the persistence of desire and of political hope.

It is remarkable that at the very height of Dos Passos's political crisis, in the very midst of his despair about the Left, he was capable of this sudden burst of affirmation. But that gesture was fragile—and fleeting. This act of mourning is followed by a swift, equivocal repudiation. Just as he could not sustain the project of the radical biographies (or even tolerate without revision those he had written earlier), Dos Passos could not leave the Sacco and Vanzetti Camera Eyes as the final statement of his own psychopolitical development. The concluding segment of the Camera Eye (51) moves forward several years, from Dos Passos's experience of the Sacco and Vanzetti executions in 1927 to his investigation of the Harlan County, Kentucky, coal strike during the winter of 1931. At the invitation of the Communist-led National Committee for the Defense of Political Prisoners, Dos Passos joined a group of radical writers under the leadership of Theodore Dreiser to investigate and write about the striking miners, who had been driven to the brink of starvation and were subjected to murderous violence by the mine owners, with the active collusion of local police and legal authorities. In *U.S.A.*'s final Camera Eye, Dos Passos records (as he had in his activist journalism at the time) the suffering of the miners and the brutal suppression of their attempts to organize.[5] Camera Eye 51 seeks to mourn for "the beaten nation" once more—but his grieving is now blocked by the reassertion of unresolved political ambivalence.

Dos Passos begins by recording the human toll of economic exploitation in Harlan County: "two wrinkled girls that might be young," but whose youth has been blighted by poverty; the miner with "cavedin mouth" and "belly swelled enormous with the wound he got working on the minetipple"; the families "scared" and helpless in the face of starvation and deprived of medical care. He records too the violence, incarceration, and political repression that has attended the miners' effort to defend themselves by striking for a union. As in the Sacco and Vanzetti Camera Eyes, Dos Passos directs his anger (and his reader's) at the economic system and the sociopolitical structures responsible for this devastation. He focuses, in particular, on the capacity of the owning class to deploy the coercive power of the state to enforce the economic exploitation of working people and to crush their resistance. The "conquering army," he explains, "stand at the minehead they stand at the polls they stand by when the bailiffs carry the furniture of the family evicted from the city tenement out on the sidewalk they are there when the bankers foreclose on a farm they are [. . .] ready to shoot down the strikers [. . .] those that the guns spare they jail." Because the owners can call out the police and the militia, they control "the power of submachineguns sawedoff-shotguns teargas and vomitinggas the power that can feed you or leave you to starve." If the workers resist this power, they stand no chance in court, where "the judge" is "an owner himself" (*TBM* 463–464).

Even as he directs his anger at this socioeconomic structure, however, Dos Passos also criticizes the divisive, self-destructive behavior of the Left itself, which has further weakened the radical movement and the efforts of working people to defend themselves. When Dos Passos goes to visit imprisoned strikers, he witnesses a member of the Communist Party offering assistance to the men in jail, but only if they give exclusive loyalty to Communist-backed unions: "the representative of the political party talks fast through the bars join up with us and no other union we'll send you tobacco candy solidarity our lawyers will write briefs speakers will shout your names at meetings they'll carry your names on cardboards on picketlines the men in jail shrug their shoulders smile thinly our eyes look in their eyes through the bars what can I say?" (*TBM* 463). Dos Passos would later claim that this experience, of watching Communist organizers refuse to assist striking miners who failed to repudiate non-Communist unions, played a decisive role in turning him against the Party.[6] In the Camera Eye, this episode stands as instance of and synecdoche for the divisive behavior of the CP, which seemed to him a stark violation of the spirit of solidarity on which the radical tradition rested—and the catastrophic international implications of which had precipitated the author's political crisis in 1934 and 1935. Here, Dos Passos implies that an inhumane sectarianism is also allied with a paternalism that he had long seen as antithetical to solidarity. In "Lover of Mankind," he had accused American radicals of undermining their own movement by failing to respond to Debs's offer of an egalitarian "brotherhood," preferring to view their leader as a "kindly uncle" who would "give them candy" (*42P* 26). Here Dos Passos suggests that the leadership of the anticapitalist movement has been transformed into a vindictive version of this avuncularity. Even as the party representatives threaten to abandon the strikers in jail if they will not toe the line, they offer a trivialized "solidarity" that has been reduced to dispensing "tobacco" and "candy"—and to a kind of publicity that Dos Passos ridicules (perhaps unfairly) as the promise that "speakers will shout your names at meetings." In these formulations, Dos Passos implies that the leading formation of the Left is itself drawing on the murderous power of the state and the tragic vulnerability of the workers to manipulate them into accepting a model of revolutionary struggle that betrays the ethos of solidarity. This perception of the movement's self-betrayal shatters the feeling of comradeship and collective belonging achieved by the Camera Eye narrator at the moment of Sacco and Vanzetti's executions. Like the passive and bewildered strikers themselves, the middle-class radical is reduced once more to the mute, paralyzed, and detached observer who wonders "what can I say?"

Although Dos Passos records the political behavior he abhorred in the Communist Party, he cannot explore or come to terms with it. In "Lover of Mankind," for example, he had focused his attention on the internal failings of the radical movement in ways that enabled him to work through, in some detail, the impulses that had compromised Debsian socialism so that he could also name and honor the impulses that were most vibrant and deserving of extension. In this final segment of the Camera Eye, in contrast, Dos Passos can only note, briefly and without elaboration, the divisive behavior of the Party. He makes no attempt to assess the motivations of such behavior, or to explore its complex, ambivalent relation to the things he valued in the revolutionary Left. Stalinism appears here, in other words, as a toxic and traumatic fact, not a complex, destructive process that grew within the radical movement itself and that required strenuous analysis and engagement. It is worth keeping in mind, for example, that it was the same Party that had helped to organize the writers' committee in which Dos Passos participated that he also here represents with such anger. But the Camera Eye cannot fully acknowledge, explore, or work through that ambivalence.

As a result, the process of mourning grinds to a halt. In the earlier Sacco and Vanzetti Camera Eyes, Dos Passos had been able to express and understand the nature of his anger at a destructive socioeconomic order—and he was then able to retrieve with considerable vitality his libidinal investments in a suppressed political movement. But in this final segment, there is an additional dimension of his rage, which he lacked the psychic resources to engage: an explosive anger at the self-betrayal of a movement to which he was also deeply bound by love. This is the tangled impasse of his political mourning. There is grief and much anger in Camera Eye 51, but there is no renewal of libidinal investment. Dos Passos can no longer declare that "the old words were made new tonight." He cannot affirm the power of memory or the persistence of desire. He dares not believe in the creative power of language to point toward a fresh, dynamic extension of a solidaristic movement crushed from without and compromised from within. As he watches the representative of his own movement threaten and cajole the frightened miners, he can only wonder helplessly: "what can I say?" As he describes the vast, murderous power of the state to perpetuate the exploitation of a defeated people, he brings the Camera Eye to a close: "we have only words against   "

The autobiographical narrative of his own political subjectivity ends with a blank space. It is not the pregnant space of desire's possibility. It is, rather, the thwarted blankness of his incapacity to name fully that which has wounded him. Immediately after the Camera Eye's ambiguous ending, the title of his biography of Samuel Insull announces the possible object of his anger—"Power Superpower"—a phrase that evokes the vast, destructive system of monopoly capitalism. And U.S.A. does indeed record, with more ambition perhaps than any work of its generation, the contours of this staggering economic formation. But it is not the exploitative ferocity of monopoly capitalism, or the repressiveness of its political self-preservation, that Dos Passos is unable to name. In the Camera Eye, as in the earlier radical biographies, he found the means to describe and to mourn for this. But the crisis of Stalinism was, for Dos Passos, a more intimately bewildering problem. At the end of the Camera Eye, the story of his own political journey, Dos Passos can no longer feel what remains of the radical movement he admired and helped to build. He cannot feel within himself the possibility of its future flourishing.

That inability to mourn the internal failings of the movement persisted—and it determined the whole of Dos Passos's subsequent political development. As other scholars have recorded, Dos Passos's violent repudiation of the

Communist branch of the movement was intensified the year after *U.S.A.*'s publication, when he came to believe that his friend, the Spanish intellectual José Robles, had been executed by Communists during the internecine violence of the Spanish Civil War.[7] He was appropriately enraged by the antidemocratic tendencies, the violent repression, and the self-destructive bloodletting of Stalinism. Perceiving the catastrophic implications of these developments within the movement, abroad and at home, Dos Passos was unable to tolerate the ambivalence he now felt toward the anticapitalist Left. Unable to acknowledge his love for a movement that he now believed was betraying and destroying itself, Dos Passos could no longer engage in the work of political mourning. That work would have required that he raise to consciousness all that he had loved, admired, and invested in American radicalism, even as he sought to clarify for himself what he now hated and how it had arisen from a movement committed to solidarity, democracy, and expressive freedom. Such a mourning would have enabled Dos Passos to contribute to the project of imagining a democratic radicalism opposed both to Stalinism and to the ravages of monopoly capitalism. But he was unable to sustain that psychic conflict. In the years ahead, and for the remainder of his life, Dos Passos attempted to resolve this crisis (as he had in the fictional narratives of *U.S.A.*) through a strategy of systematic repudiation. Moving swiftly through a brief phase as a New Deal Democrat, Dos Passos soon became a critic of welfare state liberalism and even of labor unions. By the late 1940s, he had become a defender of Joseph McCarthy. Late in life, he championed the Presidential bid of Barry Goldwater and the intellectual conservatism of the young William Buckley, condemning the emergent New Left and throwing his support behind the Vietnam War. It is true, as the writer himself claimed and as many scholars emphasized during the cold war, that Dos Passos held fast to his commitments to democracy and free expression in the course of this shift from Left to Right. But it is crucial that we acknowledge that Dos Passos inflexibly repudiated all that he—and hundreds of thousands of Americans—had valued in the anticapitalist Left. Unable to mourn the catastrophe of Stalinism, he attempted for the rest of his life to stifle the yearning for a social order liberated from the exploitation and alienation entailed by modern capitalism.

Dos Passos's story has proven to be a central one for the history of the twentieth-century American Left. American radicals of every kind have had to grieve for the external repression of a vibrant and diverse anticapitalist movement—first during the Red Scare of the teens and 1920s and, later, during the McCarthy era. And from the 1930s onward, all have had to confront, sooner or later, the disaster of Stalinism, which emerged within the movement itself. Intellectuals, activists, and artists have, to some degree, analyzed and grieved for the first of these disasters, although that task of mourning remains incomplete. It is incomplete to the degree that most Americans, including many of those who are critical of the nation's economic arrangements, remain ignorant of the richness of the democratic, anticapitalist tradition in the United States—and of its systematic, state-sponsored repression. It remains incomplete to the degree that the spectrum of electoral politics remains anomalously truncated, without even a labor party having successfully emerged over the last century.[8] And it remains incomplete to the degree that an aura of fear surrounds discussions of capitalism and its alternatives in the United States in ways that are little understood and rarely made conscious even on the part of intellectuals.

American radicals have found it even more difficult to come to terms with the legacy of Stalinism. There emerged, of course, an anti-Stalinist Left in the United States. in the middle of the twentieth century, as there did in other industrialized nations.[9] But their efforts to analyze and grieve for the failures of the Communist Left, and through such work to retrieve and extend what has been most vibrant in the anticapitalist tradition, have thus far not been widely developed by subsequent generations. The sterility, rigidity, and ferocity of cold war polemics about Communism created an intellectual and political climate in which such work was exceptionally difficult. Over the past twenty years, and especially since the collapse of the Soviet Union, the climate has been less forbidding, and a new generation of scholars are exploring more flexibly and productively the nature of the anticapitalist Left, including the revolutionary Left of the 1930s. But it is striking how commonly the phenomenon of Stalinism is bracketed even in the best recent scholarship. In this regard, we remain afraid of the ambivalence of our political legacy. Like Dos Passos, we remain too often fearful of acknowledging *both* the inspired idealism and humanity of anticapitalist radicalism in America *and* the disaster of Stalinism that blighted the socialist movement for half a century. The inability to tolerate that ambivalence makes the work of political mourning impossible. As long as that mourning remains blocked, there can be no full retrieval and no full extension of the American radical tradition. If we cannot grieve for the external repression and the internal failings of the movement, we will continue to deprive ourselves of the energies, the aspirations, the partially accomplished and persistently thwarted hopes of a movement that, over generations, was embraced by millions of Americans, including many of those who were most vulnerable and most wounded by the processes of modernization. We will remain cut off from the evolving vision of a society more just, less exploitative, less alienated.

The struggle for social change is always a psychological as well as a political challenge. Beneath the surface, it is always a struggle between mourning and melancholia. Like other radicals in his generation and our own, Dos Passos sought to grieve for the destructive effects of the social order in which he lived—and also for the disappointments and frustrations of the political movements that had arisen to remedy those social injuries. His political radicalism was a testament to his capacity for mourning: for two decades, he was able not only to name the toxic dynamics of monopoly capitalism, but also to honor in himself and others the continued desire for equality and for a less alienated way of life. But as I have shown, that capacity to mourn persistently faltered and was countered by a paralyzing and defensive melancholia. His hope for social solidarity and libidinal flourishing was persistently checked by the fear that such hopes were illusory and that the worst features of capitalism were simply an expression of the ugliness and inadequacy of an unalterable human nature. His anger at the flagrant injustices and woundings of American society were, at such moments, converted into a bitter misanthropy. That melancholic vision expressed a deep psychic pain, but it also released him from a punishing sense of responsibility. It promised too a defense against further disappointment, though that defense required a constant reassertion of misanthropy and a continuous stifling of his most expansive desires and aspirations.

This psychic and political struggle rages at the heart of American modernism. The modernist tradition voices a sustained cry of distress for the pervasive, yet dreadfully intimate, injuries inflicted by modern capitalism. These modernist writers invented ambitious new formal strategies to map and to mourn the suffering of their generation. But their efforts at social mourning were—like all processes of profound grieving—conflicted. Writers such as Hurston, H. D., Olsen, Hughes, and Williams were able to invent representational practices that expressed their rage at an alienating and exploitative social order and that affirmed their thwarted desires as potentialities that could one day flourish through social transformation. In each of these writers, there are moments when mourning gives way to melancholia, but their works are remarkable for their capacity to measure the fullness of their loss and to honor even the most frustrated of their desires. Other modernists, such as Eliot, Hemingway, Fitzgerald, Cather, Toomer, and Faulkner, produced works that gave equally powerful expression to the losses accompanying modernization, but the moments of full mourning are fewer, and the tidal pull of melancholia is stronger. In these writers, the tendency to naturalize toxic social dynamics leads to the blockage of mourning: anger is turned inward upon the self and displaced onto the most vulnerable. Disappointed desires are represented as beautiful illusions, inherently impossible of realization.

The balance between mourning and melancholia is an idiosyncratic psychic matter, which reflects the complex particularities of any circumstance of grieving. But it is also a social matter. Every culture makes available to its members a repertoire of psychic and social practices for responding to loss. Those practices are varied and they change over time: like any aspect of a culture, they reflect the complex interplay of collective inheritance and adaptation.[10] In the middle of the twentieth century, the American literary establishment lionized melancholia to a remarkable degree, celebrating melancholic modernism as the most adequate and beautiful response to social injury. Our most firmly canonized modernism is, indeed, an exceptionally poignant and expressive literature—but it also enacts a mystifying and self-destructive response to loss. The nearly exclusive celebration of that strand of modernism has had powerful cultural effects for half a century. It is time for our society to expand its repertoire of social grieving. We cannot afford to lose those practices of mourning that enabled men and women—including many from those groups most severely wounded by the processes of modernization—to affirm their desires for love, for social solidarity, for creativity and equality in the face of persistent denial. As a matter of cultural history, we should retrieve the modernism of mourning so that we can understand more fully the actual range of literary responses to the crisis of modernization. But there is more at stake than that. By retrieving the whole conflicted argument of American modernism, and not merely its melancholic half, we can grasp more clearly the enormous difficulty of grieving for the injuries of modern capitalism—and we can enhance our own capacity to mourn and resist the most destructive processes that are at work in our society.

Notes

Chapter One

1. The epigraph from Stein appears, of course, at the opening of *The Sun Also Rises*. For Kazin's observation, see *On Native Grounds: An Interpretation of Modern American Prose Literature* (1942; New York: Doubleday, 1956) 241.

2. Taking his cue (and his title) from Marx, Marshall Berman has made this case for "modernism," in its broadest historical sense, as an ambivalent response to capitalist modernization. See his influential work, *All That Is Solid Melts Into Air* (1982; New York: Penguin, 1988). For other materialist assessments of the relationship between modernism and capitalism, see Raymond Williams, *The Politics of Modernism: Against the New Conformists* (New York: Verso, 1989); Terry Eagleton, "Capitalism, Modernism and Postmodernism," *Against the Grain: Essays 1975–1985* (New York: Verso, 1986) 131–147; and Fredric Jameson, *A Singular Modernity: Essay on the Ontology of the Present* (New York: Verso, 2002).

3. John Dos Passos, e.g., explained to Malcolm Cowley that his experimental writing was an attempt to record the changes that had occurred in American life as a result of the shift from "competitive" to "monopoly capitalism." See the letter from Dos Passos to Cowley, Feb. 1932, *The Fourteenth Chronicle: Letters and Diaries of John Dos Passos*, ed. Townsend Ludington (Boston: Gambit, 1973) 404. For recent materialist accounts of the shift from "market" to "monopoly capitalism" (and cultural responses to it) see, e.g., Fredric Jameson, *Postmodernism: Or the Cultural Logic of Late Capitalism* (Durham: Duke UP, 1991); and David Harvey, *The Condition of Postmodernity: An Enquiry into the Origins of Cultural Change* (Cambridge: Blackwell, 1989).

4. I take this concept of "cognitive mapping" from Fredric Jameson. Jameson's great contribution to modernism scholarship has been this insistence on the relationship between modernist *form* (something about which Berman, e.g., is relatively unconcerned) and the cognitive difficulties posed by capitalist transformation. See Jameson, "Cognitive Mapping," *Marxism and the Interpretation of Culture*, ed. Cary Nelson and Lawrence Grossberg (Urbana: U of Illinois P, 1988) 347–360.

5. These writers' degree of political activity was quite varied, as I explain in Chapter Three. Hughes and Olsen were active in revolutionary political organizations for many years. Williams's relationship to the Left was characterized by a maverick, inconsistent sympathy for various anticapitalist causes, including public advocacy for the Social Credit movement in the 1930s. H. D. was even more wary of institutionalized politics than Williams, and her relationship to anticapitalist formations has been

little studied—but her active participation in the left avant-garde film journal *Close Up* (and the circle that surrounded it) is now well known.

6. The phrase "new modernism studies" has come into common usage relatively recently to identify the substantial changes that have taken place in the field over the past two decades. Many scholars have participated in the welcome expansion of the modernist canon, but a few of the most influential general interventions are these: on female modernists, see Shari Benstock, *Women of the Left Bank, Paris 1900–1940* (Austin: U of Texas P, 1986); Suzanne Clark, *Sentimental Modernism: Women Writers and the Revolution of the Word* (Bloomington: Indiana UP, 1991); and Bonnie Kime Scott's revisionary anthology, *The Gender of Modernism: A Critical Anthology* (Bloomington: Indiana UP, 1990); on working-class and left modernism see especially Cary Nelson, *Repression and Recovery: Modern American Poetry and the Politics of Cultural Memory, 1910–1945* (Madison: U of Wisconsin P, 1989); Walter Kalaidjian, *American Culture Between the Wars: Revisionary Modernism & Postmodern Culture* (New York: Columbia UP, 1993); Michael Denning, *The Cultural Front: The Laboring of American Culture in the Twentieth Century* (New York: Verso, 1996); and Alan Wald, *Exiles from a Future Time* (Chapel Hill: U of North Carolina P, 2002); on African American modernism, see esp. Houston Baker, *Modernism and the Harlem Renaissance* (Chicago: U of Chicago P, 1987); George Hutchinson, *The Harlem Renaissance in Black and White* (Cambridge: Harvard UP, 1995); and Brent Hayes Edwards, *The Practice of Diaspora* (Cambridge: Harvard UP, 2003).

7. I do not want to overstate the degree of isolation among these various projects of canon expansion. Particularly among literary historians, there have been a number of ambitious efforts to produce narratives that bring together formerly excluded African American, working-class, female and left modernists. Such revisionary historical narratives include Ann Douglas, *Terrible Honesty: Mongrel Manhattan in the 1920s* (New York: Farrar, Straus & Giroux, 1995); Cary Nelson, *Repression and Recovery*; Alan Wald, *Exiles from a Future Time*; and George Hutchinson, *The Harlem Renaissance in Black and White*. Among literary critics, however, concerned both with the social history of modernism and with the social implications of modernist formal experiments, there have thus far been fewer efforts at synthesis.

8. For a suggestive analysis of one part of this process, see Lawrence Schwartz's account of the cold war context of Faulkner's canonization: Lawrence H. Schwartz, *Creating Faulkner's Reputation: The Politics of Modern Literary Criticism* (Knoxville: U of Tennessee P, 1988).

9. I have noted that there were few exceptions to the posture of pained acquiescence among those admitted to the modernist canon during this period. It is not surprising that in the context of the cold war, the principal exceptions were among the reactionary critics of capitalist modernization. Despite furious debate, Ezra Pound was elevated to canonical status, although his late *Cantos* insisted that the human potentialities he valued were being crushed by capitalism and that only a new social order (embodied in Fascism) could liberate them. Similarly, Eliot's late work, suggesting that some fusion of monarchy and Anglo-Catholicism might redeem the

horrors of modernization, did not imperil his place at the center of the cold war modernist canon.

10. It is worth noting two distinct features of the cold-war shaping of the modernist canon. Most obviously, those writers whose important works were explicitly and undeniably committed to radical politics were commonly dismissed as propagandists beyond the pale of serious critical attention. But in the case of many writers whose anticapitalist politics registered itself in more allusive ways in their works, a kind of critical whitewashing often took place as a condition for canonization. This latter phenomenon can be seen, e.g, in the longstanding critical evasions of the anticapitalist commitments of such writers as Sherwood Anderson, Jean Toomer, Nathanael West, Langston Hughes, H. D.—and even, as I explain below, of John Dos Passos.

11. Despite her popularity in her own time, Cather was marginalized as the cold war modernist canon was consolidated at midcentury—and her gender certainly played an important role in this marginalization within a tradition defined along masculinist lines. Toomer's exclusion from discussions of modernism until recently stemmed in large part from his association with a racially segregated African American literary tradition. On their complex reception histories, see Deborah Carlin, *Cather, Canon, and the Politics of Reading* (Amherst: U of Massachusetts P, 1992); and Henry Louis Gates, Jr, "The Same Difference: Reading Jean Toomer, 1923-1982," in Gates, *Figures in Black: Words, Signs and the "Racial" Self* (New York: Oxford UP, 1987) 196-234.

12. Jean Toomer was drawn to radical political ideas during the period in which he wrote *Cane*. (For an assessment of the extent and limits of his relationship to the Left, see Barbara Foley, "Roads Taken and Not Taken: Post-Marxism, Antiracism, and Anticommunism," *Cultural Logic: An Electronic Journal of Marxist Theory and Practice* 1.2 [Spring 1998]; and Barbara Foley, "'In the Land of Cotton': Economics and Violence in Jean Toomer's *Cane*," *African-American Review* 32.2 [Summer 1998]: 181-198.) His case clearly indicates that it was possible for a writer to hold radical political ideas and nevertheless write literary works pervaded by a naturalizing, deterministic vision of American capitalism. (The relationship between Marxism, in particular, and social determinism is a complex matter—and one that I will address in some detail in Part Two.) But this combination of radical political commitment and a pessimistic determinism was relatively rare, and most left modernists contributed to the tradition I have called the "other" modernism—as the examples of Hughes and Olsen discussed in Chapter 3 will show.

13. Sigmund Freud, "Mourning and Melancholia," *The Standard Edition of the Complete Psychological Works of Sigmund Freud*, trans. and ed. James Strachey, vol. 14 (London: Hogarth, 1957) 243-245. Subsequent references will appear parenthetically in the text—and where necessary, will be cited as *MM*.

14. For Freud's comments on the duration of melancholia, see *MM* 244, 252, 257.

15. An early effort in this direction was Alexander Mitscherlich and Marguerite Mitscherlich, *The Inability to Mourn: Principles of Collective Behavior* (New York: Grove

Press, 1975), a study of the incapacity of Germans to grieve their losses after the end of the Second World War. Other works by historians include Wolf Lepenies, *Melancholy and Society* (Cambridge: Harvard UP, 1992); Henry Rousso, *The Vichy Syndrome: History and Memory in France since 1944* (Cambridge: Harvard UP, 1991); and Jay Winter, *Sites of Memory, Sites of Mourning: The Great War in European Cultural History* (New York: Cambridge UP, 1995). Work by sociologists on collective mourning and loss includes Peter Marris, *Loss and Change* (New York: Pantheon, 1974); and Kai Ericson, *A New Species of Trouble: The Human Experience of Modern Disasters* (New York: Norton, 1994). There has been a dramatic development of interest in mourning (sometimes including discussions of social mourning) among literary critics in recent years, which I will address below. Holocaust Studies has provided a particularly rich field in which theories of mourning—and the distinct but related domain of trauma theory—has been developed in recent years. Influential work on trauma among recent cultural critics includes Cathy Caruth, *Unclaimed Experience: Trauma, Narrative, and History* (Baltimore: Johns Hopkins UP, 1996); Caruth, ed., *Trauma: Explorations in Memory* (Baltimore: Johns Hopkins UP, 1995); Dominic La Capra, *Representing the Holocaust: History, Theory, Trauma* (Ithaca, NY: Cornell UP, 1994); and La Capra, *Writing History, Writing Trauma* (Baltimore: Johns Hopkins UP, 2001). Work on mourning in recent Holocaust scholarship includes Saul Friedlander, *Memory, History, and the Extermination of the Jews of Europe* (Bloomington: U of Indiana P, 1993); and Friedlander, ed., *Probing the Limits of Representation: Nazism and the "Final Solution"* (Cambridge: Harvard UP, 1992). Readers seeking to orient themselves in this growing field can find a useful overview of several strands of this scholarship in Peter Homans's introduction to *Symbolic Loss: The Ambiguity of Mourning and Memory at Century's End*, ed. Homans (Charlottesville: UP of Virginia, 2000) 1–42. For a recent collection of essays, see David L. Eng and David Kazanjian, ed., *Loss: The Politics of Mourning* (Berkeley: U of California P, 2002).

16. This particular kind of ambivalence—in which a person or group is struggling to grieve the loss of something that is both beloved and recognized as catastrophically (self-) destructive—creates an especially severe obstacle to mourning. This is the predicament faced by post–Second World War Germans in grieving for the Nazi regime, as noted by the Mitscherlichs and by Eric Santner in *Stranded Objects: Mourning, Memory and Film in Postwar Germany* (Ithaca, NY: Cornell UP, 1990). It has been similarly faced (or evaded) by the French people in contemplating the widespread reality of wartime collaboration, as Henry Roussou has pointed out in *The Vichy Syndrome*. As I will demonstrate at length in Chapter 2, it was a problem confronted by many canonized U.S. modernists, who were struggling to grieve for American social formations of whose toxic destructiveness they were painfully aware. To note one final case of importance to the current study, this is also a problem that socialists around the world have had to confront (and have, alas, commonly evaded) in their ambivalent relationship to the painfully complex history of international Communism.

17. One of the most striking features of recent discussions of grieving on the part of literary and cultural critics is the affirmation of melancholia as a desirable response to loss, especially to socially induced forms of loss. Those who have adopted this view have generally been motivated by an appropriate criticism of Freud's model of mourning—and, in particular, of his suggestion that a nonpathological mourning requires a withdrawal of investment (a "decathexis") from what one has loved and lost. In political contexts in which one is considering the response of vulnerable social groups to their oppression, such a model of mourning appears politically conservative as well as psychically callous. In order to respond to this limitation in Freud's account of mourning, a number of recent critics have embraced his theory of melancholia, finding in it a more adequate model for understanding how members of oppressed groups can sustain derided identities and truncated social possibilities. Philip Novak has, e.g., argued that "melancholia" is a "therapeutic" and more "ethical" response to the ongoing oppressions of African American life: to mourn, in such a context, would constitute "a surrender to the forces that produced the losses in the first place" (see "'Circles and circles of sorrow': In the Wake of Morrison's *Sula*," *PMLA* 114.2 [Mar. 1999]: 191). For similar reasons, other critics have sought to theorize a hybrid "melancholic mourning." Jose Muñoz has, for example, celebrated what he perceives as strategies of "melancholic mourning" in gay and African American visual art that "holds onto a lost object until inner feelings of ambivalence are worked out" and that enables us to "take our dead to the various battles we must wage in their names." (See "Photographies of Mourning: Melancholia and Ambivalence in Van Der Zee, Mapplethorpe, and *Looking for Langston*," *Race and the Subject of Masculinities*, ed. Harry Stecopoulos and Michael Uebel. [Durham: Duke UP, 1997] 337, 352, 356.) To celebrate the grieving processes of the oppressed as "melancholic," these and other critics ignore the self-destructive aspect of melancholia: a self-beratement that tends toward suicide. Their formulations sometimes imply that melancholia enables the bereaved to express anger at those who have harmed them, when it is precisely a mode of grieving that displaces anger onto the self and away from its actual objects. Positive assessments of melancholia also tend to ignore another central feature of this psychic dynamic: the depressed cauterization of libido. The AIDS activist and theorist Douglas Crimp has provided a valuable corrective to this theoretical tendency, pointing eloquently to the dangers posed by melancholia not only for individuals, but also for emancipatory movements organized by oppressed groups (see "Mourning and Militancy," *October* 51 [1989]: 3–18). While I share the political aims of those critics seeking to understand how oppressed people can hold onto identities and possibilities denied by unjust social structures, I believe that we can better understand such strategies of grieving through an expanded and revised model of mourning than through an embrace of melancholia. As this study points out, the veneration of melancholia (which has a long and complex literary history) has been a dominant and politically quiescent tendency within twentieth-century U.S. culture—and that tendency appears today to be receiving a new extension

into the domain of cultural theory. For a more sustained version of this argument, see Seth Moglen, "On Mourning Social Injury," *Psychoanalysis, Culture & Society* 10.2 (August 2005): 151–167. For a detailed critique of this theoretical tendency from a related position, see Greg Forter, "Against Melancholia: Contemporary Mourning Theory, Fitzgerald's *The Great Gatsby*, and the Politics of Unfinished Grief," *Differences* 14.2 (Summer 2003): 134–170. I am indebted to Forter's mapping of this critical terrain.

18. The objection may be raised that these formulations are excessively broad, and that "loss" comes in my account to describe situations in which human capacities are not so much "lost" as prevented from flourishing. The distinction is an important one. Judith Butler employs the useful formulation that social formations (in her case, homophobia) can "preempt" and "foreclos[e]" the possibility of realizing certain desires (homosexual ones, in her example) in ways that produce profound experiences of loss that may be especially difficult to grieve. (See Butler, "Melancholy Gender/Refused Identification," *The Psychic Life of Power: Theories in Subjection* [Stanford: Stanford UP, 1997] 135.) This notion of a *preemptive loss* that *forecloses* the realization of desire is a valuable one, and I believe it is quite necessary to use the term "loss" to describe experiences of this kind, while acknowledging their distinctiveness.

19. For an influential application of the Freudian concept of trauma to cultural, especially literary, representations of social injury, see Caruth, *Unclaimed Experience*.

20. Sigmund Freud, *Beyond the Pleasure Principle*, trans. and ed. James Strachey (New York: Norton, 1961) 6. Subsequent references, where necessary, will be cited as *PP*.

21. Some scholars have attempted to render the concept of trauma more flexible, specifically in order to adapt it for use in discussing the gradual, ongoing character of injurious social processes. A particularly helpful effort in this direction is Ericson, *A New Species of Trouble*. Ericson's model of "collective trauma" explicitly moves away from the emphasis on "surprise" so central to most psychoanalytic formulations about trauma. Because Ericson does not engage with psychoanalysis, or even with the details of psychic experience, however, his account does not shed much light on the psychodynamics of gradually inflicted social traumas. This work remains to be done. One possible starting point for such work within the psychoanalytic tradition would be the suggestive formulations about "cumulative trauma" offered by Massud Khan. Khan is concerned with the ways in which inadequacies in the maternal "holding environment" (a Winnicottian concept, which Khan reconceives as a maternal "protective shield") can lead to the deformation of the infant's ego as a result of injuries that may not be traumatic individually, but which may, cumulatively and often "silently," produce lasting traumatic consequences. Although socially minded scholars participating in the current trauma debates have not yet taken them up, Khan's formulations might be productively elaborated in social terms. See especially M. Massud R. Khan, "The Concept of Cumulative Trauma" (1963) and "Ego-distortion, Cumula-

tive Trauma, and the Role of Reconstruction in the Analytic Situation" (1964), *The Privacy of the Self* (London: Hogarth, 1974) 59–68.

22. The treatment of traumatic illness has, of course, remained a central concern for clinicians—and also for some social scientists who have entered more socially oriented discussions of trauma. (As a legal consultant to victims of environmental calamities, e.g., Kai Ericson has developed a limited but substantive conception of how some traumas might be redressed through the courts [see *A New Species of Trouble*]). But one of the most striking features of trauma theory as it has been developed by recent literary scholars is the common lack of concern with how the suffering of trauma (and the destructive compulsion to repeat) might be relieved. This lack of concern for the therapeutic (or social) remediation of trauma is, I believe, symptomatic of the now widespread tendency among literary critics to universalize trauma as the essence of history itself: "What does it mean," Cathy Caruth asks, e.g., "for history to be the history of a trauma?" Her answer is that "history can only be grasped in the inaccessibility of its occurrence" (Caruth, *Unclaimed Experience* 15, 18). Dominic La Capra has incisively criticized the tendency of many scholars to conflate socially induced "loss" with metaphysical forms of "absence," often assimilating purportedly historical discussions of trauma with poststructuralist arguments, e.g., about the inherent instability of language. As La Capra rightly insists, this conflation of "loss" with "absence" blunts the historical specificity of many accounts of trauma—and it also, I would add, places these phenomena outside the domain of psychic or social remedy. (See "Trauma, Absence, Loss" in La Capra, *Writing* 43–85.)

23. It is worth noting that some destructive social processes are more difficult to grasp than others. The victims of capitalist modernization may be particularly likely to experience their injuries as traumas, e.g., because the processes to which they are subject take place on such a vast scale that they are nearly impossible to conceptualize on the basis of individual experience alone. As Fredric Jameson has pointed out in "Cognitive Mapping," works of expressive culture may have a special importance in enabling individuals to map the vast and evolving structures of modern capitalism that shape (and damage) their lives, but often exceed their conscious comprehension. I would add that the work of cognitively mapping such social processes may thus be understood as psychologically (as well as politically) imperative for modern subjects to minimize (and, retrospectively, to "work through") the traumas of modernization.

24. For two particularly convincing feminist critiques of Freud's insistence on decathexis in mourning, see Louise O. Fradenburg, "'Voice Memorial': Loss and Reparation in Chaucer's Poetry," *Exemplaria* 2.1 (Mar. 1990): 169–202; and Kathleen Woodward, "Late Theory, Late Style: Loss and Renewal in Freud and Barthes," *Aging and Gender in Literature: Studies in Creativity*, ed. Anne M. Wyatt-Brown and Janice Rossen (Charlottesville: UP of Virginia, 1993) 82–101. In different ways, Fradenburg and Woodward each demonstrate that Freud's account of mourning, with its emphasis on detachment from the lost object, is characteristic of a more general

Freudian privileging of individuation and autonomy (generally marked male in our culture) over forms of attachment and relation that are culturally coded as feminine. Many critics have objected to the implicitly normative cast of Freud's distinction between a "normal" mourning and a "pathological" melancholia, and these criticisms have by and large been rooted in an appropriate sense of the coerciveness of insisting that the bereaved must withdraw their investments in things they have loved and lost. Dissatisfaction with this aspect of Freud's account has caused some critics to go so far as to reject the mourning process itself and to embrace melancholia as a possibly more satisfying alternative (see, e.g., Novak and Michael Moon, "Memorial Rags," *Professions of Desire: Lesbian and Gay Studies in Literature*, ed. George E. Haggerty and Bonnie Zimmerman. [New York: MLA, 1995] 235–239). It should be noted, further, that much of the hostility to mourning among current literary critics also stems from the largely unwarranted association of the Freudian model of mourning with the long tradition of elegy in Western literature, which has urged the bereaved to accept religious and aesthetic consolation for their worldly deprivations. See, e.g., Fradenburg and Moon, as well as Jahan Ramazani, *Poetry of Mourning: The English Elegy from Hardy to Heaney* (Chicago: U of Chicago P, 1994). See also Peter Sacks's *The English Elegy: Studies in the Genre from Spenser to Yeats* (Baltimore: Johns Hopkins UP, 1985), a work that demonstrates the relation between elegiac consolation and the process of oedipalization. As these scholars have shown, elegiac consolation does indeed enact the logic of symbolic substitution that Freud associates with mourning and that he describes in the famous fort/da section of *Beyond the Pleasure Principle*—a logic that is also enacted in the conventional "resolution" of the Oedipal complex, with all its patriarchal implications. But it is both a logical and substantive error to imagine that the Freudian model of mourning commits one theoretically to a normative reading of the Oedipal situation or to elegiac consolation. While there are many troublingly conservative presumptions in Freud's work, an affection for religious (or other transcendental) consolations is not among them.

25. It should be noted that Freud nearly recognizes as much when he asserts that mourning involves the "hypercathected" recollection of everything that binds one—"expectations" as well as "memories," he notes—to the lost object. Freud himself, however, goes on to assert that the "detachment of libido" is somehow "accomplished" by this very process of "hypercathe[xis]." Freud is reaching here for an important point: that mourning does, in a paradoxical way, involve both a holding onto and (in some sense) a letting go of what one can no longer have in reality. (This is what he calls our "compromise" with "reality.") But by characterizing the acknowledgment of loss specifically as a "detachment" or "withdrawal" of libido, he confuses matters a good deal, implying a kind of ultimate affective relinquishing of the object in a way that is belied by most mourners' experience—and in a way that actually diminishes a proper sense of the *ongoing* manner in which lost objects are held onto even in the fullest processes of mourning that lead to renewed capacity for love. See *MM* 244–245.

26. Louise Fradenburg has offered a related critique of Freud's model of "replacement" and "substitution" in "Voice Memorial." Although Fradenburg anticipates my own dissatisfactions with this Freudian vocabulary, her emphasis on the radical specificity and particularity of every love object differs from my own formulations about mourning in that I am also concerned to emphasize the persistence of libidinal impulses in the self that carry over from one attachment or love-relation to another. I see these not as alternative, but as complementary, formulations. I would also like to note in this context Kathleen Woodward's provocative and humane proposal in "Late Theory, Late Style" that very late in life, the mourning process may have distinctive dynamics of its own. Although she suggests that under such circumstances the projection of psychic possibilities into the future may be of less importance, her finely described examples from the late work of Freud and Roland Barthes actually affirm, to my mind, the capacity even late in life for these forms of creativity, dynamism, and extension in the work of mourning.

27. In thinking about an expanded conception of mourning adequate to circumstances of socially induced loss, I have been particularly inspired by the work of the AIDS activist Douglas Crimp, and by the psychoanalytic cultural theory of Judith Butler and Eric Santner. In "Mourning and Militancy," Crimp has expressed eloquently the recognition that the psychic work of mourning and the political work of social change are mutually supportive rather than opposed. In "Melancholy Gender/Refused Identification," Butler demonstrates incisively how the taboos of a homophobic culture are pervasively internalized by individual subjects as a melancholic repudiation of infantile homosexual attachments. More than this, she gestures fleetingly toward the possibility that "collective institutions for grieving" homophobic repudiations might lead to important forms of social transformation and psychosexual liberation (148). In *Stranded Objects*, Santner has offered a particularly sustained meditation on the price paid for the inability to mourn collective losses, in the context of post–Second World War Germany. In his conclusion, he offers a brief speculation on the cultural forms that such mourning might take. My own account of the modernism of mourning in Chapters 3 and 5 is intended to offer a more extended critical contribution to these speculations about the shape of cultural practices of mourning that might enable political transformation.

28. In this context, see Wendy Brown, "Resisting Left Melancholia," *Loss: The Politics of Mourning* 458–466.

CHAPTER TWO

1. On "structures of feeling," see Williams, *Marxism and Literature* (New York: Oxford UP, 1986). I have been especially influenced by Williams's critical practice in tracing structures of feeling in *The Country and the City* (London: Hogarth, 1985) and *Culture and Society, 1780–1950* (Harmondsworth: Penguin, 1985). Williams was relatively indifferent to psychoanalysis, which might have substantially enriched his

conceptualization of "structures of feeling." I have sought throughout this book to offer a psychoanalytically informed extension of Williams's cultural materialist practice.

2. T. S. Eliot, *The Waste Land*, reprinted in Eliot, *The Complete Poems and Plays, 1909–1950* (New York: Harcourt, Brace & World, 1971) 38, 46. Subsequent references are to this edition, and line numbers will be cited parenthetically, where necessary, as *Waste Land*.

3. There has been particularly strong scholarship in recent years on the problem of loss in *The Sun Also Rises*. Most of this work has focused on Hemingway's representation of the crisis in modern gender relations, and especially in normative masculinity (which I regard as one central component of the larger transformation precipitated by capitalist modernization). See, especially, Greg Forter, "Melancholy Modernism: Gender and the Politics of Mourning in *The Sun Also Rises*," *The Hemingway Review* 20.1 (Fall 2001): 22–37; Carl Eby, *Hemingway's Fetishism: Psychoanalysis and the Mirror of Manhood* (Albany, NY: SUNY P, 1999); Pamela Boker, *The Grief Taboo in American Literature: Loss and Prolonged Adolescence in Twain, Melville, and Hemingway* (New York: NYU P, 1996), introduction & chap. 5; Nina Schwartz, "Lovers' Discourse in *The Sun Also Rises*: A Cock and Bull Story," *Criticism* 26.1 (Winter 1984): 49–69; David Wyatt, *Prodigal Sons: A Study in Authorship and Authority* (Baltimore: Johns Hopkins UP, 1980), chap. 3. See also the earlier essay by Mark Spilka, "The Death of Love in *The Sun Also Rises*," *Hemingway: A Collection of Critical Essays*, ed. Robert P. Weeks (Englewood Cliffs, NJ: Prentice Hall, 1962) 127–138.

4. For a similar and related dynamic, consider Raymond Williams's account in *The Country and the City* of the way in which British authors, over many generations, responded to the effects of urbanization by the steady production of compensatory pastoral accounts of "country" life that was persistently imagined to have recently passed away. In the U.S. modernist case, as in that of the pastoral tradition, it must be emphasized that there was not, of course, a moment of fully satisfying social cohesion and libidinal gratification that preceded the advent of monopoly capitalism. Rather, a long process of historical transformation, stretching over many generations had reached a stage at which early-twentieth-century Americans felt an acute sense of intensified alienation—and some, like Hemingway and Cather, sought to understand that experience through simplified constructions of the preceding historical moment.

5. Nina Schwartz has evoked most clearly Cather's ambivalence toward the fall of this old order in "History and the Invention of Innocence in *A Lost Lady*," *Arizona Quarterly* 46.2 (1990): 33–54.

6. For a feminist account of the price paid by women in Fitzgerald's novel for this structure, see Judith Fetterley, "*The Great Gatsby*: Fitzgerald's *Droit de Seigneur*," *Major Literary Characters: Gatsby*, ed. Harold Bloom (New York: Chelsea House, 1991) 103–112.

7. Fitzgerald describes Tom's body as "cruel" in chap. 1—and he uses the word *careless* repeatedly as a term for the economic elite's destructive indifference to others

(see, e.g., Nick's description of Tom and Daisy as "careless people" who "smashed up things and creatures and then retreated back into their money" in chap. 9 and his similar judgment of Jordan Baker in chap. 3). See *The Great Gatsby* (1925; New York: Scribner, 1995) 11, 187–9, 163. Subsequent references are to this edition and will be cited parenthetically, where necessary, as *Gatsby*. There is a rich body of criticism on loss in *Gatsby*. For a recent reading that focuses the problematic of loss on a crisis in masculinity, see Greg Forter, "Against Melancholia: Contemporary Mourning Theory, Fitzgerald's *The Great Gatsby*, and the Politics of Unfinished Grief," *Differences* 14.2 (Summer 2003): 134–170. For accounts that are, in part, materialist, see especially Mitchell Breitweiser, "*The Great Gatsby*: Grief, Jazz and the Eye-Witness," *Arizona Quarterly* 47.3 (1991): 17–70 and Richard Godden, "*The Great Gatsby*: Glamour on the Turn," *American Studies* 16.3 (1982): 343–371. For an early psychoanalytic account that explores loss in Fitzgerald's work in personal rather than social terms, see Richard A. Koenigsberg, "F. Scott Fitzgerald: Literature and the Work of Mourning," *American Imago* 24 (1967): 248–270.

8. "November Cotton Flower" (line 5) in *Cane* (1923; New York: Norton, 1988) 6. Subsequent references are to this edition and will be cited parenthetically, where necessary, as *Cane*.

9. Toomer's highly sophisticated exploration of the *psychic* effects of destructive historical phenomena deserves fuller critical exploration. Recent scholars have begun to enrich our understanding of Toomer's social formation and his concrete historical and political preoccupations. See especially a series of articles by Barbara Foley, assessing Toomer's class position, relationship to socialist politics, and to particular racial and economic forces at work in rural and urban African American communities: "Jean Toomer's Sparta," *American Literature* 67.4 (Dec. 1995): 747–775; "Jean Toomer's Washington and the Politics of Class: from 'Blue Veins' to Seventh-street Rebels," *Modern Fiction Studies* 42.2 (1996): 289–321; "Roads Taken and Not Taken: Post-Marxism, Antiracism, and Anticommunism," *Cultural Logic: an Electronic Journal of Marxist Theory and Practice* 1.2 (Spring 1998); "'In the Land of Cotton': Economics and Violence in Jean Toomer's *Cane*," *African American Review* 32.2 (Summer 1998): 181–198. See also Charles Scruggs's argument that Toomer represents his "grotesques" as produced by "the historical reality of a racial past"—an argument weakened by the opposition between "personal" and "historical" causes of injury whose *relationship* Toomer's work explores as does Sherwood Anderson's: "The Reluctant Witness: What Jean Toomer Remembered from *Winesburg, Ohio*," *Studies in American Fiction* 29.1 (Spring 2000): 78–100. See also Nathaniel Mackey's lyrical account of Toomer's musical embodiment of a "wounded kinship," which evokes experiences of loss and "estrangement" produced by slavery and by the newer alienations of urban modernity: see Mackey, "Sound and Sentiment, Sound and Symbol," *Discrepant Engagement* (Cambridge, UK: Cambridge UP, 1993) 231–259.

10. An earlier generation of literary historians was more attentive to the affiliations between naturalism and modernism than the current one. Naturalism was

at least recognized as an important influence on modernism in, e.g., Richard Ellman and Charles Feidelson, Jr.'s influential early anthology, *The Modern Tradition:
Backgrounds of Modern Literature* (New York: Oxford UP, 1965) and in the important
critical overview of the movement, Malcolm Bradbury and James McFarlane, eds.,
Modernism, 1890–1930 (New York: Penguin, 1976). While these earlier critics saw
naturalism as a precursor to modernism principally in its hostility to the "genteel" literary tradition, they did not consider the persistence of specifically naturalist narrative strategies or metaphysical presumptions in works categorized as modernist—nor
have subsequent scholars of modernism. This persistence has also gone unremarked
in the sophisticated recent scholarship on U.S. naturalism such as June Howard,
Form and History in American Literary Naturalism (Chapel Hill: U of North Carolina
P, 1985); Walter Benn Michaels, *The Gold Standard and the Logic of Naturalism: American Literature at the Turn of the Century* (Berkeley: U of California P, 1987); and Mark
Seltzer, *Bodies and Machines* (New York: Routledge, 1992). I will explore in greater
detail the U.S. adaptation of the European naturalist impulse in Chapter Six.

   11. Although earlier critics have not explored the relationship of such rhetorical
maneuvers to the tradition of literary naturalism, several have approached in other
ways the universalization and metaphysicalization of historical dynamics in the novel's
concluding paragraphs: see, especially, John F. Callahan, *The Illusions of a Nation: Myth
and History in the Novels of F. Scott Fitzgerald* (Urbana: U of Illinois P, 1972) chap. 2, especially 45–48. See also Breitweiser 26–31 and Forter, "Against Melancholia" 156–161.

   12. Although she does not consider these dynamics of naturalization, Maud Ellman does emphasize *The Waste Land*'s inability to make fully conscious the losses it
records: the poem, she explains, is "compelled to re-enact the conflicts that it cannot
bring to consciousness." See Ellman, "Eliot's Abjections," *Abjection, Melancholia, and
Love: The Work of Julia Kristeva*, ed. John Fletcher and Andrew Benjamin (New York:
Routledge, 1990) 179.

   13. For a very different but not incompatible Lacanian account of Hemingway's
mystifications and disavowals, see Schwartz, "Lovers' Discourse."

   14. *The Sun Also Rises* (1926; New York: Scribner, 1986) 148. (Subsequent references are to this edition and will be cited parenthetically, where necessary, as *Sun*.)
This naturalist tendency is, perhaps, most fully enacted in *A Farewell to Arms*. In
that novel, the protagonist persistently seeks to explain the incomprehensible and
unjustifiable carnage of the First World War by recourse to mystifying and universalizing claims about the toxic destructiveness of "the world" ("If people bring so much
courage to this world the world has to kill them") and "nature" ("It's just nature giving her hell"). The author aligns himself with this vision in many ways, not least by
structuring the novel through the comparison of the social devastation of the war
with Catherine's purely accidental death in childbirth. The naturalist structure of
feeling reaches its apotheosis in the concluding pages, in which Lieutenant Henry
compares both kinds of death to the inescapable holocaust of ants on a burning log,

who will die horribly no matter which way they turn. See Hemingway, *A Farewell to Arms* (1929; New York: Scribner, 2003) 249, 320, 327–328.

15. *A Lost Lady* (1923; New York: Vintage, 1990) 70 (ellipses in original). Subsequent references are to this edition and will be cited, where necessary, as *Lost Lady*.

16. For "uncanny," see "Becky" (*Cane* 8); for "time and space have no meaning," see "Carma" (13); for "omen" and a particularly strong structure of deterministic prefiguring, see "Blood-Burning Moon" (30). Several critics have approached the question of Toomer's tendency to naturalize destructive social phenomena. Laura Doyle has argued that Toomer alternately criticizes and indulges Romantic associations of femininity with a subordinated nature: Laura Doyle, "Swan Song for the Race Mother: Late-Romantic Narrative in *Cane*," *Bordering on the Body: The Racial Matrix of Modern Fiction and Culture* (New York: Oxford UP, 1994) 81–109. Although unconcerned with the psychic aspect of these dynamics, Barbara Foley has expressed a divided assessment of Toomer's tendency to "naturalize and dehistoricize social phenomena": see Foley, "In the Land," 183 and *passim* and Foley, "Jean Toomer's Sparta," especially 748. Catherine Gunther Kodat argues that Toomer replicates in the "aesthetic register" the social phenomena of "exploitation and domination" he records—although she associates this representational violence with an undifferentiated "high modernist" practice, rather than with any particular naturalizing impulse within the tradition: see "To 'Flash White Light from Ebony': The Problem of Modernism in Jean Toomer's *Cane*," *Twentieth Century Literature* 46.1 (Spring 2000): 1–19.

17. See John Irwin's influential account of Faulkner's vision of time as an inexorable fatality that dooms both author and characters to repetition in their very efforts at resistance: *Doubling and Incest/Repetition and Revenge: A Speculative Reading of Faulkner* (Baltimore: Johns Hopkins UP, 1975). In *Faulkner and Modernism: Rereading and Rewriting* (Madison: U of Wisconsin P, 1990) 23–121, Richard Moreland has pointed out some of the naturalizing features of this vision. In an essay focusing on *Light in August*, Laura Doyle emphasizes the way in which Faulkner's novel "tells us we have made up our history even as it naturalizes and mystifies the history it makes up": "The Body Against Itself in Faulkner's Phenomenology of Race," *American Literature* 73.2 (June 2001): 339–364; quoted sentence 360.

18. For one argument claiming Fitzgerald's separation from the universalizing "myths" through which Nick seeks to evade historical particularities, see Callahan, chap. 2, especially 30–31, 56–57. On Toomer's complex ironic relationship to the naturalizations enacted by his narrators see, especially, Doyle, "Swan Song" 94–102. For two sophisticated arguments about the ways in which Faulkner simultaneously indulges in and separates himself from the naturalistic visions expressed by his characters, see Doyle, "The Body against Itself" and Moreland, chap. 1 and 2, 23–121.

19. In other early works, such as "The Love Song of J. Alfred Prufrock" or "Portrait of a Lady," one can see a similar structure of melancholic self-beratement (and misanthropic displacement of rage) at work. In these poems, however, Eliot has distanced

himself from his narrative personae to a far greater extent than in *The Waste Land*—which I read as an apocalyptically abject and melancholically fragmented lyric. My view of *The Waste Land* as a personal act of grieving follows especially the work of James E. Miller, who broke from the entrenched tradition of "impersonal," new critical readings of the poem: see *T. S. Eliot's Personal Waste Land: Exorcism of the Demons* (University Park: Penn State UP, 1977). While I share Miller's view of the "personal" character of the poem, I also insist here on the larger social phenomena that Eliot struggles, in such a painfully blocked manner, to grieve.

20. Although she is drawing on a different psychoanalytic terminology, and is not concerned with the problem of displaced aggression, Maud Ellman has powerfully explored the "abjection" of Eliot's vision in *The Waste Land*. See "Eliot's Abjection," *Abjection, Melancholia, and Love: The Work of Julia Kristeva*, ed. John Fletcher and Andrew Benjamin (New York: Routledge, 1990) 178–200. David Spurr has discussed *The Waste Land* specifically as a poem engaged in a particular kind of *mourning*—what he calls a "style of mourning that cannot name its object." While Spurr captures the poem's "inability to mourn," he understands this blockage not as a result of a melancholic displacement of rage, but of the poem's "postmodern" exposure of mourning's "hypocrisy" and its deconstructive acknowledgment of the subject's "absence" and of the "unnameability" of all objects. In Spurr's account, a theoretical naturalization (of mourning's impossibility because of an ineradicable absence in the subject) thus mirrors the forms of naturalism deployed by Eliot himself. See Spurr, "*The Waste Land*: Mourning, Writing Disappearance," *Yeats/Eliot Review* 9.4 (1988): 161–164.

21. William Shakespeare, *Hamlet*, Act II, Scene 2. Freud offers this dictum of Hamlet's as an iconic literary incarnation of the melancholic structure of displaced aggression: *MM* 246.

22. The disavowal of anger, and the retreat into hard boiled irony, is particularly evident, e.g., in his conversation with the sympathizing prostitute, Georgette, and in the hospital scene with the buffoonishly patriotic Italian officer: *Sun* 17, 30–31.

23. On the fetishistic character of the bullfighting in the novel and of Hemingway's style, see Forter, "Melancholy Modernism"—and, on the more general tendency in Hemingway, see Eby.

24. Despite the promiscuity and pervasiveness of authorial aggression in *The Waste Land*, Eliot engages in a similar focusing of particular hostility toward the most vulnerable: while even the privileged neurasthenic couple in "A Game of Chess," e.g., are abject, Eliot's poem seems to revile more intensely those further down in the social hierarchy—such as the "young man carbuncular" (lines 231–247) and, especially, the working-class women in the pub (lines 140–172). While the poet's misanthropy applies certainly to male bodies and male figures, his misogyny is especially virulent.

25. While some of the novel's aggression toward marginalized figures (e.g., its antisemitism) is systematically and self-consciously thematized by the novel itself, others (like the racist representation of the black drummer in the bar) seem more like gratuitous eruptions.

26. On Eliot's psychological condition before and during the period of *The Waste Land*'s composition, see Peter Ackroyd, *T. S. Eliot: A Life* (New York: Simon and Schuster, 1984), chaps. 5–6: 91–131. On Hemingway's psychological history, see Kenneth S. Lynn, *Hemingway* (New York: Simon and Schuster, 1987).

27. The untenable character of these distinctions is registered by both authors in their ironic distance from the narrators who seek to make them. Even as Nick tries to sustain his idealization of Gatsby to the novel's end, as Niel does with Marian, Fitzgerald and Cather make clear in the course of the novels that these idealizations are self-delusions, however beautiful they may be. Although he is not concerned with the dynamics of splitting, or with the protection of characters from authorial aggression, Ian Bell has described the peculiar "double nature" of Fitzgerald and Cather's "knowing" indulgence in nostalgic fantasies whose unreality they also acknowledge. (Bell's discussion compares this structure in *Gatsby* with Cather's later novel, *The Professor's House*: see Ian F. A. Bell, "'Newness of Beginning: The Violent Phantasies of Willa Cather and F. Scott Fitzgerald," *The Insular Dream: Obsession and Resistance*, ed. Kristiaan Versluys (Amsterdam: VU UP, 1995) 242–260.)

28. For a related argument about authorial aggression toward Tom and Gatsby, see Forter, "Against Melancholia"; and on the shifting of blame (from the machinery of American life onto those who have become "waste"), see Breitweiser.

29. I say particularly in *Absalom*, because elsewhere Faulkner does open up the space for nostalgia. In *Light in August*, e.g.,, he comes much closer to Cather and Fitzgerald's structure of splitting in the treatment of Hightower, whose fantasy of his own family's martial and quasiaristocratic past is represented with a glowing nostalgia that is at once shared and criticized by Faulkner.

30. *Absalom, Absalom!* (1936; New York: Vintage, 1990) 3. Subsequent references are to this edition and will be cited parenthetically, where necessary, as *Absalom*.

31. Moreland has offered a somewhat different account of the novel's melancholic impulses, describing Rosa's nostalgia and Compson's irony as two different strategies for evading the work of mourning. Moreland contends that in the novel's later chapters, both Rosa and Quentin become aware of the destructive consequences of their melancholic postures—and Moreland perceives Faulkner himself as gaining a greater self-consciousness about these dynamics, and as beginning a move away from a defended "modernist irony" that is completed in his later works. For a related account of Faulkner's strained self-consciousness of these dynamics, see Doyle, "The Body Against Itself."

32. The melancholia of *Cane* is produced by psychological mechanisms that are related to the suppressions evident in *Gatsby*, *Lost Lady*, and *Absalom*—but they are also quite distinct. *Cane* is unusual within the African American tradition for its refusal to express anger directly at the dehumanizing racism whose effects he records so subtly. (Although rare for his generation, he was not unique is this regard: Hurston also sought at times to deny her anger about white racism—most famously in her essay "How it Feels to Be Colored Me," though also in some ways in *Their Eyes Were Watching God*,

as I will suggest in Chapter 3.) In *Cane*, even more than in *Absalom*, authorial rage is never directly expressed: it is nowhere, even as it is implicitly everywhere. This suppression is produced by a different kind of ambivalence from the one with which Faulkner struggles. Toomer does not love what he also hates, but rather, he loves that which has emerged from something hateful—from the traumatic history of slavery and its aftermath. Toomer celebrates with a sustained, lyrical intensity the cultural beauty produced by the slaves and their descendents: they are the "purple ripened plums" from which Toomer hopes to extract the "seed" for his own artistic project, his "everlasting song" ("Song of the Son" 14). The naturalism of *Cane* serves, as in other melancholic works, to mystify the forces that have produced profound suffering—and also the beauty that he celebrates. It is as if Toomer suppresses rage at white racism for fear of assailing the very condition of what he loves and hopes to extend. This ambivalence may well have been intensified by Toomer's unusually complex racial identification—which was partly with the master class, as well as with the slaves. Because Toomer suppresses his anger at the destructive causes of slave culture, he is—as I will suggest below—unable to imagine how the culture he loves might continue to live in a future society liberated from the catastrophic conditions that produced it. (The complexity of Toomer's racial identification, and of critics' response to it, has been discussed in detail: see especially George Hutchinson, "Jean Toomer and American Racial Discourse," *Texas Studies in Literature and Language* 35.2 (Summer 1993): 226–250; and Kathryne V. Lindberg, "Raising *Cane* on the Theoretical Plane: Jean Toomer's Racial Personae," *Cultural Difference and the Literary Text: Pluralism and the Limits of Authenticity in North American Literatures*, ed. Winfried Siemerling and Katrin Schwenk (Iowa City: U of Iowa P, 1996) 49–74.

33. See Sigmund Freud, "On Fetishism" (1927), *Sexuality and the Psychology of Love*, ed. Philip Rieff (New York: Collier, 1963) 214–219.

34. See Karl Abraham and Maria Torok, *The Shell and the Kernel*, ed. and trans. Nicholas T. Rand (Chicago: U of Chicago P, 1994).

35. Of course, neither Jake nor Brett, nor their other expatriate peers, succeed in evading *all* affect. What is, perhaps, most moving in the novel are the fleeting moments of libidinally charged receptivity to the world—as, e.g., during Jake and Bill's fishing trip or at moments of collectivity with the Spanish villagers during the fiesta of San Fermin. These are brief, fragile moments at which the melancholic structure gives way, and in which connection to the world becomes possible. It should be emphasized that these moments are often enabled by aesthetic mastery (as in the fishing scene, or vicariously at the bullfights), and that they are invariably short-lived. Perhaps most importantly, these moments of connection do not involve articulate emotional intimacy between people. Momentary connection to the pleasures of food, or of nature, or of physical activity is fleetingly possible—as is occasional, unverbalized male homosocial connection (especially with men who are strangers or who are, like Bill, about to pass out of one's life). Verbal intimacy must be especially evaded, and heterosexual connection is placed invariably under the sign of loss and impos-

sibility. On the homophobic negation of intimacy between men in Hemingway, see Chapter Six below.

36. On Toomer's representation of women, see Alice Walker, "In Search of Our Mother's Gardens," *In Search of Our Mothers' Gardens: Womanist Prose* (New York: Harcourt, Brace, Jovanovich, 1983) 231–233. On "Karintha," see Doyle, "Swan Song" 83–84.

37. On Sutpen's particular inability to recognize Bon, from a psychobiographical perspective, see Judith Bryant Wittenberg, *Faulkner: The Transfiguration of Biography* (Lincoln: U of Nebraska P, 1979) 130–155. For a feminist object-relations account of Faulkner's male protagonists' need to defend themselves against recognizing women, see Gail Mortimer, *Faulkner's Rhetoric of Loss: A Study in Perception and Meaning* (Austin: U of Texas P, 1983) 97–129.

CHAPTER THREE

1. Zora Neale Hurston, *Their Eyes Were Watching God* (1937; New York: Harper & Rowe, 1990) 182. Subsequent references are to this edition and will be cited parenthetically in the text.

2. For two accounts of Janie's pursuit of self-realization through substantive and reciprocal love relations, including her friendship with Phoebe, see bell hooks, "Zora Neale Hurston: A Subversive Reading," *Matatu* 3.6 (1989): 5–23; and Carla Kaplan, "The Erotics of Talk: 'That Oldest Human Longing' in *Their Eyes Were Watching God*," *American Literature* 67.1 (Mar. 1995): 115–142.

3. For two recent analyses of the psychic effects of capitalist economic structures on characters in *Their Eyes*, see Thomas F. Haddox, "The Logic of Expenditure in *Their Eyes Were Watching God*," *Mosaic* 34.1 (Mar. 2001): 19–34; and Todd McGowan, "Liberation and Domination: *Their Eyes Were Watching God* and the Evolution of Capitalism," *MELUS* 24.1 (Spring 1999): 109–128.

4. Philip Goldstein is unusual in emphasizing the differences between Hurston's sensibility and that of canonized contemporaries such as Faulkner—and in arguing that these differences played an important role in her marginalization by cold war critics. See "Critical Realism or Black Modernism?: The Reception of *Their Eyes Were Watching God*," *Reader* 41 (Spring 1999): 54–73.

5. Hortense Spillers has argued most fully for the pessimistic evasions of the novel's ending, noting that Hurston breaks from the novel's main "pattern of revolt" in her representation of Janie as "resigned" to "geriatric retirement" in the end. Spillers also argues that Hurston's exploration of Janie's psychic evolution is truncated by her deployment of the "timeless current" of the hurricane. See "A Hateful Passion, A Lost Love," *Feminist Issues in Literary Scholarship*, ed. Shari Benstock (Bloomington: Indiana UP, 1987) 181–207. Thomas Cassidy has emphasized Janie's repression of her rage at Tea Cake, as well as the novel's change in tone after the hurricane, though he defines the novel's mode as strictly opposed to the "naturalism" he associates with

Richard Wright: see "Janie's Rage: The Dog and the Storm in *Their Eyes Were Watching God,*" *College Language Association Journal* 36.3 (Mar. 1993): 260–269. Kathleen Davies offers a more affirmative reading of Hurston's displacement of Janie's anger at Tea Cake, arguing that this narrative strategy enabled Hurston to offer a "double voiced" critique of patriarchal violence without contributing to white racist critiques of black men: see "Zora Neale Hurston's Poetics of Embalmment: Articulating the Rage of Black Women and Narrative Self-Defense," *African American Review* 26.1 (Spring 1992): 147–159.

6. The limitation of Hurston's conception of mourning is also reflected in the fact that the original "female" paradigm of mourning spelled out in the novel's opening paragraphs incorporates a strong element of repression as well as memory. In Hurston's account, women are able to act as if "the dream is the truth," not only because they "remember everything they don't want to forget," but also because they "forget all those things they don't want to remember." Hurston assumes it is necessary to forget that which is painful, I suspect, because she could not fully imagine how the destructive social processes that imperil desire could actually be resisted. Repression is, in other words, all that one has, when resistance is unimaginable.

7. There remains much work to be done to clarify Hurston's evolving but apparently skeptical attitude toward collective political action, in particular. Her first biographer, Robert Hemenway, touches fleetingly on these matters: *Zora Neale Hurston: A Literary Biography* (Urbana: U of Illinois P, 1977). In one recent effort to consider Hurston's relationship to contemporaneous political formations, Carol Batker has pointed out that, while Hurston is less daring in her sexual representations than most blues singers of her generation, she nevertheless implies a criticism of the bourgeois preoccupation with respectability characteristic of the early-twentieth-century black women's club movement: see "'Love me like I like to be': The Sexual Politics of Hurston's *Their Eyes Were Watching God,* the Classic Blues, and the Black Women's Club Movement," *African American Review* 32.2 (Spring 1998): 199–213.

8. Although the feminist implications of H. D.'s work have been explored extensively in recent decades, the more general contours of her politics deserve further inquiry. Susan Stanford Friedman has emphasized the ways in which H. D.'s "personal experience with the Harlem Renaissance played a key role in deepening and broadening her early feminism into a fully progressive modernism based in an identification with all the people who exist as 'the scattered remnant' at the fringes of culture": see "Modernism of the 'Scattered Remnant': Race and Politics in H. D.'s Development," *Feminist Issues in Literary Scholarship,* ed. Shari Benstock (Bloomington: Indiana UP, 1987) 208–231; quoted passage appears on 210. The influence of anticapitalist political currents on H. D.'s outlook—especially during the period of her involvement with the left avant-garde film journal, *Close Up*—has not been adequately studied.

9. H. D., *The Flowering of the Rod* (1944) in *Trilogy* (New York: New Directions, 1998). The phrases quoted are from poems [10] and [2], 126 and 115. Subsequent

references will be cited parenthetically as *Rod* where necessary, with poem numbers in brackets, and page numbers in this edition following.

10. For a reading that differs dramatically from my own, see Sarah H. S. Graham, " 'We have a secret. We are alive': H. D.'s *Trilogy* as a Response to War," *Texas Studies in Literature and Language* 44.2 (Summer 2002): 161–210. While Graham grants that all three parts of *Trilogy* should be read as responses to the war, she views *The Flowering of the Rod* as animated by an "urge to escape" an "apparently hopeless situation" on the part of a poet who was "exhausted and defeated by the subject of war" (200). Graham views even the gender politics of H. D.'s rewriting of the Mary story as regressive—and as an evasion of the poem's central concern with war: see especially 201–203. See, in contrast, earlier feminist accounts, especially Susan Gubar, "The Echoing Spell of H. D.'s *Trilogy*," *Contemporary Literature* 19 (1978): 196–208. While Graham is right to say that H. D. focuses more persistently on the war itself in the first two portions of *Trilogy*, I have chosen to focus on *Flowering of the Rod* precisely because it enacts the movement of mourning—the movement from war to what H. D. calls "resurrection."

11. The poet emphasizes that the work of mourning does involve a *protracted* period of withdrawal from the external world, during which one focuses on the past and on that which has been lost. She warns against any effort to circumvent or abridge that process of grieving and remembering. Those who "think, even before it is half-over, / that your cycle is at an end," risk a "foolish circling," a destructive repetition of the cycles that have produced collective loss, and have carried us all to "the pyramid of skulls" ([6] 121–2). H. D. suggests here, in effect, that melancholic repetition of the kind so persistently enacted in works like *Absalom, Absalom!* and *Cane* may be produced by a blockage in the mourning process that inhibits the sustained work of remembering what's been lost in a way that enables the retrieval of cathexes.

12. It should be emphasized, further, that this process of recollection at the heart of mourning, this "hovering," marks an effort to gain access to *un*conscious, as well as conscious, investments in that which has been lost. Susan Stanford Friedman has emphasized the role of the unconscious as the main "source of inspiration" throughout *Trilogy*: see *Psyche Reborn: The Emergence of H. D.* (Bloomington: Indiana UP, 1981) 76.

13. See Susan Stanford Friedman's account of H. D.'s effort to "rectify" the misogyny of the Western mythoreligious tradition—in *Trilogy* and throughout her corpus: *Psyche Reborn*, chap. 8, especially 243–247.

14. Something similar was even true of Cather and Toomer, despite their different (and more tenuous) forms of identification with dominant racial and gender formations. What distinguishes even Cather and Toomer from nonmelancholic writers such as H. D. or Langston Hughes was, in part, the difficulty of fully acknowledging and expressing aggression toward these dominant social formations.

15. The phrase is Olsen's, taken from the author-biography on the cover of a recent edition of the novel: Tillie Olsen, *Yonnondio: From the Thirties* (1974; New York:

Dell, 1989). Subsequent references are to this edition and will be cited parenthetically in the text. I have offered a few biographical details here because Olsen remains
less well known than other writers whom I have discussed thus far. Further details of
her biography, including her relationship to the Communist Party and the writing
of *Yonnondio*, can be found in Deborah Rosenfelt, "From the Thirties: Tillie Olsen
and the Radical Tradition," *The Critical Response to Tillie Olsen*, ed. Kay Hoyle Nelson
and Nancy Huse (Westport, CT: Greenwood, 1994) 54–89 and in Constance Coiner,
Better Red: The Writing and Resistance of Tillie Olsen and Meridel Le Sueur (Urbana:
U of Illinois P, 1998) chap. 5: 141–174.

16. For three influential feminist accounts that explore Olsen's fusion of gender and class analyses in *Yonnondio*, including the distinctively gendered forms of
exploitation endured by her female working-class characters, see Rosenfelt, "From
the Thirties," Coiner, *Better Red*, chap. 6, and Paula Rabinowitz, *Labor and Desire:
Women's Revolutionary Fiction in Depression America* (Chapel Hill: U of North Carolina
P, 1991) 97–100, 124–136.

17. It is worth emphasizing Olsen's concern with the concrete dynamics of exploitation, for these are nearly invisible in bourgeois modernism. While most middle-
class modernists in the United States were highly critical of capitalist modernization,
their texts tend to separate the phenomena of alienation from the dynamics of class
exploitation. With the exception of a small number of politically radicalized writers like Dos Passos and Steinbeck, bourgeois modernists tended to ignore the labor
that produces wealth, and their works generally obscure the causal relation between
the poverty of one class and the wealth of another. (Some bourgeois modernists are
concerned with class *inequality*—and, in particular with the forms of shame that class
subordination entails for men like Sutpen, Gatsby, or Ivy Peters. (It is striking that
bourgeois modernists rarely record the experience of class shame for women.) But
while these psychic aspects of class inequity are explored, the works of middle-class
U.S. modernists generally obscure the material foundations of class exploitation: the
labor that produces wealth.) For Olsen, however, as for most working-class writers,
the problem of alienation could not be addressed separately from the dynamics of
exploitation and the experience of poverty.

18. John Vickery is one of the few critics to consider Olsen's use of modernist
formal techniques. See "The Aesthetics of Survival: Tillie Olsen's *Yonnondio*," *American Literary Dimensions: Poems and Essays in the Honor of Melvin J. Friedman* (Newark:
U of Delaware P, 1999) 99–111. It is a testament to the power of cold war conceptions of modernism that Vickery begins his analysis by assuring the reader that "My
point, of course, is not to claim Olsen for modernism."

19. For Olsen's demonstration of the way in which industrialized work discipline
finds its alienating equivalent in women's domestic labor, compare her description of
the assembly line (114ff) to her account of Anna's kitchen work (128–129).

20. On the inability of Olsen's characters to grasp the dynamics of their own
exploitation, and their tendency to mystify these phenomena, see Anthony Dawahare, "'That Joyous Certainty': History and Utopia in Tillie Olsen's Depression-

Era Literature," *Twentieth Century Literature* 44.3 (Autumn 1998): 261–275. See also Helge Normann Nilsen, "Problems Have External Causes: *Yonnondio*, Tillie Olsen's Proletarian Novel," *Looking Inward, Looking Outward: American Fiction in the 1930s and 1940s* (The Hague: European UP, 1990) 79.

21. On Olsen's critique of aestheticization here, see also Coiner, 185–187; on Olsen's Brechtian interpolations more generally, see Coiner 182–191 and Dawahare, 265–267.

22. Open expressions of this kind of political commitment violated cold war literary norms and caused works to be dismissed and marginalized as vulgar examples of a debased "proletarian" literature. It should be clear that it is precisely this structure of feeling that Olsen herself is challenging. The continued power of those norms, however, may be indicated by the fact that, at this writing, *Yonnondio* has once again gone out of print.

23. In "Mourning and Militancy," Douglas Crimp has described the way in which some AIDS activists in the United States during the 1980s shunned the work of mourning in the name of militancy, and he has argued convincingly for the damage—both psychological and political—that follows from this false dichotomy. I want to acknowledge that there can, indeed, be forms of political militancy that seek to evade the necessary work of mourning collective trauma. In some cases, men and women attempt to deny their own feelings of vulnerability and grief by focusing on anger, and on their yearnings for retribution and security. I believe that this was, sadly, in evidence in the United States, as the government launched its so-called "War on Terrorism" as a way, in part, of evading the actual fear and grief that followed the attacks of September 11, 2001. (See Seth Moglen, "Mourning and Progressive Politics After 9/11" in *International Journal for Applied Psychoanalytic Studies* 3.2 (2006): 118–125.) A particularly dramatic, and transparent, version of this attempt to deny sorrow by converting it into aggression was recently expressed by Ehud Olmert, then mayor of Jerusalem, when he responded to the horror of suicide bombings in Israel by saying: "I saw family after family, pain after pain and tears after tears, heartbreak after heartbreak [. . .] I hope you know we will turn this pain into an iron fist, which will crush our enemies' heads. This is what the state of Israel must do, and this is what I expect them to do, and I know this will eventually happen." (See John Kifner, "Bomb Kills 6 Israelis; Army Retakes West Bank Lands," *New York Times*, 20 June 2002.) As both of these illustrations from contemporary international politics suggest, the tendency to use political violence as a means of evading the work of mourning may be particularly likely in instances where those who have suffered find it difficult to acknowledge some element of responsibility for the traumas they have experienced. While politicized aggression *can* thus in some cases be marshaled in an effort to evade grief, I am arguing here for the ways in which constructive political action in the name of social change can be consistent with—and, in fact, requires—the psychic process of mourning.

24. On determinism and misanthropy in relation to melancholic modernism, see also Chapter Six. Anthony Dawahare describes Olsen's affirmation of her characters' capacities (especially for imagination) in the context of their persistent social

determination in terms of a dialectical consciousness capable of balancing "history and utopia"—and Dawahare notes the way in which such a dialectical perspective differs from that of literary naturalists like London and Crane: see "'That Joyous Certainty,'" especially 267–268.

25. A number of critics have strongly associated mourning with the long tradition of Western elegy—and its emphasis on consolation through transcendental substitutions or redemptions of what has been lost in the present. In *Poetry of Mourning: The Modern Elegy from Hardy to Heaney* (Chicago: U of Chicago P, 1994), Jahan Ramazani, e.g., describes the modern elegy as "melancholic" because of its refusal of such consolations. My delineation of the "other" modernism is intended, in part, to emphasize that some modernist writers were strongly committed to developing forms of mourning that explicitly *refused* transcendental consolations—and that also avoided the self-destructive dynamics of melancholia.

26. In a recent edition of *Yonnondio*, Olsen included a fragmentary outline of her original plan for the novel, which includes a "lost strike," rather than a successful one (135–136). For descriptions of Olsen's intended plan, see also Coiner, *Better Red* 178–179.

27. It is worth noting that Olsen was not alone in this intuition. In *Daughter of Earth*, e.g., another important working-class novelist of this period, Agnes Smedley, emphasizes that her proletarian characters are not only unable to take in the traumas of the present, but that they blot out the past as well in an effort at psychic self-protection.

28. See especially Steven Tracey, *Langston Hughes and the Blues* (Chicago: U of Illinois P, 1998) and David Chinitz, "Literacy and Authenticity: The Blues Poems of Langston Hughes," *Callaloo* 19.1 (Winter 1996): 177–192.

29. These comments were offered by Hughes in a meditation on the blues written late in life, after decades of listening to and working in the idiom: "I Remember the Blues," originally published in the *Panorama* supplement of the *Chicago Daily News*, 26 Jan. 1964; rpt. in *Good Morning Revolution: Uncollected Writings of Langston Hughes*, ed. Faith Berry (New York: Citadel, 1992) 167.

30. In contrast to my view, Jahan Ramazani has argued that Hughes's blues poems are melancholic—and Ramazani claims Hughes as an African American exemplar of what he views as the dominant, melancholic tradition of the modern elegy. Like some other critics of Freud's model of grieving discussed in Chapter One, Ramazani associates mourning with "consolation" (and substitution), and he accordingly views as "melancholic" all forms of grieving that refuse transcendental consolations and that openly enact ambivalence toward lost objects. To some degree our different assessments of Hughes (and Williams, below) thus reflect different definitions of mourning and melancholia. But at a substantive level, Ramazani's readings of Hughes minimize both the psychic work of mourning and the political work of resistance that mine emphasize. See *Poetry of Mourning* 135–175.

31. In the original version of this poem, published in *Fine Clothes to the Jew* (1927), Hughes systematically used the dialect, "de," in place of "the"—but changed it, as

quoted here, for publication in *The Selected Poems of Langston Hughes* (New York: Knopf, 1959). Unless noted, I have relied on the version of all Hughes's poems (usually the final published version) printed in *The Collected Poems of Langston Hughes*, ed. Arnold Rampersad and David Roessel (New York: Knopf, 1994). Subsequent references to this volume will be cited in the text parenthetically as *CP*. "Hard Daddy" appears in *CP* 124.

32. It is the dialect of this blues, of course, that broadly identifies the racial and class position of its subjects.

33. This adaptation of the blues's structure of mourning to social forms of loss—and to the task of political resistance—is, of course, an impulse contained within the blues tradition itself. The blues idiom has often been adapted, in other words, to social as well as individual grieving. Angela Davis has explored these social possibilities contained within the blues in *Blues Legacies and Black Feminism: Gertrude 'Ma' Rainey, Bessie Smith and Billie Holiday* (New York: Pantheon, 1998). Among other things, I hope to suggest here that the dichotomy sometimes made between Hughes's "vernacular" and "blues" poems and his revolutionary verse is a false one: these two strands of his work are, in fact, expressions of a common sensibility.

34. Hughes was deeply sympathetic to Communism in the 1930s, and participated in a number of organizations and campaigns led by the Communist Party. I have, nevertheless, used the broader term *socialist* to describe Hughes's revolutionary ideals because his sympathy for a wide range of anticapitalist movements and ideas stretched back to his boyhood support for Eugene Debs and extended to the end of his life, decades after he had grown more distant from the strategies and programs of the Comintern. For the facts of Hughes's engagement with political radicalism, see Arnold Rampersad, *The Life of Langston Hughes, Volumes I & II* (New York: Oxford UP, 1986, 1988); as well as Faith Berry, *Langston Hughes: Before and Beyond Harlem* (1983; New York: Citadel, 1992). Hughes began publishing militantly political (including explicitly anticapitalist) poems at the very outset of his career in 1922, both in *Crisis* and the left journal *Southern Workman*: consider, e.g., "Question [1]" and "The South" (*CP* 24–25, 26–27).

35. Faith Berry played an important role in making some of Hughes's uncollected revolutionary poems available in *Good Morning Revolution: Uncollected Writings of Langston Hughes* (1973; New York: Citadel, 1992). With the publication of *The Collected Poems*, they reached a wider audience. The tenor of cold war hostility toward these poems was captured as recently as 1996, in Eric Sundquist's assertion that in his most militant vein, Hughes's poetry is "embarrassing," "trivialized by politics," and "sounds like Steinbeck's Tom Joad drunk on Marx." (See "Who Was Langston Hughes?" *Commentary* [Dec. 1996]: 55–59.) Over the last decade, there has been a slowly growing body of criticism on these poems. See, e.g., James Smethurst, *The New Red Negro: The Literary Left and African American Poetry, 1930–1946* (New York: Oxford UP, 1999); and Michael Thurston, "Black Christ, Red Flag: Langston Hughes on Scottsboro," *College Literature* 22.3 (Oct. 1995): 30–49.

36. See Seth Moglen, "Modernism in the Black Diaspora: Langston Hughes and the Broken Cubes of Picasso," *Callaloo* 25.4 (2002): 1189–1205. This article offers a detailed reading of Hughes's 1934 poem, "Cubes," from which the phrase quoted above has been taken (*CP* 175–176).

37. For an account of Hughes's politically engaged relationship to modernism—and an overview of the long critical occlusion of this—see Moglen, "Modernism in the Black Diaspora." See also Smethurst on Hughes' "popular neo-modernism" in *The New Red Negro*, as well as John Lowney's account of Hughes' "social modernism" ("Langston Hughes and the 'Nonsense' of Bebop," *American Literature* 72.2 (June 2000): 357–385), and Anita Patterson's analysis of Hughes's fusion of modernist formal experimentation and a "realist" representation of social inequities ("Jazz, Realism, and the Modernist Lyric: The Poetry of Langston Hughes," *Modern Language Quarterly* 61.4 (Dec. 2000): 651–682).

38. "Letter to the Academy" was originally published in the anticapitalist journal, *International Literature* 2 (1933): 54. Like most of Hughes's revolutionary verse, it was out of print for decades during the cold war. It was reprinted in *Good Morning Revolution: Uncollected Writings of Langston Hughes* (New York: Citadel, 1973 and 1992) 1–2, and it is also included in *CP* 169.

39. See, in this context, Rebecca L. Walkowitz's related analysis of "Ph.D." (1933) and of Hughes's self-conscious critique of the conservative cultural authority associated with poetic forms he himself deployed and scrutinized: "Shakespeare in Harlem: *The Norton Anthology*, 'Propoganda,' Langston Hughes," *Modern Language Quarterly* 60.4 (Dec. 1999): 510–511 and passim.

40. Like many prominent radicals, Hughes was subpoenaed (in 1953) to testify before the House Un-American Activities Committee about his political affiliations and about the political views expressed in his literary work. From the early 1940s on, he was also hounded by anti-Communists of various kinds, including evangelical Christians—who picketed (and tried to have cancelled) the readings and speaking tours on which he relied to support himself financially. See Rampersad, *Life* and Faith Berry, *Langston Hughes*. In the wake of these events, Hughes not only ceased writing explicitly revolutionary verse, but also excluded his militant writings of the 1920s and 1930s from the *Selected Poems of Langston Hughes*, which was for decades the only readily available volume of his poems.

41. Freud too glimpsed this, however briefly, in "Mourning and Melancholia," when he acknowledged that either form of grieving might be induced by "the loss of a loved person, or [. . .] the loss of some abstraction which has taken the place of one, such as one's country, liberty, an ideal, and so on" (38). This formulation is characteristically trenchant in it's recognition that "abstract" "ideals" may "tak[e] the place" of a "loved person"—which is surely true. But this is a limited formulation, which acknowledges only one of the many libidinal sources of political idealism (or other forms of investment in abstractions). Hughes himself—and, as we shall see in

subsequent chapters, Dos Passos—explores the libidinal sources of political idealism with a greater richness and diversity.

42. This poem has a complex history, having been published by Hughes several times in different variants. Some (though not all) of these variations are described in the notes to *Collected Poems*, 647. I have printed, and will discuss here, the final version published by Hughes in *The Panther and the Lash* (1967) and reprinted in *CP* 269.

43. It is worth noting the way in which Hughes represents "freedom" here as both an impulse within the self and as something outside that plays upon and passes through the individual: that "freedom," in other words, is a force or agent that "sings" on "the heart-strings" of the poet. In this way, Hughes emphasizes that political ideals are rooted in powerful libidinal currents within each individual, but are also collectively formulated in traditions that are passed down and shared. Consider, for example, the similar formulation offered in another poem from the same period called "Freedom": "Freedom / Is a strong seed / Planted / In a great need." Here "freedom" is represented both as something "planted" because of powerful "need[s]" within individuals, but also as a living thing that exists and endures ("a strong seed") beyond any one person. "Freedom" was originally published in 1943 under the title "Democracy": see *CP* 289 (and endnote 650).

44. The quoted phrases are from Hughes's prefatory note to *Montage of a Dream Deferred* (1951); rpt. in *CP* 387.

45. In "Mourning and Melancholia," Freud explicitly compares the work of mourning to the healing of a physical wound. The "complex of melancholia," he explains, can tax the self to the point of collapse: it "behaves like an open wound, drawing to itself cathectic energies [. . .] from all directions, and emptying the ego until it is totally impoverished" (46). In the case of mourning, in contrast, the draining of the ego is temporary, as in a wound that has not been infected.

46. This implication that a liberatory anger can explode that which thwarts desire runs throughout Hughes's poetry—not only in the early radical verse, but also in the poems of this later period. In "Jim Crow Car," e.g., written a few years later, Hughes follows the gesture of "Harlem," even more explicitly:

> Get out the lunch-box of your dreams.
> And bite into the sandwich of your heart,
> And ride the Jim Crow car until it screams
> And, like an atom bomb, bursts apart.

As in "Harlem," Hughes insists upon the explosion of a dream deferred. Here he emphasizes more definitely that this explosion will "burst apart" the system ("Jim Crow") that has constrained the flourishing of the dream—and that has attempted, moreover, to force African Americans, melancholically, to turn on ("bite into") their own yearnings. (In *CP* 467.) It strikes me as significant that in 1959—the year of "Jim Crow Car"'s first publication and the period of the civil rights movement's burgeoning—Hughes was able to render explicit the politics left abstract and implicit in "Harlem" (written at a moment of political retrenchment for the poet).

47. In "Shakespeare in Harlem," Rebecca L. Walkowitz has noted this final image's difference from the earlier similes in its rejection of "quietude" and "disintegration" (518–519). See also Paul Eggers, "An(other) Way to Mean: A Lacanian Reading of Langston Hughes' *Montage of a Dream Deferred*," *Studies in the Humanities* 27.1 (June 2000): 20–34—for a rare psychoanalytic reading of Hughes's poetry and, in particular, an account of "Harlem" as enacting both a sociopolitical *and* a psychic "tug-of-war between the Symbolic and the Imaginary" (30–31).

48. It is remarkable, e.g., to read a study as late as James Breslin's *William Carlos Williams: An American Artist* (Chicago: U of Chicago P, 1970; rpt. 1985) and to hear the tone of defensive special pleading for Williams' significance among his modernist peers. It evidently required a post-McCarthy political shift in U.S. literary studies during the late 1960s before even this degree of inclusion was possible for Williams. For an overview of Williams's critical reception, see Paul L. Mariani, *William Carlos Williams: The Poet and His Critics* (Chicago: American Library Assn., 1975).

49. Employing a conception of melancholia far broader than my own—as any form of grieving that refuses traditional elegiac consolations (see note 30 above)—Jahan Ramazani has claimed Williams as exemplary of the melancholic tradition charted in *Poetry of Mourning*: see especially "Introduction" 2–10.

50. For an account of Williams's indulgence in, and subsequent move away from, stereotypical representations of working people and people of color, see Barry Ahearn, "The Poet As Social Worker," *William Carlos Williams Review* 19.1 & 2 (Spring/Fall 1993): 15–32.

51. For a recent assessment of Williams's complex political outlook, and his relationship to the Left, see Bob Johnson, "'A Whole Synthesis of His Time': Political Ideology and Cultural Politics in the Writings of William Carlos Williams, 1929–1939," *American Quarterly* 54.2 (June 2002): 179–215. For biographical details, including Williams's shifting political attitudes and associations, see Paul Mariani, *William Carlos Williams: A New World Naked* (New York: McGraw Hill, 1981). For critical assessments of Williams's effort to negotiate the problem of political commitment in his poetry, see Paul R. Cappucci, "Negotiating the 1930s: William Carlos Williams's Struggle with Politics and Art on His Way to *Paterson*," *The Journal of Imagism* (Fall 1999): 3–21; Andrew Lawson, "Divisions of Labour: William Carlos Williams's 'The Wanderer' and the Politics of Modernism," *William Carlos Williams Review* 20.1 (Spring 1994): 1–22; and Robert Von Hallberg, "The Politics of Description: W. C. Williams in the 'Thirties," *ELH* 45.1 (Spring 1976): 131–151.

52. For his satisfaction with "The Descent" as a model for the use of "the variable foot," see Williams's brief note to the poem in the anthology *Poet's Choice*, ed. Paul Engle and Joseph Langland (New York: Dial, 1962). For his other comments about the variable foot's relation to "free verse" and iambic pentameter, see Williams's note to "Some Simple Measures in the American Idiom and the Variable Foot," *Poetry*,

March 1959. These comments are reprinted in *The Collected Poems of William Carlos Williams: Volume II, 1939–1962*, ed. Christopher MacGowan (New York: New Directions, 1988), 486, 511–512. (Subsequent references to this volume will be cited parenthetically as *CP*.) For critical analyses and assessments of the variable foot, see especially Denise Levertov, "On Williams' Triadic Line; Or How to Dance on Variable Feet," *Conversant Essays: Contemporary Poets on Poetry*, ed. James McCorkle (Detroit: Wayne State UP, 1990) 141–148; and Eleanor Berry, "William Carlos Williams' Triadic-Line Verse: An Analysis of Its Prosody," *Twentieth Century Literature* 35.3 (Autumn 1989): 364–388.

53. My emphasis on mourning's dynamism in this poem, on the power of memory to open "*new* objectives," contrasts sharply with Neil Myer's assessment in one of the few published close readings of "The Descent": "Decreation in Williams' 'The Descent,'" *Criticism* 14.4 (Fall 1972): 315–327. Myers argues that the poem marks Williams's effort to manage the psychic threat of aging and mortality through a "numbing," "aneasthetic" process that seeks to "yield to change and yet not change at all" (318), attempting to sustain a rigid psychic stasis, "to *keep* what D. H. Lawrence called 'The old stable ego of the character'" (317). Myers's reading thus attempts, in effect, to force this emblematic work of dynamic mourning into the melancholic paradigm of canonical modernism, with its privileging of self-anesthetization and psychic fixity.

54. Interestingly, Freud drew on a similar metaphor to describe the way in which desire can be alternately inhibited—and liberated—in the mourning process. Freud famously suggests that in melancholia, as a result of unacknowledged ambivalence or aggression, "the shadow of the object [falls] upon the ego" of the bereaved (*MM* 249). We have seen in the works of melancholic modernism how the entombment of precisely such lost objects (and the disavowed ambivalence that they carry) does indeed lead to a shadow being cast over all subsequent efforts to love. (Consider, for example, the "ripe mystery" and the "shades and echoes" that surround Daisy in Gatsby's mind (*Gatsby* 155–156) or the "beauty, perfect as dusk" that Karintha is forced to "carry" by the men who try unsuccessfully to love her (*Cane* 3).) Freud and Williams seem to agree that, when the process of mourning is able to run its full course, desire can liberate itself from such shadows.

55. Marjorie Perloff has argued provocatively that Williams's early love poems derive their erotic and poetic intensity from *displaced* expressions of frustrated and guilty sexual yearnings, while the later love poems offer tamer, more normative expressions of love. Although the abstractness of "The Descent" might appear to place it within this latter paradigm, I would emphasize that its open acknowledgment of the *disappointment* of love and desire separates it from *both* of Perloff's interpretive models. Perloff is not concerned with the dynamics of grieving, but the early love poems she analyzes might be described as themselves engaged in a kind of mourning that retrieves frustrated libido and projects it into fantasized domains of satisfaction, rather than turning against it melancholically. "The Descent," on my account,

marks a different and—for all its abstractness—ambitious mourning by explicitly acknowledging disappointment, and through that acknowledgment, retrieving a less disguised "desire" that risks an association with (rather than a safe segregation from) "love." See Perloff, "The Fallen Leaf and the Stain of Love: the Displacements of Desire in Williams' Early Love Poetry." *The Rhetoric of Love in the Collected Poems of William Carlos Williams* (Roma: Edizioni Associate, 1993) 189–212.

TRANSITION

1. Dos Passos "To Macolm Cowley," February 1932, Townsend Ludington, ed., *The Fourteenth Chronicle: Letters and Diaries of John Dos Passos* (Boston: Gambit, 1973) 404. (Subsequent references to this collection will be cited as *14C*.)

2. For Dos Passos's centrality to what we now call modernism, see e.g., Alfred Kazin, *On Native Grounds: An Interpretation of Modern American Prose Literature* (1942; Garden City, NY: Doubleday, 1956), especially chap. 11, in which Dos Passos received pride of place alongside Hemingway as recorder of the "lost generation" experience. For some of the significant essays about Dos Passos by these critics, see Lionel Trilling, "The America of John Dos Passos" (1938); Allen Belkind, ed., *Dos Passos, the Critics, and the Writer's Intention* (Carbondale: Southern Illinois UP, 1971) 35–43 (all subsequent references to this collection will be cited as *Writer's Intention*); Edmund Wilson, "Dahlberg, Dos Passos and Wilder" (1930); Wilson, *The Shores of Light: A Literary Chronicle of the Twenties and Thirties* (New York: Farrar, Straus and Giroux, 1952) 442–450; Malcolm Cowley, "John Dos Passos: The Poet and the World" (1932); *Writer's Intention* 22–34 and "Dos Passos: The Learned Poggius" in Cowley, *A Second Flowering: Works and Days of the Lost Generation* (New York: Viking, 1973) 74–89; Granville Hicks, "The Politics of John Dos Passos" (1950); Andrew Hook, ed., *Dos Passos: A Collection of Critical Essays* (Englewood Cliffs, NJ: Prentice Hall, 1974) 15–30 (all subsequent references to this collection will be cited as *Critical Essays*). For Sartre's comment, see his 1947 essay "John Dos Passos and 1919"; *Critical Essays* 62. See F. R. Leavis, "A Serious Writer" (1932); *Critical Essays* 72–75.

3. Scholars offered a similar set of assertions about the author himself, insisting that at the time of the trilogy's composition, Dos Passos was not a "socialist," not a "Socialist crusader," not a "marxist," not "communistic," not "a radical activist," not "committed to the radical left," not "with" those who "talked revolution," and consistently "anti-Red." (These assertions are not, of course, identical refutations—and I will address below the characteristic cold war nomenclatural confusions that they draw on and reproduce.) Most of these claims have been made repeatedly, but specific quotations can be found in Kazin, *On Native Grounds* 266–69; Walter Rideout, *The Radical Novel in the United States, 1900–1954* (Cambridge, MA: Harvard UP, 1956) 162–164; David Vanderwerken, "Dos Passos and the 'Old Words,'" *Twentieth Century Literature* (May 1977): 212; John P. Diggins, *Up From Communism: Conservative Odys-*

seys in American Intellectual History (New York: Harper & Row, 1975) 97; Ludington, *14C* 383; Linda Wagner, *Dos Passos: Artist as American* (Austin: U of Texas P, 1979) xix; Claude-Edmonde Magny, "Time in Dos Passos," *Critical Essays* 138–139; and Iain Colley, *Dos Passos and the Fiction of Despair* (London: Macmillan, 1978) 81, 116.

4. The consensus school claims that Dos Passos's apparent shift from one end of the political spectrum to another was illusory drew heavily on the author's own retrospective assertions that he had not contradicted himself politically over time. These scholars sought to identify an underlying "continuity" in his politics, emphasizing various persistent values in his thinking—values, as it happened, that were unthreatening to cold war ideology. These included a nostalgic nationalism founded on "the need of authority and moral order" (Diggins); "a temperamental individualistic dissidence" (Chase); "the ideal of self-government" (Sanders); and a stable personal identity as "a man always opposed to power" (Ward). The assertion quoted in the text, and the first claim in this note, are from the most impressive of the consensus accounts: Diggins, *Up From Communism* 97, 106. For other versions of this argument, see Richard Chase, "The Chronicles of Dos Passos," *Critical Essays* 176; David Sanders, "The 'Anarchism' of John Dos Passos," *Writer's Intention* 122, 135; John William Ward, "Dos Passos, Fitzgerald, and History," *Critical Essays* 126. For another variant, see Wagner xvii. The emergence of the consensus school, as a response to intellectual currents within the American Left, is an important historiographical equivalent of the literary critical currents that produced the politically quiescent modernist canon. For one revealing account of the consensus history, see Christopher Lasch, foreword to Richard Hofstadter, *The American Political Tradition and the Men Who Made It* (New York: Vintage, 1974) vii–xxiv.

5. See Arthur Mizener, "The Gullivers of Dos Passos," *Critical Essays* 165–167; Magny 139; Colley 66–119.

6. In developing my account of *U.S.A.*, I have benefited from the recent renaissance in Dos Passos scholarship—a revival enabled in large part by the waning of cold war anxieties in the United States after 1989 and the opening of a slightly broader cultural space for discussions of anticapitalism. The intellectual groundwork for this revival was laid during the cold war itself—especially by Melvin Landsberg, whose *Dos Passos' Path to U.S.A.: A Political Biography* (Boulder: Colorado Associated UP, 1972) remains the most accurate and least partisan guide to Dos Passos's political evolution, and by Barbara Foley, whose early essays on Dos Passos sought to understand the relationship between *U.S.A.*'s formal ambitions and its political preoccupations (see especially Foley, "History, Fiction and Satirical Form: The Example of Dos Passos' *1919*," *Genre* XII [Fall 1979]: 357–378; and Foley, "The Treatment of Time in *The Big Money*: An Examination of Ideology and Literary Form," *Modern Fiction Studies* 26 [Autumn 1980]: 447–467). For recent work on various aspects of Dos Passos's politics and *U.S.A.*, see Janet Galligani Casey, *Dos Passos and the Ideology of the Feminine* (New York: Cambridge UP, 1998); Michael Denning, "The Decline and

Fall of the Lincoln Republic: Dos Passos' *U.S.A.*," *The Cultural Front: The Laboring of American Culture in the Twentieth Century* (New York: Verso, 1997) 163–199; Barbara Foley, *Radical Representations* (Durham: Duke UP, 1993) 425–436; Fred Pfeil, "Montage Dynasty: A Market Study in American Historical Fiction," *Another Tale to Tell: Politics & Narrative in Postmodern Culture* (New York: Verso, 1990) 151–192; and John Trombold, "From the Future to the Past: the Disillusionment of John Dos Passos," *Studies in American Fiction* 26.2 (Autumn 1998): 237–256.

CHAPTER FOUR

1. Several scholars have called attention to factors that, while not affecting Dos Passos's class position, may have complicated his sense of social status. These include the fact that he was an illegitimate child until the age of fourteen (when his father finally married his mother); that he was harassed to some degree by his American schoolmates because of the "foreign" accent he had acquired during a childhood spent largely in Europe; and finally, the fact that Dos Passos's father was himself only one generation away from the working-class immigrant experience of his own father, a cobbler who had emigrated from Portugal before the civil war. For Dos Passos's own impressionistic autobiographical account of his early years, see chap. 1 of *The Best Times* (New York: New American Library, 1966) 1–40. For fuller biographical accounts, see Townsend Ludington, *John Dos Passos: A Twentieth Century Odyssey* (New York: E. P. Dutton, 1980) 2–85; and Virginia Spencer Carr, *Dos Passos: A Life* (New York: Doubleday, 1984) 3–45. See also Alfred Kazin's remarks about Dos Passos's proximity to the immigrant experience, *On Native Grounds: An Interpretation of Modern American Prose Literature* (1942; Garden City, NY: Doubleday, 1956) 269.

2. The gendered overtones of this particular epithet—that a bad, exclusionary culture is like a physically constrained (and, by implication, sexually repressed) woman—is characteristic of Dos Passos's idiom throughout his career. On the one hand the image carries a significant misogyny, which I will discuss at length below: the sexually repressed woman stands in for all that is wrong with his society. At the same time, the metaphor carries a sexually liberatory, and even potentially feminist content: that the liberation of a culture is symbolized by the physical and sexual liberation of women. (For Dos Passos's ambivalent relationship to femininity, see also Janet Galligani Casey, *Dos Passos and the Ideology of the Feminine* [New York: Cambridge UP, 1998].)

3. Quotations in this paragraph come from letters to Rumsey Marvin dated May 29, 1916; Spring 1916; Aug. 24, 1916; and Sept. 28, 1916, *The Fourteenth Chronicle: Letters and Diaries of John Dos Passos*, ed. Townsend Ludington (Boston: Gambit, 1973) 36–40, 45–46, 47–49. (Subsequent references to this work will be cited as *14C*.) For the reference to "four years under the ethercone," see Camera Eye 25 in *The 42nd Parallel* (1930); rpt. in *U.S.A.* (Boston: Houghton Mifflin, 1960) 271.

4. Dos Passos, "A Humble Protest" (*Harvard Monthly*, June 1916); rpt. in *John Dos Passos: The Major Nonfictional Prose*, ed. Donald Pizer (Detroit: Wayne State UP, 1988) 30–34. (All subsequent references to this collection will be cited as *MNP*.)

5. See "A Humble Protest" 33–34. It is worth emphasizing in this context that Dos Passos's populist impulse extended to the *objects*, as well as the agents, of aesthetic experience. From very early on, he condemned the highbrow aesthetic fussiness that prevented people from perceiving the immediate, sensual beauty of ordinary things. Championing "modern realism and the new poetry," he insisted that "every subject under the sun which has any thing to do with human beings [. . .] is susceptible of poetic treatment," whether "love" and "war" or "tin pans" and "lawnmowers." (See DP, "To R. Marvin," fall 1915, *14C* 26–27.)

6. Dos Passos himself began using the term *exploitation* by 1919 to describe the process by which the rich "extract money from other people," like "parasite[s] living off other peoples brains, off other people's work" (see, e.g., his letter to Rumsey Marvin, Oct. 15, 1919, *14C* 265–266)—and he would continue to do so throughout the next two decades. Despite his growing familiarity with Marxism in the 1920s and 1930s, he never adopted the word *alienation*—although the term aptly captures one of Dos Passos's most persistent criticisms of capitalist society.

7. It would, of course, be a mistake to draw too strict, or static, a separation between Romantic anti-industrialism and a socialist anticapitalism—in the case of Dos Passos, or in the American Left more generally. It is clear that Dos Passos's early criticism of industrialism was partly fostered and influenced by his reading of American Romantics, particularly Whitman and Thoreau. And the continued and distinctive centrality of alienation in Dos Passos's critique of capitalism over the next two decades probably owed as much to his reading of these Romantics as to the later influence of Marxism (which deepened his concern with exploitation and class conflict, as we will see.) This Romantic influence was shared by many radical intellectuals of his generation and those preceding him. Daniel Aaron, e.g., has emphasized the importance of the Transcendentalists in the socialist thought of the generation who founded *The Masses*. (See Daniel Aaron, *Writers on the Left: Episodes in American Literary Communism* (1961; New York: Columbia UP, 1992) particularly chap. 1, 5–29.) It is also striking to find how persistently such radicals as Emma Goldman and Eugene Debs invoked the writing of Emerson and Thoreau in making their case for a revolutionary anticapitalist politics. (See, e.g., Emma Goldman, "Anarchism: What It Really Stands For" in *Anarchism and Other Essays* [1911; New York: Dover, 1969] 47–69.) For an illuminating comparative perspective on this development of anticapitalist politics from the traditions of Romanticism in Britain, see E. P. Thompson's studies of William Morris (*William Morris: Romantic to Revolutionary* [1955; New York: Pantheon, 1976]); and William Blake (*Witness Against the Beast: William Blake and the Moral Law* [New York: New Press, 1993]); and Raymond Williams, *Culture and Society* (Harmondsworth, UK: Penguin, 1985).

8. In another article published in the same issue of *Harvard Monthly* as "A Humble Protest," for example, Dos Passos suggested that the U.S. government should follow a policy of "forceful commonsense" on the European war, "steer[ing] clear" both of "'grape-juice' moralizing" and "long-haired ultra-socialism." (See "A Conference on Foreign Relations"; rpt. *MNP* 35.)

9. Goldman's statement appeared in the June 1916 issue of *The Masses* (and is reprinted in the anthology, *Echoes of Revolt: The Masses, 1911–1917*, ed. William L. O'Neill [Chicago: Quadrangle, 1966] 211–212.) Some readers may be puzzled by my inclusion of Emma Goldman's anarchism alongside the discussion of other radical tendencies—including socialist ones. This is an important point, as my subsequent analysis will show, because Dos Passos consciously understood himself to be a socialist with distinctively anarchist leanings. There has, of course, been a strong tendency within certain Marxist traditions (from the time of Marx's own critique of "Utopian Socialism") to draw a stark line of separation between anarchism and socialism. I wish to emphasize here that such a separation would have been foreign to most American radicals of Dos Passos's generation—not only among Greenwich Village intellectuals, but throughout the anticapitalist movement. Anarchists like Goldman explicitly understood themselves to be offering the most faithful version of the original "socialist" impulse (see, e.g., her essay arguing this point, "Socialism: Caught in the Political Trap," *Red Emma Speaks: Selected Writings and Speeches by Emma Goldman*, ed. Alix Kates Shulman [New York: Vintage, 1972] 78–85; and Alexander Berkman, *What Is Communist Anarchism?* [New York: Vanguard, 1929], especially chap. 12 and 23). Many socialists in this period, while disagreeing with the strategic emphases of anarchism, commonly viewed anarchists as comrades within the anticapitalist struggle. (Readers uncertain of this contention might wish, e.g., to consult Eugene Debs's letters to Goldman, Sacco and Vanzetti, and Big Bill Haywood, which clearly adopt this tone of strategic disagreement within a common anticapitalist solidarity. See *Gentle Rebel: Letters of Eugene V. Debs*, ed. Robert J. Constantine [Urbana: U of Illinois P, 1995].)

10. The fullest account of this radical bohemia can be found in Leslie Fishbein, *Rebels in Bohemia: The Radicals of "The Masses," 1911–1917* (Chapel Hill: U of North Carolina P, 1982). My own view of this bohemian radical milieu is also indebted to Daniel Aaron's description in *Writers on the Left* (see particularly chap. 1–3). In *Writers and Partisans: A History of Literary Radicalism in America* (New York: John Wiley and Sons, 1968), James Burkhart Gilbert has traced the relationship between the bohemian radicalism of the teens and the later formation of *Partisan Review*. For the relationship between feminism (and sexual liberation) and the radical movement more generally, see Mari Jo Buhle, *Women and American Socialism, 1870–1920* (Urbana: U of Illinois P, 1981). It should, perhaps, be emphasized that contributors and editors of *The Masses* were not unified in their assessments of political and cultural formations: the journal, rather, fostered lively debate on many topics, including, e.g., occasionally tart criticisms of anarchist strategy and avant-garde art as well as celebrations.

11. In letters written in New York during the summer of 1917, Dos Passos spoke excitedly of being in "the outer circle" of Emma Goldman's coterie in the cafes of Greenwich Village, and of attending "anarchist and pacifist meetings." By the time he got back from the war in France, he wrote to his more conventionally minded correspondent Rumsey Marvin, "you'll disown me entirely, I'll be so red, radical and revolutionary" (*14C* 73–75). Even a half century later, when he had long since broken from the Left entirely, Dos Passos would recall the exhilaration he had felt in 1917 reading "each issue of *The Masses* damp from the press." (See Dos Passos, *The Best of Times* 46.)

12. See, e.g., Dos Passos's diary entry from July 31, 1917: "I'm dying to write—but all my methods of doing things in the past merely disgust me now, all former methods are damned inadequate.

"How damned ridiculous it all is! The long generations toiling—skimping, lashing themselves screwing higher and higher the tension of their minds, polishing brighter and brighter the mirror of intelligence to end in this— My God what a time—All the cant and hypocrisy, all the damnable survivals, all the vestiges of old truths now putrid and false infect the air, choke you worse than German gas—The ministers from their damn smug pulpits, the business men—the heroics about war—my country right or wrong—oh infinities of them! Oh the tragic farce of the world" (*14C* 89–90).

13. Dos Passos was by no means the only American writer to pass through what Alfred Kazin has called "the most distinguished of all the lost generation's finishing schools" (*On Native Grounds* 270) with the lessons of a radical politics already in mind. It was in the ambulance corps, e.g., that he met John Howard Lawson, another aspiring radical writer with whom Dos Passos collaborated after the war in the socialist and modernist venture of the New Playwrights Theatre. But Dos Passos's response to the war was, e.g., very different from that of his Harvard classmate e. e. cummings or his subsequent friend Ernest Hemingway, neither of whom could draw on the resources of a radical political analysis in their efforts to understand their wartime disillusionments. As one reads Malcolm Cowley's famous "lost generation" autobiography, *Exile's Return*, one can see that some elements of Dos Passos's radical formation were shared by many of his literary contemporaries—particularly the adolescent bohemianism, the interest in a "revolt" against stuffy bourgeois social life and education (and later against the war). But one feels, equally, that Dos Passos was rare among his cohort in the depth (and relative longevity) of his attachment of this prewar bohemianism to a political (and explicitly anticapitalist) radicalism. (See *Exile's Return: A Literary Odyssey of the 1920s* [New York: Viking, 1968], particularly chap.1–2, 3–73.)

14. See, e.g., Dos Passos's diary entries for July 31, 1917; Aug. 23, 1917; Apr. 8, 1918 (*14C* 90, 93, 170–171); "A Humble Protest" 34; and DP, "Jose Giner Pantoja," Feb/Mar. 1918 (*14C* 152).

15. See diary entries for Jan. 28, 1918 and Apr. 8, 1918 (*14C* 134, 171); and DP, "To Pantoja," op cit.

16. DP, "To Pantoja," Feb/Mar. 1918, and diary entry Feb. 8, 1918 (*14C* 153, 142). It is also worth noting that Dos Passos's anxious query about being shot for refusing military discipline was deep enough to provide the emotionally powerful conclusion to his second novel about the war, *Three Soldiers*, in which the main character (one of many partially autobiographical heroes in his early fiction) is taken off by military police at the end, perhaps to be shot for desertion.

17. Dos Passos's political essays were published primarily in *The Liberator* (the postwar successor to *The Masses*, which functioned independently until 1922, when it became the official organ of the Workers' Party)—and also in *The Freeman* (a left literary journal that provided a more domestically focused alternative to *The Dial*) and in the left-liberal weekly, *The Nation*. The political range of these journals—from left-liberalism to the revolutionary communist Left—reflects the range of Dos Passos's own political interests and sympathies in these years.

18. For Dos Passos's exposure to anarchism in the summer of 1917, see, e.g., DP, "To R. Marvin" June (?) and June 15, 1917 (*14C* 73–74). The influence of anarchist ideas is particularly pronounced in letters and diary entries from succeeding months, in which Dos Passos condemned all forms of "overorganization" and repudiated the state as "an incubus" that "must be thrown off." See, e.g., diary entries for July 21 and Aug. 30, 1918 (*14C* 193, 208). I will discuss Dos Passos's relationship to the IWW, to Debs, and to the Socialist Party below. It is perhaps worth noting here that he already included Debs in his list of socialist "heroes" as early as the summer of 1917 (see *The Best Times* 46).

19. Dos Passos had first expressed his admiration for the Spanish anarchists in 1917 (see, e.g., "Young Spain" (*Seven Arts*, Aug. 1917), and his continued respect can be seen in other essays also collected and published in 1922 as *Rosinante to the Road Again*. Although anarchism was largely destroyed as a practical force on the American Left during the postwar Red Scare, Dos Passos's continued sympathy is clearly expressed in his writings about the immigrant anarchism of Sacco and Vanzetti in the late 1920s (consider, e.g., "The Pit and the Pendulum" [*New Masses*, Aug. 1, 1926], rpt. in *MNP*, particularly 89–91). On Dos Passos's relationship to the Portuguese syndicalists, see in particular "In Portugal" (*Liberator*, Apr. 1920); rpt. in *MNP* 51–54. For Dos Passos's heightened interest in European social democracy, consider as an example his letter to Rumsey Marvin, Dec. 29, 1920, in which he explained that he was "bitterly disappointed by the defeat of the British Labor Party" in the general elections of 1918 (*14C* 240). I will discuss Dos Passos's relationship to the Russian Revolution and the Communist movement below.

20. The breadth of Dos Passos's political sympathies reflected the particular moment and subculture in which he had initially been radicalized. In the years before and during the First World War, the anticapitalist movement in the United States was a highly heterodox yet relatively cohesive political phenomenon, with a far greater degree of ideological flexibility and tolerance for internal variation than it became in the factionalized decades that followed. On the greater heterodoxy of the Socialist

Party see, e.g., James Weinstein, *The Decline of Socialism in America, 1912–1925* (New York: Monthly Review, 1967); and David Shannon *The Socialist Party of America: A History* (Chicago: Quadrangle, 1967). For the greater flexibility of radical intellectual circles, see Daniel Aaron, *Writers on the Left*; and, on the greater openness of *The Masses* in particular, see Irving Howe's comparison with later Left journals in his introduction to *Echoes of Revolt* 5–8.

21. For his assertion that "the Soviets are a system of government based on the idea of 'pure democracy,'" see DP, "To Rumsey Marvin," Feb. 2, 1920 (*14C* 276). For his celebration of popular education and access to the arts, and his criticisms of the "new tyranny," see Dos Passos, "In a New Republic" (*Freeman*, 5 Oct. 1921) and "The Caucasus Under the Soviets" (*Liberator*, Aug. 1922). Both rpt. in *MNP*: see particularly 60–61, 66–67.

22. On this wartime political repression, and the Red Scare that followed the Armistice, see William Preston, *Aliens and Dissenters: Federal Suppression of Radicals, 1903–1933* (Cambridge: Harvard UP, 1963); and Robert K. Murray, *Red Scare: A Study in National Hysteria, 1919–1920* (Minneapolis: U of Minnesota P, 1955). For a more specific account of the suppression of the Wobblies, see Dubofsky's vivid and detailed treatment in part four of *We Shall Be All*. While American Socialists mostly maintained their internationalist opposition to the war (in stark contrast to their European counterparts), there were some important divisions within the Party. For Socialist attitudes toward the war, and the suppression of Socialists, see Weinstein, chap. 3 and Shannon, chap. 4 and 5.

23. On the suppression of the socialist press, the destruction of Socialist Party locals, and the prosecution of Socialist Party leaders see Shannon, chap. 4–5 and Weinstein chap. 3. On the mass trial of the Wobblies, prosecutions of leaders, and the amazing scale of vigilante violence directed at Wobblies (including the incident at Bisbee, Arizona, where the mayor and police chief deputized two thousand men to round up twelve hundred suspected Wobblies, drove them into cattle cars, and left them stranded in the New Mexico desert, after having cut off telephone and telegraph lines to seal off the town), see Dubofsky, part four.

24. Although radicals had been suppressed for opposing the war in 1917 and 1918, during the postwar Red Scare they were persecuted explicitly for their anti capitalist convictions. During the infamous Palmer Raids, launched in 1919, many thousands of radicals were indiscriminately arrested, and many of the foreign born were deported. The prosecutions and jailings continued, now authorized by vague "criminal syndicalism" statues—as did the vigilante violence, often more systematically organized than before by the newly formed American Legion. Legislative bodies, from Congress to city councils, simply refused to seat duly elected Socialist representatives. (The House of Representatives, e.g., refused in April 1919 to seat Victor Berger who had been popularly elected from his Milwaukee constituency—and when he was reelected in a special election that December, he was once again denied his seat. The same year, the New York state assembly refused to seat five fairly

elected Socialists simply because of their party affiliation—and two New York City Socialists were prevented for two years from taking up their elected municipal posts for the same reason. See Shannon 122–124.)

25. Sacco and Vanzetti were picked up by the police at the height of the Palmer Raids in May 1920 and interrogated as "Reds"—and only subsequently charged with armed robbery and the murder of a paymaster and payroll guard in South Braintree, Massachusetts. Despite the weakness of the evidence against them, and the sworn testimony of twenty people who had seen Vanzetti in North Plymouth at the time of the holdup, both men were convicted of first-degree murder. For those interested in the details and larger ramifications of the case, there is, of course, an extensive historical literature. For a full-length study that explores, among other things, the significance of the Sacco and Vanzetti case for the American Left, see Herbert B. Ehrmann, *The Case That Will Not Die* (Boston: Beacon, 1969); and for a collection of more recent discussions, see Robert D'Attilio and Jane Manthorn, eds., *Sacco-Vanzetti: Developments and Reconsiderations* (Boston: Boston Public Library, 1979).

26. Dos Passos, "An Open Letter to President Lowell" (*The Nation*, Aug. 1927); rpt. in *MNP* 97–98.

27. For Dos Passos's developing attitudes toward, and statements about, the Sacco and Vanzetti case, see the pamphlet he wrote and edited for the Defense Committee, *Facing the Chair: Story of the Americanization of Two Foreignborn Workingmen* (Boston, 1927; New York: Da Capo, 1970), as well as the following shorter pieces (rpt. in *MNP*): "The Pit and the Pendulum" (*New Masses* 1, Aug. 1926), "An Open Letter to President Lowell" (*Nation*, Aug. 24, 1927), and "Sacco and Vanzetti" (*New Masses*, Nov. 1927).

28. One of the most easily quantifiable indications of the effect of the splits of 1919 on the socialist movement can be found in membership statistics. While the Socialist Party, still reeling from the onslaught of the Red Scare, had managed to build its eviscerated membership back up to 109,000 in the first months of 1919, within a year of the split the *combined* membership of the Socialist Party, the Communist Party, and the Communist Labor Party was 36,000. See Weinstein 232–233.

29. The splits within the socialist movement precipitated by the Third International and the rise of Communist parties in the United States have been described, and debated, in detail elsewhere. For the classic (and highly critical) account of the Communist Party's role in this process, see Theodore Draper, *The Roots of American Communism* (rpt. Chicago: Elephant Paperbacks, 1989), chap. 9–13. For the effect of the splits on the Socialist Party, see Shannon, chap. 6–7 and Weinstein, chap. 4–5. For divisions among the Wobblies, see Dubofsky, chap. 18. And for the increasing factionalization of socialist intellectual life, see Aaron and Weinstein.

30. The Communist Party was, of course, buoyed by the enormous prestige of the successful Bolshevik Revolution, and it was in many respects better adapted to survive—even to flourish in— the conditions of external repression and internal factionalization that overwhelmed the prewar formations.

31. The shift in Dos Passos's organizational affiliations can, perhaps, be usefully symbolized by his relationship to the radical periodical, *The New Masses*. When Dos Passos was contacted in 1925 by a group of writers and activists who wanted to relaunch a journal like *The Masses*, the main voice of pre-war bohemian radicalism, Dos Passos wrote back enthusiastically: "I'm absolutely with you and would gladly do anything to help. *The MASSES* was the only magazine I ever had any use for." (See *14C* 338.) The new journal—which was called *The New Masses*—became Dos Passos's principle venue for activist journalism in the late 1920s and early 1930s, and he served on the initial executive board. Although *The New Masses* was, in the years of Dos Passos's involvement, institutionally independent of the Communist Party, it was always actively involved in Party concerns and Party debates—and it did ultimately become officially affiliated with the Party. Thus, Dos Passos's explicit desire to participate in extending institutionally the anticapitalist radicalism of the teens involved founding and promoting a publication that was very much in the orbit of the Communist Party. (His ultimate break from *The New Masses* in the mid-1930s, because of what he perceived to be its Communist sectarianism was also, in this context, illustrative.)

32. Although I speak here and elsewhere of *the* Communist Party, the early history of Communism in the United States is complex and highly factionalized, from the founding of two competing parties (the Communist Party and the Communist Labor Party) in 1919 through the ensuing decade of organizational splits, fusions, and conflicts. The single, unified Communist Party U.S.A. was not successfully established until 1929. Because Dos Passos's relationship to Communism was always a highly independent one, based neither on Party membership nor particular institutional loyalty, there is no need here to specify the particular incarnations of the Party in existence at any given moment of Dos Passos's radical activity. For the sake of nomenclatural clarity, however, I should emphasize that when I use the word *Communist* with an uppercase spelling, I refer specifically to the politics of parties officially affiliated with the Comintern—and not to broader, more general "communist" traditions.

33. A second visit to the USSR. in 1928 intensified his initial criticisms of Soviet Communism (particularly of antidemocratic tendencies, hierarchical rigidities, and excessively centralized authority)—and these infused his attitude toward the Communist Party in the United States. His ambivalent feelings toward the development of the Communist experiment in the USSR—strongly positive and strongly negative—were so pronounced at the end of this second visit that, as he poignantly reported in his travel writing, he was unable even to answer clearly one way or the other when a sympathetic Moscow theater director simply asked him to explain "where you stand politically. Are you with us?" See Dos Passos, *In All Countries* (London: Constable & Co., 1934) 6.

34. See DP to Edmund Wilson Jan. 14(?), 1931 (*14C* 398). It is perhaps worth noting that this mixture of practical participation in Communist Party campaigns with a continued anarchist antistate temperament—although odd—was not peculiar to Dos

Passos. For another example, consider Dwight Macdonald's account of a similar fusion in the political autobiography that he republished as an introduction to *Memoirs of a Revolutionist* (New York: Meridian, 1958); see particularly 27–28.

35. For Dos Passos's responses to the *Modern Quarterly* questionnaire, see *MNP* 149–150; for his comments to Edmund Wilson see two letters to Wilson, Jan. 14(?), 1931, and May 1932 (*14C* 396–398, 409).

36. Comment reprinted in *MNP*, 150. When Fredericka Field, editor of *The Golden Book*, misconstrued this comment as an endorsement of the Socialist Party, an exasperated Dos Passos demanded that she "rectify this error," and explained his meaning more explicitly: "I don't see how you can have failed to notice that what I intended was that the Socialist Party was near beer in distinction to the Communist Party (good 7 1/2 pc). However much we may cavil at the Communists they mean it when they say they are fighting for socialism, i.e. the cooperative commonwealth." (See DP, "To Fredericka Field," Nov. 29, 1932 [*14C* 413].)

37. Although he never abandoned a nostalgic devotion to the IWW (as well as to the Debsian Socialist Party) he was explicit about their practical inadequacy to the current situation. As early as 1927, he published an article in which he asserted that "[t]he protest that expressed itself in such movements as the I.W.W. and the Non-Partisan League" (the latter was one of several short-lived farmer-labor parties that attempted to succeed the Socialist Party after the splits of 1919) "has pretty well petered out." (See "A Great American" [*New Masses*, Dec.1927]; rpt. in *MNP*, 105.) More frankly still, in the letter to Edmund Wilson in which he reasserted his preference for "the IWW theory" over the "methods" of the Communist Party, he promptly acknowledged that "practically all [the Wobblies] did was go to jail." (See *14C* 398.)

38. In the 1950s, after Dos Passos had abandoned the Left altogether, he would claim that this public support for Foster and Ford was merely a "protest vote." Although some scholars (including Townsend Ludington) have accepted this retrospective assertion at face value, I believe that this is one of many efforts on Dos Passos's part to deny and rewrite the radical commitments of his youth. If Dos Passos had merely intended to register his protest against the mainstream political parties, he could have endorsed Norman Thomas in 1932, whose candidacy on the Socialist ticket was far more widely supported by socialist and left-liberal intellectuals. Dos Passos weighed his public statements and endorsements carefully throughout his life, and his support for Ford was one among many gestures by which he explicitly identified himself (however independently) with the revolutionary wing of the anticapitalist movement. (For Dos Passos's later repudiation, see *The Theme is Freedom* 103; and for Ludington's acceptance of this claim see *John Dos Passos* 309–310.)

39. Dos Passos was treasurer of the Emergency Committee for Southern Political Prisoners and chairman of the National Committee to Aid Striking Miners Facing Starvation. Among other Communist Party-led organizations, he worked actively for the Scottsboro Boys' defense committee and for the National Students League. See Landsberg 163.

40. Some of the most significant campaigns about which Dos Passos wrote in the years between 1926 and 1934 were the Passaic textile strike; the Sacco and Vanzetti trial and executions; the suppression of Communists in New Jersey, Pennsylvania, California, and Georgia; the Scottsboro Boys' trial; the violent labor conflict in the coalfields of Harlan County, Kentucky; the Hunger March on Washington; the Bonus March; and a meeting of leaders of the unemployed. Some of Dos Passos's activist journalism from these years has been reprinted in *MNP*. For a complete bibliography, see David Sanders, ed., *John Dos Passos: A Comprehensive Bibliography* (New York: Garland, 1987) 111–157.

41. In stressing his active participation in these campaigns, I am seeking to counter the tendency within cold war scholarship to claim that Dos Passos was never a radical, even during these years of his most strenuous commitment. Townsend Ludington—editor of Dos Passos's letters and author of a full-length biography—has, e.g., summarized the writer's political position in these years by saying that "though he may have seemed committed to the radical left he was not" (*14C* 383). More recently, Joseph Epstein endorsed a similar judgment in his centenary evaluation of Dos Passos. Asserting that "[t]he exact nature of Dos Passos's politics has long been in dispute," Epstein acknowledges that "at times he seemed close to being a fellow-traveler" but he then apparently concurs with Dawn Powell "that Dos Passos's leftism was in part legendary." (Despite the fact that Epstein appears to be familiar with Dos Passos's radical writings, he accepts as evidence for this claim Powell's assertion "that Communist rallies were always advertising him when he wasn't even present, that he never led meetings, had a horror of organizations, etc.") (See Joseph Epstein, "'U.S.A.' Today" in *The New Yorker* LXXII.22 (Aug. 5, 1996): 70.)

42. "Thank You Mr. Hitler!" *Common Sense* (Dec. 5, 1932); rpt. in *MNP* 156–57. Especially after the onset of the Great Depression, Dos Passos saw a resurgence of the kinds of antidemocratic repression that had prevailed at the height of the Red Scare—and it was this that made fascism seem a plausible danger in the United States. As early as 1930, in an article titled "Back to Red Hysteria," e.g., he asserted that "the struggle against working-class radicalism" on the part of "the American governors and owners" was "going back to the acute stage of 1919"—only now "the arch-enemy is Communism instead of the I.W.W." (See Dos Passos, "Back to Red Hysteria," *New Republic* [July 2, 1930]; rpt. in *MNP* 127–30.)

43. For the "radical fringe" quote, see "Whom Can We Appeal To?" *New Masses* (1930); rpt. in *MNP* 133; for "white collar workers" and intellectual "producers" see, e.g., "Toward a Revolutionary Theatre" (*New Masses*, 1927); rpt. in *MNP* 101; and "Thank You Mr. Hitler!" 156. As in many matters, Dos Passos was somewhat inconsistent in his terminology about (and conceptualization of) the class position of intellectuals and writers. As I've suggested, he frequently referred to writers as intellectual "producers" or "white collar workers"—although he almost always emphasized the fact that writers' class position was complicated by the fact that they often earned their living by legitimating the power of the capitalist class. (In response to a 1932

Modern Quarterly questionnaire, e.g., he characteristically wrote that "As a producer and worker, any writer who's not a paid propagandist for the exploiting group [and most of them will be] will naturally find his lot with the producers." See *MNP* 150.)

One particular bit of idiosyncratic terminology has caused much confusion among Dos Passos scholars. In "Back to Red Hysteria" (1930), Dos Passos states that he is a "middle class liberal"—and a number of scholars (including Ludington) have used this as evidence that Dos Passos was not committed to "the radical left." Dos Passos, however, explicitly explains in his essay that this term is not intended as a description of his political views, but rather of his class position as an intellectual (a position that does not create a *necessary* affiliation in the class war): "By middle-class liberals I mean everybody who isn't forced by his position in the economic structure of society to be pro-worker or anti-worker." In both this essay and in "Whom Can We Appeal To?" published the following month, Dos Passos clearly distinguishes between the "neutrality" that such "middle class liberals" (or "technicians") can "afford"—and his own active endorsement of the working-class movement (as part of "the radical fringe" of this "middle class").

44. See "Toward a Revolutionary Theater" 101 and "Thank You Mr. Hitler" 157. For the Communist Party as "the most advanced outpost" of "the radical movement" to build "a workers' and producers' commonwealth," see Dos Passos, "Unintelligent Fanaticism" in *New Masses* X (Mar. 27, 1934): 6, 8.

45. The rally was organized to protest against the fascist suppression of the Austrian Left. In addition to the Socialist Party, the protest's organizers included the International Ladies Garment Workers Union, the Amalgamated Clothing Workers of America, the Cap and Millinery Workers International Union, the Workmen's Circle, and the Forward Association. Prominent left-liberals, including Mayor Fiorello La Guardia and the American Federation of Labor's vice president Matthew Woll, were also invited to address the meeting. For an account of the protest meeting and the ensuing riot, see Landsberg 180.

46. Dos Passos had, e.g., one particularly intense personal encounter with Communist factionalism on his fact-finding trip to Harlan County, Kentucky in November 1931. When he went to visit some of the striking miners who had been jailed by local authorities, he was shocked and disgusted to discover that Communist organizers were refusing to assist those strikers who were members of non-Communist unions. This behavior seemed so profound a repudiation of the spirit of socialist solidarity that it rankled in Dos Passos for years afterward. He included the incident, significantly, in the final Camera Eye of *U.S.A.*, and in later years, he would claim that it had been one of many turning points in his relationship to the revolutionary Left. See Landsberg 169–170, and see my discussion in the Conclusion below.

47. For a succinct description of the Comintern's turn to this policy of "left extremism"—and its contribution to the rise of fascism in various countries, see Franz Borkenau's classic account in *World Communism: A History of the Communist International* (rpt., Ann Arbor: U of Michigan P, 1962), chap. 20 and 22.

48. This letter offers particularly strong and explicit evidence refuting the notion that Dos Passos was never "committed to the radical left." Here he publicly reiterated his commitment to "the radical movement" (which he defined as "the whole trend, in politics, social organization and in men's minds, in the direction of a workers' and producers' commonwealth") and his support for the Communist Party as "the most advanced outpost" of the movement. He then went on, in the context of this commitment, to assert his "growing conviction that only a drastic change of policy and of mentality [could] save the radical movement in this country from the disastrous defeats suffered in Italy, Germany, Austria and Spain." The Communists' behavior at Madison Square Garden, he argued, indicated "the growth of unintelligent fanaticism that, in my opinion, can only end in the division of the conscious elements of the exploited classes into impotent brawling sects, and in the ruin for our time of the effort towards a sanely organized society." See Dos Passos, "Unintelligent Fanaticism" 6, 8.

49. See DP, "To Edmund Wilson," Mar. 23, 1934 and DP, "To John Howard Lawson," Oct. (?) 1934; *14C* 435–436, 446–448.

50. The masculinist presumptions underlying this epithet—and ambiguously infusing Dos Passos's relationship to the anticapitalist movement generally—will be discussed in some detail in Chapters Five and Six.

51. For one account of the history of Kirov's assassination and the state repression and terror that followed in the USSR, see Isaac Deutscher, *Stalin: A Political Biography* (New York: Oxford UP, 1982), chap. 9, especially 353–359.

52. DP, "To Edmund Wilson," Dec. 23, 1934; *14C* 458–459.

53. Dos Passos's repudiation was the sudden culmination of a long process. He had always evaluated the Soviet experiment on the basis of humanist and democratic commitments—and his judgments had, accordingly, been mixed from the beginning. When he wrote to Edmund Wilson in January 1935 to describe his unfolding crisis of conscience, he explained that his "enthusiastic feelings, personally, about the U.S.S.R. have been on a continual decline since the early days," and he listed some of the "steps" of the process: "the Kronstadt rebellions, the Massacres by Bela Kun in the Crimea, the persecution of the S.R.'s, the N.E.P., the Trotsky expulsion, the abolition of factory committees, and last the liquidating of the Kulaks and the Workers and Peasants Inspection—which leaves the Kremlin absolutely supreme." DP, "To Wilson," Jan. 1935; *14C* 462.

54. DP, "To Edmund Wilson," Jan. 1935; *14C* 460–462. It is interesting to note that, despite the fact that Dos Passos would presumably have been more sympathetic to the intellectual position of the revisionists within the Party, he asserted his preference for the "orthodox" (against "the Adamics and Stolbergs and even possibly against the ingenious Mr. Hook") for practical reasons—"more for what they do than for what they say." Dos Passos was no more willing to relinquish his pragmatic assessments of political effectiveness in the name of his idealism than he was to abandon his principles during this crisis.

55. DP "To Robert Cantwell," Sept. 1934; *14C* 441–442. Dos Passos's continued democratic anticapitalism was equally in evidence, e.g., when he publicly endorsed a national student strike against war in Apr. 1935. Here he not only made the general anticapitalist argument that "[w]ar is the last line of defense for the entrenched interests that arrogate to themselves the name of the nation they exploit," but went on to warn more specifically that "the next war [. . .] will be a war against the mass of the people in behalf of monopolies drunk with financial power. It will bring with it the complete obliteration of personal liberty." See Dos Passos, "Two Views of the Student Strike" (*Student Outlook*, Apr. 1935); rpt. in *MNP* 168.

56. While Freud emphasized the decisive role of ambivalence in the blockage of mourning, Melanie Klein's later conceptualization is particularly relevant here. For Klein, the most central challenge of psychic life is the capacity to recognize and tolerate the coexistence of the good and the bad, the gratifying and the frustrating, the beloved and the hated, in those objects most important to us. The infant's negotiation of such ambivalence toward the primary caretaker, and the move from what Klein calls the paranoid-schizoid to the depressive position, is the model on which similar subsequent challenges are based. The political crisis posed by Stalinism for Dos Passos represented a massive challenge of this kind—a challenge that Dos Passos was, as I will suggest below, unable to negotiate fully. See Melanie Klein, *Envy and Gratitude: A Study of Unconscious Sources*. (London: Tavistock, 1957).

57. The unstable combination of social analysis and naturalization can be seen particularly starkly in Dos Passos's letter to Wilson of Dec. 23, 1934, in which he explains that the Kirov assassination marks the "Napoleonic" degeneration of the Soviet regime and then goes on to insist upon "The horrid law of human affairs by which any government must eventually become involved in power for itself, killing for the pleasure of it" (*14C* 459).

58. See DP, "To Edmund Wilson" Feb. 5, 1935; *14C* 465 and Dos Passos, "The Writer as Technician" (1935); rpt. in *MNP* 172. Dos Passos might, of course, have offered a quite consistent *political* analysis of the antidemocratic (and antihumanist) tendencies shared by capitalism and Stalinism. Other anti-Stalinist socialist intellectuals did develop such a position—and Dos Passos attempted briefly to do this himself. His most substantive effort to do so is, in fact, the very essay from which I have taken my second example here. (It was, significantly, his contribution to the 1935 Communist-organized American Writers Congress). The essay is, in effect, an attempt to argue for an anti-Stalinist democratic socialism founded upon the proposition that intellectual freedom must be a constitutive goal and uncompromisable principle of socialist struggle. The fact that this essay ends on the naturalistic note I have quoted above has, therefore, a particular poignance and significance. The psychic and intellectual inability to sustain this kind of anti-Stalinist democratic socialism has had enormous consequences for progressive politics throughout the capitalist world, and especially in the United States. For the position developed by those within the anti-Stalinist Left, see Aaron, *Writers on the Left*; Burkhart, *Writers and Partisans*; and Alan

Wald, *The New York Intellectuals: The Rise and Decline of the Anti-Stalinist Left* (Chapel Hill: U of North Carolina P, 1987).

59. For an account that places more emphasis on the persistence of Dos Passos's ambivalent attitude toward this kind of chauvinism, see John Smith, "John Dos Passos, 'Anglo-Saxon,'" *Modern Fiction Studies* 44.2 (1998): 282–305.

60. These letters are all reprinted in *14C*. For Dos Passos's anti-Semitic letter to John Howard Lawson, Oct. 1934, see 446–448. For his use of the "Anglo Saxon democracy" terminology see, e.g., DP, "To E. Wilson," Feb. 23, 1934 (435–436), Dec. 23, 1934 (458–460), and Jan. 1935 (460–462). Michael Denning touches on these sentiments, though he does not consider their distinctive intensity during this period of political crisis for Dos Passos: see Denning 197.

61. DP, "To Edmund Wilson," Mar. 23, 1934 and Jan. 1935; *14C* 436 and 461.

62. For Dos Passos's anxious jokes, see again DP, "To Lawson," Oct. 1934 and DP, "To Edmund Wilson," Dec. 23, 1934; *14C* 446–448 and 460. I should perhaps make clear that Dos Passos's writings contain some racist and nationalist elements before the mid-1930s. While there are occasional racist jokes in his earlier letters, however, these tend to be casual or incidental, rather than ideologically systematic and politically purposeful as they are here. The same is roughly true of his relation to U.S. nationalism, although there are occasional instances earlier of a romantic U.S. exceptionalism. The latter was not, however, racialized before the mid-1930s (i.e., associated with distinctively "Anglo Saxon" traits)—and there is a dramatic intensification of this rhetoric after 1934.

63. DP, "To Edmund Wilson," Mar. 23, 1934; DP, "To Robert Cantwell," Sept. 1934; and DP, "To Edmund Wilson," Jan. 1935; *14C* 436, 442, 461.

CHAPTER FIVE

1. Dos Passos, "An Open Letter to President Lowell," *Nation*, Aug. 24, 1927; "Sacco and Vanzetti," *New Masses*, Nov. 1927; and "The Pit and the Pendulum," *New Masses*, Aug. 1926; all rpt. in Donald Pizer, ed., *John Dos Passos: the Major Nonfictional Prose* (Detroit: Wayne State UP, 1988) 97–98, 99, and 85–91. Subsequent references to this collection will be cited as *MNP*.

2. Dos Passos, "Sacco and Vanzetti" 99. Ellipses here, and in all quotations, appear in the original text. My own editorial elisions will be marked with bracketed ellipses ([. . .]).

3. On the demographics of the radical movement in the teens—a majority of whose members were native born—see David A. Shannon, *The Socialist Party of America: A History* (1955; Chicago: Quadrangle, 1967) chap. 1, 2, 6, & 7; and James Weinstein, *The Decline of Socialism in America, 1912–1925* (New York: Monthly Review, 1967) chap. 2 & 4. Michael Denning has emphasized the nativist tendencies of *U.S.A.* and Dos Passos's relative lack of interest in immigrant and nonwhite constituencies within the Left: see "The Decline and Fall of the Lincoln Republic: Dos

Passos's *U.S.A.*," *The Cultural Front: The Laboring of American Culture in the Twentieth Century* (New York: Verso, 1997) 163–200.

4. While Dos Passos and many others saw them as martyrs to the radical cause, it should be noted that Hill at least, like Sacco and Vanzetti, was officially accused of other crimes.

5. George Knox has noted Dos Passos's use of the *Who's Who* entry in "Dos Passos and Painting"; rpt. in *Dos Passos, the Critics and the Writer's Intention*, ed. Allen Belkind (Carbondale: Southern Illinois UP, 1971) 261.

6. In the course of his research, Dos Passos read—and reviewed—some of the more conventional recent biographies of the figures whom he included in *U.S.A.* These reviews attest to Dos Passos's scholarship, and they offer revealing, more prosaic, early explorations of these historical figures. See, e.g., "Edison and Steinmetz," *New Republic*, Dec 18, 1929; rpt. in *MNP* 123–127.

7. This modernist documentary technique—factually "accurate," yet suffused with "fiery" subjective investments—is also evident in other Left documentary experiments of the 1930s. In the literary domain, James Agee's *Let Us Now Praise Famous Men* offers a massively elaborated version of this documentary subjectivism. Agee documents the concrete (and politically explosive) realities of southern sharecroppers' constrained and impoverished lives in the late 1930s, and his account is also drenched with his own subjectivity, with his expressive meditations on his own experience of and relation to the people whose lives he is recording. The photographs of Agee's collaborator, Walker Evans, like those of other documentary photographers of the 1930s—including, most notably, Dorothea Lange—offer an equivalent fusion, in the domain of visual representation. These images call our attention to the hard facts of impoverished lives (a pair of worn workboots; a migrant mother's distracted grimace of anxiety) but, through their careful, self-conscious composition, they not only remind us of the photographer's aesthetic subjectivity, but deploy that aesthetic agency specifically in order to emphasize, elicit, and honor their hard-pressed subjects' capacity for beauty (e.g., in the arrangement of a kitchen, or a straw hat). With respect to the literary form of the biographical prose poem itself, the one clear modernist precursor is William Carlos Williams's *In the American Grain*. Published two years before Dos Passos began writing *U.S.A.*, this volume attempts to identify and explore distinctively American traditions of sensibility and aspiration through highly compressed, metaphorical treatments of historical figures and events. Although Williams's book does not concern itself explicitly with radical politics, and although his technique is (ironically) less condensed and more prosaic than Dos Passos's, Williams's project clearly suggested the ways in which intensely subjective, metaphorically structured, prose poems might function as tools of historical inquiry and tradition building. For two discussions that help to suggest the complexity of 1930s documentary photography, see Lawrence W. Levine, "The Historian and the Icon" and Alan Trachtenberg, "From Image to Story," *Documenting America: 1935–1943*, Carl Fleischhauer and Beverly W. Brannan, eds. (U of California P, 1988). For an

account of documentary practices more generally in the period, see William Stott, *Documentary Expression and Thirties America* (New York: Oxford UP, 1973).

8. "Sacco and Vanzetti" 99.

9. Dos Passos, *42nd Parallel* in *U.S.A.* (1936; Boston: Houghton Mifflen, 1960) 25. All references in this chapter are to this edition of *U.S.A.* and will be cited parenthetically in the text (according to volume) as *42P*, *1919*, and *TBM*.

10. This kind of shorthand revolutionary contextualization is characteristic of Dos Passos's biographies and suggests the insistence of the tradition-building imperative. He commonly weaves these lines of tradition, both domestic and international, even when they are tangential to the central biographical subject. In the biography of Steinmetz, e.g., he goes out of his way to tell us that the inventor's first employer was "a German exile from fortyeight"—just as he reminds us here of the significance of Alsace in 1849, despite the fact that Debs's father was not actually a refugee from the revolution. For more information about Jean Daniel Debs's actual motivations for emigration, see Nick Salvatore, *Eugene Debs: Citizen and Socialist* (Urbana: U of Illinois P, 1982) 9.

11. This emphasis on the fact that Debs's father came to America from Alsace also embodies, in another way, Dos Passos's deep ambivalence about nationalism. On the one hand, his explicit hostility toward all forms of nationalism, intensified by the First World War, would find a fitting symbol in Alsace—annexed by the Germans in 1871 and then returned to France as one of the prominent geopolitical pawns at Versailles in 1919. On the other, Dos Passos's radical version of American nationalism, which was mostly latent in the 1920s and early 1930s, is also captured by the recurrent image in the biographies of America as the destination of disappointed European revolutionaries and refugees, who hoped to find freer and more fertile ground in the New World.

12. The paucity of careful textual analysis is one of the most remarkable features of *U.S.A.*'s critical history. A rare example of a sustained close reading of one of the biographies ("Body of an American") can be found in William Solomon, "Politics and Rhetoric in the Novel in the 1930s," *American Literature* 68.4 (Dec. 1996): 799–818.

13. Dos Passos even ambivalently criticizes, e.g., the Progressive demagoguery of William Jennings Bryan, whose "silver tongue chanted" "out of [his] big mouth" and whose "voice charmed the mortgageridden farmers" (*42P* 154–155). (It is this criticism that causes Dos Passos to treat Bryan as one of the political manipulators, rather than one of the radical heroes, in the biographies.) For Dos Passos's hostility toward vanguardism and antidemocratic practices within the socialist movement, see my discussion in Chap. Four and Six.

14. It is worth noting that the very end of this passage indicates that the wealthy are "scared" of Debs and of the "crowd" that might make him president. In this way, Dos Passos indicates that class conflict is part of the context of Debs's socialism—but, interestingly, he places class hostility here on the side of the rich (who fear the "bogy of a Socialist President"), rather than in the minds of the exploited workers. In this

portrait, Dos Passos is concerned above all to emphasize that Debs's socialism stems from the lyrical, utopian sense of fraternity which I have been exploring—and not principally from envy or resentment of the exploiters.

15. Dos Passos's persistent use of work-related metaphors in the biographies reflected a long-standing, materialist conviction that most people's sensibilities were decisively shaped by the work they performed. In 1919, for example, he cautioned a friend who was considering a career in business that "[a] man's mind is moulded by his occupation, willy nilly. The ideas of a shoemaker are those which are useful in shoemaking, the ideas of a banker those useful in banking. Think what your mind will be like after forty years of exploiting other people." Dos Passos "To Rumsey Marvin," Oct. 15, 1919; *The Fourteenth Chronicle: Letters and Diaries of John Dos Passos*, ed. Townsend Ludington (Boston: Gambit, 1973) 266.

16. It is worth noting that there is a dark implication to this image of Debs being "burned *up*" by the fire of fraternity. The suggestion of self-destructiveness, which appears here as a subdued, minor theme in the imagery, becomes central in the last volume of the trilogy—and I will discuss this development below and in Chap. Six. For now, I want only to emphasize that this metaphor insists that Debs himself shares whatever risks (or destruction) may be entailed by his political vision.

17. The selectivity of this account is particularly revealing in one respect: in order to enforce his interpretive emphasis on Debs's betrayal and isolation, Dos Passos notably omits any mention of the fact that Debs earned about as many votes for the presidency in 1920, while in prison, as he had in 1912.

18. Dos Passos's account of the desire for and fear of socialism mirrors Freud's late drive theory, which posits a conflict between Eros (the drive to form ever-greater, libidinally charged unities) and the death drive (the impulse to eliminate all tension and excitation, to return to stasis). While Freud himself was conscious of the ways in which the drive theory might be used to explain the movement for socialism, his temperamental pessimism made him cautious: see *Civilization and Its Discontents*, trans. James Strachey (1930; New York: Norton, 1989) esp. 70–71 and 109. It fell to Left Freudians like Herbert Marcuse and Norman O. Brown in the 1960s to explore in theoretical detail this psychoanalytic reading of socialism: see, respectively, *Eros and Civilization: A Philosophical Inquiry into Freud* (1955; New York: Vintage, 1961); and *Life Against Death: The Psychoanalytical Meaning of History* (Middletown, CT: Wesleyan UP, 1959).

19. Roughly the same story was told a generation later, by two other psychologically oriented socialist writers, Herbert Marcuse and Norman O. Brown. Elaborating Freud's allegorical account in *Totem and Taboo* within an explicitly socialist framework, Marcuse and Brown both argued that the "revolution of the sons" is always undone when they seek to elevate one of their own into the vacated position of the father. All the libidinal possibilities of solidarity and equality, they suggest, are destroyed in this single act. The deformation of a democratic socialism into an authoritarian Stalinism was already weighing on Dos Passos's mind at the time he composed *U.S.A.*, as

I have explained in Chapter Four—and the preoccupation with this catastrophe in the later years of the twentieth century helps to explain its persistent importance to Brown and Marcuse. See Marcuse, *Eros and Civilization*, especially chap. four, where he discusses the "element of *self-defeat* . . . involved in this dynamic," as a result of which "every revolution has also been a betrayed revolution" (82–83). See also Norman O. Brown, particularly *Love's Body* (New York: Knopf, 1966), chap. one, where he explains that "the history of Marxism shows how hard it is to kill the father" (8). While Marcuse and Brown largely replicate the patriarchal cast of Freud's original account of these dynamics, a later generation of feminists thinkers—including Gayle Rubin, Juliet Mitchell, and Jessica Benjamin—have demonstrated the role of gender hierarchy in vitiating the emancipatory impulses of earlier psychoanalytic and socialist projects. In this context, see especially, Jessica Benjamin, *The Bonds of Love: Psychoanalysis, Feminism and the Problem of Domination* (New York: Pantheon, 1988).

20. The association of venereal disease with *illicit* sexuality (usually between frustrated men and prostitutes) is repeated with remarkable frequency in the trilogy's fictional story lines, as discussed in Chap. Six. Later in this chapter, I will discuss in some detail Dos Passos's persistent association of socialism with the desire for an active, unfettered (hetero)sexuality, and the rejection of socialism with a conventional bourgeois fear of sex. This pattern of representation significantly complicates Dos Passos's treatment of women. On the one hand, the desexualized woman (or the woman who is merely fearful of the ramifications of sex) becomes a persistent symbol for (and the active enforcer of) the constrained, repressive realities of bourgeois society. On the other, the possibility of a truly free society is equally associated with the possibility of women fearlessly embracing their own sexuality. Frequently, as in "Lover of Mankind," the ambivalence toward socialism that is explicitly explored in terms of male choices is also, in effect, acted out through representations of women that alternate—with a disorienting instability—between the explicitly misogynistic and the implicitly feminist. Janet Galligani Casey has recently discussed some aspects of Dos Passos's ambivalence toward femininity in *Dos Passos and the Ideology of the Feminine* (New York: Cambridge UP, 1998).

21. I will explore the tension between the implicitly sexual cast of these male homosocial bonds between Left comrades and its disavowal in Dos Passos's representations in Chap. Six.

22. It is worth emphasizing that Debs's words imply no gendered restriction to this expansive solidarity. Dos Passos's own yearning for such an inclusive solidarity is, of course, persistently undermined by the limits of his own capacity for identification—as, e.g., in the misogyny present in this biography and throughout the trilogy.

23. *1919* 10–14 and 154–158; all italics in quotations in this paragraph have been added for interpretive emphasis.

24. Dos Passos prefigures, here as elsewhere, the theoretical speculations of the Frankfurt school about the utopian potential of expressive culture. Marcuse's assertion in *Eros and Civilization* that "art opposes to institutionalized repression the 'image

of man as a free subject'" (131) could, for example, function as a gloss on Dos Passos's biography of Joe Hill. It is worth emphasizing, however, that in contrast to Marcuse's (and Adorno's) tendency to celebrate the utopian implications of unique artistic masterpieces, Dos Passos's emphasis on the *collaborative* prefiguring of a liberated society through shared expressive activity contains an appealing populism—and a greater attention to creative process as an ordinary part of life. This emphasis on the utopian aspect of popular creativity runs throughout the populist strand of modernist writing in the 1930s: consider, e.g., Hurston's *Their Eyes Were Watching God* and Steinbeck's *The Grapes of Wrath* (particularly chap. 23). It is worth noting that there was something especially evocative for Dos Passos in the image of radicals enacting socialism in prison through singing: more than a decade earlier, he had recorded a similar image in a journalistic account of jailed Portuguese syndicalists. (See Dos Passos, "In Portugal," *Liberator* (Apr. 1920); rpt. in *MNP* 52.)

25. In nearly all the radical biographies, Dos Passos highlights some physical weakness or disability that functions implicitly in this way, as a means of highlighting the men's vulnerability: Debs is "shamblefooted"; Haywood has "lost an eye"; Bourne too is a "hunchback" (a "tiny twisted bit of flesh"). The vulnerability of others is revealed only in their suppression: La Follette becomes "a sick man" "choked" by the "breathed out air of committee rooms"; Reed "caught typhus and died"; Hill is shot by a firing squad; Everest is lynched; and Hibben's Princeton classmates "had a noose around his neck" at a class reunion.

26. It is worth noting that Dos Passos's male modernist contemporaries persistently deployed and explored the castration metaphor. Such disparate works, e.g., as Hemingway's *The Sun Also Rises*, Toomer's *Cane*, and Faulkner's *Light in August* invoke castration as a metaphor for the ways in which structures of social relations (the First World War in Hemingway and race relations in Faulkner and Toomer) have destroyed the possibility of full male development. In these works (as in *U.S.A.*), castration stands either for the irrevocable loss of, or for the perpetual exclusion from, creative or relational fulfillment.

27. Douglas Crimp, who has expressed more clearly than any other commentator the relationship between mourning and political militancy, has pointed out the way in which Joe Hill's famous remark requires precisely this revision for those concerned with political movement building. See Crimp, "Mourning and Militancy," *October* 51 (1989): 5.

28. Melvin Landsberg was the first critic to note these revisions and to suggest their main political implications: see Landsberg, *Dos Passos' Path to U.S.A: A Political Biography* (Boulder, CO: Colorado Associated UP, 1972) 221.

29. Quoted from the first edition of *The 42nd Parallel* (New York: Harper and Brothers, 1930) 97.

30. See, e.g., his hope that the United States would be "a workers' and producers' commonwealth": Dos Passos, "Unintelligent Fanaticism," *New Masses* X (Mar 27, 1934): 6, 8.

31. Although he dates Dos Passos's turn away from the Left as taking place after *U.S.A.*'s completion, John Trombold has offered a related account of the writer's shift from the present to the past: see "From the Future to the Past: The Disillusionment of John Dos Passos," *Studies in American Fiction* 26.2 (Fall 1998): 237–256.

32. Both quotations are from the first edition of *The 42nd Parallel* (New York: Harper and Brothers, 1930) 378.

Chapter Six

1. John Dos Passos, "The Pit and the Pendulum," *New Masses* 1 (Aug. 1926); rpt. in Donald Pizer, ed., *John Dos Passos: The Major Nonfictional Prose* (Detroit: Wayne State UP, 1988) 89. (Subsequent references to this volume will be cited as *MNP*.)

2. Although Dos Passos makes no effort to fictionalize the locations of the Passaic strike or the Sacco and Vanzetti trial, he does dramatize the demoralizing conflicts between Communist and non-Communist miners in Harlan County in the shifted location of the Pennsylvania coalfields in Mary French's narrative. The resonance between the actual events in Kentucky and the fictional enactment in Pennsylvania is made explicit by Dos Passos's account of his own trip to Harlan County in Camera Eye 51, which echoes in many respects Mary's experiences in the final phase of her narrative.

3. John Dos Passos, *The 42nd Parallel* in *U.S.A.* (Boston: Houghton Mifflin, 1960) 13. Subsequent references are to this edition of *U.S.A.* and will be cited parenthetically, by volume, as *42P*, *1919* and *TBM*.

4. Barbara Foley, "From *U.S.A.* to *Ragtime*: Notes on the Forms of Historical Consciousness in Modern Fiction," *American Literature* 50 (Mar. 1978): 92. For Foley's emphasis on *U.S.A.*'s contribution to the development of American historical fiction, see also Foley, "History, Fiction and Satirical Form: The Example of John Dos Passos' *1919*," *Genre* XII (Fall 1979): 357–378; and Foley, "The Treatment of Time in *The Big Money*: An Examination of Ideology and Literary Form," *Modern Fiction Studies* 26 (Autumn 1980): 447–467.

5. While some critics have defended the "fullness and complexity" of naturalist tragedy (see, e.g., Donald Pizer, *Twentieth-Century American Literary Naturalism: An Interpretation* [Carbondale: Southern Illinois UP, 1982] 6–7), my analysis here is more in agreement with those who have emphasized the ways in which fully deterministic naturalisms eliminate the forms of meaning upon which most conceptions of tragedy rely (such a view goes back, e.g., as far as Vernon Parrington, *Main Current in American Thought: The Beginnings of Critical Realism in America (1860–1920)* (New York: Harcourt Brace & World, 1958) 326.). I have particularly benefited from Raymond Williams's formulations in *Modern Tragedy* (London: Chatto and Windus, 1966), as in the following passage (69): "The tragedy of naturalism is the tragedy of passive suffering, and the suffering is passive because man can only endure and can never really change his world. The endurance is given no moral or religious valuation; it is wholly

mechanical, because both man and his world, in what is now understood as rational explanation, are the products of an impersonal and material process which though it changes through time has no ends."

6. There is, of course, a painful masochism to this kind of storytelling, this kind of grieving. It is a masochism that particularly concerned Freud in his meditations on trauma in *Beyond the Pleasure Principle*, trans. James Strachey (1920; New York: Norton, 1961). Seeking to understand the psychic tendency to repeat traumatic loss, Freud famously turned to the "fort/da" game, in which his infant grandson threw away a beloved toy spool (declaring "fort," German for "gone"), and then retrieved it by a string, crying out "da" (German for "here"). Freud himself proposes that such a game is psychically gratifying to a child struggling to come to terms with the painful but quotidian departures of his mother, because the child here repeats a loss originally experienced passively as a phenomenon that he can now control. Freud also remarks that by making the beloved object go away, the child experiences a displaced aggression and revenge against the mother for her departure. Freud minimizes the more obvious point that, through such a game, the child experiences not only the loss of a beloved object, but the reassuring experience of retrieval. If we emphasize this dimension of the game, we can understand it more centrally as an infantile attempt to *mourn*: to recognize that a frustrated desire may be endured—and later gratified in some new way. Dos Passos's mode of grieving loss in the radical storylines of *U.S.A.* resembles this "fort/da" game far less than it does the more primitive—and to Freud "disturbing"—grieving game enacted by his grandson in the months before he invents the game of loss and retrieval. In this earlier version, the child merely throws away his toys, rendering them inaccessible. Here, the child seems simply to enact, over and over again, the painful and bewildering experience of loss, as if to reassure himself that, indeed, beloved things vanish. I would propose that this activity might be understood as a melancholic practice—an infantile version of the complex game that Dos Passos plays in these fictions: a masochistic behavior that seeks, preemptively, to shield the ego from further disappointment by attempting to convince oneself of the inevitability of loss. While Freud views both games in *Beyond the Pleasure Principle* as expressions of the masochistic impulse of the "death drive," my account here seeks to resist the naturalizing tendency of the late drive theory in order to emphasize, rather, the alternative (and culturally varied) forms that grieving may take—in adult, as in infantile, life.

7. For some of the many animal comparisons, see, e.g., Stephen Crane, *Maggie: A Girl of the Streets* in *Great Short Works of Stephen Crane*, ed. James B. Colvert (New York: Harper & Rowe, 1968) 141, 152, 164; for schoolyard fight, see 127–130; for "hereditary evil," see Frank Norris, *McTeague* (New York: Norton, 1977) 19.

8. Theodore Dreiser, *Sister Carrie* (1900; New York: Signet, 1980) 273–274, 304–305.

9. Alfred Kazin, *On Native Grounds: An Interpretation of Modern American Prose Literature.* (1942; Garden City, NY: Doubleday, 1956) 268.

10. See DP, "To Edmund Wilson," June 27, 1939; rpt. in Townsend Ludington, ed., *The Fourteenth Chronicle: Letters and Diaries of John Dos Passos*. (Boston: Gambit, 1973) 522. (Subsequent references to this volume will be cited as *14C*). Wilson was, at that time, commenting on Dos Passos's later novel, *Adventures of a Young Man*— but their exchange concerns the same literary technique so visible in the fictional narratives of *U.S.A.*.

11. John Dos Passos, "Sacco and Vanzetti" in *New Masses* 3 (Nov. 1927): 25; rpt. in *MNP* 99.

12. It is worth noting that the Newsreel segments that run throughout the *U.S.A.* trilogy imply the same analysis as that offered here in Dos Passos's journalism. The primary purpose of these segments is to show, through actual snippets of newspaper headlines, newsreel stories, and popular songs, the relentlessness with which the mass media was manipulating political consciousness (and primary human emotions—especially romantic love) through the technique I am describing: by reducing them to vacuous and ideologically partisan clichés. Even in the Newsreels, however, Dos Passos does not focus his political analysis quite so sharply as he does in his nonfictional writings.

13. See Camera Eye segments 49 and 50 (*TBM* 391, 413).

14. "An Open Letter to President Lowell"; rpt. in *MNP* 97–98.

15. Dos Passos, "To Edmund Wilson," Jan 14(?) 1931; *14C* 397–398.

16. Dos Passos's letters "To Edmund Wilson," (May 1932) and "To Robert Cantwell," (Jan. 25, 1935); *14C* 409 and 463–464.

17. "The Writer as Technician" and "Introductory Note to *The 42nd Parallel*; both rpt. in *MNP* 172 and 180.

18. The phrase is from Dos Passos's May 1932 letter "To Edmund Wilson," quoted earlier; rpt. in *14C*, 409. Also consider in this context, Dos Passos's pithy assertion that "[s]omebody's got to have the size to Marxianize the American tradition before you can sell the American worker on the social revolution. Or else Americanize Marx." ("Whither the American Writer?" in *Modern Quarterly* 6 [Summer 1932]; rpt. in *MNP* 150.)

19. According to a leading historian of the IWW, "no more complete amalgamation of workers had ever existed in the American labor movement": those organized in the same local included "newsboys, waiters, bartenders, cooks, clerks, maids, hard-rock miners, reporters." As a result, the Wobblies exercised for a brief time a remarkable degree of control over hours and working conditions in Goldfield. Ultimately, the mine owners were able, with the assistance of federal troops, to break the Wobblies' hold over the town in the course of a particularly bitter and protracted strike. See Melvyn Dubofsky, *We Shall Be All: A History of the Industrial Workers of the World*. (Chicago: Quadrangle, 1969) 120–125.

20. For Dos Passos's own comments about the sources of this Marxist cliché about the intellectual as "wellsharpened instrument," see Melvyn Landsberg, *Dos Passos' Path to U.S.A.: A Political Biography* (Boulder, CO: Colorado Associated UP, 1972) 216.

21. For an argument that goes particularly far in emphasizing Dos Passos's identification with, and positive representation of, Mary, see Janet Galligani Casey, *Dos Passos and the Ideology of the Feminine* (New York: Cambridge UP, 1998) 171–174.

22. I have borrowed the term *reification* from Dos Passos's contemporary, the literary theorist Georg Lukacs. Lukacs named most precisely the way in which the intensification of capitalism causes people at every level of the social order to become ever more alienated from their creative capacities, which they experience as "reified" things, as increasingly mysterious and alien processes of which they are the passive objects. Lukacs himself warned that "bourgeois attempts to comprehend [...] reification"— including the attempts of thinkers "clear in their own minds about its humanly destructive consequences"—often lead to a "'deepening' of the problem" itself. In particular, Lukacs argued that such observers tend to "divorce" the "manifestations" of reification "from their real capitalist foundation and make them independent and permanent by regarding them as the timeless model of human relations in general." (It is precisely this kind of naturalization in which Dos Passos engages throughout the fictional story lines of *U.S.A.* Like most materialists, Lukacs did not concern himself with the *psychological* dynamics that motivate such acts of naturalization (even on the part of writers "who have no desire to deny or obscure" capitalism's destructive effects)—and my aim here is, centrally, to illuminate those dynamics. See Lukacs, "Reification and the Consciousness of the Proletariat" in *History and Class Consciousness: Studies in Marxist Dialectics*, ed. and trans. Rodney Livingston (Cambridge, MA: MIT P, 1982) esp. 92–95. For an influential account of the problem of reification in the American literary tradition, see Carolyn Porter, *Seeing and Being: The Plight of the Participant Observer in Emerson, James, Adams and Faulkner* (Middletown, CT: Wesleyan UP, 1981).

23. For Eliot's derisive representation of working-class speech, see *The Waste Land*, lines 139–172. For Crane's characteristic use of repetitive dialogue to make working-class characters appear foolish, see, e.g., the conversation between Pete and Jimmie in *Maggie*, chap. 5, 24. For Norris's trivialization of political conversation, see, e.g., chap. 1, 8.

24. A long and varied critical tradition has, in particular, explored this authorial aggression in *U.S.A.* in terms of the idiom of "satire"—and Dos Passos was, indeed, a lifelong admirer of the satirical tradition. (See, e.g., Arthur Mizener, "The Gullivers of John Dos Passos"; Townsend Ludington, *Dos Passos: A Twentieth Century Odyssey* [New York: E. P. Dutton, 1980] 355 ff; and Foley, "History, Fiction and Satirical Form.") Sartre offered perhaps the most compelling *celebration* of Dos Passos's treatment of language in the fictions of *U.S.A.*, arguing that this mode of representation produces in readers a kind of existential nausea, a revolt against the intellectual bad faith embodied in these pervasive ways of speaking and thinking. See Jean-Paul Sartre, "John Dos Passos and *1919*" in Andrew Hook, ed., *Dos Passos: A Collection of Critical Essays* (Englewood Cliffs, NJ: Prentice Hall, 1974) 80–96.

25. Judith Butler, "Melancholy Gender/Refused Identification" in Butler, *The Psychic Life of Power: Theories in Subjection* (Stanford: Stanford UP, 1997) 132–166.

26. Feminist analysis was a central component of the bohemian radical subculture of the teens that Dos Passos encountered in New York. He was certainly familiar, e.g., with Emma Goldman's fierce critique of bourgeois marriage and her celebration of "free love"—and with the male feminists like Max Eastman who were prominent at *The Masses*. The influence of feminist writers and intellectuals within the Communist Left of the 1930s—including, e.g., Tillie Olsen and Agnes Smedley—deserves further study, but such voices were certainly a part of the Left literary subculture that, among others, Dos Passos inhabited. On feminism within the radical movement of the teens and 1920s, see, e.g., Mari Jo Buhle, *Women and American Socialism, 1870–1920* (Urbana: U of Illinois P, 1981); and Leslie Fishbein, *Rebels in Bohemia: The Radicals of "The Masses," 1911–1917* (Chapel Hill: U of North Carolina P, 1982). On the feminist analysis of some writers affiliated with the Communist Party in the 1930s, see Constance Coiner, *Better Red: The Writing and Resistance of Tillie Olsen and Meridel Le Sueur* (Urbana: U of Illinois P, 1998); and Deborah Rosenfelt, "From the Thirties: Tillie Olsen and the Radical Tradition," *The Critical Response to Tillie Olsen*, ed. Kay Hoyle Nelson and Nancy Huse (Westport, CT: Greenwood, 1994) 54–89.

27. It is worth emphasizing that this mingling of feminist insight and misogyny was characteristic of quite a number of the authors I have described as melancholic modernists, including, especially, Faulkner and Cather. On Dos Passos's ambivalent gender politics, and his complex relationship to normative masculinity, see, in particular, Casey, *Dos Passos and the Ideology of the Feminine*. See also Michael Denning, *The Cultural Front*, especially 182–186. On Dos Passos's attitudes toward masculinity, see also Mark A. Graves, "A World Based on Brotherhood: Male Bonding, Male Representation, and the War Novels of John Dos Passos," *College Literature Association Journal* 38.12 (Dec. 1994): 228–246. There remains much work to be done on Dos Passos's relationship to homosexuality and homophobia.

28. It is interesting to note, that this image of the Jewish woman as a sexually unappealing but powerfully maternal figure seems to have characterized Dos Passos's first personal encounter with Emma Goldman, the woman radical whom he also most admired in his youth. He bragged to his confidant of the time, Rumsey Marvin, of "sitting next to Emma Goldman's table" in a New York cafe, but his description seeks to domesticate her as a maternal figure, even as he depicts her as a woman of appetite and great power over her unquestioning (presumably male) followers, whom Dos Passos alludes to as "myrmidons": "She's a Bronxy fattish little old woman who looks like a rather good cook. She has a charmingly munchy fashion of eating sandwiches and pats her myrmidons on the head and kisses them in a motherly fashion" (DP "To Marvin," June 5, 1917; *14C* 75). This comment, which resonates with his more explicitly phobic representation of Helen Mauer and Fanya Stein, may help to explain Dos Passos's exclusion of Goldman from the pantheon of the radical biographies.

CONCLUSION

1. The Camera Eye segments are numbered in the text (and table of contents) of *U.S.A.* I have cited them here, and throughout the conclusion, with the abbreviation CE.

2. For earlier biographical readings of the Camera Eye, see Janet Galligani Casey, *Dos Passos and the Ideology of the Feminine* (New York: Cambridge UP, 1998) 148–154, 173–174; Donald Pizer, "The Camera Eye in *U.S.A.*: The Sexual Center," *Modern Fiction Studies* (Autumn 1980): 417–430; and Townsend Ludington, "The Ordering of the Camera Eye in *U.S.A.*," *American Literature* 49 (Nov. 1977): 443–446.

3. CE 49 in Dos Passos, *The Big Money* in *U.S.A.* (Boston: Houghton Mifflin, 1960) 390–391. Subsequent references are to this edition of *U.S.A.* and will be cited parenthetically, by volume, as *42P*, *1919*, and *TBM*.

4. It should be noted that Dos Passos's relationship to nativism in this Camera Eye and the two that follow is, in fact, deeply divided. On the one hand, he is explicitly condemning the ethnic nationalism that contributed to the persecution of Sacco, Vanzetti, and many other immigrant radicals. At the same time, however, he is actively engaged in Camera Eye 49 in the creation of a heroic Anglo-Saxon origin story, which associates the virtuous founding of America with the "roundheads," who are identified as the original "haters of oppression." Dos Passos goes so far as to write that these English immigrants brought their liberationist ideology to an empty continent "that belonged to no one." Dos Passos appears to be somewhat self-conscious about this nostalgic vision of European conquest when he acknowledges that this land was not, in fact, "empty": he notes that the "redskins grew their tall corn in patches forever into the incredible west." This formulation enacts a peculiar instability in Dos Passos's view, at once indulging in a pastoral rewriting of European imperialism and implicitly registering its falsity. (This representational instability about the founding myths of America strongly resembles those enacted by Cather in *A Lost Lady* and by Fitzgerald at the end of *Gatsby*.) In this Camera Eye, as in those that follow, Dos Passos is, then, both condemning modern U.S. nativism and seeking to create an idealized image of the Anglo-Saxon roots of America that he looks back to nostalgically if uneasily. As I argue in Chapter Four and at the end of Chapter Five, that nostalgic Anglo-Saxon nationalism became an increasingly powerful compensatory prop as Dos Passos's faith in radical social change faltered. The ambivalent indulgence in these late Camera Eyes in a nostalgic nationalism he also criticized is an indication of the precariousness of his final gesture of mourning.

5. For Dos Passos's account of this trip, see "Harlan: Working Under the Gun," *New Republic* 69 (December 2, 1931) 62–67, rpt. in *John Dos Passos: The Major Nonfictional Prose*, ed. Donald Pizer (Detroit: Wayne State UP, 1988), 136–145. (Subsequent references to this volume will be cited as *MNP*). See also Melvin Landsberg, *Dos Passos' Path to U.S.A.: A Political Biography* (Boulder: Colorado Associated UP, 1972) 163–70; Daniel Aaron, *Writers on the Left: Episodes in American Literary Com-*

munism (1961; New York: Columbia UP, 1992) 178–182; and Townsend Ludington, *John Dos Passos: A Twentieth Century Odyssey* (New York: Dutton, 1980) 297–300.

6. See Landsberg 169–170. For Edmund Wilson's similar reaction to these organizing tactics in Harlan County the following year, see Aaron 182.

7. For Dos Passos's public account of his view of Robles's execution, see "The Death of José Robles," *New Republic* (July 1939), 308–309; reprinted in *MNP* 193–195. For this episode in Dos Passos's life, and his public break from the Communist Party, see Ludington 362–399 and Carr 357–413. John Trombold emphasizes the decisiveness of this political break and explores some of its subsequent literary effects in Dos Passos's writing in "From the Future to the Past: The Disillusionment of John Dos Passos," *Studies in American Fiction* 26.2 (Autumn 1998): 237–256. For two other discussions of this episode in literary contexts, see John Rohrkemper, "The Collapse of Faith and the Failure of Language: John Dos Passos and the Spanish Civil War," *Rewriting the Good Fight: Critical Essays in the Literature of the Spanish Civil War*, ed. Frieda S. Brown et. al. (East Lansing: Michigan State UP, 1989): 215–228; and Robert Sayre, "Anglo-American Writers, the Communist Movement and the Spanish Civil War: The Case of Dos Passos," *Revue Francaise D'études Américaines* 11.29 (May 1986): 263–274.

8. For a new assessment of the anomalous absence of a labor party in the United States, see Robin Archer, *Why Is There No Labor Party in the United States?* (forthcoming, Princeton UP).

9. On the emergence of the anti-Stalinist Left in the United States, see Aaron, *Writers on the Left*; and for a fuller, more recent account of its development and denoument, see Alan Wald, *The New York Intellectuals: The Rise and Decline of the Anti-Stalinist Left from the 1930s to the 1980s* (Chapel Hill: U of North Carolina P, 1987).

10. See Raymond Williams, "Culture Is Ordinary," rpt. in Williams, *Resources of Hope* (London: Verso, 1989), 3–18.

Works Cited

Aaron, Daniel. *Writers on the Left: Episodes in American Literary Communism.* 1961. New York: Columbia UP, 1992.

Abraham, Karl, and Maria Torok. *The Shell and the Kernel.* Trans. and ed. Nicholas T. Rand. Chicago: U of Chicago P, 1994.

Ackroyd, Peter. *T. S. Eliot: A Life.* New York: Simon and Schuster, 1984.

Agee, James. *Let Us Now Praise Famous Men.* 1941. New York: Ballantine, 1969.

Ahearn, Barry. "The Poet As Social Worker." *William Carlos Williams Review* 19.1–2 (Spring/Fall 1993): 15–32.

Archer, Robin. *Why Is There No Labor Party in the United States?* (Forthcoming, Princeton UP).

Baker, Houston. *Modernism and the Harlem Renaissance.* Chicago: U of Chicago P, 1987.

Batker, Carol. "'Love me like I like to be': The Sexual Politics of Hurston's *Their Eyes Were Watching God*, the Classic Blues, and the Black Women's Club Movement." *African American Review* 32.2 (Spring 1998): 199–213.

Belkind, Allen, ed. *Dos Passos, the Critics and the Writer's Intention.* Carbondale: Southern Illinois UP, 1971.

Bell, Ian F. A. "'Newness of Beginning': The Violent Phantasies of Willa Cather and F. Scott Fitzgerald." *The Insular Dream: Obsession and Resistance.* Ed. Kristiaan Versluys. Amsterdam: VU UP, 1995. 242–260.

Benjamin, Jessica. *The Bonds of Love: Psychoanalysis, Feminism, and the Problem of Domination.* New York: Pantheon, 1988.

Benstock, Shari. *Women of the Left Bank, Paris 1900–1940.* Austin: U of Texas P, 1986.

Berkman, Alexander. *What Is Communist Anarchism?* New York: Vanguard, 1929.

Berman, Marshall. *All That Is Solid Melts Into Air.* 1982. New York: Penguin, 1988.

Berry, Eleanor. "William Carlos Williams' Triadic-Line Verse: An Analysis of Its Prosody." *Twentieth Century Literature* 35.3 (Autumn 1989): 364–388.

Berry, Faith, ed. *Good Morning Revolution: Uncollected Writings of Langston Hughes.* 1973. New York: Citadel, 1992.

———. *Langston Hughes: Before and Beyond Harlem.* 1983. New York: Citadel, 1992.

Boker, Pamela. *The Grief Taboo in American Literature: Loss and Prolonged Adolescence in Twain, Melville, and Hemingway.* New York: New York UP, 1996.

Borkenau, Franz. *World Communism: A History of the Communist International.* Ann Arbor: U of Michigan P, 1962.

Bradbury, Malcolm, and James McFarlane, eds. *Modernism, 1890–1930.* New York: Penguin, 1976.

Breitweiser, Mitchell. "*The Great Gatsby*: Grief, Jazz and the Eye-Witness." *Arizona Quarterly* 47.3 (1991): 17–70.

Brown, Norman O. *Life Against Death: The Psychoanalytical Meaning of History.* Middletown, CT: Wesleyan UP, 1959.

———. *Love's Body.* New York: Knopf, 1966.

Brown, Wendy. "Resisting Left Melancholia." *Loss: The Politics of Mourning.* Ed. David Eng and David Kazanjian. Berkeley: U of California P, 2002. 458–466.

Breslin, James. *William Carlos Williams: An American Artist.* 1970. Chicago: U of Chicago P, 1985.

Buhle, Mari Jo. *Women and American Socialism, 1870–1920.* Urbana: U of Illinois P, 1981.

Burkhart, James. *Writers and Partisans: A History of Literary Radicalism in America.* New York: John Wiley and Sons, 1968.

Butler, Judith. *The Psychic Life of Power: Theories in Subjection.* Stanford: Stanford UP, 1997.

Callahan, John F. *The Illusions of a Nation: Myth and History in the Novels of F. Scott Fitzgerald.* Urbana: U of Illinois P, 1972.

Cappucci, Paul R. "Negotiating the 1930s: William Carlos Williams's Struggle with Politics and Art on His Way to *Paterson*." *The Journal of Imagism* (Fall 1999): 3–21.

Carlin, Deborah. *Cather, Canon, and the Politics of Reading.* Amherst: U of Massachusetts P, 1992.

Carr, Virginia Spencer. *Dos Passos: A Life.* New York: Doubleday, 1984.

Caruth, Cathy. *Unclaimed Experience: Trauma, Narrative and History.* Baltimore: Johns Hopkins, 1996.

———, ed. *Trauma: Explorations in Memory.* Baltimore: Johns Hopkins, 1995.

Casey, Janet Galligani. *Dos Passos and the Ideology of the Feminine.* New York: Cambridge UP, 1998.

Cassidy, Thomas. "Janie's Rage: The Dog and the Storm in *Their Eyes Were Watching God*." *College Language Association Journal* 36.3 (Mar. 1993): 260–269.

Cather, Willa. *A Lost Lady.* 1923. New York: Vintage, 1990.

Chase, Richard. "The Chronicles of Dos Passos." *Dos Passos: A Collection of Critical Essays.* Ed. Andrew Hook. Englewood Cliffs, NJ: Prentice Hall, 1974. 171–180.

Chinitz, David. "Literacy and Authenticity: The Blues Poems of Langston Hughes." *Callaloo* 19.1 (Winter 1996): 177–192.

Clark, Suzanne. *Sentimental Modernism: Women Writers and the Revolution of the Word.* Bloomington: Indiana UP, 1991.

Coiner, Constance. *Better Red: The Writing and Resistance of Tillie Olsen and Meridel Le Sueur.* Urbana: U of Illinois P, 1998.

Colley, Iain. *Dos Passos and the Fiction of Despair.* London: Macmillan, 1978.

Constantine, Robert J., ed. *Gentle Rebel: Letters of Eugene V. Debs.* Urbana: U of Illinois P, 1995.

Cowley, Malcolm. *Exile's Return: A Literary Odyssey of the 1920s.* New York: Viking, 1968.

———. "John Dos Passos: The Poet and the World." *Dos Passos, the Critics and the Writer's Intention.* Ed. Allen Belkind. Carbondale: Southern Illinois UP, 1971. 22–34.

———. *A Second Flowering: Works and Days of the Lost Generation.* New York: Viking, 1973.

Crane, Stephen. *Maggie: Girl of the Streets.* 1893. *Great Short Works of Stephen Crane,* Ed. James B. Colvert. New York: Harper and Rowe, 1968. 127–189.

Crimp, Douglas. "Mourning and Militancy." *October* 51 (1989): 3–18.

D'Attilio, Robert, and Jane Manthorn, eds. *Sacco-Vanzetti: Developments and Reconsiderations.* Boston: Boston Public Library, 1979.

Davies, Kathleen. "Zora Neale Hurston's Poetics of Embalmment: Articulating the Rage of Black Women and Narrative Self-Defense." *African American Review* 26.1 (Spring 1992): 147–159.

Davis, Angela. *Blues Legacies and Black Feminism: Gertrude 'Ma' Rainey, Bessie Smith and Billie Holiday.* New York: Pantheon, 1998.

Dawahare, Anthony. "'That Joyous Certainty': History and Utopia in Tillie Olsen's Depression-Era Literature." *Twentieth Century Literature* 44.3 (Autumn 1998): 261–275.

Denning, Michael. *The Cultural Front: The Laboring of American Culture in the Twentieth Century.* New York: Verso, 1996.

Deutscher, Isaac. *Stalin: A Political Biography.* New York: Oxford UP, 1982.

Diggins, John P. *Up from Communism: Conservative Odysseys in American Intellectual History.* New York: Harper & Row, 1975.

Dos Passos, John. *The Best Times.* New York: New American Library, 1966.

———. *Facing the Chair: Story of the Americanization of Two Foreignborn Workingmen.* 1927. New York: Da Capo, 1970.

———. *The 42nd Parallel.* New York: Harper and Brothers, 1930.

———. *In All Countries.* London: Constable & Co., 1934.

———. *John Dos Passos: The Major Nonfictional Prose.* Ed. Donald Pizer. Detroit: Wayne State UP, 1988. 149–150.

———. *Rosinante to the Road Again.* New York: George H. Doran, 1922.

———. *The Theme Is Freedom.* New York: Dodd, Mead, 1956

———. *Three Soldiers.* 1921. New York: Houghton Mifflin, 1964.

————. "Unintelligent Fanaticism." *New Masses* 10 (Mar. 27, 1934): 6, 8.

————. *U.S.A.* 1936; Boston: Houghton Mifflin, 1960.

Douglas, Ann. *Terrible Honesty: Mongrel Manhattan in the 1920s.* New York: Farrar, Straus and Giroux, 1995.

Doyle, Laura. "The Body against Itself in Faulkner's Phenomenology of Race." *American Literature* 73.5 (2001): 339–364.

————. *Bordering on the Body: The Racial Matrix of Modern Fiction and Culture.* New York: Oxford UP, 1994.

Draper, Theodore. *The Roots of American Communism.* 1957. Chicago: Elephant Books, 1989.

Dreiser, Theodore. *Sister Carrie.* 1900. New York: Signet, 1980.

Dubofsky, Melvyn. *We Shall Be All: A History of the Industrial Workers of the World.* Chicago: Quadrangle Books, 1969.

Eagleton, Terry. "Capitalism, Modernism and Postmodernism." *Against the Grain: Essays 1975–1985.* New York: Verso, 1986. 131–148.

Eby, Carl. *Hemingway's Fetishism: Psychoanalysis and the Mirror of Manhood.* Albany: SU New York P, 1999.

Edwards, Brent Hayes. *The Practice of Diaspora: Literature, Translation, and the Rise of Black Internationalism.* Cambridge: Harvard UP, 2003.

Eggers, Paul. "An(other) Way to Mean: A Lacanian Reading of Langston Hughes' *Montage of a Dream Deferred.*" *Studies in the Humanities* 27.1 (June 2000): 20–34.

Ehrmann, Herbert B. *The Case That Will Not Die.* Boston: Beacon, 1969.

Eliot, T. S. *The Complete Poems and Plays, 1909–1950.* New York: Harcourt, Brace & World, 1971.

Ellman, Maud. "Eliot's Abjection." *Abjection, Melancholia, and Love: The Work of Julia Kristeva.* Ed. John Fletcher and Andrew Benjamin. New York: Routledge, 1990. 178–200.

Ellman, Richard, and Charles Feidelson, Jr., eds. *The Modern Tradition: Backgrounds of Modern Literature.* New York: Oxford UP, 1965.

Eng, David L., and David Kazanjian, eds. *Loss: The Politics of Mourning.* Berkeley: U of California P, 2002.

Engle, Paul, and Joseph Langland, eds. *Poet's Choice.* New York: Dial, 1962.

Epstein, Joseph. "'U.S.A.' Today." *The New Yorker* 72.22 (Aug. 5, 1996): 68–74.

Ericson, Kai. *A New Species of Trouble: The Human Experience of Modern Disasters.* New York: Norton, 1994.

Faulkner, William. *Absalom, Absalom!* 1936. New York: Vintage, 1990.

————. *Light in August.* 1932. New York: Vintage, 1987.

Fetterley, Judith. "*The Great Gatsby*: Fitzgerald's *Droit de Seigneur.*" *Major Literary Characters: Gatsby.* Ed. Harold Bloom. New York: Chelsea House, 1991. 103–112.

Fishbein, Leslie. *Rebels in Bohemia: The Radicals of "The Masses," 1911–1917.* Chapel Hill: U of North Carolina P, 1982.

Fitzgerald, F. Scott. *The Great Gatsby.* 1925. New York: Scribner, 1995.

Fleischhauer, Carl, and Beverly W. Brannan, eds. *Documentary America: 1935–1943.* Berkeley: U of California P, 1988.

Fletcher, John, and Andrew Benjamin, eds. *Abjection, Melancholia, and Love: The Work of Julia Kristeva.* New York: Routledge, 1990.

Foley, Barbara. "From *U.S.A.* to *Ragtime*: Notes on the Forms of Historical Consciousness in Modern Fiction." *American Literature* 50 (Mar. 1978): 85–105.

———. "History, Fiction and Satirical Form: The Example of John Dos Passos' *1919.*" *Genre* XII (Fall 1979): 357–378.

———. "'In the Land of Cotton': Economics and Violence in Jean Toomer's *Cane.*" *African-American Review* 32.2 (Summer 1998): 181–198.

———. "Jean Toomer's Sparta." *American Literature* 67.4 (Dec. 1995): 747–775.

———. "Jean Toomer's Washington and the Politics of Class: from 'Blue Veins' to Seventh-street Rebels." *Modern Fiction Studies* 42.2 (1996): 289–321.

———. *Radical Representations.* Durham: Duke UP, 1993.

———. "Roads Taken and Not Taken: Post-Marxism, Antiracism, and Anticommunism." *Cultural Logic: An Electronic Journal of Marxist Theory and Practice* 1.2 (Spring 1998).

———. "The Treatment of Time in *The Big Money*: An Examination of Ideology and Literary Form." *Modern Fiction Studies* 26 (Autumn 1980): 447–467.

Forter, Greg. "Against Melancholia: Contemporary Mourning Theory, Fitzgerald's *The Great Gatsby*, and the Politics of Unfinished Grief." *Differences* 14.2 (Summer 2003): 134–170.

———. "Melancholy Modernism: Gender and the Politics of Mourning in *The Sun Also Rises.*" *The Hemingway Review* 20.1 (Fall 2001): 22–37.

Fradenburg, Louise O. "'Voice Memorial': Loss and Reparation in Chaucer's Poetry." *Exemplaria* 2.1 (Mar. 1990): 169–202.

Freud, Sigmund. *Beyond the Pleasure Principle.* Trans. and ed. James Strachey. 1920. New York: Norton, 1961.

———. *Civilization and Its Discontents.* Trans. and ed. James Strachey. 1930. New York: Norton, 1989.

———. "Mourning and Melancholia." 1917. *The Standard Edition of the Complete Psychological Works of Sigmund Freud.* Trans. and ed. James Strachey. vol. 14. London: Hogarth Press, 1957. 239–258.

———. "On Fetishism." 1927. *Sexuality and the Psychology of Love.* Ed. Philip Rieff. New York: Collier, 1963. 214–219.

Friedlander, Saul. *Memory, History, and the Extermination of the Jews of Europe.* Bloomington: U of Indiana P, 1993.

Friedlander, Saul, ed. *Probing the Limits of Representation: Nazism and the "Final Solution."* Cambridge: Harvard UP, 1992.

Friedman, Susan Stanford. "Modernism of the 'Scattered Remnant': Race and Politics in H. D.'s Development." *Feminist Issues in Literary Scholarship.* Ed. Shari Benstock. Bloomington: Indiana UP, 1987. 208–231.

———. *Psyche Reborn: The Emergence of H. D.* Bloomington: Indiana UP, 1981.

Gates, Henry Louis, Jr. *Figures in Black: Words, Signs and the "Racial" Self.* New York: Oxford UP, 1987.

Gilbert, James Burkhart. *Writers and Partisans: a History of Literary Radicalism in America.* New York: John Wiley and Sons, 1968.

Godden, Richard. "*The Great Gatsby*: Glamour on the Turn." *American Studies* 16.3 (1982): 343–371.

Goldman, Emma. *Anarchism and Other Essays.* 1911. New York: Dover, 1969.

———. "Emma Goldman's Defense." *The Masses* (June 1916). Rpt. in *Echoes of Revolt: The Masses, 1911–1917.* Ed. William L. O'Neill. Chicago: Quadrangle, 1966. 209–212.

———. "Socialism: Caught in the Political Trap." *Red Emma Speaks: Selected Writing and Speeches by Emma Goldman.* Ed. Alix Kates Shulman. New York: Vintage, 1972. 78–85.

Goldstein, Philip. "Critical Realism or Black Modernism?: The Reception of *Their Eyes Were Watching God.*" *Reader* 41 (Spring 1999): 54–73.

Graham, Sarah H. S. "'We have a secret. We are alive': H. D.'s *Trilogy* as a Response to War." *Texas Studies in Literature and Language* 44.2 (Summer 2002): 161–210.

Graves, Mark A. "A World Based on Brotherhood: Male Bonding, Male Representation, and the War Novels of John Dos Passos." *College Literature Association Journal* 38.12 (Dec. 1994): 228–246.

Gubar, Susan. "The Echoing Spell of H. D.'s *Trilogy.*" *Contemporary Literature* 19 (1978): 196–208.

H. D. *The Flowering of the Rod.* 1944. *Trilogy.* New York: New Directions, 1998.

Haddox, Thomas F. "The Logic of Expenditure in *Their Eyes Were Watching God.*" *Mosaic* 34.1 (Mar. 2001): 19–34.

Harvey, David. *The Condition of Postmodernity: An Enquiry into the Origins of Cultural Change.* Cambridge: Blackwell, 1989.

Hemenway, Robert. *Zora Neale Hurston: A Literary Biography.* Urbana: U of Illinois P, 1977.

Hemingway, Ernest. *A Farewell to Arms.* 1929. New York: Scribner, 2003.

———. *The Sun Also Rises.* 1926. New York: Scribner, 1986.

Hicks, Granville. "The Politics of John Dos Passos." *Dos Passos: A Collection of Critical Essays.* Ed. Andrew Hook. Englewood Cliffs, NJ: Prentice Hall, 1974. 15–30.

Homans, Peter, ed. *Symbolic Loss: The Ambiguity of Mourning and Memory at Century's End.* Charlottesville: UP of Virginia, 2000.

Hook, Andrew, ed. *Dos Passos: A Collection of Critical Essays.* Englewood Cliffs, NJ: Prentice Hall, 1974.

hooks, bell. "Zora Neale Hurston: A Subversive Reading." *Matatu* 3.6 (1989): 5–23.

Howard, June. *Form and History in American Literary Naturalism.* Chapel Hill: U of North Carolina P, 1985.

Howe, Irving. Introduction. *Echoes of Revolt: The Masses, 1911–1917*. Ed. William L. O'Neill. Chicago: Quadrangle, 1966. 5–8.

Hughes, Langston. *The Collected Poems of Langston Hughes*. Ed. Arnold Rampersad and David Roessel. New York: Knopf, 1994.

———. "I Remember the Blues." *Good Morning Revolution: Uncollected Writings of Langston Hughes*. Ed. Faith Berry. New York: Citadel, 1992. 167.

———. *The Selected Poems of Langston Hughes*. New York: Knopf, 1959.

Hurston, Zora Neale. *Their Eyes Were Watching God*. 1937. New York: Harper and Rowe, 1990.

———. "How it Feels to Be Colored Me." 1928. *The Norton Anthology of African American Literature*. Ed. Henry Louis Gates, Jr. and Nellie Y. McKay. New York: Norton, 1997. 1008–1011.

Hutchinson, George. *The Harlem Renaissance in Black and White*. Cambridge, MA: Harvard UP, 1995.

———. "Jean Toomer and American Racial Discourse." *Texas Studies in Literature and Language* 35.2 (Summer 1993): 226–50.

Irwin, John T. *Doubling and Incest/Repetition and Revenge: A Speculative Reading of Faulkner*. Baltimore: Johns Hopkins UP, 1975.

Jameson, Fredric. "Cognitive Mapping." *Marxism and the Interpretation of Culture*. Ed. Carey Nelson and Lawrence Grossberg. Urbana: U of Illinois P, 1988. 347–360.

———. *A Singular Modernity: Essay on the Ontology of the Present*. New York: Verso, 2002.

———. *Postmodernism: Or the Cultural Logic of Late Capitalism*. Durham: Duke UP, 1991.

Johnson, Bob. "'A Whole Synthesis of His Time': Political Ideology and Cultural Politics in the Writings of William Carlos Williams, 1929–1939." *American Quarterly* 54.2 (June 2002): 179–215.

Kalaidjian, Walter. *American Culture Between the Wars: Revisionary Modernism & Postmodern Culture*. New York: Columbia UP, 1993.

Kaplan, Carla. "The Erotics of Talk: 'That Oldest Human Longing' in *Their Eyes Were Watching God*." *American Literature* 67.1 (Mar. 1995): 115–142.

Kazin, Alfred. *On Native Grounds: An Interpretation of Modern American Prose Literature*. 1942. Garden City, NY: Doubleday, 1956.

Khan, M. Massud R. *The Privacy of the Self*. London: Hogarth, 1974.

Kifner, John. "Bomb Kills Six Israelis; Army Retakes West Bank Lands." *New York Times* June 20, 2002.

Klein, Melanie. *Envy and Gratitude: A Study of Unconscious Sources*. London: Tavistock, 1957.

Knox, George. "Dos Passos and Painting." *Dos Passos, the Critics and the Writer's Intention*. Ed. Allen Belkind. Carbondale: Southern Illinois UP, 1971. 242–264.

Kodat, Catherine Gunther. "To 'Flash White Light from Ebony': The Problem of Modernism in Jean Toomer's *Cane*." *Twentieth Century Literature* 46.1 (Spring 2000): 1–19.

Koenigsberg, Richard A. "F. Scott Fitzgerald: Literature and the Work of Mourning." *American Imago* 24 (1967): 248–270.

La Capra, Dominic. *Representing the Holocaust: History, Theory, Trauma*. Ithaca, NY: Cornell UP, 1994.

———. *Writing History, Writing Trauma*. Baltimore: Johns Hopkins UP, 2001.

Landsberg, Melvin. *Dos Passos' Path to U.S.A: A Political Biography*. Boulder, CO: Colorado Associated UP, 1972.

Lasch, Christopher. Foreword. *The American Political Tradition and the Men Who Made It*, by Richard Hofstadter. New York: Vintage, 1974. vii–xxiv.

Lawson, Andrew. "Divisions of Labour: William Carlos Williams's 'The Wanderer' and the Politics of Modernism." *William Carlos Williams Review* 20.1 (Spring 1994): 1–22.

Leavis, F. R. "A Serious Writer." *Dos Passos: A Collection of Critical Essays*. Ed. Andrew Hook. Englewood Cliffs, NJ: Prentice Hall, 1974. 72–75.

Lepenies, Wolf. *Melancholy and Society*. Cambridge: Harvard UP, 1992.

Levertov, Denise. "On Williams' Triadic Line; Or How to Dance on Variable Feet." *Conversant Essays: Contemporary Poets on Poetry*. Ed. James McCorkle. Detroit: Wayne State UP, 1990. 141–148.

Levine, Lawrence W. "The Historian and the Icon." *Documenting America: 1935–1943*. Ed. Carl Fleischhauer and Beverly W. Brannan. Berkeley: U of California P, 1988. 15–42.

Lindberg, Kathryne V. "Raising *Cane* on the Theoretical Plane: Jean Toomer's Racial Personae." *Cultural Difference and the Literary Text: Pluralism and the Limits of Authenticity in North American Literatures*. Ed. Winfried Siemerling and Katrin Schwenk. Iowa City: U of Iowa P, 1996. 49–74.

Lowney, John. "Langston Hughes and the 'Nonsense' of Bebop." *American Literature* 72.2 (June 2000): 357–385.

Ludington, Townsend, ed. *The Fourteenth Chronicle: Letters and Diaries of John Dos Passos*. Boston: Gambit, 1973.

———. *John Dos Passos: A Twentieth Century Odyssey*. New York: E. P. Dutton, 1980.

———. "The Ordering of the Camera Eye in *U.S.A.*" *American Literature* 49.3 (Nov. 1977): 443–446.

Lukacs, Georg. "Reification and the Consciousness of the Proletariat." *History and Class Consciousness: Studies in Marxist Dialectics*. Trans. and ed. Rodney Livingston. Cambridge, MA: MIT P, 1982. 83–222.

Lynn, Kenneth S. *Hemingway*. New York: Simon and Schuster, 1987.

MacDonald, Dwight. *Memoirs of a Revolutionist*. New York: Meridian, 1958.

MacGowan, Christopher, ed. *The Collected Poems of William Carlos Williams: Volume II, 1939–1962*. New York: New Directions, 1988.

Mackey, Nathaniel. "Sound and Sentiment, Sound and Symbol." *Discrepant Engagement*. Cambridge: Cambridge UP, 1993. 231–259.

Magny, Claude-Edmonde. "Time in Dos Passos." *Dos Passos: A Collection of Critical Essays*. Ed. Andrew Hook. Englewood Cliffs, NJ: Prentice Hall, 1974. 128–144.

Marcuse, Herbert. *Eros and Civilization: A Philosophical Inquiry into Freud*. 1955. New York: Vintage, 1961.

Mariani, Paul L. *William Carlos Williams: A New World Naked*. New York: McGraw Hill, 1981.

———. *William Carlos Williams: The Poet and His Critics*. Chicago: American Library Association, 1975.

Marris, Peter. *Loss and Change*. New York: Pantheon, 1974.

McGowan, Todd. "Liberation and Domination: *Their Eyes Were Watching God* and the Evolution of Capitalism." *MELUS* 24.1 (Spring 1999): 109–128.

Michaels, Walter Benn. *The Gold Standard and the Logic of Naturalism: American Literature at the Turn of the Century*. Berkeley: U of California P, 1987.

Miller, James E. *T. S. Eliot's Personal Waste Land: Exorcism of the Demons*. University Park: Penn State UP, 1977.

Mitscherlich, Alexander, and Marguerite Mitscherlich, *The Inability to Mourn: Principles of Collective Behavior*. New York: Grove, 1975.

Mizener, Arthur. "The Gullivers of John Dos Passos." *Dos Passos: A Collection of Critical Essays*. Ed. Andrew Hook. Englewood Cliffs, NJ: Prentice Hall, 1974. 165–167.

Moglen, Seth. "Modernism in the Black Diaspora: Langston Hughes and the Broken Cubes of Picasso." *Callaloo* 25.4 (2002): 1189–1205.

———. "Mourning and Progressive Politics After 9/11." *International Journal for Applied Psychoanalytic Studies* 3.2 (2006): 118-125.

———. "On Mourning Social Injuries." *Psychoanalysis, Culture & Society* 10.2 (August 2005): 151–167.

Moon, Michael. "Memorial Rags." *Professions of Desire: Lesbian and Gay Studies in Literature*. Ed. George E. Haggerty and Bonnie Zimmerman. New York: MLA, 1995. 235–239.

Morland, Richard C. *Faulkner and Modernism: Rereading and Rewriting*. Madison: U of Wisconsin P, 1990.

Mortimer, Gail L. *Faulkner's Rhetoric of Loss: A Study in Perception and Meaning*. Austin: U of Texas P, 1983.

Muñoz, Jose. "Photographies of Mourning: Melancholia and Ambivalence in Van Der Zee, Mapplethorpe, and *Looking for Langston*." *Race and the Subject of Masculinities*. Ed. Harry Stecopoulos and Michael Uebel. Durham: Duke UP, 1997. 337–358.

Murray, Robert K. *Red Scare: A Study in National Hysteria, 1919–1920*. Minneapolis: U of Minnesota P, 1955.

Myer, Neil. "Decreation in Williams' 'The Descent.'" *Criticism* 14.4 (Fall 1972): 315–327.

Nelson, Cary. *Repression and Recovery: Modern American Poetry and the Politics of Cultural Memory, 1910–1945*. Madison: U of Wisconsin P, 1989.

Nilsen, Helge Normann. *Looking Inward, Looking Outward: American Fiction in the 1930s and 1940s*. The Hague: European UP, 1990.

Norris, Frank. *McTeague*. 1899. New York: Norton, 1977.

Novak, Philip. "'Circles and circles of sorrow': In the Wake of Morrison's *Sula*." *PMLA* 114.2 (Mar. 1999): 184–193.

Olsen, Tillie. *Yonnondio: From the Thirties*. 1974. New York: Dell, 1989.

O'Neill, William L., ed. *Echoes of Revolt: The Masses, 1911–1917*. Chicago: Quadrangle, 1966.

Parrington, Vernon. *Main Currents in American Thought: The Beginnings of Critical Realism in America (1860–1920)*. New York: Harcourt Brace & World, 1958.

Patterson, Anita. "Jazz, Realism, and the Modernist Lyric: The Poetry of Langston Hughes." *Modern Language Quarterly* 61.4 (Dec. 2000): 651–682.

Perloff, Marjorie. "The Fallen Leaf and the Stain of Love: The Displacements of Desire in Williams' Early Love Poetry." *The Rhetoric of Love in the Collected Poems of William Carlos Williams*. Rome: Edizioni Associate, 1993. 189–212.

Pfeil, Fred. "Montage Dynasty: A Market Study in American Historical Fiction." *Another Tale to Tell: Politics & Narrative in Postmodern Culture*. New York: Verso, 1990. 151–192.

Pizer, Donald. "The Camera Eye in *U.S.A.*: The Sexual Center." *Modern Fiction Studies* 26.3 (Autumn 1980): 417–430.

———. *Twentieth-Century American Literary Naturalism: An Interpretation*. Carbondale: Southern Illinois UP, 1982.

Porter, Carolyn. *Seeing and Being: The Plight of the Participant Observer in Emerson, James, Adams and Faulkner*. Middletown, CT: Wesleyan UP, 1981.

Preston, William. *Aliens and Dissenters: Federal Suppression of Radicals, 1903–1933*. Cambridge: Harvard UP, 1963.

Rabinowitz, Paula. *Labor and Desire: Women's Revolutionary Fiction in Depression America*. Chapel Hill: U of North Carolina P, 1991.

Ramazani, Jahan. *Poetry of Mourning: The Modern Elegy from Hardy to Heaney*. Chicago: U of Chicago P, 1994.

Rampersad, Arnold. *The Life of Langston Hughes, Volumes I & II*. New York: Oxford UP, 1986, 1988.

Rideout, Walter. *The Radical Novel in the United States, 1900–1954*. Cambridge: Harvard UP, 1956.

Rohrkemper, John. "The Collapse of Faith and the Failure of Language: John Dos Passos and the Spanish Civil War." *Rewriting the Good Fight: Critical Essays in the Literature of the Spanish Civil War*. Ed. Frieda S. Brown et al. East Lansing: Michigan State UP, 1989. 215–228.

Rosenfelt, Deborah. "From the Thirties: Tillie Olsen and the Radical Tradition." *The Critical Response to Tillie Olsen*. Ed. Kay Hoyle Nelson and Nancy Huse. Westport, CT: Greenwood, 1994. 54–89.

Rousso, Henry. *The Vichy Syndrome: History and Memory in France since 1944*. Cambridge: Harvard UP, 1991.

Sacks, Peter. *The English Elegy: Studies in the Genre from Spenser to Yeats*. Baltimore: Johns Hopkins UP, 1985.

Salvatore, Nick. *Eugene Debs: Citizen and Socialist*. Urbana: U of Illinois P, 1982.

Sanders, David, ed. *John Dos Passos: A Comprehensive Bibiliography*. New York: Garland, 1987.

———. "The 'Anarchism' of John Dos Passos." *Dos Passos, the Critics and the Writer's Intention*. Ed. Allen Belkind. Carbondale: Southern Illinois UP, 1971. 122–135.

Santner, Eric. *Stranded Objects: Mourning, Memory and Film in Postwar Germany*. Ithaca, NY: Cornell UP, 1990.

Sartre, Jean Paul. "John Dos Passos and *1919*." *Dos Passos: A Collection of Critical Essays*. Ed. Andrew Hook. Englewood Cliffs, NJ: Prentice Hall, 1974. 61–69.

Sayre, Robert. "Anglo-American Writers, the Communist Movement and the Spanish Civil War: The Case of Dos Passos." *Revue Francaise D'études Américaines* 11.29 (May 1986): 263–274.

Schwartz, Lawrence H. *Creating Faulkner's Reputation: The Politics of Modern Literary Criticism*. Knoxville: U of Tennessee P, 1988.

Schwartz, Nina. "History and the Invention of Innocence in *A Lost Lady*." *Arizona Quarterly* 46.2 (1990): 33–54.

———. "Lovers' Discourse in *The Sun Also Rises*: A Cock and Bull Story." *Criticism* 26.1 (Winter 1984): 49–69.

Scott, Bonnie Kime. *The Gender of Modernism: A Critical Anthology*. Bloomington: Indiana UP, 1990.

Scruggs, Charles. "The Reluctant Witness: What Jean Toomer Remembered from *Winesburg, Ohio*." *Studies in American Fiction* 29.1 (Spring 2000): 78–100.

Seltzer, Mark. *Bodies and Machines*. New York: Routledge, 1992.

Shannon, David. *The Socialist Party of America: A History*. 1955. Chicago: Quadrangle, 1967.

Shulman, Alix Kates, ed. *Red Emma Speaks: Selected Writings and Speeches by Emma Goldman*. New York: Vintage, 1972.

Smedley, Agnes. *Daughter of Earth*. 1929; New York: The Feminist Press, 1987.

Smethurst, James. *The New Red Negro: The Literary Left and African American Poetry, 1930–1946*. New York: Oxford UP, 1999.

Smith, John. "John Dos Passos, 'Anglo-Saxon.'" *Modern Fiction Studies* 44.2 (Summer 1998): 282–305.

Solomon, William. "Politics and Rhetoric in the Novel in the 1930s." *American Literature* 68.4 (Dec. 1996): 799–818.

Spilka, Mark. "The Death of Love in *The Sun Also Rises*." *Hemingway: A Collection of Critical Essays*. Ed. Robert P. Weeks. Englewood Cliffs, NJ: Prentice Hall, 1962. 127–138.

Spillers, Hortense. "A Hateful Passion, A Lost Love." *Feminist Issues in Literary Scholarship*. Ed. Shari Benstock. Bloomington: Indiana UP, 1987. 181–207.

Spurr, David. "*The Waste Land*: Mourning, Writing, Disappearance." *Yeats/Eliot Review* 9.4 (1988): 161–164.

Steinbeck, John. *The Grapes of Wrath*. 1939. New York: Penguin, 1985.

Stott, William. *Documentary Expression and Thirties America*. New York: Oxford UP, 1973.

Strachey, James, ed. and trans. *The Standard Edition of the Complete Psychological Works of Sigmund Freud*. London: Hogarth, 1957.

Sundquist, Eric. "Who Was Langston Hughes?" *Commentary* (Dec. 1996): 55–59.

Thompson, E. P. *William Morris: Romantic to Revolutionary*. 1955. New York: Pantheon, 1976.

———. *Witness Against the Beast: William Blake and the Moral Law*. New York: New Press, 1993.

Thurston, Michael. "Black Christ, Red Flag: Langston Hughes on Scottsboro." *College Literature* 22.3 (Oct. 1995): 30–49.

Toomer, Jean. *Cane*. 1923. New York: Norton, 1988.

Tracey, Steven. *Langston Hughes and the Blues*. Chicago: U of Illinois P, 1998.

Trachtenberg, Alan. "From Image to Story." *Documenting America: 1935-1943*. Ed. Carl Fleischhauer and Beverly W. Brannan. Berkeley: U of California P, 1988. 43–73.

Trilling Lionel. "The America of John Dos Passos." *Dos Passos, the Critics and the Writer's Intention*. Ed. Allen Belkind. Carbondale: Southern Illinois UP, 1971. 35–43.

Trombold, John. "From the Future to the Past: The Disillusionment of John Dos Passos." *Studies in American Literature* 26.2 (Autumn 1998): 237–256.

Vanderwerken, David. "Dos Passos and the 'Old Worlds.'" *Twentieth Century Literature* (May 1977): 195–228.

Vickery, John. "The Aesthetics of Survival: Tillie Olsen's *Yonnondio*." *American Literary Dimensions: Poems and Essays in Honor of Melvin J. Friedman*. Newark: U of Delaware P, 1999. 99–111.

Von Hallberg, Robert. "The Politics of Description: W. C. Williams in the 'Thirties.'" *ELH* 45.1 (Spring 1976): 131–151.

Wagner, Linda. *Dos Passos: Artist as American*. Austin: U of Texas P, 1979.

Wald, Alan. *Exiles from a Future Time*. Chapel Hill: U of North Carolina P, 2002.

———. *The New York Intellectuals: The Rise and Decline of the Anti-Stalinist Left*. Chapel Hill: U of North Carolina P, 1987.

Walker, Alice. *In Search of Our Mothers' Gardens: Womanist Prose*. New York: Harcourt, Brace, Jovanovich, 1983.

Walkowitz, Rebecca L. "Shakespeare in Harlem: *The Norton Anthology*, 'Propoganda,' Langston Hughes." *Modern Language Quarterly* 60.4 (Dec. 1999): 495–519.

Ward, John William. "Dos Passos, Fitzgerald, and History." *Dos Passos: A Collection of Critical Essays*. Ed. Andrew Hook. Englewood Cliffs, NJ: Prentice Hall, 1974. 120–127.

Weinstein, James. *The Decline of Socialism in America, 1912–1925.* New York: Monthly Review Press, 1967.

Williams, Raymond. *The Country and the City.* London: Hogarth, 1985.

———. *Culture and Society, 1780–1950.* Harmondsworth: Penguin, 1985.

———. "Culture Is Ordinary." *Resources of Hope.* Ed. Robin Gable. London: Verso, 1989. 3–18.

———. *Marxism and Literature.* New York: Oxford UP, 1986.

———. *Modern Tragedy.* London: Chatto and Windus, 1966.

———. *The Politics of Modernism: Against the New Conformists.* New York: Verso, 1989.

Williams, William Carlos. *The Collected Poems of William Carlos Williams: Volume II, 1939–1962.* Ed. Christopher MacGowan. New York: New Directions, 1988.

——— *In the American Grain.* 1925. New York: New Directions, 1956.

Wilson, Edmund. *The Shores of Light: A Literary Chronicle of the Twenties and Thirties.* New York: Farrar, Straus & Giroux, 1952.

Winter, Jay. *Sites of Memory, Sites of Mourning: The Great War in European Cultural History.* New York: Cambridge UP, 1995.

Wittenberg, Judith Bryant. *Faulkner: The Transfiguration of Biography.* Lincoln: U of Nebraska P, 1979.

Woodward, Kathleen. "Late Theory, Late Style: Loss and Renewal in Freud and Barthes." *Aging and Gender in Literature: Studies in Creativity.* Ed. Anne M. Wyatt-Brown and Janice Rossen. Charlottesville: UP of Virginia, 1993. 82–101.

Wyatt, David. *Prodigal Sons: A Study in Authorship and Authority.* Baltimore: Johns Hopkins UP, 1980.

Index

Aaron, Daniel, 265n7, 266n10, 269n20, 270n29, 276n58, 288n5, 289n9
Abraham, Karl, 40, 250n34
Abstract Expressionism, 10
Ackroyd, Peter, 249n26
Adorno, Theodor, 282n24
aestheticization of loss, 45, 63–65, 73–74, 81–82, 255n21. *See also* melancholic modernism.
African Americans: and grieving for slavery, 18, 19; civil rights movement, 24, 259n46; in Dos Passos's *U.S.A.*, 127, 204; in Faulkner's *Absalom, Absalom!*, 31, 42; in Hemingway's *Sun Also Rises*, 37, 248n25; in Hughes' poetry, 70–81, 129; in Hurston's *Their Eyes Were Watching God*, 47–53; and melancholia, 239n17; and modernism, 6, 8, 11, 30, 34, 236nn6-7, 237n11,252n8, 258n37; and naturalism, 187–88; in Toomer's *Cane*, 30–31, 34, 41–42, 245n9, 249n32. *See also* race; slavery
Agee, James: *Let Us Now Praise Famous Men*, 278n7
Ahearn, Barry, 260n50
alienation: and capitalism, xiii–xiv, xvii, 5–6, 9, 10, 11, 14, 28–29, 30, 31, 34, 35, 39, 45, 48, 52, 54, 55, 60–61, 67–68, 82, 89–90, 91, 98, 99, 102, 103, 124, 149, 158, 166, 177, 180–81, 201, 216, 217, 232, 233, 244n4, 254nn17,19, 265n6; in Dos Passos's political vision 95–99, 102–103; in Dos Passos's *U.S.A.* trilogy, 91–92, 149–51, 156, 158–59, 166, 177, 180, 186–217, 222; in Eliot's *Waste Land*, 28–39, 55, 60, 166; in Faulkner's *Absalom, Absalom!*, 31; in H.D.'s *Flowering of the Rod*, 54, 58; in Hemingway's *The Sun Also Rises*, 29, 34; in Hurston's *Their Eyes Were Watching*

God, 48–49, 52; in Olsen's *Yonnondio*, 60–62, 65, 67–69, 254nn17,19,20; as self-alienation, 61, 67–68; in Toomer's *Cane*, 30–31, 34.
Amalgamated Clothing Workers of America, 274n45
American Civil Liberties Union (ACLU), 112
American Legion, 269n24
American Workers Party, 115
American Writers' Congress of 1935, 193, 276n58
anarchism, 91, 110, 126, 177–78; and Dos Passos, 100, 103, 127, 204, 266n9, 267n11, 268nn18,19, 271n34, 287n28; Goldman, 98–99, 106, 127, 265n7, 266n9, 267n11, 287nn26,28; of Sacco and Vanzetti, 106–7, 124, 131, 182, 266n9; in Spain, 103, 268n19. *See also* IWW (Industrial Workers of the World)
Anderson, Sherwood, 237n10
anger: ability to identity proper objects of, 20–21, 23, 25, 35–36, 46, 49–53, 58, 59, 65–66, 69–70, 75, 82, 126, 130–31, 147, 149, 159–60, 167, 179, 222–23, 225–27, 228–29, 253n14; displacement of, 13–14, 17, 23, 25, 36–37, 38, 45, 52–53, 61–62, 142–44, 147, 161, 167, 168, 193–94, 200, 233, 239n, 247n19, 248nn21,22,24,25, 249n32, 251n5, 253n14, 284n6; of Dos Passos, 92, 125, 126, 130–31, 139–49, 159–61, 172, 173, 179, 193–94, 200, 219, 220, 222–23, 226–27, 228–29; Freud on, 13–14, 15, 16–17, 20, 23; and Hughes, 71–73, 74–75, 77–78, 80–81, 233, 259n46; and Hurston, 52–54, 233, 251n5; in melancholic modernism, 17, 35–37, 38–39, 59, 92, 200, 233, 238n, 247n19,

305